Modern Monetary Theory

In Association with the Gower Initiative for Modern Money Studies

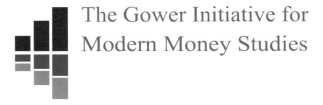

The Gower Initiative for
Modern Money Studies

Modern Monetary Theory

Key Insights, Leading Thinkers

Edited by

L. Randall Wray
Senior Scholar, Levy Economics Institute, Professor of Economics, Bard College, USA

Phil Armstrong
York College, UK

Sara Holland
Founder, The Gower Initiative for Modern Money Studies, UK

Claire Jackson-Prior
Founder, The Gower Initiative for Modern Money Studies, UK

Prue Plumridge
Founder, The Gower Initiative for Modern Money Studies, UK

Neil Wilson
Associate, The Gower Initiative for Modern Money Studies, UK

 Edward Elgar
PUBLISHING

Cheltenham, UK • Northampton, MA, USA

Cover design based on an original concept by www.marke.photography with images from Shutterstock.

Published by
Edward Elgar Publishing Limited
The Lypiatts
15 Lansdown Road
Cheltenham
Glos GL50 2JA
UK

Edward Elgar Publishing, Inc.
William Pratt House
9 Dewey Court
Northampton
Massachusetts 01060
USA

A catalogue record for this book
is available from the British Library

Library of Congress Control Number: 2022948485

This book is available electronically in the **Elgar**online
Economics subject collection
http://dx.doi.org/10.4337/9781802208092

Printed on elemental chlorine free (ECF)
recycled paper containing 30% Post-Consumer Waste

ISBN 978 1 80220 808 5 (cased)
ISBN 978 1 80220 809 2 (eBook)

Printed and bound in the USA

Contents

Figures

Contributors

Phil Armstrong has been a teacher for 40 years, in the main economics but latterly, engineering. He completed his PhD in Economics in 2020 at the University of Solent and recently authored, *Can Heterodox Economics Make a Difference? Conversations with Key Thinkers* (Edward Elgar, 2020) based upon his thesis research. He is a strong advocate of Modern Monetary Theory (MMT) and supports pluralism in economics. Phil regularly interviews leading MMT economists as part of the GIMMS' events programme.

Andrew Berkeley's background is in marine geology and oceanography. He earned a PhD in 2008 and has since worked in several contexts including academic research, scientific and analytical software development, environmental regulation and the renewables sector. Following the Global Financial Crisis in 2007–08, Andrew became interested in economics and decided to apply his research experience to understanding the manner in which the UK government interacts with the banking sector and the monetary system as a whole – a topic which is seemingly poorly understood by many but crucial to the public, political discourse. This ongoing work seeks to shed well-evidenced light on the constraints and privileges with which the UK government operates.

Deborah Harrington is Co-Director of Public Matters, an independent research and information partnership focused on public service. Public Matters provided the secretariat for an All-Party Parliamentary Group on Health in All Policies from 2017 to 2020. Deborah was a founder member of the Leathermarket Community Benefit Society, a community-based organisation in London which builds small-scale social housing developments and sat on the board of directors from 2014 to 2021. Her interest in economics is a corollary of her work on health, especially the social determinants of health. She was a founder member of the Gower Initiative.

John T. Harvey is Professor of Economics at Texas Christian University, where he has worked since 1987. His areas of speciality are international economics (particularly exchange rates), macroeconomics, history of economics and contemporary schools of thought. During his time in Fort Worth, he has served as department chair, Executive Director of the International Confederation of Associations for Pluralism in Economics, a member of the board of directors of the Association for Evolutionary Economics, and a member of the editorial boards of the *American Review of Political Economy*, the *Critique of Political Economy*, the *Encyclopaedia of Political Economy*, the *Journal of Economics Issues* and the *Social Science Journal*. His research consists of over 40 refereed publications, two edited volumes and two books.

Sara Holland is GIMMS' social media lead. She came to MMT from a persistent curiosity on the back of home repossession and homelessness following the early 1990s recessions and exchange rate mechanism (ERM) interest rate/currency debacle. She is a carer and has worked on community youth and fundraising projects, is a keen advocate and campaigner for social housing, public services and the National Health Service (NHS).

Claire Jackson-Prior is GIMMS' website manager. A campaigner for social justice, Claire is appalled by the levels of wealth inequality, not only in the UK, but worldwide. She is determined to promote an understanding of our monetary system to help return the NHS and other public services to public provision, and to work towards rebalancing the sharing of resources fairly around the world so that every person has a decent chance in life and can live free from poverty. Claire has a degree in Geology from University College London and stood as the Green Party Candidate for the Sutton and Cheam Constituency in the 2017 and 2019 General Elections.

Daniel Kostzer is an Economist at ITUC-CSI (International Trade Unions Confederation-Confederacion Sindical Internacional) and a research scholar at the Global Institute for Sustainable Prosperity, having worked at the office of the International Labour Organization (ILO) up to February 2021. He was previously an Alternate Executive Director at the World Bank (2014–16). His earlier positions include Senior Economic Advisor at the United Nations Development Programme (UNDP), Myanmar, Head of the Socio-Economic Unit at United Nations Integrated Mission (UNMIT) in Timor-Leste, Coordinator of the Social Development Cluster at the UNDP, Argentina, Director of Research and Macroeconomic Coordination at the Argentine Ministry of Labor and Senior Advisor of the National Lower Chamber. He has served as a consultant for the ILO, ECLAC, World Bank, IICA, and UNDP on economic development, poverty reduction, income distribution and employment and labour policies, and was a member of the Knowledge Networks of the World Commission on the Social Dimension of Globalization, ILO. He has been a visiting professor at the University of Missouri at Kansas City, Drew University, and lecturer at the Master of Applied Labor Economics for Development (MALED) at Turin, Italy, and the ILO, University of Turin and the Institute d'Etudes Politiques de Paris between 2011 and 2020. He was also Professor at the University of Buenos Aires, the University of Tucuman and University of Jujuy in Argentina. He has published in academic and professional journals on the topics of economic development, labour markets, poverty alleviation and income distribution. He did graduate studies in Development Studies at the International Institute of Social Studies, Erasmus University, The Hague, the Netherlands; Applied Statistics at the University of Tucuman; and Rural Planning at the Universidad Simon Rodriguez in Venezuela.

Stuart Medina Miltimore is an economist and a founding member of Red MMT Spain, of which he is the current President. He has developed his professional career in the biotechnology sector where he has held management positions such as Controller and Director of Business Development. He also founded the consulting firm Metas Biotech and the biopharmaceutical company, ProRetina Therapeutics. He is currently an advisor to the Elkarrekin Podemos political party in the Basque Parliament and the Regional Assembly of Biscay. He is the author of two books on Modern Money Theory in Spanish: *El Leviatán desencadenado: siete propuestas de política económica, 21 razones para salir del euro* (Lola Books, 2016) and *La moneda del pueblo* (El viejo Topo, 2017).

William Mitchell is Professor of Economics at the University of Newcastle, New South Wales, Australia, and a leading proponent of Modern Monetary Theory. He is a director of CofFEE, the Centre of Full Employment and Equity promoting research aimed at restoring full employment and achieving an economy that delivers equitable outcomes for all. He has written extensively in the fields of macroeconomics, econometrics and public policy including his book *Reclaiming the State: A Progressive Vision of Sovereignty for a Post-Neoliberal World* (Pluto Press, 2017).

Jamie Morgan is Professor of Economic Sociology at Leeds Beckett University. He has published widely in the fields of economics, political economy, philosophy, sociology and international politics. His recent books include *Realist Responses to Post-Human Society: Ex machina* (co-edited with I. Al-Amoudi, Routledge, 2018); *Brexit and the Political Economy of Fragmentation: Things Fall Apart* (co-edited with H. Patomäki, Routledge, 2018); *Trumponomics: Causes and Consequences* (co-edited with E. Fullbrook, College Publications, 2017); *What Is Neoclassical Economics?* (editor, Routledge, 2015); and *Piketty's Capital in the Twenty-first Century* (co-edited with E. Fullbrook, College Publications, 2014).

Warren Mosler is a financial economist who independently originated – and has spent the last 25 years promoting – the school of thought that has been popularised as Modern Monetary Theory (MMT). In 2010 he authored *The Seven Deadly Innocent Frauds of Economic Policy* (Valance Co., 2020). Warren also formally entered MMT into the mainstream economic literature in 2017, co-authoring 'Maximizing Price Stability in a Market Economy' with

Professor Damiano Silipo. Published in the *Journal of Policy Modelling* (2017), a leading peer-reviewed mainstream economics journal, it proposes the European Central Bank fund and managing an employed buffer stock policy.

Yeva Nersisyan is Associate Professor of Economics at Franklin and Marshall College in Lancaster, PA. She received her BA in Economics from Yerevan State University in Armenia, and her MA and PhD (2013) in Economics and Mathematics from the University of Missouri–Kansas City. She is a macroeconomist working in the Modern Money Theory, Post Keynesian and Institutionalist traditions. Her research interests include banking and financial instability, fiscal and monetary theory and policy. She has published a number of papers on the topics of shadow banking, liquidity creation, the Glass–Steagall Act, the Green New Deal and Modern Money Theory. Currently, she is working on editing the *Elgar Companion to Modern Money Theory* with L. Randall Wray.

Jessica Ormerod is Co-director of Public Matters, an independent research and information partnership focused on public service, working closely with Deborah Harrington. Jessica worked in the campaign and policy team for the National Health Action Party.

Prue Plumridge is GIMMS' events facilitator and author of the 'MMT Lens' which aims to connect the latest news with MMT concepts. Coming originally to MMT through an interest in gaining a better understanding of how the monetary system operated, it soon became clear how the framework could assist in delivering progressive public policy aiming to bring about a fairer society and sustainable prosperity. In 2015 she co-organised the first official MMT Event in London at which Professor Bill Mitchell was the guest speaker and then went on two years later to co-host a fringe event in Brighton. From there it was a short leap to becoming a co-founder of GIMMS. Prue has a degree in Business Studies from Anglia Ruskin University, a Diploma in French Language Studies awarded by the Institut-Francais in London and Mastery Level Italian from Essex University.

Pavlina R. Tcherneva is Program Director and Associate Professor of Economics at Bard College and a Research Associate at the Levy Economics Institute. She conducts research in the fields of Modern Monetary Theory and public policy and has collaborated with policymakers from around the world on developing and evaluating various job-creation programmes. Her work on the Job Guarantee spans over 20 years. In her recently published book *The Case for a Job Guarantee* (Polity, 2020), she challenges us to imagine a world where the phantom of unemployment is banished and anyone who seeks decent living-wage work can find it – guaranteed. Her work will be of particular relevance as we begin to grapple with the economic fall-out of the COVID-19 pandemic and for anyone passionate about social justice and building a fairer economy her work is essential reading.

Richard Tye was born in Bristol in 1974 and raised in the North of Scotland from the age of three. He attended Edinburgh University reading Geology and Geophysics, after which he moved abroad, working in Italy and Croatia in the offshore oil construction industry for three years. Moving to the United States in 1999, he gained a commercial helicopter pilot's licence in 2000 and has specialised in Search and Rescue flying for the last 17 years, living and working in the Netherlands and all over the UK. He now lives in Lincolnshire with his wife and three teenage boys, spending too much of his free time researching the history of the UK monetary system.

Neil Wilson is an expert in finance and information systems and one of the UK's leading thinkers about Modern Monetary Theory. After more than 30 years in the systems business, Neil learned the hard way that operations rarely follow the manual. Moving from network crashes to financial crashes, Neil was intrigued as to whether the economy could be fixed with a reboot – which led him to MMT. His work challenges the high priesthood of 'Important Grey Men' who refer to people as 'resources' and who believe debt is bad for government and good for you. He dreams of a world where everyone who wants a living-wage job can find one, close to their home, their friends and family.

L. Randall Wray is a Senior Scholar at the Levy Economics Institute and Professor of Economics at Bard College. He is one of the original developers of Modern Money Theory.

Wray's most recent books are *Why Minsky Matters* (Princeton University Press, 2016), and A *Great Leap Forward* (Academic Press, 2020). Randall is the author of *Money and Credit in Capitalist Economies* (Edward Elgar, 1990), *Understanding Modern Money* (Edward Elgar, 1998), *The Rise and Fall of Money Manager Capitalism* (with É. Tymoigne, Routledge, 2013), *Modern Money Theory* (Palgrave Macmillan, 2012, 2nd revision, 2015), and a textbook, *Macroeconomics* (with William Mitchell and Martin Watts, Red Globe Press, 2019). Randall previously taught at the University of Missouri–Kansas City and at the University of Denver, and has been a visiting professor at the Universities of Paris and Rome, as well as UNAM in Mexico City. He holds a BA from the University of the Pacific and an MA and a PhD from Washington University, where he was a student of Minsky. He has held a number of Fulbright Grants, including most recently at the Tallinn University of Technology in Estonia.

Preface

The Gower Initiative for Modern Money Studies and the motivation behind this volume

Phil Armstrong

The Gower Initiative for Modern Money Studies (GIMMS) was founded by a group of five women, Sara Holland, Claire Jackson-Prior, Prue Plumridge, Deborah Harrington and Jessica Ormerod, who share a keen interest in politics and economics. The project was launched in central London in October 2018 at an event at which Modern Monetary Theory (MMT) co-founding academic, Professor Bill Mitchell of the University of Newcastle, was the keynote speaker. Since that foundation, GIMMS have developed their scope and become the UK's foremost organisation for the promotion of the insights of MMT – and globally, one of the most important – at all levels. At the outset, GIMMS established an Advisory Board made up of the world's major MMT academics who continue to be a source of encouragement for GIMMS' work. This volume represents the latest and one of the most significant manifestations of this support.

GIMMS is an independent, non-profit organisation which is part of a growing international movement challenging the economic orthodoxy of the last four decades. Whilst coming together from different directions, the founders share a common understanding that the current dominant orthodoxy in economics is deeply flawed. Its methodological and theoretical failings are such that it is unable to address the questions of how best to utilise our real resources and how to design government policies that are likely to promote human flourishing and environmental sustainability. GIMMS' strategy has always been to broaden public awareness of MMT as a body of economic thought and, in the spirit of solidarity for economic and ecological justice, to develop international links with nations facing similar challenges.

All the founding members of GIMMS passionately believe that economic theory should shed light on the operation of a monetary economy. They recognise that MMT provides the richest explanation of how our monetary system works and, crucially, it considers government economic policy in relation to the world's real resources: the planet and its people. Public awareness of

MMT as a lens for understanding the nature of monetary operations is growing around the world and it is the aim of the Gower Initiative to offer a UK portal for promoting and developing that understanding.

The GIMMS' website offers a variety of resources from introductory level to more in-depth analysis. As well as FAQs and factsheets it offers a portal to a wide range of videos, books and academic resources forming the basis for a more comprehensive study. GIMMS' searchable database provides scholars from around the world with the material they need to support their work. Since its launch, the website has proved extremely popular and is currently averaging around 500 visits per day. The website's factsheets are available in PDF, and data shows that these resources are frequently used by activists in support of real-world teaching and for sharing with family, friends and colleagues in the 'Each One Teach One' style, inspired by MMT activists at Real Progressives in the United States. In addition to the website, GIMMS has a social media presence on Twitter and Facebook and its posts are shared to over a hundred different activist group sites. GIMMS also produces a fortnightly news blog, 'MMT Lens', which provides its audience with an analysis of current economic or social affairs from an MMT perspective and has proven to be a popular format and draw to the website. Alongside its social media activities and as part of its objectives, GIMMS continues to work hard to reach out to community and activist groups around the UK.

Since its launch, GIMMS has provided an opportunity for people to hear directly from MMT founders Warren Mosler and Professor Bill Mitchell, hosting events in London, Manchester and Birmingham as well as supporting MMT Scotland with events in Glasgow and Edinburgh. I have been very fortunate to be given the role of Associate Member, alongside Alan Hutchinson, Neil Wilson (who contributes two chapters to this work) – and Christian Reilly and Patricia Pino (the latter two provide the excellent MMT Podcast which works closely with GIMMS). GIMMS have organised very successful meetings across the country, notably in Leeds, Manchester, Nottingham and London with more planned in the future. The GIMMS' team also took a stand at the 2019 Green Party Conference, at which I was able to give a presentation that was both well attended and well received by delegates. Many of these events have been filmed and posted on GIMMS' website and YouTube Library where they have proved to be well-used, shared resources. In addition, GIMMS looks to promote MMT beyond the UK and has forged links with internationally acclaimed economists (many of whom contribute to this work) and numerous activist groups which are growing rapidly around the world, particularly in Europe.

The international profile of MMT has grown considerably, in recent years in particular, due to its explanatory and predictive success relative to mainstream mathematical modellers during the Global Financial Crisis and its aftermath, and also as a result of its ability to provide intelligibility to the global fiscal responses of governments to the COVID-19 pandemic. For those with an open mind, it has become increasingly clear that MMT provides a sound basis for developing an understanding of the operation of a monetary economy, enabling economists and political analysts to better understand the nature of the opportunities that are available for policy.

I would point out that the approach taken by MMT authors has used 'Modern Money' as the designation of the theory as well as 'Modern Monetary'. In this context, Modern Money is state money, Chartalist money or sovereign currency. In practice, the two terms, 'Modern Monetary Theory' and 'Modern Money Theory' are used interchangeably, the first being the most common, especially in the UK, Europe and Australia.

Over many years, the leading MMT economists have written widely in peer-reviewed journals. They have also written numerous books, contributed chapters to books and produced a very popular university textbook. In addition, as MMT's profile has grown, it has faced exacting criticism from mainstream and heterodox economists. MMT economists have consistently been able to rebut this criticism, however, it seems clear that MMT's further development would be enhanced by the publication of a new volume allowing all the world's major MMT economists to examine an area or areas of expertise. This book realises GIMMS' ambition of delivering an unmatched and ground-breaking academic resource which provides in a single volume, for the first time globally, the most important distinctive insights of MMT in the words of the leading MMT thinkers and authors.

Acknowledgements

I would like to thank Alison, Jonny and Catherine for their love and support during this project.
Phil Armstrong

My thanks to all the serious minds that have contributed to this book, I'm thrilled to have been a part of this project and I hope with all my heart it contributes to making the UK a fairer place to live. This is for you Dad, I hope you can check out a copy of this in your dream library, for Flora Joan and Penelope and my long-suffering family.
Sara Holland

I would like to thank Paul, Quinn and Ethan for their encouragement and for their patience in accepting all the hours I spent looking at a computer at weekends during this endeavour. I would also like to thank my fellow editors for their work, advice, support and kindness.
Claire Jackson-Prior

I would like to thank Sue Davies without whose knowledge and encouragement I would not have embarked upon my MMT journey or understood the vital message that sits at its heart; the role government can play, if it so chooses, in creating a fairer society and a sustainable planet.

My appreciation also goes to Deborah Harrington and Peter Martin with whom I collaborated in the organisation of two key MMT events in London and Brighton. Their enthusiasm and hard work sowed the seeds for the founding of GIMMS in 2018, and its success in bringing MMT to a wider UK audience.
Prue Plumridge

I thank the GIMMS team for all their work.
L. Randall Wray

The whole editorial team would like to thank all of the chapter contributors and those who have reviewed the book for their time and work on this project. We would also like to thank Mark Epstein for his work on the cover design.

Introduction to *Modern Monetary Theory: Key Insights, Leading Thinkers*

by The Gower Initiative for Modern Money Studies

Sara Holland, Claire Jackson-Prior and Prue Plumridge

The purpose of studying economics is not to acquire a set of ready-made answers to economic questions, but to learn how to avoid being deceived by economists.
Joan Robinson

The esoteric ideas of mainstream economists have seemingly made no useful contribution to the development of a general understanding of how the economy around us actually works, indeed, trying to understand the economic thinking of politicians and journalists in the context of real-world events has often left us frustrated.

So much of the media narrative at the time of various economic crises makes little sense and is at odds with our lived experience. Born of this frustration and out of curiosity, we individually sought to establish in our own minds why the economy is failing ordinary people and why our governments get away with the neglect of our public services and infrastructure in one of the richest and most advanced nations on Earth. This curiosity led, via social media, to the insights of Modern Monetary Theory, the exquisitely simple explanation of our economy and how the monetary system actually works, thanks largely to Stephanie Kelton's Angry Birds lecture, a lightbulb moment shared now by millions around the world. In Modern Monetary Theory, we found explanations that did make sense and explained the reasons for the various crises (the Global Financial Crisis especially) and that did shine a light on what had made governments' responses to these crises so detrimental to the majority of the people.

The insights offered by the 'MMT Lens' can show us a wider, more appropriate range of policy options, ways to help communities make the best of the resources they have available, rather than believing that some things are impossible because of a lack of money. We believe that an understanding of how monetary systems work is a vital base for creating public policy. Just as it would be madness to ignore the theory of gravity when trying to send a spacecraft to the moon, ignoring Modern Monetary Theory (MMT) makes creating public policies that will achieve their aims a much more treacherous task. We are passionate about sharing MMT insights with the public, economists and policymakers because we know that so much suffering could be alleviated if appropriate policies were pursued by governments around the world, not only for humans but also for the other varieties of life with whom we share this Earth.

We came together with the intention of creating a space where the layperson can access the materials and resources necessary to grasp an understanding of MMT and in 2018 The Gower Initiative for Modern Money Studies (GIMMS) was born.

One of the obstacles in our way was an excess of US-centric material, making it difficult for us to put the explanations in the context of other countries. GIMMS' intention is to present a UK perspective of MMT, but we also see that its implications are important for countries all over the world.

In addition, from the very beginning of our project it became clear that if MMT is to gain credibility in the UK and really make a difference, then the exact mechanism by which the government spends needed to be established and that knowledge needed to be shared beyond the layperson and to reach academic institutions and policymakers. To drive the MMT stake in the academic ground in the UK, an academic text is needed, a reference book specific to the UK, that is both a showcase for the painstakingly researched UK Exchequer Paper (Chapter 1), and for the key insights established by MMT's principal developers.

We wanted this book to answer the criticisms we most often hear when discussing MMT with members of the public generally and also with those who have a background in economics. Arguments such as MMT only being relevant to the US, the idea that MMT-inspired policies would be inflationary or that the UK risked suffering the same problems as Greece if the government had not implemented austerity policies after the Global Financial Crisis. We feel that it is important to answer such critiques because the views held by mainstream economists and repeated by politicians and journalists leave our society stuck where we are, with poverty commonplace, housing for many being expensive and of poor quality, public services being privatised and hollowed out and jobs being poorly paid and becoming less secure. Such views also keep the Global South trapped in a cycle of poverty, resource extraction and foreign currency debt. The subjects of the individual chapters were selected with these points in mind; however, all the chapters are the views of the authors, and each author has their own perspective within a broad MMT framework.

In Chapter 1, Andrew Berkeley, Richard Tye and Neil Wilson show the means by which the UK government spends. This is an extremely important piece of work and is ground-breaking in its depth and scope. The authors draw on historical sources, testimonies from government departments, official documentation and parliamentary abstracts, forensically disassembling the components of the UK government's finances, debunking ideology and half-truths along the way. This is a Wizard of Oz moment, the pulling back of the curtain to reveal the myths and obfuscation that has enabled decades of needless austerity to wreck the lives of millions in the UK and around the world.

Chapter 2 by Richard Tye explores the history of 'money' both English, then British, to show what insights this history gives on our financial system as it is today. He then argues that today's Exchequer is in need of reform and that many of its departments should be eliminated as they are unnecessary, given that they are composed of layer upon layer of conventions that have conspired to create a complex web preventing the type of transparency necessary in a functioning democracy.

In Chapter 3, Yeva Nersisyan and L. Randall Wray show how MMT builds on the Chartalist approach to money and how the constraints on spending in government are often self-imposed, and that the insights of MMT apply to many countries, not just those who issue reserve currencies. They explore the relevance of MMT to developing countries and discuss why the popular belief that it does not apply in these nations is detrimental to those countries.

Chapter 4 is by Warren Mosler, one of the founders of MMT. He delivers one of MMT's key insights, 'a unique understanding of inflation' in direct contrast to the frequent accusations that MMT economists ignore inflation. Mosler shows how a currency-issuing government creates a demand for its currency by imposing a tax liability and that the price level is dictated by the prices paid by government when it spends, not by the total amount of money that the government spends.

In Chapter 5, MMT's principal developer, William Mitchell, explains how the ending of the Bretton Woods system changed the constraints on government spending from financial to real resource ones instead. Mitchell also explains the key MMT insight ignored by other schools of economic thought, that at a macroeconomic level, exports are a real cost to a nation, and imports in real terms are a benefit. The erroneous belief that our exports are a benefit to the nation has enabled generations of political lobbying by exporters to put downward pressure on domestic wages and living standards. This, again, is in contrast to the orthodox narrative which sees exports as a policy target because they provide income to nations, rather than a balanced economy that focuses on strategic self-sufficiency.

In Chapter 6, John T. Harvey addresses the argument that MMT-inspired policies will cause the currency to collapse. He shows how the

MMT-as-currency-killer argument is based on models and assumptions that are at odds with reality as well as misrepresenting MMT. Harvey presents a realistic model that shows that MMT-informed policies would not cause a currency collapse, nor would high inflation or stagflation be the result.

Chapter 7, by Stuart Medina Miltimore and William Mitchell, examines the European Union and the Euro currency. They argue that the diversity of the nations in the Eurozone and the lack of a fiscal union make it unlikely that the Euro will be successful in the long term, and that nations will more than likely exit the Union.

In Chapter 8, Phil Armstrong and Jamie Morgan show how methodology and philosophy support MMT within broader heterodoxy and argue that MMT is a variant of open systems theory. They show that MMT economists understand that institutions that are made by humans can be directed by humans for better or for worse, and that in the light of the climate crisis, care is needed to direct these institutions wisely.

Chapter 9, by Neil Wilson, explains the vital importance of taxation and that, contrary to the belief of many economists, MMT does not ignore it. He then presents his view on what is needed in an effective tax system and his own proposals for a new system for the UK that makes use of existing state structures to simplify taxation whilst driving the currency and releasing the resources needed by the public sector.

In Chapter 10, Daniel Kostzer examines the Jefes Plan, an employment guarantee initiative which ran in Argentina until 2009 and had begun as a response to the financial crisis of 2001 there. Kostzer describes the programme and explores what the experience of Argentina can teach us about the options for a Public Employment Programme, including the Job Guarantee.

Chapter 11, by Pavlina R. Tcherneva, explores the lessons that can be learned from the response of governments to the COVID-19 pandemic. She shows how the response corroborated key MMT insights about money, employment and inflation and argues that these lessons should be heeded in the future to improve public health, reach and maintain full employment, control inflation and protect the environment.

Chapter 12 sees Deborah Harrington and Jessica Ormerod use the 'MMT Lens' to examine the crucial role of the State in provisioning itself with the real resources necessary to meet its public purposes mandate. They examine the history of government investment in infrastructure and public services, their subsequent neglect, and the privatisation models which have in recent years failed to meet the needs of the population and have left millions lacking in decent housing, healthcare, and the skills necessary both for now and to pass on to future generations.

We believe that an understanding of the insights of MMT is a vital base for the creation of a world where people have the opportunity to live lives free from poverty and hunger and also to have the ability to contribute to their communities. MMT is the starting point for improvements to our lives, the seed from where good policy can grow and flourish. Once the knowledge of the realities of our monetary system shows the true extent of policy options, it will be up to the people to choose those policies that will be most advantageous to humans and the environment in which we live.

1. How does the government spend? A functional model of the UK Exchequer

Andrew Berkeley, Richard Tye and Neil Wilson

1.1 INTRODUCTION

The last decade began with the Prime Minister of the United Kingdom warning of an impending crisis in government finances. In the wake of the Global Financial Crisis of 2008 and unprecedented interventions to stabilise the financial system by his predecessor, David Cameron announced that:

> the more the Government borrows, the more it has to repay; the more it has to repay, the more lenders worry about getting their money back, and the more lenders start to worry ... we run the risk of higher interest rates ... Greece stands as a warning of what happens to countries that lose their credibility.[1]

These concerns were paramount in the justification for the incoming coalition government's policy of spending cuts from 2010.

Despite this focus, manifested as sharp and damaging cuts to crucial government services over the subsequent years, UK government debt levels continued to rise steadily, with the absolute value up by 80 per cent on the eve of the Covid-19 pandemic a decade later.[2] That this scale of debt was not only unproblematic but even presented no barrier to the government engaging in another economic intervention of staggering scale was difficult to miss, as was the glaring observation that only the government is in a position to backstop continuing economic activity. Equally clear was that years of underfunding had left the UK ill-prepared for such a health crisis. Regardless, the BBC's most senior reporter stated that a limit had – this time – been reached: 'This is the credit card, the national mortgage, everything absolutely maxed out.'[3]

Government finances have been at the forefront of the UK political landscape for over a decade, but despite attempts from many in the economics profession as well as a burgeoning activist scene, mainstream debates have barely moved on from concerns raised and prescriptions given in 2010. The concerns raised reveal a poor understanding of the way in which the UK government interacts financially with the rest of the economy, the significance of the government in the monetary system, and the constraints within which the government must operate. These issues are, on the face of it, complicated, obscured perhaps by the many institutions and conventions involved and the absence of any coherent, up-to-date official description of the whole system. But these obstacles are in no way mitigated by the quality of debate in public discussions which often rely on politically motivated tropes rather than well-evidenced research.

In this chapter, we seek to remedy this by presenting a coherent and detailed description of how spending arises from the UK Exchequer according to legislation, banking arrangements and policy conventions. The consequences which flow from this functioning are then examined. Notably, the study of these spending mechanisms helps contextualise the government's other financial activities – taxing and borrowing – which are able to be understood from a different perspective than that usually presented. We explain the crucial role of the government to the UK monetary system and wider economy, and in that context show how alternative policies which support a more equitable society are possible.

1.2   THE UK FINANCIAL SYSTEM

Figure 1.1 gives an overview of the institutional landscape within which the UK government's financial activities are undertaken. The economy is classified into a public sector and a private sector, with the private sector represented by individuals, businesses and other non-bank financial institutions (e.g., pension funds), all connected by a commercial banking system. In the public sector we can differentiate Parliament from what is known as the Exchequer – the system of institutions around which the UK government's financial activities are organised. It will be seen that the role of Parliament is fundamental to the government's finances, though this is often understated. At the interface between the public and private sectors is the Bank of England ('the Bank'). The Bank is wholly owned by the government and so is objectively part of the public sector. It is shown spanning both sectors, however, in order to emphasise its crucial role in connecting and serving each sector. Parliament is connected to the Exchequer in an administrative sense through HM Treasury but from an accounting and legislative perspective via the 'Central Funds'. The Exchequer and private sector interface through two channels – the Government Banking Service and the Debt Management Office – both via accounts at the Bank of England.

The majority of the money used by individuals and businesses in the UK takes the form of commercial bank deposits. These are liabilities of commer-

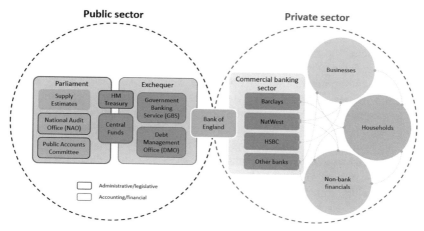

Figure 1.1   *A sketch of the institutions involved in the government's financial activities*

cial banks which are issued to customers when a bank receives a corresponding asset, for example, a loan agreement, and as such, most of the bank deposits held within the UK banking system are the result of private sector borrowing, for example through mortgages, loans and credit cards. The deposits created in this manner by individual commercial banks operate as a single form of money because each bank agrees to deliver a common form of money to their customers on request. This form of money is known as Sterling, is a liability of the Bank of England, and can take the form of banknotes or deposits held by commercial banks in accounts at the Bank. Sterling is thus used to settle transactions made using commercial bank deposits, either by way of a cash withdrawal or transfer between banks using their respective accounts at the Bank of England. As such, banks require sufficient access to central bank money in order to successfully accommodate the business of their customers.

The Bank of England ('the Bank') is the central bank of the United Kingdom. It has a delegated responsibility for conducting monetary policy, regulating the financial services sector, as well as managing the primary payment settlement systems. These activities are formalised under the 'Sterling Monetary Framework' (SMF), which underpins the commercial banking system. The entire capital, comprising £14,553,000 of Bank Stock, is held by the Treasury Solicitor on behalf of HM Treasury following nationalisation of the Bank in 1946. The Bank is therefore part of the public sector, though not central government. Section 4(1) of the Bank of England Act 1946 declared the right of HM Treasury to 'give such directions to the Bank as, after consultation with the Governor of the Bank, they think necessary in the public interest'. This authority has been qualified by subsequent Acts of Parliament. The Bank of England Act 1998 s10 – commonly understood to represent the granting of 'independence' to the Bank – added the clause 'except in relation to monetary policy', and the Bank of England and Financial Services Act 2016 added a similar exemption relating to Prudential Regulation. HM Treasury retains a public interest power to give directions to the Bank regarding monetary policy,[4] sets the Bank's financial stability objectives, appoints or approves all of the members of the Monetary Policy Committee, and has been closely involved with most prominent monetary policy initiatives since 2008.

Compared to other central banks, the Bank of England facilities are open to a wide range of financial firms[5] including banks, building societies, broker/dealers, central counterparties and International Central Securities Depositories. Each of these can obtain a deposit account at the Bank of England (reserve settlement account) allowing them final and immediate settlement in Sterling with other firms in the framework. In addition, they have access to Operational Standing Facilities where they can retain spare funds in their reserve settlement account, or tender high-quality collateral (typically government securities) with which to borrow funds from the Bank. Banks, building societies and broker-dealers also have access to liquidity upgrade facilities, whereby the Bank of England will lend government securities in exchange for lower-quality collateral such as mortgages and corporate bonds. Since the Bank of England is also the bank supervisory authority, if a bank meets the supervisory threshold conditions to operate and has signed up to the framework, it will be able to use these 'lender of last resort' facilities.[6] Government securities are used widely within the current Sterling Monetary Framework, a feature which will be discussed in detail below.

1.3   THE PARLIAMENTARY BASIS FOR UK GOVERNMENT SPENDING

1.3.1   The Central Funds

The UK government maintains several core accounting structures known as the Central Funds. These sit apart from any specific governmental department and represent the legal entities from which all government expenditure arises, from which all government securities are issued, and to which most[7] government revenue is ultimately surrendered. The Central Funds comprise the Consolidated Fund (CF), the National Loans Fund (NLF), the Contingencies Fund (CCF) and the Exchange Equalisation Account (EEA), and are connected to the banking system via two distinct interfaces: (1) Government Banking Service, which administers government expenditure and the receipt of revenue; and (2) the Debt Management Office, which deals in the trading of government securities. It will be seen that the balance of flows through these two interfaces represents one of the fundamental organising principles of the Exchequer.

The Central Funds each provide an accounting framework for distinct aspects of the government's financial activities. The Consolidated Fund was established in 1787 as '... one fund into which shall flow every stream of public revenue and from which shall come the supply for every service'.[8] The National Loans Fund was established in 1968[9] in order to account for the government's lending and borrowing activities separately. As such, the Consolidated Fund is, today, sometimes conceptualised as the government's 'current account', dealing ostensibly with the cash flows associated with daily expenditure and revenue, while the National Loans Fund records many of the government's financial assets and liabilities. The Contingencies Fund is used to enable urgent expenditure beyond that which is provided by routine procedures. The Exchange Equalisation Account is used to manage the government's foreign exchange and other financial reserves. An additional account, the Debt Management Account (DMA), is not formally one of the Central Funds, but operates as an agent of the National Loans Fund and exhibits some of the characteristics of the Central Funds. It is useful, therefore, to consider the DMA along with the other Central Funds.

The Central Funds were likened, in a debate in the House of Lords in 1968,[10] to the Holy Trinity – being jointly and severally 'incomprehensible'. They can perhaps be best understood by analogy to a Russian Doll. The Debt Management Account and the Exchange Equalisation Account are both funded, either implicitly or explicitly, by the National Loans Fund, and can therefore be considered to be dependents of the latter. The National Loans Fund is, in turn, automatically funded by the Consolidated Fund, of which it is therefore a dependent. Similarly, the Contingencies Fund draws its provisions exclusively from the Consolidated Fund. It follows that the Consolidated Fund is the accounting entity which is the backstop on all of the others and understanding the nature of the Central Funds system can be somewhat reduced to an exercise in understanding the Consolidated Fund specifically.

1.3.2   The Exchequer and Audit Departments Act 1866

The Consolidated Fund is governed by the Exchequer and Audit Departments Act 1866 (the '1866 Act'),[11] which states the conditions and mechanisms under which money can be issued out of the Fund for the purposes of public expenditure. Paramount among these conditions is the stipulation in section 11 that

> this enactment shall not be construed to empower the Treasury or any authority to direct the payment … of expenditure not sanctioned by any Act whereby services are or may be charged on the Consolidated Fund, or by a vote of the House of Commons, or by an Act for the appropriation of the supplies annually granted by Parliament.

Sections 13 and 15 of the 1866 Act then specify the mechanism which relates two forms of Parliamentary authorisation explicitly to the provision of money: Standing Services and Supply Services.

Standing Services are forms of government expenditure which are authorised from the Consolidated Fund permanently by virtue of specific Acts of Parliament. For example, the Commissioners for Revenue and Customs Act 2005 permits His Majesty's Revenue and Customs (HMRC) to issue out of the Consolidated Fund when necessary for purposes of making tax repayments or for provisioning the National Insurance Fund. Equally, HM Treasury may issue from the Consolidated Fund in order to make urgent advances to government departments,[12] for making interventions in the banking sector for purposes of financial stability,[13] and for making interest payments on government debt.[14] These are all, therefore, Consolidated Fund Standing Services.

Supply Services, in contrast, are voted annually and result in the passing of Supply and Appropriation Acts[15] by Parliament. There are usually two such Acts each year (in March and July) and they itemise what would typically be considered to be the routine expenditure of government, including allowances for individual government departments and other public bodies (e.g., health, education, defence, etc.). These Acts explicitly authorise the itemised expenditure to be issued from the Consolidated Fund.

Sections 13 (Standing Services) and 15 (Supply Services) of the 1866 Act detail how provisions made in such legislation are discharged within the banking system. In both cases, the mechanism is, for all intents and purposes, identical. The first step is the passing of legislation through Parliament which authorises an issue from the Consolidated Fund. Next is a requisition by the Treasury for funds granted by Parliament to the Comptroller and Auditor General (today, the head of the National Audit Office) whose responsibility it is to verify that the request is consistent with the terms under which Parliament authorised the expenditure. If satisfied, the Comptroller and Auditor General grants 'a credit' on the Consolidated Fund account and this approval permits HM Treasury to order the Bank of England to make an 'issue' to a 'Principal Accountant'.

1.3.3   Principal Accountants

The 'Principal Accountants', to which issues out of the Consolidated Fund are made, are public entities holding accounts at the Bank of England. Today, the most important of these accounts fall under the auspices of the Commissioners for Revenue and Customs due to their specific responsibility for the activities of HMRC but more generally to their oversight of Government Banking Service (GBS). The latter was established in 2008 to consolidate the government's banking arrangements into a single, 'shared service'. Previously, much of the government's banking activities were concentrated in the Office of Her Majesty's Paymaster General (OPG) with the exception of HMRC which had held alternative banking arrangements with commercial partners. The consolidation expanded the existing OPG banking model across the whole of government and parts of the wider public sector.

The Office of HM Paymaster General was established in 1836 as a consolidated payment office for the armed forces and, later, the civil service.[16] The office was responsible for the administration and settlement of payments between government departments and the private sector and functioned analogously to a commercial bank in some respects. For example, the Paymaster would keep detailed ledger records of the Parliamentary allowances granted to departments which, akin to commercial bank deposits, would represent a departmental claim over the Paymaster for future settlement of their expenditure. Equally, the Paymaster would hold, like a commercial bank, cash balances in accounts at the Bank of England which could be drawn upon in order to satisfy such settlement obligations. These accounts were, in turn, provisioned from the Consolidated Fund according to the process described above in conjunction with the 1866 Act. Oversight of these functions was transferred to HMRC in 2006 though the accounts 'remain the property of the Paymaster General'.[17]

With the establishment of the Government Banking Service, the OPG was expanded and rebranded with the accounts and overall banking model remaining in place. The main difference was the introduction of commercial banking partners for the provision of retail banking transmission services previously provided by the Bank of England. Currently, NatWest provides accounts for most government departments, facilitating spending into the banking sector, while Barclays serves HMRC and the Driver and Vehicle Licensing Agency (DVLA) and thus administers the majority of the government's revenue. Settlement on behalf of these accounts is nevertheless provided by accounts held within the Exchequer at the Bank of England and the commercial partner's balance sheets are impacted only transiently or not at all depending on the type of transaction undertaken[18] (Figure 1.2).

Therefore, the consequence of the 1866 Act is that, following the granting of Parliamentary authorisation for expenditure, a cash balance is credited by the Bank of England to an Exchequer account within the Government Banking Service. These credits are made primarily to the Supply Account[19] of the Paymaster General (PMG) for the purposes of facilitating the spending by most government departments, but may also be made to, amongst others, the General Account of the Commissioners of Inland Revenue and the General Account of the Commissioners of Customs and Excise for purposes relating to tax and National Insurance. Once balances exist in these accounts, they can be deployed into the banking system.

1.3.4   The Consolidated Fund Account

The issue of money by the Bank of England under order of HM Treasury takes the form of a credit being made to the account of a designated public entity (e.g., PMG, HMRC, etc.) and a corresponding debit being charged on the Consolidated Fund. A fundamental design feature of the modern-day Exchequer is that the Consolidated Fund starts every day with a zero cash[20] balance, yet regardless, orders for issues out of the account are nevertheless made and fulfilled.[21] It follows that credits to the Principal Accountants arise as a straightforward balance sheet expansion for both the Bank and the Exchequer, with each granting a new liability to the other. In this manner, spending proceeds as new money under order of the Treasury but with ultimate provenance in Parliament.

The terms under which the Bank of England issues money on behalf of Parliament pre-dates the 1866 Act and has been somewhat simplified in the intervening period. A fundamental aspect of this relationship through the nineteenth and early twentieth centuries was the stipulation of a quarterly accounting period over which debits (expenditure) and credits (receipts) on the Consolidated Fund would accumulate before being reconciled. At the end of each quarter, if it was established that the total revenue was not sufficient to defray the cumulative charges on the account (i.e., the debits representing issues for expenditure), a formal advance was arranged with the Bank of England in order to close the quarterly accounts, and which would be repayable in the subsequent quarter. Prior to 1866 an issue of Exchequer bills to the Bank, known in this context as 'Deficiency bills', was made in order to provide the counterpart security for the advance on the Bank's balance sheet. Following the 1866 Act, this security took the form of a simple accounting memorandum which would later become known as the government's 'Ways and Means Account'.

The Bank of England Act 1819 mandated that any lending to the government by the Bank must be explicitly authorised by Parliament. The 1866 Act

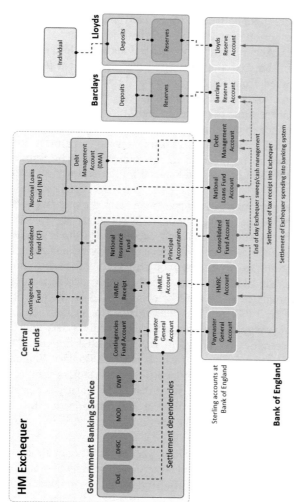

Note: The commercial banking sector is represented here by Barclays and Lloyds which hold internal ledger records describing the allocation of deposit liabilities to their customers, and also accounts at the Bank of England for the purpose of settling customer payments with other institutions. The Exchequer also holds a number of accounts at the Bank of England which are used to settle payments with the commercial banking system and make internal transfers within the Exchequer. Government Banking Service resembles the commercial banks by organising a system of ledger deposits representing the allowances of governmental departments and other entities, all serviced by settlement accounts held at the Bank of England. A wide range of transactions occur between the accounts shown at the Bank of England and the 'settlement transfer' arrows shown are not exhaustive.

Figure 1.2   *Schematic diagram showing the banking interrelationships between the Central Funds, Government Banking Service, the Bank of England and the banking sector* (and the 1834 Exchequer Reform Act before it) granted such authority in the context of the quarterly deficiencies described above. However, the very fact that issues from the Consolidated Fund could exceed receipts over the quarter meant that advances were implicitly being made *during* each quarter and prior to any formal reconciliation and recognition at the end of the quarter. It was therefore possible to differentiate between a routine advance of money *within* the mandated accounting period, and the more formal advancing of money *across* accounting periods. Accordingly, more general authority for advances was typically specified in the Acts that permitted the government to spend annually. Expenditure issued from the Consolidated Fund was, thus, never dependent on the existence of a provisioning balance. Indeed, this feature was codified in each pertinent piece of spending legislation, enacted annually or otherwise, with a reference to the charges being made 'out of the growing produce of the Consolidated Fund'.[22] This phrasing served to connect issuances with 'all the revenues to be received in the future',[23] thereby framing expenditure implicitly as a form of credit advanced on the security of future tax revenues.

Several changes to these arrangements were made from the mid-twentieth century though none changed the overall implications substantively. In 1954, the requirement for the preparation of quarterly accounts and the associated system of quarterly deficiency advances was repealed, leaving advances to be managed simply according to day-to-day requirements. At the same time, a blanket provision was made such that 'Any sum charged by any Act, whenever passed, on the Consolidated Fund shall be charged also on the growing produce of the Fund.'[24] In 1968, the National Loans Act established the National Loans Fund which would adopt responsibility for the government's borrowing and lending activities on behalf of the Consolidated Fund. The Act repealed the Bank of England Act 1819 which required Bank of England advances to be explicitly authorised by Parliament, but nevertheless stipulated a blanket authority for the Bank to lend any sums that HM Treasury is permitted to borrow.[25] As with the 'growing produce' clause, authorisation for the Bank to lend to the government ceased to be explicitly required in individual items of legislation thereafter.

The National Loans Act 1968 also defined a *daily* accounting cycle under which the Consolidated Fund Account would be zeroed each night by transfers to or from the National Loans Fund. This provision explicitly anticipated the possibility of end-of-day deficiencies much as quarter-end deficiencies had been anticipated earlier.[26] As a consequence, money would be advanced in the first instance on an *intraday*, rather than *intra-quarter*, basis and either cleared by the close of business or formalised as a Ways and Means advance[27] overnight. The context at the time was one in which negotiable government securities were managed by the Bank of England on behalf of the government in conjunction with daily monetary policy operations. In that context, the use of Ways and Means advances was often simply a means of reconciling the objectives of monetary policy with the government's daily net financial flows.[28] This changed in 2000 when responsibility for the government's daily cash management activities was formally transferred to the Debt Management Office (DMO). As a consequence, a policy objective was undertaken to avoid the routine use of the Ways and Means Account, with the implication that any intraday advances would be eliminated by the close of business each day via exchange for other government securities. This effectively completed the historical trend from a quarterly accounting cycle, within which money would be advanced and issued, to a daily one. It can be noted that while the treaties of Maastricht (1993) and Lisbon (2009) prohibited central bank lending to state governments of the signatories, intraday credit and the UK Government's Ways and Means Account were explicitly exempted from any prohibitions. This arrangement was written directly into UK law in 2019 with the UK's departure from the European Union.[29]

1.3.5 The National Loans Fund Account

The daily flows accounted for directly on the Consolidated Fund are those associated with most forms of routine expenditure and revenue. The National Loans Fund is involved with additional forms of financial inflow and outflow and these relate to the government's borrowing activities,[30] such as those associated with the issuance of government securities and the provision of National Savings and Investment products, as well as the provision and repayment of loans to public bodies. On any given day, therefore, the National Loans Fund Account at the Bank of England may be required to make and receive payments in service of these activities. Perhaps the most conspicuous form of expenditure chargeable on the National Loans Fund is the repayment of the principal associated with maturing government securities.

As with the Consolidated Fund, issues for expenditure out of the National Loans Fund proceed via the granting of a credit on the Fund by the Comptroller and Auditor General, in accordance with section 1 of the National Loans Act 1968. Unlike the Consolidated Fund, however, there is no direct provision within the 1968 Act which confers the subsequent right of HM Treasury to order the Bank of England to make an issue in association with such an approved credit. Instead, there is simply a stipulation that any charges on the National Loans Fund have 'recourse to the Consolidated Fund' and, as such, qualify for the provisions of section 13 of the 1866 Act described earlier. As such, expenditure from the National Loans Fund, including the redemption of government debt, proceeds irrefutably, by law, via the issue of money by the

Bank of England, in the same manner as those forms of expenditure charged explicitly on the Consolidated Fund.[31]

1.4   THE FUNCTIONING OF THE UK EXCHEQUER

The reason for emphasising, in some detail, the legislative context in which government expenditure occurs is that a clear understanding of the mechanics and controls under which spending proceeds affects how the government's other financial activities are perceived. Taxation and the sale of government securities are invariably understood as being exercises which are undertaken in order to enable the government to spend. With a clear picture of how spending is actually enacted, the 'money sourcing' motivations of tax revenue and debt sales become redundant and these activities need to be reframed. This section will describe the functioning of the UK Exchequer more holistically.

1.4.1   The Allocation of Money

We're now in a position to describe the money allocation process and this is illustrated in Figure 1.3 which seeks to show the balance sheet impacts of the various entities involved when the government spends. These are the Consolidated Fund, Government Banking Service, a notional government department and the Bank of England. The Bank can be considered to hold a balance sheet in the first instance comprising reserve deposit liabilities to commercial banks and government securities held as the balancing asset. All other entities have, for purposes of illustration, no assets or liabilities at the outset (Figure 1.3, step 1).

The first step is for the Treasury to make a requisition for expenditure, which typically occurs on a monthly basis. As explained previously, should this request be approved by the Comptroller and Auditor General, it results in the granting of a credit on the Consolidated Fund. At this point, although the expenditure has been approved, there is no 'money' available in the form of cash balances at the Bank of England. Indeed, this requires another step, and one that is typically taken only on a daily basis in order to direct cash flows optimally to those government entities whose payments are imminently due for settlement. However, the existence of an authorised 'credit' on the Consolidated Fund means that the Treasury can, at any time subsequently, order such a balance to be realised. The authorised credit thus represents an asset that can be 'cashed' at the Bank. This asset is held by the Government Banking Service and represents a claim on the Consolidated Fund. With this asset in hand, the Government Banking Service can extend ledger credits to the department that is the subject of the requisitioned expenditure. At this point, therefore, a government department has an allowance, granted by Parliament, and manifested as a balance within the Government Banking Service.[32] The Government Banking Service holds a claim over the Consolidated Fund as an asset, but has a liability to the department in the form of an allowance and an obligation to provide payment settlement when a payment instruction is received. The Consolidated Fund holds a liability to the Government Banking Service for the provision of cash when needed (Figure 1.3, step 2).

From day to day, HM Treasury and the Government Banking Service seek to manage imminent cash flows. The next step, therefore, is for the Treasury to order the Bank to make cash available for the settlement of anticipated expenditure. This is at the discretion of the Treasury to the extent that approved credits on the Consolidated Fund are available and proceeds via the crediting of the account of a Principal Accountant according to the 1866 Act. This account, in the present case, is held by the Government Banking Service at the Bank of England, and in receiving such a credit has essentially swapped a claim on the Consolidated Fund for a cash claim on the Bank of England. Correspondingly, the Consolidated Fund has reduced its liability to the Government Banking Service, but undertaken a new liability to the Bank, that is, a cash debt. As such, the balance sheets of both the Government Banking Service and the Consolidated Fund have changed in composition but not in overall size. The Bank of England, on the other hand, has increased its balance sheet by issuing cash to the Government Banking Service but holds an equal claim over the Consolidated Fund (Figure 1.3, step 3).

There now exists a cash balance in an Exchequer account which can be spent into the banking system. This balance is classified as 'public deposits' on the Bank of England's balance sheet, rather than the 'reserves', which are uniquely held by commercial banks operating within the Sterling Monetary Framework. When a government department elects to spend some of its Parliamentary allowance, this results in the reduction of the ledger credits administered by the Government Banking Service and the transfer of cash from the Government Banking Service account at the Bank of England to the reserve settlement account of the recipient bank. As such, the Government Banking Service sees a reduction in its own balance sheet, having effectively used up some of its Parliamentary credits. The Bank of England's balance remains the same in size at this stage having merely transferred a public deposit liability for a reserve deposit one, while the balancing claim on the Consolidated Fund remains outstanding. In the commercial banking sector (not shown in Figure 1.3), additional central bank reserves held are mirrored by the creation of commercial bank deposits which are allocated to the final recipients of the spending (Figure 1.3, step 4).

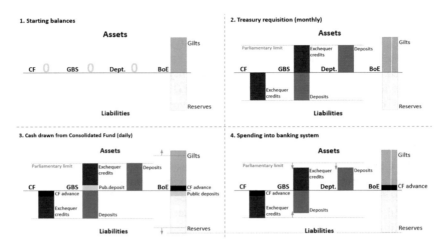

Figure 1.3   Sequence of balance sheet adjustments in the allocation of
              money to the Exchequer

1.4.2   The Receipt of Money

The 1866 Act specified that the gross revenue received by the Commissioners
for Inland Revenue and the Commissioners for Customs and Excise should
be surrendered to the Consolidated Fund at such times as the Treasury pre-
scribe. The 2005 Commissioners for Revenue and Customs Act combined
the responsibilities of each into HM Revenue and Customs but reaffirmed the
principle that receipts be transferred to the Consolidated Fund. As such, the
Consolidated Fund represents the legally mandated, final destination for most
of the government's revenue.

   Following the establishment of the Government Banking Service and the
current commercial banking partnerships, HMRC is supported in its revenue
collection activities by Barclays Bank PLC. Government revenue accumulates
in accounts at Barclays and is transferred to HMRC accounts[33] at the Bank of
England several times each day. These transfers have the opposite impact on
the balance sheets of the Government Banking Service and the commercial
banking sector, principally reducing the reserves held by the commercial
banking sector and increasing the public deposits held within the Government
Banking Service. It can be noted that all money is transferred into the
Exchequer via the medium of central bank money. Tax revenue is not received
in the form of commercial bank deposits for the simple reason that the destination account(s) are held at the Bank of England and not commercial banks.

1.4.3 The Daily Accounting Cycle

The Exchequer undertakes an end-of-day process that seeks to rationalise all cash balances held, known as the 'sweep'. This does not affect the Exchequer credits held by the Government Banking Service or the GBS deposits held by departments which are entirely internal to the Exchequer. Rather, the consolidation refers only to sterling balances held in accounts at the Bank of England and which are, by definition, liabilities of the Bank. This process culminates in all balances being transferred, ultimately, to the National Loans Fund, and takes place by way of permanent transfers as well as overnight lending. The overarching aim of this consolidation is to rationalise the Exchequer position with respect to balances held at the Bank of England. The result represents the net position of the Exchequer which, by accounting identity, also represents the net position of the banking sector due to the government's activities.

A diagrammatic representation of the end-of-day sweep of Exchequer accounts is shown in Figure 1.4. Represented are the Consolidated Fund and the National Loans Fund, as well as two of the accounts described previously that are administered by the Government Banking Service. These are: the Drawing Account of HM Paymaster General (PMG) which is involved in settling expenditure into the banking system; and (one of) the HMRC General Account(s) which receives incoming revenue. All of these accounts start each day with a nil balance, as shown in step 1.

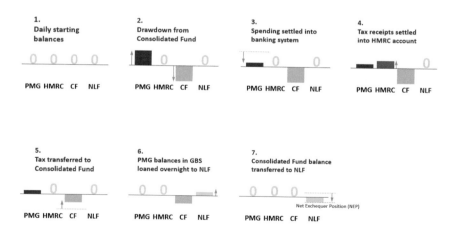

Figure 1.4   *Example of the daily activity and end-of-day cycle with which Exchequer accounts held at the Bank of England are involved*

The first activity shown is the issuance of money for expenditure purposes which is manifested as a credit to the PMG account and an equal and opposite debit on the Consolidated Fund (step 2). This places the Consolidated Fund into a deficit position. When this spending is deployed into the banking system the PMG account is depleted but the debt on the Consolidated Fund remains (step 3). Transfers of tax from the commercial banking sector during the day result in balances accumulating within the HMRC accounts (step 4). At the end of the day (step 5) tax is transferred from the HMRC account(s) to the Consolidated Fund. This is a direct, permanent transfer as obliged by law. Note that, in the example illustrated, this has the effect of zeroing the HMRC account and reducing the deficit on the Consolidated Fund. Next, the remaining balance in the PMG account is loaned overnight to the National Loans Fund (step 6). This has the effect of zeroing the PMG account and, in the example shown, producing a positive balance on the National Loans Fund. Finally, the remaining balance on the Consolidated Fund is also transferred to the National Loans Fund. This zeroes the Consolidated Fund, as mandated by the National Loans Act 1968 s18.

The upshot is that there is a 'Net Exchequer Position' (NEP) on the National Loans Fund which represents the overall position of the Exchequer with respect to the Bank of England. In the example shown, the positive balances held on some accounts were able to cancel against some of the cash debt on the Consolidated Fund, thereby minimising the end-of-day debt to the Bank of England. In the scenario described the Exchequer has ended the day with a net debt to the Bank of England having spent into the banking system more than it drew out through taxation.

There are a couple of aspects of this process that should be noted. First, spending and revenue are both anchored to the Consolidated Fund but proceed during each day via separate accounts at the Bank of England. These accounts are only reconciled at the end of each day and the Consolidated Fund can therefore only ever have a positive balance – by virtue of receiving a transfer over its initial zero starting position – at the *end* of each day. It follows that any and all expenditure from the Consolidated Fund occurs when the Fund has a nil or negative balance and there is never a situation wherein a deposit of tax revenue furnishes a balance that is subsequently used for spending. In this sense, all spending arises as new money advanced under credit and not 'from taxation'.

Second, as alluded to earlier, there is a formal relationship between the Bank and the National Loans Fund for recording an end-of-day debt known as the Ways and Means Account. Often construed as the government's overdraft facility, the Ways and Means Account also represents a form of government security which backs the Bank's money issuance. The logical consequence of the mechanisms set out in the 1866 Act is for spending – in the absence of any additional undertakings – to be formalised as a Ways and Means advance at the end of the day. Such an outcome is entirely within the discretion of HM Treasury and explains how and why *any* spending authorised by Parliament can happen without constraint in all circumstances. Under routine circumstances, however, HM Treasury seeks to avoid such an outcome and this *policy objective* is achieved via the practice known as 'cash management'.

1.4.4   Cash Management and the Exchequer's Neutrality Objective

The daily accounting cycle results in a net cash surplus or cash debt being held in the National Loans Fund. Under the current policy framework, this end-of-day position motivates reactive policy undertaken by the DMO known as 'cash management' and which involves the trading of government securities with the private sector. This activity is usually construed as a 'borrowing' exercise where the government has to raise funds in order to spend. As we've seen, though, the government has no requirement to source cash from the private sector in order to be able to spend because cash is made available by the legislative processes described.

This cash management process and associated policy objective is outlined in the DMO Annual Review:[34]

> The DMA [Debt Management Account] is used to manage the Exchequer's net cash position. Balances in central government accounts contained within the Exchequer pyramid are swept on a daily basis into the NLF and the DMA is required to offset the resultant NLF balance through its borrowing and lending in the money markets. The DMA is held at the Bank of England and a positive end-of-day balance must be maintained at all times; it cannot be overdrawn. Automatic transfers from the government Ways and Means (II) account at the Bank of England would offset any negative end-of-day balances, though it is an objective to minimise such transfers. Thus, evidence of meeting this objective is provided by reference to the number of occasions the DMA goes overdrawn.
>
> KPI 1.1: Ways and Means end-of-day transfers for cash management purposes must be avoided by ensuring that there is always a positive DMA balance.

The motivation for cash management activities is that, by accounting identity, the Exchequer's net position also represents a measure of the impact of the government's financial flows *on the banking sector*. Specifically, an end-of-day *positive* balance on the National Loans Fund Account indicates that cash has been drawn *out of* the banking sector overall, whereas an end-of-day *negative* balance indicates that money has been *added to* the banking sector. Such an effect on the banking sector has the possibility of influencing the interest rate policy which is undertaken by the Bank of England (as a form of inflation management) and therefore needs to be considered if monetary policy is to be conducted coherently.

Prior to the establishment of the DMO in 1998, the government's cash management responsibilities were undertaken directly by the Bank of England in conjunction with daily monetary policy operations. These operations were aimed solely at achieving the appropriate level of central bank money held by commercial banks – as defined by monetary policy objectives – in lieu of the various flows across the banks' balance sheets each day. The Bank would typically trade in Treasury bills,[35] selling bills with a view to producing a systemic shortage of central bank money which could then be alleviated at the Bank's monetary policy rate. As explained above, the government's own activities would affect the 'bankers' balances' by adding or removing money from the banking sector. Other factors, such as the demand for foreign exchange, banknotes or advances to the banks, would also influence aggregate reserve levels. As such, the quantity of Treasury bills traded on a daily or weekly basis was not solely a function of the government's net expenditure and revenue flows, but would instead be influenced by the wider monetary context. In cases wherein the level of market operations conducted by the Bank did not exactly match the government's own daily surplus or deficit, simple accounting adjustments between the Exchequer and the Bank would arise, for example as a change to the balance of the Ways and Means Account or the direct repurchase by the government of bills held by the Banking Department of the Bank. Under this process, therefore, the net effect of the government's daily spending and revenue activities on the banking sector would be somewhat unwound on a daily basis through purchases or sales of Treasury bills, though only to the extent that monetary policy objectives required. The overarching concern of the authorities was the bringing about of a perceived balance to the banking system.

This system was changed following the granting of independence for monetary policy to the Bank of England in 1998 when it was felt that perceptions of a conflict of interest may arise if the authority responsible for monetary policy is also involved with the government's securities trading activities. As such, the DMO was established in 1998 and adopted responsibility for government cash management in 2000. This meant that it was no longer possible to deal with the effect of the government's cash flows alongside the management of the wider monetary system as part of a single, overarching objective, and two distinct objectives, to be enacted by two different institutions, were now required in order to coherently arrive at the same result. The solution was that the DMO would be tasked with offsetting any Net Exchequer Position by the end of each day, and this would present a neutral monetary backdrop to the Bank of England which could then undertake its own objective of explicitly managing outcomes in the banking sector without having to consider the government's financial flows.

The principle of neutrality means that, by design, the Exchequer is to accumulate no cash balances or cash debts on its accounts at the Bank of England by the end of each day, as these would reflect an equal and opposite impact on the banking sector. One implication of this aim is that accounting adjustments between the Exchequer and the Bank, such as a change to the Ways and Means Account, are to be avoided. The DMO's remit is therefore, by the close of business each day, to drain any reserves which have been added to the banking system on days of net spending, or to return reserves which have been removed from the banking sector on days of net revenue. This is achieved by way of the trading of government securities in quantities which reflexively match the (anticipated) Net Exchequer Position. Accordingly, the net result of the Exchequer's activities each day is manifested in changes to the quantity of government securities on issue rather than adjustments to reserve (and, by identity, Exchequer) balances.

Cash management operations are undertaken using an account at the Bank of England called the Debt Management Account. Current practice is for the DMA to hold a positive balance which is maintained from day to day.[36] This balance functions identically to a notional target balance of zero in the sense that credits and debits to the account during any day must be equal if the balance is to be maintained. The intention is that the balance provides a contingency for situations in which the Exchequer experiences a swing in expenditure or revenue which is too late in the day for the DMO to react.[37]

The cash management process is illustrated in Figure 1.5 which describes two scenarios: that of a daily Exchequer deficit (above), and a daily Exchequer surplus (below). In the first step illustrated, the Consolidated Fund and the National Loans Fund start the day with a nil balance whereas the DMA has its prescribed target balance. During the day, activity on the Consolidated Fund and National Loans Fund (see Section 1.4.3) causes variations in their respective balances (step 2), and at the end of the day the balance on the Consolidated Fund is swept into the National Loans Fund (step 3). The resulting balance then represents the Net Exchequer position and it is the DMO's task to offset that quantity. In the case of an Exchequer deficit, the DMO achieves its objective by selling government securities which serves to increase its own balance over the mandated target balance (step 4). The DMO then transfers its excess balance to the National Loans Fund which has the effect of zeroing the latter and restoring the Debt Management Account to its target level (step 5). In the case of an Exchequer daily surplus, the process is similar except the DMO needs to *buy* securities from the private sector in order to dispose of the excess cash.

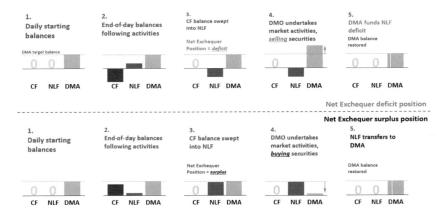

Note: Above, an Exchequer daily net deficit; below, an Exchequer daily net surplus.

Figure 1.5   *Example variations in the balances held at the Bank of England by the Consolidated Fund, the National Loans Fund and the Debt Management Account, describing the end-of-day Net Exchequer Position and the resulting cash management remit*

1.5   SIGNIFICANCE OF THE UK EXCHEQUER IN THE MONETARY SYSTEM

It is commonly claimed, or at least implied, that the UK government is a passive user of sterling with the implication that the government has no agency to create money and must instead obtain existing units of the currency from taxpayers or lenders. This has been belaboured in the era of central bank independence where it is claimed that the UK government has little or no influence over the central bank which it owns. The reality, however, is that the UK government is fundamental to the sterling monetary system, including the creation and issuance of monetary instruments and guarantees that underpin the entire monetary framework.

1.5.1   The UK Government and the Banking System

The primary function of the banking system is to create credit via the issuance of loans against suitable collateral. This essentially transforms the liabilities (the promise of repayment) of individuals, businesses and other entities into a standard form (commercial bank deposits) that can circulate effectively within the country's payment systems. Bank deposits created in this way by distinct commercial banks can be exchanged seamlessly with one another because they are implicitly pegged to a common medium of exchange – central bank money – which is used to settle interbank transfers or cash withdrawals. If we consider the term 'money' to describe only the deposits that are created by the banking system in this manner, then it is trivial to conclude that the UK government does not literally create money. Such a conclusion would, however, disregard the extent to which the UK government exerts an influence on the banking sector to, amongst other things, create 'money' on its behalf.

As explained previously, UK government spending arises following the granting of central bank deposits to specific Exchequer accounts by the Bank of England, and the establishment of a corresponding debt on the Consolidated Fund. These central bank deposits are then transferred to a commercial bank which in turn grants deposits to the ultimate recipient of the spending. It can be argued that by taking on a debt in exchange for deposits, the government's interaction with the banking system is essentially the same as that wherein private sector entities (e.g., individuals, businesses) take on loans. There are at least two important distinctions, however, both of which are a consequence of the government's unique status with respect to legislation.

First, and most straightforwardly, the government compels the Bank of England to advance central bank deposits by virtue of the 1866 Act. Under these provisions, the Bank of England has no discretion over whether to extend credit (and accept the counterpart debt asset).[38] This legislative privilege is not available to other entities within the economy which must instead be judged as creditworthy by the banking system in order to be the counterparty to money creation. As such, though the government may not literally create money itself (under this definition), it has the power and the mechanisms to delegate this activity to the banking system on its own terms.

Second, and perhaps more fundamentally, the UK government is the only entity within the UK economy which can compel the payment of taxes. This privilege gives the government, uniquely, a guaranteed claim over the resources of the country and as such makes the government the most creditworthy agent in the economy. This uniquely elevated credit standing can be discerned from the various ways in which the government supports the banking sector. For example, almost the entirety of the Bank of England's assets are represented by government securities and therefore the cash and central bank deposits which are collectively known as 'base money' are underpinned by liabilities of the government.[39] Moreover, there are provisions in law for ensuring that the government reflexively provides such securities to back the banknote issue,[40] while additional injections of capital[41] or granting of indemnities[42] to support the Bank's business more generally are also provided by HM Treasury. It follows that the creditworthiness of the central bank – which manages the currency – derives from the financial security inherent in the government. Equally, HM Treasury stands ready to provide financial assistance for purposes of economic stability in the event of commercial bank failure. Such stabilisation powers include the transfer of banking entities into public ownership[43] and the provision of deposit insurance[44] both of which featured in the response to the Global Financial Crisis from 2008. As the only entity within the economy which is in a position to extend such support, it is clear that the financial security of the government surpasses even that of the banking system which creates the instruments we typically consider to be money. From this perspective, it is clear why the banking sector would be satisfied to advance credit to the government in exchange for the most robust financial promises available, even without explicit compulsion.

This concept of supreme creditworthiness represents the fundamental link between taxation and spending. Taxes *do* allow a government to spend, but not in the way that is usually implied whereby each individual pound must be received before it can be spent. Instead, the guaranteed claim over national resources that the imposition of taxes provides generates the unsurpassed creditworthiness that enables the government to leverage the banking system for its own purposes. This notion is enshrined in UK law with the provision that expenditure from the Consolidated Fund is charged 'on the growing produce of the Fund',[45] explicitly linking *current* spending to *future* tax revenue. The imposition of taxes in the abstract, therefore, regardless of their quantitative or other characteristics, is a sufficient basis for the government to spend and to cause the creation of money in the process.

1.5.2   The Role and Function of Government 'Debt'

The creditworthiness of the UK government derives from the direct linkage between the authority to tax and the authority to spend which is realised in the Consolidated Fund.[46] Given the provisions in legislation which anchor the other Central Funds (and the Debt Management Account) to the Consolidated Fund, it follows that any claim on the Central Funds is ultimately a claim on the Consolidated Fund and inherits the same, paramount creditworthiness. It is instructive to examine the various types of claims on the Central Funds that can be held in order to further understand and characterise the role of government in the monetary system.

The most conspicuous forms of claim over the Central Funds are gilts and Treasury bills which are issued from the National Loans Fund and the Debt Management Account respectively.[47] Gilt-Edged securities ('gilts') are time-limited bonds sold with maturities exceeding one year and which pay a six-monthly 'coupon' (analogous to an interest payment) and principal upon maturity. Treasury bills are zero-coupon securities with maturities of less than one year and typically sold at discount to their face value whereby they confer a yield to the holder upon maturity. A fundamental feature of gilts and Treasury bills is that they are negotiable instruments and are thus widely traded in financial markets. Other types of claims on the Central Funds are not negotiable. For example, National Savings & Investments (NS&I) is an Executive Agency of HM Treasury which offers personal savings facilities to individuals, while Ways and Means advances (W&M), as explained previously, are held only by the Bank of England. Both of these essentially represent deposits made by counterparties in the National Loans Fund.[48]

These various forms of claim upon the Central Funds serve broadly two functions within the UK economy. First, they are used as fundamental instruments in the management of the monetary system. In this context, gilts (and to a lesser extent today, Treasury bills and Ways and Means advances) represent almost the entirety of the assets held by the Bank of England. This is, at least partly, a reflection of the predominant use of government securities by the Bank in the implementation of monetary policy. For example, the circulating stocks of gilts and Treasury bills are traditionally used as a buffer stock with which to regulate the price of central bank reserve deposits and, by extension, interest rates more generally. More specifically, the Bank may buy or sell these government securities (in exchange for central bank reserves) in order to direct prices in wholesale, interbank lending markets towards the Bank's policy rate.[49] Monetary policy therefore requires a sufficient supply of government securities and the Bank has agreements in place for the DMO to issue such securities on request for this reason. Equally, commercial banks may require additional central bank reserves for settlement purposes at their own discretion and therefore hold government securities for use as collateral or outright trading with the Bank of England (or other banks).

As explained by Monetary Policy Committee member Gertjan Vlieghe, 'When a central bank issues reserves, the main counterpart asset on the central bank balance sheet is generally some form of government financing.'[50] Evidently, government securities share a very close relationship with central bank reserve deposits: they represent the residual stock of reserves drained out of the central bank's reserve settlement account system according to monetary policy objectives, and the medium of exchange with which the banking sector can obtain new reserves. This coupling is exemplified by recent monetary policy initiatives wherein the Bank of England supplied gilts (Discount Window) and Treasury bills (Special Liquidity Scheme, Funding for Lending Scheme) to banks and building societies in exchange for eligible private sector collateral in order to enable access to central bank money more readily.[51]

The second main function for claims upon the Central Funds is that of a highly secure store of value. In this context, HM Treasury holds a contingent liability to the Financial Services Compensation Scheme for the provision of commercial bank deposit insurance.[52] This effectively associates bank deposits up to a value of £85,000 per person with a claim on the National Loans Fund and the creditworthiness inherent therein. Balances in excess of this threshold amount are therefore vulnerable to the risk of bank failure. NS&I provides an alternative, highly secure way for individual savers to deposit money with the National Loans Fund. Larger institutional investors, such as pension funds and insurance companies, are not eligible for NS&I products and therefore tend to hold negotiable government securities, particularly gilts, for this purpose. In this sense, gilts represent a saving instrument of the same creditworthiness as central bank reserves, but which can be held in large quantities by individuals and non-banking institutions.[53]

The claims upon the Central Funds which are represented by gilts, Treasury bills, NS&I deposits and Ways and Means advances are collectively known as the 'national debt'. This debt is often characterised as being a consequence of government profligacy, with the implication that it should be reduced or eliminated. As explained, however, these instruments play specific roles within the existing monetary system, being fundamental to the implementation of monetary policy and the provision of secure forms of saving. Given these functions, there is an inherent demand for these 'debt' instruments – from individuals, non-banks, and banks including the central bank – much as there is a demand for bank deposits, banknotes and coins. Indeed, government securities exhibit money-like qualities, with negotiable securities being an important medium of exchange (for purchasing or borrowing central bank money), and all exhibiting a store of wealth property which is the most secure in the monetary system. The reduction or elimination of government debt would therefore have significant implications for private sector wealth and the functioning of the monetary system, though these consequences are scarcely referenced by those anxious about government debt.

1.5.3   The Government's Monetary Circuit

From this perspective, we can widen the definition of 'money' and consider claims upon the Central Funds to be, in effect, a form of money. The creation of such claims represents the creation of a monetary asset which can circulate and be held by parties within the economy, in some cases as assets backing other forms of money issuance, but invariably according to demand. In this manner, it is straightforward to see the monetary-asset creating role of the government through the functioning of the Exchequer. These are either held by counterparties or discounted[54] into 'sterling' pounds (a claim on the Bank of England) by the banking system in order to provide access to the sterling payment clearing systems. A circuit through which such government money originates, circulates and is extinguished can be described.

Claims upon the Central Funds originate with a vote in Parliament granting government expenditure. These claims are then transferred to the Bank of England via the process mandated by the 1866 Act, with the Bank subsequently holding a claim over the Central Funds (specifically an intraday debt of the Consolidated Fund) and granting its own form of money (sterling) to the Exchequer. In effect, the historic use of gold and silver tokens within the UK monetary system still exists. The Exchequer issues 'gold' pounds ('gilt-edged stocks and bills'), and the Bank of England issues 'silver' pounds (sterling). As the entity which facilitates the interchanging of gold and silver pounds,[55] the Bank of England thus sits with both on its balance sheet as asset and liability, respectively. When the government chooses to spend, this simply results in a transfer of the (silver) central bank deposits to a third-party bank, but they remain liabilities on the Bank of England's balance sheet balanced by a (gold) claim on the Consolidated Fund.

Due to cash management policy, the Exchequer seeks to offset central bank money added to the banking system (and correspondingly the Bank's claim on the Consolidated Fund) and creates a new claim on the National Loans Fund in the form of a gilt (or, equally, a Treasury bill or NS&I deposit). This gilt is exchanged for the new central bank money held in the banking system and subsequently the Exchequer holds a claim on the Bank of England equivalent in size to the claim that the Bank holds on the Consolidated Fund. Since the issuers of gold and silver pounds hold one another's liabilities, these mutual claims cancel, leaving only the gilts now held in the private sector. The claim upon the Central Funds held by the Bank of England has effectively been transferred into the private sector, though the form has changed from an intraday central bank claim on the Consolidated Fund to a negotiable claim on the National Loans Fund. The overall effect of the spending operation is that the private sector was paid in gold pounds,[56] albeit facilitated via the payment infrastructure which is enumerated in silver pounds.

Once gold pounds are held by the private sector, they can be exchanged into silver pounds in a variety of ways. Simple trading of gilts and Treasury bills enables the ownership of gold and silver pounds to be switched, though this does not affect the aggregate quantities of each in circulation. More generally, gold pounds can be discounted into silver pounds with the involvement of the Bank of England. For example, the Bank may elect to purchase gilts from the private sector by issuing central bank deposits under monetary policy objectives, as is typified by conventional open market operations or the more recent initiative known as Quantitative Easing. Alternatively, a commercial bank may seek additional liquidity in the form of central bank deposits and submit gilts or Treasury bills to the Bank of England as collateral.[57] Such a process is routine, for example, in the Bank's provision of intraday credit for Real-Time Gross Settlement (RTGS) transactions. Equally, maturing gilts and Treasury bills, as well as withdrawals from the NS&I, are served under the National Loans Act 1968 'with recourse to the Consolidated Fund'. As such, a new claim on the Consolidated Fund is allocated to the Bank of England under the terms of the 1866 Act, and the Bank duly produces the silver pounds for payment to the holder of the expiring claim over the Central Funds. In each of these cases, a third-party claim over the Central Funds is effectively transferred to the Bank of England.

When tax revenue arrives at the Exchequer – in the form of silver, central bank money – it has the effect of cancelling gold pounds. This arises in one of two ways depending on intraday conditions. If the tax received is less than the Exchequer's spending on any given day, then it directly cancels against some of the Bank of England's outstanding (gold) intraday claim on the Consolidated Fund. If, on the other hand, daily tax receipts exceed daily spending, the Exchequer ends the day with a surplus of central bank money which it then uses to buy back gilts or Treasury bills from the private sector. (When the issuer of gold pounds itself holds gold pounds, they are effectively cancelled.) Either way, taxes received serve to reduce the outstanding claims upon the Central Funds that originated in Parliament.

1.5.4   The Government's Macroeconomic Context

Although monetary conditions and particularly price stability are paramount in the motivation for monetary policy and, by extension, much of the functioning of the Exchequer, the government operates within a context which features several inherently deflationary factors. Among these are the desire of the domestic private sector to *net* save and to *net* import.

A well-known consequence of the decision of private sector individuals or businesses to seek to accumulate financial wealth is for aggregate incomes to fall. This is because the withholding of spending – that is, the choice to spend less than one's income – causes a leakage from the circular flow of money that determines aggregate levels of spending and income. The contractionary effects produced by the saving activities of some in the private sector can be counteracted by others spending *more* than their income – that is, by borrowing. Depending on the balance between saving and borrowing activities, aggregate income may adjust upwards or downwards, but in any case, the private sector can have no *aggregate* financial savings if all of the monetary assets in the sector held are matched by a corresponding debt (e.g., as loans with the banking system).

In general, it is not possible for any whole sector (however defined) to save in *aggregate* unless there is a source of money from *outside* of the sector. This arises from the simple principle that any financial asset – including those we call 'money' – is also a liability for some counterparty. *Within* a sector, these assets and liabilities invariably sum to zero and therefore the only way for a given sector to accumulate a positive, net quantity of financial assets is to hold those which are issued by another sector. If the government injects money into the private sector, for example, then there exist financial assets which can be accumulated that have no counterpart debt within the private sector. These can be termed *net financial assets* – assets held as financial wealth in excess of liabilities. Such a supply of financial assets enables the private sector to accumulate aggregate savings while maintaining aggregate levels of spending and income.

By accounting identity, the accumulation of net assets by one sector must mean an accumulation of net liabilities by another. Therefore, the cumulative net savings of the private sector – if they exist – must be associated, by definition, with an 'indebted' government. In principle, it would be possible for the domestic private sector to accumulate assets from the rest of the world (the 'external' sector) rather than the government, by exporting more than it imports. Such a scenario could be consistent with a stable economy and increasing private sector savings, but with no requirement for a government debt. However, in recent decades, the UK has tended to import more than it exports. This means that there is typically a net *outflow* of income to people resident abroad rather than an inflow, and this operates as another leakage of demand from the domestic economy, analogous to that of domestic saving. Indeed, net importing can be seen as a generalisation of net saving – the distinction being that the saving is done by foreigners in exporting nations (and who therefore choose to hold gold or silver pounds).

Moreover, in determining the size of the government's debt (and, by identity, the private sector's net savings), the government is subordinate to the private sector. The government can, with a high degree of discretion, set the absolute quantity of its own expenditure. Taxes, on the other hand, are typically set in percentage terms and therefore the government's revenue is effectively proportionate to overall domestic economic activity. It follows that tax revenue – and therefore the government's budget outcome – is determined not only by government policy but also by the spending and saving decisions of the private sector, which contribute to overall activity. Depending on sentiments, the private sector as a whole may seek to net save and/or to net import. In such a case the government will invariably have a budget deficit, irrespective of budgetary aspirations. This is because, within any given time period, not all of the money spent by the government into the domestic private sector will continue to recirculate within that sector, stimulating further economic activity and accrual of tax. Instead, some fraction will be held static (by foreign or domestic savers), fulfilling no taxable activity, and the government will not recover the entirety of its spending. The government may try to reduce the size of such a budget deficit, but as long as the non-government sectors seek to net save that can only be achieved at the expense of contracting the entire economy, and cannot be eliminated entirely.

This provides the macroeconomic perspective on the demand for gold pounds. The claims upon the Central Funds which are held outside of government represent the provision of a net money supply which supports the non-government sector's (domestic and foreign) desire to accumulate sterling-denominated net financial assets. This net money supply is expressed in two ways. Either the gold pounds are held by the UK banking system (as gilts, Treasury bills, Ways and Means advances or intraday central bank credit), in which case they serve to accommodate a demand for central bank and commercial bank deposits *without* the requirement for a counterpart private sector debt claim. Alternatively, they are held directly by non-bank entities (individuals, businesses, pension funds, etc.) as explicit savings instruments in the form of gilts, Treasury bills and NS&I deposits. This allocation of net financial assets occurs reflexively, according to spending decisions made in the private sector, and serves to mitigate any contractionary or deflationary effects that these decisions would otherwise produce. The *distribution* of gold pounds across the central bank, banking system and non-banks is influenced by monetary policy (which uses gold pounds to control the price of silver pounds), but the total *quantity* is determined by private sector sentiments manifested through successive government budget outcomes.

1.6   THE UK GOVERNMENT'S POLICY SPACE

1.6.1   Constraints on Government

It is tempting, in light of the Exchequer's policy of day-to-day cash neutrality, to understand the role of taxation and the cash management activities of the DMO as 'funding' for the Exchequer's expenditure. After all, on a daily basis, the objective is for receipts from taxation and sales of government securities to be equal to government expenditure, and this therefore presumably presents the Exchequer with a number of apparent constraints. While this 'funding' or 'provisioning' framing is familiar and may be somewhat useful depending on its precise definition and analytical purpose, the constraints on government which emerge from the structure and functioning of the Exchequer deviate from those which are often implied.

For example, it is clear that government expenditure is not dependent on any *pre*-funding activities. That is to say that there is no requirement for a provisioning of money balances through taxation and 'borrowing' activities to occur *before* spending can be undertaken. As such, there are no circumstances whereby it can be said that the government has insufficient money for expenditure to be able to take place, or that the government is at risk of 'running out of money'. Indeed, one of the fundamental organising principles of the Exchequer is for cash balances to be minimised, and the accumulation of 'provisioning balances' would be contrary to this objective. Instead, all spending arises via the creation of new money (as intraday credit) in the first instance and this process is independent of tax and securities dealing activities. The upshot, which HM Treasury acknowledges,[58] is that there is no aspect of the government's banking arrangements which can prevent government expenditure from being realised once it has been authorised by Parliament.

The uninhibited discharge of expenditure extends to the payment of principal and interest on government 'borrowing', which is permanently authorised by Parliament by the National Loans Act 1968. As such, default on national debt repayments, for example those associated with maturing gilts and Treasury bills, or NS&I withdrawals, can only occur with an express or implied repeal by Parliament of the relevant legislation. Neither the government nor HM Treasury has any discretion in the matter. From this perspective, government securities function analogously to time-deposits, representing an interest-earning, secure alternative to other forms of money[59] for a fixed or discretionary duration before reverting seamlessly to sterling.

Equally, sales of negotiable securities – typically required to meet end-of-day 'offsetting' objectives – do not present some of the challenges to HM Treasury that are commonly believed. In this context, it is often claimed that the government is at the behest of an investor market which may refuse to purchase the government's securities or otherwise demand punitive terms. However, as explained by the Bank of England half a century ago, the banking sector will purchase by the end of each day any securities which need to be sold in accordance with policy requirements.[60] That is because banks are *already* holding excess[61] central bank deposits that have been injected into the banking system during the day by virtue of the Exchequer's net spending.[62] The quantity of the balances added during the day exactly matches the DMO's offsetting remit – by definition – and the banks will reflexively switch these excess balances for something of the same creditworthiness but a higher rate of return. The DMO is not, therefore, faced with a market holding scarce funds and seeking to bid up the prices charged to the government. Instead, as the monopoly issuer of sterling safe-assets, the DMO needs only to offer terms which are infinitesimally greater than that earned on the excess central bank reserves that the banks already hold. As such, short-term rates on government securities converge to the Bank's policy rate, rather than being determined by market forces. Given the role of government securities in the functioning of monetary policy, interest payments on government debt can be seen simply as an expression of the interest rate targeting monetary framework. Sales of government securities are not at the discretion of markets, but are simply a routine feature of the functioning of the Exchequer and the Sterling Monetary Framework.[63]

There may be occasions where uncertainty within markets has the potential to disrupt the process described above. In such cases, it should be noted that while the government's spending process is rooted in legislation and is therefore incontrovertible, the cash management activities which seek to trade securities in order to balance any net expenditure flows are motivated by government *policy* and are therefore discretionary. In times of crisis and if the government determines that the conditions and consequences are unfavourable, it can suspend or alter its policy. An example occurred on 9 April 2020 when HM Treasury announced its intention to use the Ways and Means Account in response to the Covid-19 pandemic should it be required. This collapsed the interest rate in three-month money, which was the intention, and the government was able to maintain its cash management policy in any case. The Ways and Means Account remained unused.

It is often claimed that the government should reduce the quantity of outstanding government debt, or that the government budget should be balanced, or even in surplus, rather than in deficit. As explained, however, government securities function as a form of money and the total magnitude of the government's outstanding liabilities in this respect represents the provision of a net money supply to the private sector. Rather than being a burden that must be reduced, it is an important component in the functioning of the current monetary system and private sector net wealth. Moreover, the size of government debt is not even subject to the sole discretion of government policy, but rather is determined by demand in the form of private sector spending and saving decisions. Decreasing the deficit in lieu of private sector net saving/importing objectives can only be achieved at the expense of economic output, and therefore it is not possible for the government to target both deficit reduction and maximise economic activity and participation at the same time.

It follows that the government is not exposed to the alleged risks associated with running out of money, defaulting on debt obligations, the sentiments of bond markets or a need to reduce levels of government debt below those demanded by the economy. Instead, the functioning of the Exchequer, in particular the daily accounting cycle and trading activities, is geared towards the maintenance of monetary policy. Given that the primary objective of monetary policy is macroeconomic price stability, it follows that inflation is the fundamental concern around which Exchequer policy is organised. Inflation remains a valid constraint on the government's activities and the only context within which other government objectives should be weighed.[64]

1.6.2   Achieving Full Employment and Macroeconomic Stability in the UK

The limitations that the UK government is subject to are significantly fewer than those which have motivated official policy in the past decade. Given a clearer understanding of these constraints, we can consider the policy space that is made available to improve domestic economic and social conditions. Paramount in this consideration is the interplay between the government's fiscal policy and price stabilisation mechanisms.

Current approaches to price stability are based on the use of interest rates to adjust aggregate demand. When inflation is above target, the Bank of England increases its benchmark lending rate and this is believed to cascade through the banking system to retail interest rates. The increased price of borrowing allegedly causes a reduction in spending, reducing pressure on aggregate prices. If inflation is below target, rates are reduced, which encourages borrowing and increases demand. This system has several disadvantages when considering the transmission mechanism through which prices are considered to be adjusted.

The use of a baseline interest rate as a calibration parameter for the whole economy may be considered rather blunt for a variety of reasons. For example, adjustments to aggregate demand operate at the national level and cannot reflect or adapt to differences in conditions in different geographic areas. As such, distinct areas of the country may be disproportionately affected. The efficacy and coherency of the approach can also be called into question as it is associated with a substantial time lag (e.g., 18 months to 2 years), and a breakdown of policy space when interest rates are close to zero. Furthermore, the inherent requirement, under interest rate targeting policy, for the government to pay interest on the net financial assets held by the private sector serves as a government transfer payment to holders of financial wealth. Not only is this highly regressive, it may cause contradictory effects when interest rate rises that are intended to suppress spending power cause an elevated flow of income to the private sector.

Perhaps more fundamentally, under the existing monetary policy regime, changes to aggregate demand are used as a proxy for influencing the price level. Invariably, the reduction of aggregate spending causes a reduction of incomes and consequently employment levels and, as such, unemployment represents a systematic component of the policy transmission mechanism. In effect, the quantity of unemployed persons within the economy operates as a buffer stock which can be adjusted in order to optimise aggregate prices. It follows that long-term full employment is a systemic impossibility, and this has obvious negative ramifications for individuals and society in general. Employment policy in the UK also suffers from another inherent bias wherein private sector employment is reflexively preferred to public sector employment. As such, private sector businesses are treated somewhat like community centres, depended upon and saluted for their provision of jobs. At the same time, however, the firms are expected to increase productivity through competition and innovation, an objective which essentially requires a reduction in labour inputs.[65] Such a viewpoint is obviously incoherent and a disservice to society.

Modern Monetary Theory proponents propose solutions to these deficiencies that include two main components, both of which could be readily implemented in the UK given the political will. The first component is the provision of a guaranteed job, which offers any individual the opportunity to work in their local area for up to 35 hours per week at a fixed, living wage.[66] As such, the Job Guarantee produces genuine full employment at all times. When economic conditions are contractionary and non-government sector employment is reducing, workers can shift from the non-government sector into the Job Guarantee sector. Under more buoyant conditions, workers can transition to the private sector in order to take advantage of higher wage opportunities. In all cases, no person seeking to undertake paid work is unable to find it.

Moreover, the Job Guarantee provides macroeconomic stabilisation via two channels. The first is as a powerful spend-side automatic stabiliser. When an individual moves from the Job Guarantee to the private sector, government spending reduces just as private sector spending increases. Equally, when private sector activity reduces and wages are replaced with the Job Guarantee wage, government spending is accordingly increased as the private sector spending is withdrawn. In this regard, the Job Guarantee provides a more powerful stabilisation effect in comparison with existing Universal Credit support for the unemployed, because the Job Guarantee wage is equivalent to one in the private sector. As such, any swings in aggregate demand caused by increasing or decreasing private sector activity are dampened to a much greater degree than under conventional policy. For example, when a person transitions into a booming private sector, the size of the reduction in government spending through the removal of a Job Guarantee wage is much greater than with the removal of existing out-of-work benefits, and this therefore curbs the potential inflationary conditions to a greater extent. Moreover, the adjustments are spatially targeted precisely where they are required: in an area where private sector employment is increasing, government spending on Job Guarantee wages will reduce, while at the same time increasing in weaker areas elsewhere in the country.

The second stabilisation channel comes via the development of more competitive conditions which ensure that wages and prices more closely track increases in productivity. The Job Guarantee wage represents a floor on the price of labour, and this serves to stifle potential deflationary conditions by limiting any downward pressure on wages and thus overall spending. With the introduction of a Job Guarantee paying living wages, and because workers can choose to take the guaranteed job, workers no longer have to accept exploitative, low-paid work with poor conditions elsewhere. Instead, firms are required to offer improved terms that reflect the risk and reward of the work in order to attract labour, or deliver their products with fewer labour inputs by increasing productivity. Equally, though, employers have the opportunity of hiring from the pool of labour on a guaranteed job if the demands of workers are judged to exceed their productivity. Again, in comparison to existing policies which maintain a stock of people out of work, often for long periods, the Job Guarantee ensures that the pool of potential private sector workers is industrious and work-ready and thereby compete more effectively with existing private sector workers. Both of these stabilisation channels exert an expectational anchoring effect on the economy-wide wage structure. In turn, prices in general are anchored: if prices outgrow wages, firms will struggle to sell what they produce and the unsold stock will cause prices to fall. The result is that firms are treated like cattle rather than pets: those which drive increases in productivity are favoured; those that don't fail.[67] Firms can shed labour as automation proceeds, safe in the knowledge that the Job Guarantee will support those displaced. At the same time, demand remains high and productivity is driven forward, and this provides the source of sustainable, stable wage growth.

As we've seen, there is no financial constraint on the UK government in providing such a programme. Indeed, the government is the only entity which can divorce the offering of work from the profitability of hiring workers and thereby maintain the infinitely elastic demand for labour required to effectuate a price anchor. Moreover, several components of the necessary infrastructure are already up and running. The National Insurance (NI) system provides a unique reference for all working-age individuals in the UK and records their payment history and eligibility for the UK state pension. All individuals with a NI number would be eligible for the Job Guarantee. The Department for Work and Pensions (DWP) Universal Credit[68] (UC) system is used to assess eligibility for, and to administer, a variety of social security payments including jobseeker's allowance and other benefits. The DWP pays certain 'in-work' benefits on the basis of information relayed to HMRC via the Pay-As-You-Earn (PAYE) wage calculation and tax deduction system. This information details how much an individual has been paid, what their tax deductions are, and an indication of how many hours they have worked in that period, and enables the DWP to pay the right amount of 'top up' Universal Credit to those eligible. Extending this scheme to support the payment of hours worked under a Job Guarantee would be straightforward, as demonstrated by the successfully delivered furlough scheme which was administered by the UK authorities during the Covid-19 pandemic. The difference would be that the

PAYE scheme that the guaranteed job workers would be paid through would be operated by a public authority rather than a private company. The main area of policy development would involve extending the capability of work coaches to establish initiatives to create socially beneficial work, and extending the existing public sector job creation systems to provide a guaranteed job to everybody that wants one.[69]

With a Job Guarantee providing the primary macroeconomic stabilisation function, there is no requirement for an interest rate targeting monetary policy. Therefore, the other main policy proposal would be to peg the silver pound to the gold pound and eliminate the interest rate between them. Under such a framework there is no need for central bank reserves to be reflexively drained from the banking system in order to push rates upwards, and negotiable government securities thereby become obsolete. The DMO would no longer be required and this significantly simplifies the functioning of the Exchequer. The government would have no interest costs, and this would further increase general productivity levels since an equivalent flow of income from the government to the private sector could be associated with useful activity, rather than regressive transfer payments to holders of monetary wealth.

Although the UK government has no need for sterling from anybody, there are entities within the economy that need to save very safely. Individuals, for example, have a justifiable need for growing savings backed by the government, if the society considers that private saving for retirement is the way to deal with pension provision. Pension funds cannot provide that support by private means alone, which is why index-linked gilts were developed.[70] An alternative approach could involve a form of annuity issued by NS&I on a non-negotiable basis, where an individual can build up an annual additional pension by purchasing 'Granny Bonds' directly. These would have limited residual capital value and no capital uplift, but would give a secure additional income in retirement for ordinary people who decide to be thrifty and save. The precise level and nature of the instruments is open to debate.[71] Beyond that, deposit insurance in banks would cover rainy day funds. The current value is £85,000 but unlimited deposit insurance for individuals (directly and on trust – to cover client accounts at solicitors, for example) would be as much as is required. As for everybody else, the market will provide. For corporations, the default option for their cash pile deposit is an involuntary investment in a bank, though society doesn't want them to have a cash pile, it wants them to run their working capital on an overdraft.[72]

Proponents of Modern Monetary Theory understand that a permanent zero per cent policy rate is the base case for analysis of a floating exchange rate currency, since that is the natural rate of interest in such a system.[73] It concludes that it is better to pay government money out to people as wages via a guaranteed job than to banks as interest, and that has far greater automatic stabilisation effect than any other option. This, in turn, will lead to an economy that can run at a higher real output than it is capable of doing under the current regime of targeting inflation with discretionary interest rate adjustments. It is this capacity to run the economy at a higher output level and yet still maintain stable prices that is the Modern Money Advantage. Thanks to accidents of history and centuries of trial and error, the UK monetary system and legislative framework is uniquely placed to press home that advantage.

NOTES

1. Cameron 2010.
2. Munro 2021.
3. Aldrick 2020.
4. Bank of England Act 1998, s19.
5. Bank of England Market Operations Guide n.d.
6. Carney 2013.
7. Statutorily, National Insurance contributions are not formally surrendered to the Central Funds, as other public receipts are (typically the Consolidated Fund). However, National Insurance receipts are, as a matter of policy, managed in the form of a deposit within the Debt Management Account where they become, implicitly, a liability of the Consolidated Fund. The National Insurance Fund is therefore managed, ultimately, with recourse to the Central Funds.
8. See Berkeley et al. 2020, Appendix H for a short history of the Consolidated Fund.
9. National Loans Act 1968.
10. 'For my own part, I am afraid that the Bill itself and the noble Lord's explanation of it remind me a good deal of the Athanasian creed: the Consolidated Fund is incomprehensible; the National Loans Fund incomprehensible; the Local Loans Fund incomprehensible; and yet there are not three incomprehensibles, but one incomprehensible' (Earl of Dundee 1968).
11. Exchequer and Audit Departments Act 1866.
12. Contingencies Fund Act 1974.
13. Banking Act 2009.
14. National Loans Act 1968.
15. The organisation of these functions in legislation has evolved through time with Supply and Appropriation Acts being the most recent incarnation, in place since 2011. Previously, annually authorised spending would be presented via separate Appropriation Acts and Consolidated Fund Acts, amongst others.
16. Ulph 1985.
17. The Transfer of Functions (Office of Her Majesty's Paymaster General) Order 2006, explanatory memorandum.
18. BACS payments, for example, use the BACS3 'government grade' protocol which substitutes Exchequer accounts for the GBS commercial partners' own reserve accounts in the transaction settlement chain.
19. Parliamentary credits are first allocated to the Paymaster General Supply Account from which they are transferred to the Drawing Account for use in transaction settlement. This is a technical distinction and the activities can be satisfactorily modelled by a single account.

20.   'Cash' in this sense means sterling, that is, a liability of the Bank of England.
21.   On a typical working day some £400 million of state pension payments will be settled into the banking system by BACS at 9:30 am, all from an account with a zero balance at the start of the day.
22.   Finance Act 1954, s34(3).
23.   Brittain 1959.
24.   Finance Act 1954, s34(3).
25.   National Loans Act 1968, s12(7).
26.   National Loans Act 1968, s18.
27.   The Ways and Means Account is formally a liability of the National Loans Fund.
28.   Equally, the direct purchase of government securities, from the Bank of England's Banking Department, by the government would represent the opposite type of accounting adjustment, in cases where the Bank's monetary operations left the Exchequer with a cash surplus.
29.   The European Union Budget, and Economic and Monetary Policy (EU Exit) Regulations 2019, s6.
30.   'Borrow' from the Central Funds' point of view is strictly the Oxford dictionary meaning: 'acquire temporarily with the promise or intention of returning'. There is no further constraint: express or implied.
31.   Although the Consolidated Fund provides a backstop on the National Loans Fund, the routine responsibilities of the latter fund such as debt repayments are not formally recognised as Consolidated Fund Standing Services, despite having their roots in a permanently enacted item of legislation. This is because of the unique relationship between the two funds which involves mutual funding activities which wash-out in the end-of-day accounting.
32.   These balances are administered by the GBS commercial banking partners (NatWest and Barclays) and can therefore be considered as pseudo-commercial bank deposits. They are not commercial bank deposits proper, however, as they arise directly from Parliament and are supported by settlement responsibilities of Exchequer accounts held at the Bank of England.
33.   The General Account of the Commissioners of Inland Revenue and the General Account of the Commissioners of Customs and Excise.
34.   DMO Annual Review 2020, p. 35.
35.   Gilt repurchases became the primary instrument for the Bank's operations in the mid-1990s.
36.   Strictly speaking it represents a weekly average target balance and so can vary from day to day, but not over timescales beyond one week.
37.   This function – designed so that use of the Ways and Means Account can be avoided – essentially acts as a pre-funded Ways and Means advance. See Berkeley et al. 2020, section 6.4, p. 69.
38.   Equally, under the terms of the Sterling Monetary Framework, commercial banks have no discretion to refuse the receipt of a central bank reserve transfer and the corresponding issuance of their own deposit liabilities to their customers.
39.   It is possible for the Bank of England to hold private sector assets on its balance sheet though since the 1990s the major form of security used in Bank operations has been gilts. These may not appear explicitly on the Bank's balance sheet when used as collateral or held by a subsidiary. In the past couple of decades any purchase of private sector securities by the Bank has been accompanied by indemnities against potential losses or capital injections provided by HM Treasury.
40.   Currency and Banknotes Act 1928, s3(1) and National Loans Act 1968, s9(3).

41. Financial relationship between the Treasury and the Bank of England 2018, §20, p. 5.
42. Financial relationship between the Treasury and the Bank of England 2018, §9, p. 2.
43. Between 2007 and 2009, four banking institutions were nationalised: the Royal Bank of Scotland, Lloyds, Northern Rock and Bradford & Bingley (Mor 2021).
44. For example, £20 billion was loaned from the National Loans Fund to the Financial Services Compensation Scheme in 2008 in order to compensate four million customers of the failed banks Bradford & Bingley, Heritable Bank plc, Kaupthing Singer & Friedlander Limited (KSF), Landsbanki Islands hf and London Scottish Bank plc (Mor 2021, p. 17).
45. Finance Act 1954, s34(3).
46. Contributions to the National Insurance Fund are dematerialised into claims upon the National Loans Fund via the National Insurance Fund Investment Account and the Debt Management Account, plus the National Insurance Fund is topped up periodically by Parliamentary vote. Transitively these are all backstopped by the Consolidated Fund.
47. The National Loans Fund may also issue Treasury bills though this is not currently routine.
48. In general, deposits made in the National Loans Fund are known as 'Ways and Means borrowing'. Similarly, governmental and other public bodies can place deposits with the Debt Management Account which also represent a (non-negotiable) claim upon the Central Funds. Such deposits in the NLF and DMA are made by public sector entities on a day-to-day basis as part of the Exchequer's cash management cycle.
49. This function is somewhat weakened by the introduction of interest on central bank reserve deposits from 2006 which alone provides a floor to interbank lending rates, leaving Bank interventions via the gilt market to secure only the upper bound on rates. In any case, the Bank's Quantitative Easing programme, from 2009, represents an unprecedented, ongoing purchase of gilts in order to push rates (including long-term rates) down to the policy rate.
50. Vlieghe 2020.
51. These initiatives can be considered as 'collateral upgrade' services whereby the Bank agrees to exchange lower- for higher-quality collateral in an attempt to stimulate banking activity.
52. HM Treasury Annual Report and Accounts 2020, p. 193.
53. Public sector entities such as the National Insurance Fund, National Lottery and local authorities are also permitted to hold gilts as a store of wealth but can additionally access deposit facilities provided by the Debt Management Office which represent an equivalent claim on the Central Funds.
54. 'Discounting' in banking is the practice of taking on an asset in return for issuing one's own liabilities. The discrepancy between the values of the asset and the liabilities is known as a 'haircut'. The difference between the amount of liabilities received and the amount required to repurchase the asset in the future is known as the 'discount' which can be construed as a fee or an interest rate and will convey an income to the issuer.
55. In principle, either of the issuers of gold (DMO) or silver pounds (Bank of England) could fulfil this function as long as they can maintain an adjustable buffer stock of each other's pounds. In practice, the DMO is prevented by policy from varying its balance of silver pounds whereas the Bank has policy freedom

to accommodate demand on its own terms and the DMO guarantees a supply of gold pounds to the Bank if required.

56. This is reminiscent of Michał Kalecki's postulation that the government effectively 'pays its suppliers in government securities'. It can be argued that the current regime of 'gold' pounds and 'silver' pounds are effectively separate currencies with a floating exchange rate between them and that a Zero Interest Policy would merely be Parliament forcing the Bank of England to peg 'silver' pounds to 'gold' pounds at a one-to-one exchange rate.

57. Non-overnight liquidity will show up on the Bank of England balance sheet as loans and advances to banks and other financial institutions.

58. HM Treasury – FOI2020/02182 2020.

59. Sterling balances at the Bank of England currently earn interest though this has not always been policy.

60. Bank of England Quarterly Bulletin 1964.

61. 'Excess' in this case is defined with respect to the start of the day.

62. Not to mention the colossal quantity of excess reserves the banks hold thanks to Quantitative Easing.

63. Note that this represents one important distinction between the UK system and that of the Eurozone. In the Eurozone, national governments also inject money into their national banking systems via intraday credit but the holders of such excess funds have a *choice* of national jurisdictions from which to buy euro-denominated government bonds. As such, the demand for any particular government's bonds does not necessarily match that government's daily net spending (and therefore offsetting objective) and rates on government bonds issued by states across the Eurozone thereby can diverge according to market perception (assuming no intervention by the European Central Bank).

64. 'There is no reason to assume that MMT-inspired policies will cause a depreciation of the domestic currency. Indeed, it is more likely to cause an appreciation' (Harvey, Chapter 6, page 125, this volume).

65. It could be said that the task of the private sector is to fully automate everything and put everybody out of work.

66. Likely at or above the living wage proposed by the Living Wage Foundation, about £10 per hour in 2021, with no London weighting.

67. The 'what about the jobs, can I have a bailout' cries can be ignored, because everybody has an alternative guaranteed job to go to. Anybody paid more than the living wage has an alternative bid in the economy – or they are overpaid – and everybody else has the Job Guarantee.

68. Universal Credit can be considered to be a one-sided job provision system whereby individuals are paid a (much) lower-than-living wage to undertake the full-time job of searching for alternative work which – in aggregate – does not exist. It cannot discipline firms because people cannot choose to take Universal Credit. The contrast of this economically and socially inept mechanism with the Job Guarantee could not be starker.

69. It's interesting that the HM Prison and Probation Service can create jobs on demand to service Unpaid Work Orders ordered by the courts (Brookes 2021), but creating jobs on demand is supposedly impossible anywhere else in the public sector.

70. Oliver and Rutterford 2020.

71. Wilson 2021.

72. Wilson 2021.

73. Forstater and Mosler 2005.

REFERENCES

Aldrick, P. (2020), 'BBC "Misled Viewers" on Scale of National Debt', *The Times*, 30 November, accessed 15 August 2021 at https://www.thetimes.co.uk/article/bbc -misled-viewers-on-scale-of-national-debt-ckvkcwc7j

Bank of England Act (1998), accessed 29 August 2021 at https://www.legislation.gov .uk/ukpga/1998/11/introduction

Bank of England Annual Report and Accounts (2021), Bank of England, 28 February, accessed 15 August 2021 at https://www.bankofengland.co.uk/-/media/boe/files/ annual-report/2021/boe-2021.pdf?la=en&hash=965204F6565CB8CAD29A 86E595CB7F02E8A54E07#page=129

Bank of England Market Operations Guide (n.d.), accessed 15 August 2021 at https:// www.bankofengland.co.uk/markets/bank-of-england-market-operations-guide/our -tools

Bank of England Quarterly Bulletin (1964), 'The Treasury Bill', 3, 186–93, 1 September.

Banking Act 2009 (2009), accessed 26 August 2022 at https://www.legislation.gov.uk/ ukpga/2009/1/introduction

Berkeley, A., R. Tye and N. Wilson (2020), United Kingdom: The Gower Initiative for Modern Money Studies, 26 December, accessed 26 December 2020 at https://gimms .org.uk/2020/12/26/accounting-model-uk-exchequer/

Brittain, H. (1959), *The British Budgetary System*, London: Allen & Unwin.

Brookes, A. (2021), 'Offenders Tidy up Barking as Part of Unpaid Work Scheme', *Barking and Dagenham Post*, 28 June, accessed 17 August 2021 at https://www.ba rkinganddagenhampost.co.uk/news/offenders-do-unpaid-work-to-tidy-up-barking -8092494

Cameron, D. (2010), David Cameron: We Must Tackle Britain's Massive Deficit and Growing Debt: Conservative Party Speeches, Speech, 7 June, accessed 15 August 2021 at http://conservative-speeches.sayit.mysociety.org/speech/601466

Cameron, D. (2010), David Cameron: We Must Tackle Britain's Massive Deficit and Growing Debt: Conservative Party Speeches: Speech, 7 June, accessed 28 September 2022 at https://www.gov.uk/government/speeches/prime-ministers -speech-on-the-economy

Carney, M. (2013), The UK at the Heart of a Renewed Globalisation, Speech presented at the 125th anniversary of the *Financial Times*, London, 24 October, accessed at https://www.bankofengland.co.uk/-/media/boe/files/speech/2013/the-uk-at-the -heart-of-a-renewed-globalisation.pdf

Contingencies Fund Act (1974), accessed 26 August 2022 at https://www.legislation .gov.uk/ukpga/1974/18/introduction

Currency and Banknotes Act (1928), accessed 15 August 2021 at https://www .legislation.gov.uk/ukpga/Geo5/18-19/13/section/3

DMO Annual Review (2020), United Kingdom Debt Management Office, 16 October, accessed 15 August 2021 at https://dmo.gov.uk/media/17019/gar1920.pdf

Earl of Dundee (1968), 'National Loans Bill', in Hansard, vol. 289, UK Parliament, Column 704.

Exchequer and Audit Departments Act 1866 (1866), accessed 17 August 2021 at https://www.legislation.gov.uk/ukpga/Vict/29-30/39/contents

Finance Act (1954), accessed 15 August 2021 at https://www.legislation.gov.uk/ukpga/ Eliz2/2-3/44/section/34

Financial Relationship between the Treasury and the Bank of England (2018), accessed 15 August 2021 at https://assets.publishing.service.gov.uk/government/uploads/system/uploads/attachment_data/file/718481/The_Financial_Relationship_between_the_Treasury_and_the_Bank_of_England_-_MoU_web.pdf

Forstater, M. and W. Mosler (2005), 'The Natural Rate of Interest Is Zero', *Journal of Economic Issues*, 39(2), 535–42.

HM Treasury – FOI2020/02182 (2020), Freedom of Information Response.

HM Treasury Annual Report and Accounts (2020), HM Treasury, 29 September, accessed 15 August 2021 at https://assets.publishing.service.gov.uk/government/uploads/system/uploads/attachment_data/file/922357/HMT_Group_Annual_Report_and_Accounts_2019-20__003__for_web_accessible.pdf

Mor, F. (2021), Bank Rescues of 2007–09: Outcomes and Cost, 16 August, accessed 16 August 2021 at https://commonslibrary.parliament.uk/research-briefings/sn05748/

Munro, F. (2021), Government Deficit and Debt Return, accessed 16 August 2021 at https://www.ons.gov.uk/file?uri=/economy/governmentpublicsectorandtaxes/publicsectorfinance/datasets/governmentdeficitanddebtreturn/current/previous/v24/rftm19tables1.xls

National Loans Act (1968), accessed 15 August 2021 at https://www.legislation.gov.uk/ukpga/1968/13

Oliver, M. J. and J. Rutterford (2020), '"The Capital Market Is Dead": The Difficult Birth of Index-Linked Gilts in the UK', *The Economic History Review*, 73(1), 258–80.

The European Union Budget, and Economic and Monetary Policy (EU Exit) Regulations (2019), accessed 9 January 2022 at https://www.legislation.gov.uk/uksi/2019/484/introduction

The Transfer of Functions (Office of Her Majesty's Paymaster General) Order (2006), accessed 15 August 2021 at https://www.legislation.gov.uk/uksi/2006/607/memorandum/contents

Ulph, C. (1985), *150 Not Out: The Story of the Paymaster General's Office, 1836–1986*, Crawley, West Sussex: Her Majesty's Paymaster General's Office.

Vlieghe, G. (2020), Monetary Policy and the Bank of England's Balance Sheet, Speech by Gertjan Vlieghe, Bank of England, 23 April, accessed 15 August 2021 at https://www.bankofengland.co.uk/-/media/boe/files/speech/2020/monetary-policy-and-the-boes-balance-sheet-speech-by-gertjan-vlieghe.pdf

Wilson, N. (2021), 'The Only Bonds We Need Are Granny Bonds', accessed 17 August 2021 at https://new-wayland.com/blog/the-only-bonds-we-need-are-granny-bonds/

2. Credit and the Exchequer since the Restoration

Richard Tye

2.1 INTRODUCTION

English sovereigns maintained the medieval 'Free-Minting' system for at least six centuries, under which the nation's coin was produced from silver bullion according to very strict standards of weight and fineness as defined by the Sovereign Mint indentures.[1] Minters were men of high social standing and the mints under their control were subject to tight regulation. The Trial of the Pyx[2] tested the quality of coin produced and woe betide the minter whose coin failed the test. The Royal Mints sourced silver bullion from the population, predominantly the merchant classes, who gave it to the Mints and received money coined from it in return. Naturally, the Mints kept a few coins back as their fee which the merchants willingly paid, as coin was required to trade in the closely controlled market towns of the nascent English medieval economy. Conceptually, the premium paid for coined money distinguished it from the underlying commodity from which it was produced. Money in these times was explicitly understood to be an expression of Royal power and prerogative, a circulating unit of account accepted principally by tale,[3] that the ancient literature calls the sovereign's 'lawful money of England'.[4] In summary, money was a recognisable social construct whose focal point was the centre of power.

Coin became trapped between two medieval ideas: the notion of seigniorage, that a sovereign could just declare the value of the coin by proclamation, and the notion of intrinsic value, that coins could only be worth the 'natural' value of the substance from which they were minted. Both views had their adherents, and both were wrong.

It was under Charles II, in the post-Restoration period, however, that financial reform was undertaken in order to solve growing financial pressures needed to prosecute the Anglo-Dutch wars. Wars are a recurring theme during periods of monetary system evolution. The 17th century was such a period, involving great financial re-engineering and innovation that culminated, towards the very end of the century, in Parliament asserting its growing power over Royal finances and the nation's money, and which included the incorporation of the Bank of England. It was during the 1660s that the government scrapped the mint fees and began to finance the production of coined money itself. The production process was also mechanised, improving the quality of coined money and securing it from counterfeiting and clipping. With the disappearance of mint fees, silver bullion exchanged for money pound for pound. As a result, the distinction between commodity and the unit of account in the form of counted coin became blurred. Seen through the eye of emergent political liberalism, money came to be conceptualised, incorrectly, as a tangible commodity.[5]

Coins were heavy and difficult to move around. Moving them backwards and forwards to the Exchequer in London caused a shortage of coins in the right place at the right time, which would impede commerce. Moreover, taxes were paid at the end of a year of production when spending needed to happen at the beginning. Since medieval times, mechanisms had been in place for the sovereign to work around these problems and credit had been issued in the form of 'Tallies'[6] – hazelwood sticks split into two with an amount marked and which could be 'returned' to the Exchequer at the end of the year in payment of taxes owed.

Consequently, the sovereign monetary system of England became based upon twigs, not metal. Tallies were issued by the Exchequer in anticipation of revenue and returned to the Exchequer in lieu of revenue in the form of coin. Because most individuals were not directly taxed, the actual coin of the realm remained in the local area with little of it entering the Exchequer. Instead, the Exchequer became largely a clearing house for late medieval wooden cheques.

All of this worked fine during peace time throughout England where the King's ability to tax kept the tally sticks circulating, but when the King decided to go to war in foreign parts the system started to break down.

2.2   BY ORDER OF THE TREASURY

In the 1660s, Charles II had a war to fight against the Dutch. Soldiers fighting wars in foreign parts would only accept coin and the 'Merry Monarch', saddled as he was with an Exchequer that preferred to deal in sticks, was particularly short at the time. Parliament passed an Act to issue paper repayment orders alongside tallies in return for cash loans to the Exchequer and together these instruments were known as 'Tallies of Loan'.[7] Tallies of Loan diverged from earlier, much more ancient 'Tallies of Pro', itself an innovation of the original 'Tally of Receipt (Sol)'. In conception, the Tally of Receipt was a record of receipt for money paid into the Exchequer and the Exchequer Receipt Rolls a record of tallies issued. So, whenever a cash payment was made to the Exchequer, the payment was recorded in the Receipt Rolls and a Tally of Receipt was struck for the sum received. However, to solve the perennial problem of cash shortages, the Exchequer took to striking Tallies of Pro as a means of payment. They functioned much like a modern cheque. It entitled the creditor to cash it upon the revenues in hand of a tax collector whose name was inscribed on its side. This transaction was simultaneously recorded in both the Exchequer Issue and Receipt Rolls, as if cash had been received and paid out, when of course neither was the case. Consequently, a Tally of Pro was known as a tally of anticipation or a tally of assignment, anticipating and assigning tax revenues that never physically entered the Exchequer.

The Tally of Loan was different, however. According to the 'ancient course', as a loan to the Exchequer constituted a receipt of money, it was duly recorded in the Receipt Rolls and a tally struck. In contrast to a Tally of Pro, a Tally of Loan and its accompanying repayment order was only recorded in the Issue Rolls when it was later presented for encashment.[8] First, this represented an accurate record of the facts, with issue occurring after receipt. Second, the design of the Tally of Loan and its method of recording in the books of the Exchequer opened the door to creating an entirely different and new financial instrument.

The repayment orders issued alongside Tallies of Loan were exactly that. They prescribed the numbered order in which each holder would be repaid, regardless of status or class. These repayment orders attracted a rate of interest of 6 per cent payable every six months and the Act creating them detailed the specific revenues against which they were secured. As well as attracting interest, the repayment orders became negotiable and thus tradable assets of the person holding them.[9]

Owing to the enduring shortfall of revenues, the Exchequer issued a further type of Treasury Order.[10] Although authorised by the same Act as Tallies of Loan, they were distinct from the loan repayment orders as they were issued in response to a certificated supply of goods or services to the army or navy and did not attract any interest.[11] As a promissory note, they became the first example of an English paper currency.[12] Bearer status was for the future though; changes of ownership still had to be registered at the Exchequer. The scope of these Orders was extended via an Additional Aid Act passed in 1667[13] and they started to be used to allocate funds directly to departmental officials, such as the Paymaster of the Forces for the payment of wages.[14] It is this innovation, requiring government officials to obtain money directly in the market by selling Exchequer paper, that gave rise to the name 'Fiduciary Order'. They were issued in numbers greatly exceeding the amount specified in the original Act and became secured, not upon a parliamentary guarantee of specified revenues, but simply upon the 'ordinary' revenues and the King's promise to repay.[15]

As they were negotiable, Fiduciary Orders could be sold for coin to finan-ciers in the City of London,[16] or transferred to creditors who then cashed them with goldsmiths. However, they lacked a crucial characteristic of the other circulating forms of money,[17] namely, 'they could not be used in lieu of cash for taxes'.[18] Had the decision been made to accept them in payments to the Exchequer, and thereby avoid the requirement to cash them, it is quite possible that Fiduciary Orders would have been successfully deployed as a national paper currency and as a consequence the Bank of England may not have come into existence.

By 1672, the ability of the Exchequer to settle the orders in coin was stretched to its limit and ultimately King Charles II was forced to bring about the infamous 'Stop of the Exchequer', when he suspended cash repayments on Fiduciary Orders at the Exchequer.[19] This brought about the ruin, over the next decade, of some of the famous goldsmith bankers of London, who, having cashed the great bulk of the Orders, ultimately bore the financial consequences of their failure.[20] Despite the drama, 'The Stop' had little effect on the wider economy and 'the financial affairs of the country went on much as they had before'.[21]

Neither did the Stop prevent Parliament proposing such suspensions of repayments in the future. The Bank of England Act 1696, given Royal assent on 1 April 1697,[22] contained a hastily added clause stating that Exchequer Bills 'shall be current onely for the Aids Taxes or Supplies granted', with encash-ment reinstated upon Royal Proclamation.[23] It was only a short suspension, however, and the Royal Proclamation was issued on 23 April 1697.[24]

2.3   THE RISE OF THE BANK

In the early years of the reign of King William III, to meet the heavy cost of continental wars, coin continued to be raised by Tallies of Loan. The repay-ment system was now reliant on the flow of this coin through the Exchequer, and the revenue flow became 'over-mortgaged'. 'Tallies fell to a heavy dis-count, and it became necessary to invent some new method of borrowing.'[25]

In 1693, the first tontine loan was tried, but it raised only £108,000 out of the £1,000,000 required.[26] The rest was raised by simple life annuities. For the first time, a permanent funded debt was proposed, and secured upon the incorporation of the Bank of England by Royal Charter via the Bank of England Act of 1694.[27] The principal sum of the £1,200,000 loan from the Bank of England was to remain outstanding, but the interest on that loan was serviced by the levying of customs, duties and taxes as determined by Acts of Parliament. These became known as 'the funds' and any surplus on these revenues was allocated to 'sinking funds', which would be intended for paying down existing debts.

In the latter years of the 17th century silver became more valuable, so much so that the value of English coins was greater melted down as bullion in Europe than they were at face value, and this resulted in a severe shortage of coins in England.[28] The value of the government's tallies declined further as a consequence. The Bank of England Act 1696 allowed the Bank to increase its capital stock.[29] This time, however, the subscription for the stock was not to be in coin. Instead, stock was issued in exchange for government tallies and for bank notes issued by the Bank of England, both at face value.[30] This consolidation by the Bank removed tallies from the market and improved the rate the government could obtain for new tallies.[31] In return, the nominal rate of interest on the tallies the Bank now held was raised, and the repayment of principal on the tallies by the government indefinitely delayed.[32] It was also the first time money created by the Bank against loans, in the form of bank notes, was swapped for new bank equity, allowing the Bank to make more loans.[33]

Issuance of shares precluded the need to repay capital regularly; moreover, shareholders derived an income from shareholding dividends while also retaining liquidity as share markets developed. Insurance markets also developed from the mid-17th century, reducing risk of loss due to shipwreck, fire or premature death.[34]

2.4 EXCHEQUER BILLS

The Bank of England Act 1694 made no reference to the very close financial relationship that would evolve between the Treasury and the Bank. The relationship between the two institutions developed primarily via the medium of a further government innovation, 'Exchequer bills'. Provision for the issuance of Exchequer bills was first granted by clauses slipped into an Act of 1696 by the Chancellor of the Exchequer, Charles Montagu (1694–1699) for providing credit in the event that the project to establish the National Land Bank failed.[35] The intention was to alleviate the shortage of coinage in circulation resulting from the Great Recoinage that had commenced that year and provide crucially needed credit to the government in the event that the National Land Bank project failed to get off the ground.

From their first introduction in 1696, Exchequer bills were solely and exclusively prepared by and issued from the Exchequer. Initially, Exchequer bills were instruments of credit, a currency in their own right circulating as interest-bearing promissory notes, rivalling the Bank of England's bills and notes. In essence they were a repeat of the earlier attempt via Fiduciary Orders to turn the Exchequer into a bank by issuing credit upon general taxation. They were issued to Paymasters, who made payments with, or raised loans upon, them. Later, however, once the Treasury started to use the Bank more and more, Exchequer bills became the tool by which the government settled with the Bank of England. While the National Land Bank subscription ultimately failed, the Exchequer bill became of fundamental importance, binding the Treasury and the Bank in ever closer relations over the next 200 years. The Bank of England 'had so much to do with Exchequer bills that the issue is really part of its own story'.[36]

The Act of 1696, as well as authorising subscriptions to a National Land Bank, authorised lending to the Exchequer of £1.5 million 'upon the Creditt of Bills to be made Payable upon Demand with Interest'.[37] They were not a great success and only £133,709[38] were issued. The bills accrued interest at under 5 per cent,[39] less than that of Tallies of Loan and repayment orders at 7 per cent, which were also authorised by the Act. Outside the scope of the Act, Montagu organised the assistance of businessmen in four cities around the country, who raised money to aid cashing and circulation of the bills locally. The Treasury Lords even sent official notification to tax receivers requiring them to accept Exchequer bills in payment of taxes, though this was never written into law.

Despite these terms, the principal reason behind their poor floatation was a political rivalry between the Tory supporters of the National Land Bank[40] and the Whig Treasury Lords. In correspondence to Montagu, William Blathwayt, Secretary of War, wrote that there was much malicious sentiment among 'all those that deal in money' that they 'endeavour to defeat and disappoint' the project.[41] The commissioners for the National Land Bank were attempting to force the Treasury to bend to their will by ridiculing Montagu's attempt to raise a reserve loan to aid circulation of the bills. Moreover, they sought to reduce the terms of the National Land Bank subscription, which, after long meetings, the Lords Justices refused to countenance.

The friction between the parties resulted in the failure to raise the reserve loan. This was a £200,000 loan to the Exchequer in coin which would allow the bills to be cashed upon demand and, it was believed, give them credit in the public mind. The terms of the loan set by the Exchequer were very generous: lenders were permitted to contribute with clipped silver (old coins were being demonetised in the Great Recoinage) and were to be paid a premium of 10 per cent above the current market price. Furthermore, lenders were to be issued tallies, accruing a rate of interest at 7 per cent, though later this figure was reduced to 6 per cent. Despite Montagu's efforts, it was all to no avail and as a result of the wranglings, the bill issue was cut short and abandoned.[42]

Similarly, the opposing National Land Bank subscription ended in dismal failure, raising a tiny fraction of the required £2.6 million, and it too was abandoned. Instead, the Treasury Lords decided to turn to the Bank of England for a loan of £200,000 to gain much needed credit for the continuation of payments to conduct the war.[43] This played to the Bank of England's advantage and suited Charles Montagu, who was opposed to the National Land Bank and whose Exchequer bills depended on its failure.

Montagu was to strike again in 1697, when a further Act authorised the creation of £1.5 million of Exchequer bills for the payment of war supplies.[44] Crucially, it went one step further: the Act made Exchequer bills redeemable for taxes, either directly to the Exchequer or, like Tallies of Pro, to revenue collectors.[45] Now tax payment by bill was embedded in the law of the land, rather than at the whim of the Treasury Lords. This important innovation undoubtedly empowered Exchequer bills to persist where the earlier Fiduciary Order had not.

Inevitably, the Nine Years War (1688–97) created deep financial deficiencies and the Bank of England Act 1696, passed in spring 1697, extended the role of Exchequer bills so they could be used to pay for any supply authorised by Parliament (rather than just war supplies), and extended their credit for any payment due at the Exchequer.[46] In addition, interest was added, paid at around 7.6 per cent.[47] Exchequer bills could be used for payment of taxes, but because tax bills could also be paid in coin, this wasn't sufficient to drive the acceptance of Exchequer bills. The mindset was still that credit had to be pushed,[48] rather than pulled by creating an unavoidable demand.[49]

The Bank of England Act 1696 'temporarily' enlarged the capital stock of the Bank of England[50] in order to absorb, and take off the market, Treasury floating debt consisting of Tallies of Loan and Treasury Repayment Orders that were trading at a 'heavy discount'.[51] Capital stock subscriptions were authorised payable at four-fifths in Tallies of Loan and Treasury Orders, and one-fifth in Bank of England notes. This aided the Bank's other interventions, and more importantly the Treasury's credit, in the open tally market, bringing the heavy discounts at which they were transacting to near par. The Act also continued the Bank of England's banking monopoly and the Bank's charter was renewed and extended until 1710 with Treasury debt owing to the Bank redeemable by Parliament 12 months later. The Act established the 'General Fund' into which various duties and excises were now paid, rather than being maintained separately.[52] At first, the Treasury approached the Bank of England to aid in the circulation of the Exchequer bills, however, despite the Bank director's recommendations to accept the Treasury's proposals, the General Board voted against.[53] Accordingly, a clause was written into the Act authorising the Treasury to contract with 'Trustees', market makers like the modern GEMMs,[54] for the circulation of Exchequer bills.[55]

The Trustees were City financiers and 12 in number initially, three of whom were Bank of England directors (Eyles, Janssen and Heathcote). Their number dropped to three in total by 1702. A subscription list was opened with the public in order to obtain the necessary money, a quarter of which was paid in 'milled money or guineas'. The Trustees kept these subscriptions as a reserve fund under their management to be utilised for 'exchanging and circulating' the bills. In all, 16 contracts for the circulation of Exchequer bills were entered into with the Trustees between 1697 and 1709.[56]

With the commencement of the Wars of the Spanish Succession, however, the Bank of England was finally brought into the fray, bringing to bear its considerable financial power to aid in the successful issuance and circulation of Exchequer bills. In 1707 following an Act of Parliament, the Bank underwrote an issuance of £1.5 million of Exchequer bills for which it received a return of 4½ per cent on the principal of outstanding bills in circulation, and the House Duties upon which they were secured from 1 August 1710 for repayment were continued under the Act.[57] However, until that date the Bank agreed to accept Exchequer bills for interest payments in quarterly instalments.

The issue went badly for the Bank and 'its specie stores had come under considerable, indeed unprecedented pressure'.[58] The Bank was forced to issue several cash calls to its members, and after October 1708 the Bank's holding of the bills settled above £1 million, displacing the higher interest-bearing tallies it had held previously. This decreased the income of the Bank and its return to holders of stock.

Given the necessary expansion of Exchequer bills for supply due to increasing war expenditures, the Treasury approached the Bank to renegotiate its charter and secure its ongoing support for their circulation. Despite misgivings, and with its existence on the line, the Bank agreed to support a further issuance of £2.5 million funded at a rate of 3 per cent and agreed to immediately advance the Treasury £400,000. In return the Bank's charter was extended from 1710 to 1732. To underwrite this, Parliament passed the Bank of England Act 1708 to increase the capital of the Bank, doubling it to £4,402,343.[59]

Under this same Act, the first consolidation and funding of Exchequer bills occurred, converting short-term floating debt to long-term permanent debt. Existing bills to the value of £1.5 million issued in 1707 were purchased by the Bank and the interest funded at 6 per cent. The Bank received its interest in Exchequer bills until 1710, after which the House Duties were charged to pay the annual interest. This permanent funding of Exchequer bills, one of many similar episodes over the next century and a half, was an efficient means of consolidating the Treasury's debt into a long-term financial commitment and was directly linked with the Bank's increases of its capital.

To try to encourage the circulation of Exchequer bills, the Bank was not required to exchange them for cash until they had passed through the Exchequer at least once.[60] Bills that hadn't passed through the Exchequer became known as 'non-specie' bills.

Further financial pressure forced the government's hand in late 1710. By 1711, the Treasury had agreed to pay the Bank an annual circulation sum of £45,000 charged yet again on the same customs revenues, so that the Bank would once again agree to cash 'non-specie' bills.[61] And in 1713, £1.2 million worth of Exchequer bills were issued which the Bank agreed to circulate for an additional payment of £8,000 per annum on top of the annual £45,000.[62]

To empower the Bank to circulate Exchequer bills it established a separate fund called the 'subscription for the circulation'.[63] Subscribers pledged £1 million, of which the Bank called in only 10 per cent. The fund was formed in 1711 and underwrote the Bank's obligations to cash bills at sight. The subscription fund was hugely profitable for the Bank and remained in place until it was finally dissolved in 1759. At the same time, the Bank opened an asset account in its books titled 'Account for Exchequer bills', through which Exchequer bills passed – received in exchange for cash money or bank notes, and reissued again if bank note holders preferred.[64]

From 1720, the Bank began liquidation of its holdings of bills following the Treasury's establishment of the 'Aggregate Fund' in 1715. The fund provided some £270,000 per annum for bill cancellation.

Due to lobbying by the Bank, the Exchequer came to issue bills in standard £100, £50 and £25 denominations, in contrast to the ad hoc amounts they were made out for when first introduced. By 1713, Exchequer bills were in £100 denominations only, which became the standard until 1742 when £1000 denominations were introduced.[65]

The bills so far discussed have been termed 'supply bills' and contrasted with bills that anticipated tax revenues. These latter bills were paid off as tax revenues flowed into the Exchequer. Supply bills resembled to all intents and purposes a national paper currency, and were exactly analogous to the Fiduciary Orders from the Restoration period, except that they attracted interest and could be used to settle taxes.

In 1722, a new circulation contract was agreed and signed by the Treasury and the Bank: £1 million of bills were created to repay Navy debts.[66] A further £100,000 of bills were issued and charged on the new Roman Catholic tax.[67] In 1725, £1 million more were issued,[68] which followed the creation of the new office of Paymasters for Exchequer bills in 1723, whose duties included the paying of the Bank's quarterly circulation allowance and the cancellation of bills when instructed by the Treasury. In October 1725, the office of Comptroller of Exchequer bills was formed. Its duties were defined in 1755 as the weekly cancellation of bills following their repayment by the Paymasters, auditing the Bank's accounts to calculate the quarterly circulation fee. By century's end the office was still in commission running under the title of 'Office for the Issue of Exchequer bills'.

From the mid-1720s, the Treasury innovated the issuance of Exchequer bills. Bills were issued for advances on the annual Land and Malt taxes from 1725 to 1726. When the taxes were received at the Exchequer the bills would be repaid and cancelled. For the next 140 years, until the passing of the Exchequer and Audit Departments Act 1866, Exchequer bills were the primary means of obtaining advances upon revenue flows mandated by Act of Parliament. This system was very obviously analogous to the former system of Tallies of Loan and Treasury Repayment Orders.

Up until 1760, the Treasury and the Bank agreed annual contracts signed each July, which obliged the Bank to cash upon demand bills worth £2.5 million. The Bank received interest of 3 per cent when the number of bills in circulation exceeded £1 million and 1 per cent when below this figure. The Bank's records show how this system worked: it would receive the bills in batches and cash them. It would then return them to the Exchequer for cancellation as the tax monies were received. This system excluded other lenders and effectively demonstrated the Bank's monopolisation of government fiscal operations.

During the American War of Independence, the Bank's advances on the Land and Malt taxes, secured by Exchequer bills, grew considerably. For example, in 1779 the Bank advanced £6 million but reached their peak in 1813 to the tune of £54 million. Further innovation followed too during the 19th century, when Exchequer bills were issued for public works, providing grants for the building of churches for example. But as the 18th century progressed, and with the rise of the Napoleonic Wars, the records show clearly that the other private London banks, which were growing in strength and number, became extensive holders of Exchequer bills.

2.5   THE FALL OF THE ANCIENT EXCHEQUER

The road to the Exchequer and Audit Departments Act of 1866 was a long one, starting two centuries earlier at the beginning of the Restoration period. It was painfully clear by the 1660s that the 'ancient course' of the Exchequer, so beloved by its tenured inhabitants, was completely incapable of producing an accurate and comprehensive account of what was happening to public funds.[69]

Throughout the majority of the 18th century the Exchequer remained protected by political forces and vested interests, until finally in 1780 Lord North was forced to sidestep reform proposals headed by Edmund Burke in the Commons by appointing a Commission of Accounts. This commission consisted of expert laymen, rather than politicians, and succeeded where the 17th-century attempts had failed. The Commissioners for Examining the Public Accounts produced 15 reports between 1780 and 1786 that 'permanently influenced the character of British government'.[70]

The commission discovered, as its 17th-century predecessor had, that accounts were 20 years in arrears, huge sums were being detained by public officials, and the Exchequer procedures were a costly, inaccurate and inconsistent farce, with audits that matched the greatest works of fiction. The commission demanded simplicity, for where there is simplicity there is economy, and this philosophy was developed throughout the reports. Archaic, anachronistic, overly complex processes were to be swept away and a new streamlined mechanism introduced. 'The wooden tallies, the Exchequer-Latin, and unique hieroglyphics could be left to the antiquarians, clearing the way for speedy and intelligible accounting.'[71]

The Receipt of the Exchequer Act of 1783 abolished the tally offices on the death of the current incumbents.[72] Tallies were replaced by indented paper cheque receipts. However, the tallies persisted until the last chamberlain died in 1826.[73] William Pitt's Act of 1785 initiated the reform of the Exchequer, by implementing the recommendations of the Commissioners. The two Auditors of Imprest were replaced with a professional board of auditors working under Treasury direction, and the multiple funds that had sprung up over the decades were replaced, in 1787, with a single 'Consolidated Fund,' which remains the Government's principal account today.

However, the reforms fell short of what was required. Although, in 1806, Acts of Parliament required revenue collectors to bank at the Bank of England, they had, in practice, been banking with the Bank for many decades with the fiction of paying cash into the Exchequer maintained using cancelled bank notes.[74] The 'redundant formalities of the ancient course' still hamstrung the audit office obtaining control of the public funds, waiting as they did for the 'King's Remembrancer to issue his cumbersome writs'.[75] In 1810, a Select Committee of the House concluded that the audit changes had simply preserved the evils of the old system, and its findings led to the abolition of the sinecures within the Exchequer in 1817. In 1831, the 'Commissioners of Public Accounts' led by Sir Henry Parnell published their first and only report. Titled a 'Report on the Exchequer', it recommended that responsibility for making Exchequer payments should be transferred to the Bank of England and that the Exchequer should be retained solely for purposes of control and audit. Following the death of the last Auditor of Receipt, Lord Greville, these recommendations were afterwards brought into effect by Act of Parliament and Treasury Minute, bringing to an end the ancient Exchequer.[76]

The Exchequer was finally abolished on 10 October 1834. The day after, two cart loads of tally sticks, kept faithfully in store since 1826, were cleared out and burnt in the understoves of the House of Lords. That evening fire swept through the estate razing both Houses of Parliament to the ground.[77] The last act of the ancient Exchequer was to bring into being the Palace of Westminster we know today.

2.6   CREDIT AND THE CONSOLIDATED FUND

The establishment of the Consolidated Fund in 1787 simplified and secured the methods of making good financial deficiencies and dealing with surplus funds.[78] By the Act of 1787 and under every Act up until 1817, revenues paid into the Consolidated Fund could only be appropriated towards the payment of interest on the national debt, the civil list and other permanent charges payable out of the fund. These direct charges on the fund were termed 'prior charges'.[79] Exclusively by special grant of Parliament could surpluses on the fund, arising after prior charges, be appropriated for other branches of supply.

From inception the Consolidated Fund ran on a quarterly accounting cycle.[80] Revenues were paid into the Consolidated Fund at the Exchequer, accumulating as balances at the Bank of England throughout the quarter from the first to the last day. The total revenues and charges were then ascertained. If a deficiency to make the charges payable for the quarter over revenues received was apparent, then an advance was made immediately from other aids and supplies. If, however, a surplus was apparent, then this was applied in the first instance to repay such aids and supplies advanced in previous quarters. Having repaid previous advances, the remaining surplus simply accumulated at the Bank awaiting parliamentary process to appropriate the funds. Thus, surpluses were unavailable to make good deficiencies of previous quarters until the end of the quarter in which they arose and, furthermore, accumulating balances remained in the Bank and could not be issued for quarterly charges due until the succeeding quarter. Clearly, this system of financial management was highly inefficient and unsatisfactory, and hence was ripe for reform, which occurred in 1817.

Under the reforms authorised by Act of Parliament in 1817, to make good any deficiency on the Consolidated Fund, the Commissioners of the Treasury were empowered to issue Exchequer bills from 'time to time', instead of having to immediately pay for deficiencies on advances from other revenues.[81] These Exchequer bills, known as 'Deficiency bills', were interest bearing at half the Bank's discount rate, and repayable from time to time out of the 'growing produce' of the fund during the quarter in which they were issued. Operationally, under the Act, the bills were issued to the Bank of England which was 'empowered to advance money on the credit of such Exchequer bills.'[82]

An Act of Parliament was passed in 1830 and under its provisions the surplus sums on the Consolidated Fund were for the first time appropriated towards making good the annually voted Supply Services.[83] Thus, when deficiencies arose on the surplus funds appropriated to meet grants of supply, the Treasury was authorised to issue Exchequer bills termed 'Ways and Means bills'. Ways and Means bills, however, were repayable from time to time out of the growing produce of the fund in the *following* quarter. They also bore interest at the Bank's full discount rate. There were instances, though infrequent, when surpluses failed to materialise and consequently these bills could not be repaid. The Treasury responded by transforming these floating bills into funded bills.[84]

In 1846, the law was reformed once more and since this time all annually voted Ways and Means have been transferred to the Consolidated Fund.[85]

As well as seeing the demise of the ancient Exchequer, the Office of the Receipt of the Exchequer Act 1834 required the opening of 'The Account of His Majesty's Exchequer' in the books of the Bank of England.[86] However, the reforms of 1834 still led to needless issuing of paper between the Bank and the Treasury. Consequently, another influential report was commissioned and published in 1857. The report from the Select Committee on Public Monies recommended, among many other reforms including requiring all departments to use double-entry bookkeeping, ending the practice of issuing Deficiency bills and Ways and Means bills to the Bank of England as security for advances on temporary deficiencies on the Consolidated Fund.[87] The commissioners proposed that advances of money by the Bank of England were to be granted upon written application by HM Treasury, replacing the bills with simple 'book debts' – simple accounting entries in the books of both the Bank and the Treasury.[88]

On the death, in February 1866, of Baron Monteagle of Brandon, the belligerent Comptroller who took office in 1839 and opposed the reforms proposed by the Select Committee on Public Monies, change started to take place.[89] The Comptroller position had been created following the abolition of the Office of the Exchequer of Receipt in 1834, but it had been a transfer of function, not a reappraisal of the roles. Now it was reimagined as the Comptroller and Auditor General to include not only the 'issue of parliamentary grants from Bank of England accounts', but also the critical evaluation of expenditure and reporting those findings back to the Public Accounts Committee of the House of Commons.[90] It is through this officer of Parliament that parliamentary control of public money is asserted. Gladstone's words, the genius behind these latter reforms, fittingly summarise the principle, 'it is undoubtedly the business of the House of Commons to be responsible, not only for the inception of all public expenditure but also follow money raised by taxation until the last farthing is accounted for'.

Finally, in 1866, these simplifications and reforms came together in the Exchequer and Audit Departments Act, which still forms the legal basis by which government spending is undertaken from the Consolidated Fund, and accounted for to Parliament.[91]

Following recommendations from the Select Committee, under the Exchequer and Audit Departments Act 1866, quarterly Deficiency bills and Ways and Means bills were dropped and replaced with 'book debt'.[92] Related to this decision, the report concluded that remaining Exchequer bills, issued for supply purposes, should be repayable out of the Consolidated Fund rather than its surplus.

The mode of issuing and repaying Exchequer bills was regulated by several Acts of Parliament. An Act of 1808[93] separated the preparing and issuing of bills from that of paying them. Preparation and issuance remained a responsibility of the Receipt of the Exchequer, under audit authority from the Office for the Issue of Exchequer Bills, but responsibility for paying them transferred to the Paymaster of Exchequer bills. With later reform of the Paymaster's Office, paying of Exchequer bills became the duty of the Paymaster General where it remained until the demise of the Exchequer bill. The influential Report on the Exchequer of 1831 recommended that the task of preparing Exchequer bills should transfer to the Treasury, however, by 1857 this responsibility had still not been transferred. Indeed, in the Select Committee report,[94] some discussion focused on transferring the responsibility for preparing bills to the Bank of England. Objections were raised, but, despite these, it came to pass in the Exchequer Bills and Bonds Act 1866 that 'all Exchequer Bills which shall be made out and issued under the Authority of any Act or Acts of Parliament shall be prepared and made out at the Bank of England'.[95] According to Dickson, Exchequer bills reigned supreme until 1877 when, under Stafford Henry Northcote's leadership, the Treasury bill supplanted it.[96] Exchequer bills were formally withdrawn and discontinued in 1897, 200 years after their lacklustre beginning.

2.7   A SINKING FEELING

The visceral desire to eliminate the National Debt started almost as soon as the first bank credit was issued to the government. In the eyes of many, national debt constituted a moral wrong, rather than financial assets in the hands of the private sector – an attitude that persists to this day. Since the floating debt[97] was of the greatest concern, proposals were put forward to create a 'sinking fund',[98] which would purchase government debt and take it out of circulation.

In 1716, the revenue items appropriated for the service of the national debt were grouped into four funds, the Aggregate, South Sea, General and Sinking funds. The latter so-called because it received the surpluses from the other three, while being appropriated to the sinking of the national debt 'and to no other purpose'.[99] This Walpole–Stanhope fund appeared to do its job for a while, but as soon as the economic tide turned and wars needed financing, the fund was raided and it fell into disrepair.

The biggest proponent of sinking funds was not a financier but a theologian, Dr Richard Price, a prominent pamphleteer, Unitarian minister, radical Whig and all-round self-promoter in 18th-century Britain. Dr Price had an interest in interest thanks to his extensive actuarial work that influenced the insurance industry for decades.

In a widely circulated treatise, Price called down the power of compound interest to show how the national debt could be paid off[100] but there was a flaw in his thinking. Once the entirety of the government accounts had been assessed, it became clear that one part of the state was paying another. Yet Price believed that if interest rates were higher, it would pay off the national debt even faster.[101]

Price's theories[102] penetrated the mind of a certain up-and-coming politician by the name of William Pitt.[103] In the National Debt Reduction Act 1786[104] he created a new sinking fund, vested in a 'Board of Commissioners of the Sinking Fund'.[105] It took until 1828 before an essay by Lord Grenville,[106] a former ardent fan of the sinking fund concept, finally exposed the truth – the government had been issuing new debt at 5 per cent to purchase old debt at 4½ per cent.[107]

In 1875 the moralists gained the political upper-hand again and a 'new' sinking fund created a 'permanent annual charge for National Debt' upon the Consolidated Fund, replacing the ad hoc budgetary provisions that had failed to make any difference over the previous 50 years.[108]

The First World War put paid to the permanent annual charge and caused a huge increase in the national debt, including for the first time national debt borrowed in US dollars.[109] The boom times of the 1920s saw the revival of the sinking fund concepts with several finance acts implementing further 'new' sinking funds, culminating in the Finance Act 1928.[110]

However, the Great Depression and the Second World War once again suspended the permanent charge, which continued until the provision was eventually abolished in the Finance Act 1954:[111] 'It is unnecessary to go through the farce, year after year, of solemnly suspending that provision, and therefore we propose its abolition.'[112]

Even then, it took until the National Loans Act 1968 before the sinking fund Acts and their provisions were finally repealed.[113] And there the idea stayed until the Great Financial Crisis of 2008 and the introduction of the Asset Purchase Facility by the Bank of England, which buys up government securities from the market and retains them rather than passing them back to the owner of the Bank of England, HM Treasury, to write off.[114]

The sinking fund has returned, repurposed for a new age.

2.8   NEW LABOUR, NEW PAPER

During the 1990s, the idea took root that government debt management and cash management should be institutionally divorced from interest rate setting, and that central banks should always be independent of Parliament,[115] along with the judiciary.[116] Monetary policy was redefined to a narrower role[117] and the Bank of England became 'independent',[118] given the power to determine monetary policy which started as little more than trying to adjust the Bank Rate by undertaking transactions in a new wider market for gilts and Treasury bills. A market that went beyond the traditional discount houses to a whole raft of newly created, and subsequently newly enriched, middlemen.

The catalyst for the change was the 1995 Report of the Debt Management Review, which led to the government adopting a 'full funding rule'.[119] This formalised a policy that had been adopted in 1985 to ensure that the financial transactions of the public sector had no effect on the M4 money aggregate so beloved at the time.

Although this review was initiated by a Conservative Government, it was under the Labour Government of 1997, and the stewardship of Gordon Brown, that wholesale changes were made. Institutional separation and 'Chinese Walls' were the order of the day, and Brown introduced a tripartite separation between the Bank of England, the new Financial Service Authority and HM Treasury.[120] As part of this, debt and cash management were transferred to a new Debt Management Office that took over responsibility from the Bank of England for implementing the government's 'full funding rule' policy. Specific within this was a decision to halt the previous habitual use of the Ways and Means account for end-of-day balancing,[121] primarily to bring the UK into line with the convergence criteria required to join the Euro.[122]

The early years of the new millennium bedded in this new, more complex institutionally separate structure and this resulted in reviews of the operations. The first was a review of the Bank of England's operations initiated by the Governor in 2003[123] and implemented in 2006.[124] The primary reason for change was that the existing operational framework left sterling overnight rates considerably more volatile than desired, and the result was a new reserve averaging scheme and standing facilities. This included introducing the concept of reserves into UK banking for the first time and the payment of interest on reserves.[125]

Alongside this HM Treasury initiated a review into the cash and debt management operations within the Debt Management Office.[126] The key conclusion of the review was to refocus cash management 'to minimise the cost' instead of 'and to do so in a cost-effective way'. In addition, it identified that the institutional split between HM Treasury and the Debt Management Office had caused differences in the way forecasts were viewed. The review attempted to refocus both institutions on a single performance target. The downsides of Chinese Walls were beginning to surface.

However, it was the Great Financial Crisis of 2007–08 that finally caused these walls to come tumbling down. Caught flat-footed, with out-of-date beliefs and with parts of the process in different institutions, the collapse in the financial system led to 'Britain's first bank run in 141 years',[127] even though systemically there was no reason for that to happen.[128]

The limited deposit insurance scheme, following the European Union model and covering only 90 per cent of deposits over £2000 and with a cap of only £31,700, failed to provide depositors with any confidence and the bank run commenced.[129] Government was forced to extend the scheme to cover 100 per cent of deposits and increase the limit, eventually reaching £85,000. The Bank of England, obsessed with controlling monetary growth, limped into action with a mere £10 billion liquidity injection. The result was two years of crisis after crisis, where bad loans in the banks mounted up and more and more interventions were required. The Bank of England slashed rates to record lows, the reserve averaging scheme was suspended in March 2009 as the Bank of England started to purchase gilts to try and bring longer-term interest rates down. This was the start of the modern notion of Quantitative Easing (QE) which followed a similar pattern to those of the 17th century: the Bank buying higher yielding gilts and replacing them with lower yielding Bank of England liabilities.

The fiction of the full funding rule was exposed, with the Debt Management Office forced on 15 October 2008 to use the overnight Ways and Means facility to the tune of £700 million,[130] with £3.8 billion funded through the traditional main Ways and Means Advance.[131] Every year the ability to use this mechanism is mentioned in the annual review,[132] and if a crisis occurs the market is reminded to keep it in line.[133]

Since the financial crisis, interest rates have remained low and QE has continued apace as the economy has limped along. The Westminster village is still convinced that interest rates have magical powers to revive or suppress an economy and that the all-powerful 'star chamber' of the Monetary Policy Committee will maintain stability in the economy.[134] Lobbying of these few individuals is intense and their every utterance reported in the press.[135]

We are now left in a similar situation to the one that faced Burke in the 1780s. We have an Exchequer system that is overly complex, providing well-paid tenures to many individuals who are wedded to beliefs that Modern Monetary Theory shows are incorrect. Power over the purse has moved between Parliament, the Crown and the Bank over the centuries. In recent history the idea that the Bank is in charge has become popular, but that idea has failed to keep even to the targets it has set itself, largely because the processes it follows simply do not have the effect its proponents believe. It is time that the Exchequer system was reformed again, with the power over the purse returning to Parliament. The Debt Management Office, the National Loans Fund and the Monetary Policy Committee, along with the associated hangers-on in the finance industry, should meet the same fate as the Ancient Exchequer – consolidated down to a single account at the Bank of England.[136]

NOTES

1. A contract cut in two along an 'indenture' line with each party retaining one half. The indentures were '(*edictum* [by Order] or *licentia* [*by Licence*]) made between the sovereign and Master and Worker of the Royal Mint' (Fox and Ernst 2016, p. 206).
2. An ancient judicial process dating back to Edward I that tests the weight, size and fineness of coins produced by the Royal Mint and which is still mandated by law. See Coinage Act 1971, s8 and The Royal Mint 2014.
3. By count, rather than weight and composition of the item. From the same root as 'tally'. The sovereign proclaims the value of each coin in England, and that is the value the law applies to it no matter what it is made of or where it came from. Even some foreign coins were given fixed value in England by proclamation (e.g., Proclamation 406, Mary I, 4 March 1554).
4. Fox and Ernst 2016, p. 206.
5. The works of John Locke were very influential in this period and deeply held the view that money was only worth what it was made from.
6. For a brief history of the English Tally and the changes during the Restoration, see Tye 2019.
7. 17 Car. II, c. 1, VII (Raithby 1819a, pp. 570–4). For an overview of the novel and revolutionary mechanisms introduced into this Act by Sir George Downing, see Roseveare 1973, pp. 22–5.
8. Tallies of Pro had become limited in their use by the 1660s because they gave the owner the legal right to specific tax revenues (Nichols 1971, p. 96).
9. 17 Car. II, c. 1, X (Raithby 1819a, pp. 570–4). Until then tallies could only be paid out to the original payee (Philippovich et al. 1911, p. 60). 19 & 20 Car. II c.4 (Raithby 1819a, p. 629), prevented assignors revoking their assignment.
10. Attempts to reform the corrupt Tax Farming tax collection system resulted in even less tax revenue being raised (Nichols 1971, pp. 92–4).
11. And as such, they ought to be described as 'Certificated Orders' to distinguish them from the other types.
12. Shaw 1906, Clapham 1945, Nichols 1971.
13. 18 & 19 Car. II c. 13, VI (Raithby 1819a, pp. 616–23)
14. 18 & 19 Car. II c. 13, X (Raithby 1819a, pp. 616–23).
15. The ordinary revenues were the King's hereditary income that occurred every year, including income Parliament had voted 'for life'. The Glorious Revolution of 1688 brought a change to parliamentary practice where Parliament would only grant revenue to the Crown for the forthcoming year, to prevent the Crown proroguing Parliament and ruling alone as Charles II had done in the 1670s, and James II in 1685.
16. The Goldsmith Bankers.
17. In other words, coins and tallies.
18. Desan 2014, p. 261.
19. Berkeley et al. 2020, Appendix J. The Stop was brought about on advice from the 'Cabal', a term coined from the initials of five Privy Councillors who were close advisors to the King: Clifford, Arlington, Buckingham, Ashley and Lauderdale.
20. A famous legal battle ensued called the 'Case of the Bankers' that eventually found in favour of the bankers. They were finally recompensed by an Act of Parliament in 1705.

21. Richards 1930.
22. House of Lords Journal 1696–1701 1697, pp. 141–2.
23. 8 & 9 Wm III c.20 LXVIII (Raithby 1820, pp. 218–38).
24. William 1697.
25. Cox 1901, p. 359.
26. McKeever 2010.
27. 5 & 6 Will & Mary c.20 XVIII–XX (Raithby 1819b, pp. 487–8).
28. A period of time known as the Great Recoinage, after which Isaac Newton became Master of the Mint (Isaac Newton, Warden and Master of the Royal Mint 1696–1727 n.d.).
29. For a list of Acts extending the capital of the Bank of England, see Berkeley et al. 2020, Appendix E.
30. Philippovich et al. 1911, p. 74.
31. Along with a call in of subscriptions, optionally payable in tallies and notes, and direct purchases of tallies by the bank for notes (Kleer 2017, p. 37).
32. This was, in effect, the first example of Quantitative Easing by the Bank, consolidating the public debt.
33. The Bank of England Acts (both 1694 and 1696) imposed a limit on the loans the Bank may advance before the shareholders became personally liable. 'But they give their Cashire's Notes for all sums (ad infinitum) which neither charge the Fund nor the Proprietors, which seems to be a Credit beyond the Intention of the Act of Parliament, and never practised before by any Corporation' (Bank of England 1969).
34. Dickson 1993.
35. 7 & 8 Will III c.31 LXVII–LXXIII (Raithby 1820, pp. 142–5).
36. Clapham 1945.
37. 7 & 8 Will III c.31 LXVII (Raithby 1820, p. 142).
38. Kleer 2017, Clapham 1945 and Dickson 1993 state the figure at £158,589.
39. 'Three pence per diem for every one hundred pounds', 7 & 8 Will III c.31 LXVII (Raithby 1820, p. 142).
40. The Land Bank was an early form of mortgage lending and intended to issue notes secured on land. It was supported, amongst others, by Nicholas Barbon, a property speculator and early economic theorist. Unlike John Locke, Barbon considered money to be symbolic. See Barbon 2016.
41. Kleer 2017.
42. They were issued between 10 July and 28 September 1696.
43. Clapham 1945, p. 40.
44. 8 & 9 Wm III c.6 XCIV (Raithby 1820, p. 187).
45. 8 & 9 Wm III c.6 XCV (Raithby 1820, p. 187).
46. 8 & 9 Wm III c.20 LXIII (Raithby 1820, p. 236).
47. 'Five pence per day for every one hundred pounds', 8 & 9 Wm III c.20 LXIV (Raithby 1820, p. 236).
48. Charles Montagu tried many things to drive his innovation, adjusting interest rates, cajoling, begging, getting the King to order merchants to take them. All of them failed. See Graham 2019.
49. What Montagu didn't try is making Exchequer bills the exclusive instrument for the settlement of taxes. This unavoidability is the fundamental point missed in Kleer (2015, p. 201) where it states 'So Chartalists are simply wrong …'.
50. 8 & 9 Wm III c.20 XX–XXXVI (Raithby 1820, pp. 224–8).

51.   Tallies and Orders in circulation were all drawn against inadequate tax revenues and were due at an uncertain future date, hence their trading at heavy discount and their having a negative impact on the Treasury raising further credit.
52.   8 & 9 Wm III c.20 XXXVIII (Raithby 1820, pp. 224–8).
53.   Clapham 1945, p. 55.
54.   Gilt-Edged Market Makers.
55.   8 & 9 Wm III c.20 LXVI (Raithby 1820, pp. 218–38) extended later in the year by 8 & 9 Wm III c.24 XIX–XX (Raithby 1820, pp. 259–66).
56.   Dickson 1993.
57.   6 Anne c.21 VI (Raithby 1821, p. 595) (5 Anne c.13 in the CPE).
58.   Kleer 2015, Chapter II, pp. 188–90.
59.   7 Anne c.30 IV (Raithby 1822, p. 114) (c.7 in the CPE).
60.   7 Anne c.30 LVII (Raithby 1822, p. 128).
61.   9 Anne c.7 III (Raithby 1822, pp. 384–5).
62.   12 Anne c.11 III (Raithby 1822, p. 772).
63.   Clapham 1945, p. 68.
64.   Dickson 1993.
65.   Dickson 1993.
66.   8 Geo 1 c.20 (Pickering 1765a, p. 422).
67.   9 Geo 1 c.18 (Pickering 1765b, p. 70).
68.   11 Geo 1 c.17 (Pickering 1765b, pp. 219–21).
69.   Roseveare 1973, p. 48.
70.   Roseveare 1973, p. 61.
71.   Roseveare 1973, p. 62. See also the 8th report of the Commissioners (Journals of the House of Commons 1803, pp. 56–7).
72.   57 Geo 3 c.84 (Great Britain 1817, pp. 273–4).
73.   Records of the Exchequer of Receipt and Successors 1901.
74.   'The payment of cash into the Exchequer was superseded, in practice but not in theory, by different arrangements. Revenue was now paid direct into the Bank of England, and disbursements paid out similarly. The fiction of an active Exchequer of Receipt was maintained by the attendance of a Bank of England clerk at the Exchequer to receive cancelled bank notes from the receivers general of the principal revenue departments (all of which banked at the Bank), and to give each receiver general credit for these notes with the tellers' (Records of the Exchequer of Receipt and Successors 1901).
75.   Roseveare 1973, p. 64.
76.   4 & 5 Will 4 c.15 (Great Britain 1834, pp. 103–14); and Treasury Minute dated 26 September 1834.
77.   Great Fire 1834.
78.   27 Geo III c.13, XLII (Pickering 1787, p. 44).
79.   Select Committee on Public Monies 1857.
80.   Quarterly accounts were abolished by Finance Act 1954, s34(3).
81.   'It was usual formerly for the Paymaster General to apply to the Treasury every Four Months, each time for about a third part of the sum voted for the Services of the Army, under the general Head of Subsistence and Pay of the Forces at Home and Abroad; but since the Year 1759, the practice has been to ask of the Treasury, from "Time to Time", for the sums voted under distinct Heads of Service, and not until the Time when the Demands for the Services are near approaching.'
82.   57 Geo III c.48 IX (Great Britain 1817, p. 138).
83.   11 Geo IV c.2 1830 (Great Britain 1830, p. 2).

84. Select Committee on Public Monies 1857. Footnote p. 40.
85. 9 & 10 Vict. c.47 (Rickards 1846).
86. 4 & 5 Will IV c.15 VIII (Great Britain 1834, p. 104).
87. Double-entry bookkeeping, as opposed to the ancient charge and discharge accounting, started to be used in some departments from the 1820s.
88. 'Book-debt' being a straightforward overdraft at the Bank of England, like today's Ways and Means Advance from the Issue Department to the National Loans Fund. The Bank still prefers to keep book debt short term though, changing it for long-term Treasury issued paper – Treasury bills, and latterly gilts.
89. 'Monteagle believed that the basis of financial control must be mistrust' (Roseveare 1973, p. 71).
90. Roseveare 1973, p. 72.
91. Exchequer and Audit Departments Act 1866.
92. Select Committee on Public Monies 1857.
93. 48 Geo III c.1 (Great Britain 1808, p. 2).
94. Select Committee on Public Monies 1857.
95. Exchequer Bills and Bonds Act 1866, s3.
96. Dickson 1993.
97. Categories of debt arose over time: 'funded debt' was perpetual debt where only the interest was paid. 'Unfunded debt' was debt at a fixed interest, but which had to be paid at a specific time (like today's gilts), and 'floating debt' was debt that had to be repaid in the current period or shortly thereafter (which today are repo contracts, overnight Ways and Means and Treasury bills). See Lombard Street Research 2000.
98. When debt was issued it was 'floated', therefore to get rid of it required 'sinking'.
99. Ross 1892.
100. Price 1772.
101. DeMatos 2020.
102. '[T]hough clearly refuted by a few obscure writers' (Ross 1892, p. 14).
103. Cone 1951.
104. National Debt Reduction Act 1786.
105. Who became the Commissioners for the Reduction of the National Debt, now part of the DMO (About the CRND 2021).
106. Grenville 1828.
107. 'Even in peace-time the Sinking Fund was an absurd and masochistic ritual; it was simply a little more absurd in war. But, as a proof of public virtue, the Sinking Fund was of incalculable psychological value' (Roseveare 1969, p. 128).
108. Sinking Fund Act 1875, s1(1).
109. And which was defaulted upon in 1934 during the Great Depression (Gill 2018).
110. Finance Act 1928, s23.
111. Finance Act 1954, s34(1).
112. Boyd-Carpenter 1954, Hansard, column 33.
113. National Loans Act 1968, Schedule 6.
114. Asset Purchase Facility Annual Report 2021.
115. 'If the freedom of capital movement was the belt, then central bank independence was the buckle on the free-market Washington Consensus of the 1990s' (Tooze 2020).
116. This view resulted in the judiciary moving out of Parliament into its own Supreme Court in 2009, replacing the ancient right of appeal to the monarch in Parliament embedded in the Law Lords sitting in the House of Lords.

117. 'The view that debt management is not part of monetary policy (or that it should not be part of monetary policy) seems to be a recent development in some Anglo-American macroeconomics circles. By traditional standards, it is unorthodox and strange' (Lombard Street Research 2000).
118. Bank of England Act 1998, s10.
119. 'To review the existing arrangements for the setting of debt management policy, the selling of Government debt and the management of outstanding debt' (HM Treasury and Bank of England 1995).
120. Managed by the Tripartite Standing Committee on Financial Stability. See Blei 2008.
121. HM Treasury 1997, §49, p. 19.
122. HM Treasury 1998, §20, p. 8, 'A previous consultation paper indicated that the Ways and Means overdraft facility at the Bank of England would be frozen at the time of the transition to the new cash management system. The outstanding balance would subsequently be repaid in accordance with the Maastricht Treaty (Articles 104 and 109e(3), the UK Protocol (Paragraph 11) and Council Regulation 3603/93).' And 'In order to be Maastricht compliant (if the UK were to join Stage 3), the Bank of England cannot lend overnight to make up the shortfall' (§43, p. 16).
123. 'The Governor announced a review of the Bank's operations in the sterling money markets in a speech in Leicester on 14 October 2003' (Tucker 2004).
124. Bank of England 2006a.
125. 'UK banks and building societies that are members of the scheme undertake to hold target balances (reserves) at the Bank on average over maintenance periods running from one MPC decision date until the next. If a member's average balance is within a range around their target, the balance is remunerated at the official Bank Rate' (Bank of England 2006b).
126. DMO Annual Review 2005, pp. 28–34.
127. Blei 2008.
128. Berkeley et al. 2020, s4.
129. Edmonds 2010, p. 5.
130. 'The DMO ensured a positive end-of-day DMA balance on each day during 2008–09 except for the 15 October 2008 when a transfer from the Bank of England's Ways and Means (II) facility was required. This facility was required to prevent the DMA from going overdrawn after a large unexpected payment of £700 million occurred after the wholesale money market had closed for same-day settlement' (DMO Annual Review 2009, p. 86).
131. '[A] temporary increase of £3.8 billion in short-term borrowing from the Ways and Means Advance in order to smooth the impact of the financing of part of the Bank of England's loans to the FSCS' (DMO Annual Review 2009, p. 17).
132. 'Automatic transfers from the government Ways and Means (II) account at the Bank of England would offset any negative end-of-day balances' (DMO Annual Review 2020, p. 35).
133. HM Treasury 2020.
134. Britannica 2019.
135. Lynch 2021.
136. This time the main Ways and Means Advance (Berkeley et al. 2020, p. 126).

REFERENCES

About the CRND (2021), accessed 25 October 2021 at https://www.dmo.gov.uk/responsibilities/public-sector-funds-crnd/about-crnd/.

Asset Purchase Facility Annual Report (2021), Bank of England, 17 June, accessed 27 October 2021 at https://www.bankofengland.co.uk/-/media/boe/files/asset-purchase-facility/2021/annual-report-2021.pdf.

Bank of England (1969), 'The Bank of England Note – a Short History', Bank of England Quarterly Bulletin, (Q2), 1 June, accessed 4 November 2021 at https://www.bankofengland.co.uk/-/media/boe/files/quarterly-bulletin/1969/the-boe-note-a-short-history.pdf.

Bank of England (2006a), Reforms to the Bank of England's Operations in the Sterling Money Markets: Target Launch Date for the New Framework, 29 March, accessed 22 October 2021 at https://www.bankofengland.co.uk/-/media/boe/files/news/2006/march/reforms-to-the-boes-operations-in-the-sterling-money-markets.pdf.

Bank of England (2006b), The Framework for the Bank of England's Operations in the Sterling Money Markets, accessed 22 October 2021 at https://www.treasurers.org/ACTmedia/redbook0506.pdf.

Bank of England Act (1998), accessed 22 October 2021 at https://www.legislation.gov.uk/ukpga/1998/11/introduction.

Barbon, N. (2016), 'A Discourse Concerning Coining the New Money Lighter (1696)', in *Essential Writings*, Germany: Jazzybee Verlag, p. 92.

Berkeley, A., R. Tye and N. Wilson (2020), An Accounting Model of the UK Exchequer, United Kingdom: The Gower Initiative for Modern Money Studies, 26 December, accessed 26 December 2020 at https://gimms.org.uk/2021/02/21/an-accounting-model-of-the-uk-exchequer/.

Blei, S.K. (2008), 'The British Tripartite Financial Supervision System in the Face of the Northern Rock Run', Supervisory Policy Analysis Working Papers 2008–01, Federal Reserve Bank of St. Louis, accessed 22 October 2021 at https://EconPapers.repec.org/RePEc:fip:fedlsp:2008-01.

Boyd-Carpenter, J. (1954), Finance Bill, accessed 25 October 2021 at https://api.parliament.uk/historic-hansard/commons/1954/may/03/finance-bill#column_33.

Britannica (2019), 'Star Chamber | Definition, History, & Facts', accessed 24 October 2021 at https://www.britannica.com/topic/Star-Chamber.

Clapham, J.H. (1945), *The Bank of England: A History*, vol. 1–1694 to 1797, Cambridge: The University Press.

Coinage Act (1971), accessed 5 November 2021 at https://www.legislation.gov.uk/ukpga/1971/24/introduction.

Cone, C.B. (1951), 'Richard Price and Pitt's Sinking Fund of 1786', *The Economic History Review*, 4 (2), 243.

Cox, H. (1901), 'The Public Debt of Great Britain', *The North American Review*, 173 (538), 355–76.

DeMatos, D. (2020), 'Britain's Sinking Fund', accessed 25 October 2021 at https://thetchblog.com/2020/05/18/britains-sinking-fund/.

Desan, C. (2014), *Making Money: Coin, Currency, and the Coming of Capitalism*, Oxford: Oxford University Press.

Dickson, P.G.M. (1993), *The Financial Revolution in England: A Study in the Development of Public Credit, 1688–1756*, 2nd edn, Aldershot, UK: Gregg Revivals.

DMO Annual Review (2005), United Kingdom Debt Management Office, July, accessed 22 October 2021 at https://dmo.gov.uk/media/14483/gar0405.pdf.

DMO Annual Review (2009), United Kingdom Debt Management Office, August, accessed 24 October 2021 at https://dmo.gov.uk/media/14487/gar0809.pdf.

DMO Annual Review (2020), United Kingdom Debt Management Office, 16 October, accessed 24 October 2021 at https://dmo.gov.uk/media/17019/gar1920.pdf.

Edmonds, T. (2010), 'Financial Services Compensation Scheme', House of Commons Library, accessed 24 October 2021 at https://researchbriefings.files.parliament.uk/documents/SN04466/SN04466.pdf.

Exchequer and Audit Departments Act (1866), accessed 17 August 2021 at https://www.legislation.gov.uk/ukpga/Vict/29-30/39/introduction.

Exchequer Bills and Bonds Act (1866), accessed 6 November 2021 at https://vlex.co.uk/vid/exchequer-bills-and-bonds-808072721.

Finance Act (1928), accessed 25 October 2021 at https://www.legislation.gov.uk/ukpga/Geo5/18-19/17/section/23/enacted.

Finance Act (1954), accessed 15 August 2021 at https://www.legislation.gov.uk/ukpga/Eliz2/2-3/44/introduction.

Fox, D. and W. Ernst (eds) (2016), *Money in the Western Legal Tradition: Middle Ages to Bretton Woods*, 1st edn, New York: Oxford University Press.

Gill, D.J. (2018), 'The UK's Unpaid War Debts to the United States, 1917–1980', accessed 25 October 2021 at https://ehs.org.uk/the-uks-unpaid-war-debts-to-the-united-states-1917-1980/.

Graham, A. (2019), 'Credit, Confidence and the Circulation of Exchequer Bills in the Early Financial Revolution', *Financial History Review*, 26 (1), 63–80.

Great Britain (1808), *Statutes of the United Kingdom*, London: J. Butterworth.

Great Britain (1817), *Statutes of the United Kingdom*, London: J. Butterworth.

Great Britain (1830), *Statutes of the United Kingdom*, London: J. Butterworth.

Great Britain (1834), *A Collection of the Public General Statutes*, London: J. Richards.

Great Fire (1834), accessed 30 October 2021 at https://www.parliament.uk/about/living-heritage/building/palace/architecture/palacestructure/great-fire/.

Grenville, W.W. (1828), *Essay on the Supposed Advantages of a Sinking Fund*, John Murray.

HM Treasury (1997), The Future of UK Government Debt and Cash Management: A Response to Consultation, HM Treasury, December, accessed 1 November 2021 at https://www.dmo.gov.uk/media/14580/cons290797.pdf.

HM Treasury (1998), UK Government Cash Management: The New Framework, accessed 1 November 2021 at https://www.dmo.gov.uk/media/14613/cmfwork041298.pdf.

HM Treasury (2020), 'HM Treasury and Bank of England Announce Temporary Extension of the Ways and Means Facility', GOV.UK, 9 April, accessed 24 October 2021 at https://www.gov.uk/government/news/hm-treasury-and-bank-of-england-announce-temporary-extension-of-the-ways-and-means-facility.

HM Treasury and Bank of England (1995), Report of the Debt Management Review, July, accessed 24 October 2021 at https://www.dmo.gov.uk/media/2083/report95.pdf.

House of Lords Journal 1696–1701 (1697), vol. 16, London: His Majesty's Stationery Office.

Isaac Newton, Warden and Master of the Royal Mint 1696–1727 (n.d.), accessed 24 October 2021 at https://www.royalmintmuseum.org.uk/journal/people/isaac-newton/.

Journals of the House of Commons (1803), vol. 39, HM Stationery Office.

Kleer, R.A. (2015), '"A New Species of Mony": British Exchequer Bills, 1701–1711', *Financial History Review*, 22 (2), 179–203.

Kleer, R.A. (2017), *Money, Politics and Power: Banking and Public Finance in Wartime England, 1694–96*, London: Routledge.

Lombard Street Research (2000), House of Commons – Treasury – Appendices to the Minutes of Evidence, accessed 22 October 2021 at https://publications.parliament.uk/pa/cm199900/cmselect/cmtreasy/154/154ap08.htm.

Lynch, R. (2021), 'Brace for Interest Rate Rises, Warns Bank of England Rate-setter', *Telegraph*, 9 October, accessed 24 October 2021 at https://www.telegraph.co.uk/business/2021/10/09/brace-interest-rate-rises-warns-bank-england-rate-setter/.

McKeever, K. (2010), 'A Short History of Tontines', *Fordham Journal of Corporate & Financial Law*, 15, 491.

National Debt Reduction Act (1786), accessed 24 November 2021 at https://www.legislation.gov.uk/apgb/Geo3/26/31/introduction.

National Loans Act (1968), accessed 15 August 2021 at https://www.legislation.gov.uk/ukpga/1968/13/introduction.

Nichols, G.O. (1971), 'English Government Borrowing, 1660–1688', *Journal of British Studies*, 10 (2), 83–104.

Philippovich, Eugen von, United States National Monetary Commission, and Sixty-First Congress (1911), History of the Bank of England and Its Financial Services to the State, accessed 24 October 2021 at https://fraser.stlouisfed.org/title/634.

Pickering, D. (ed.) (1765a), *The Statutes at Large from the Fifth to the Ninth Year of King George I*, vol. 14, Cambridge, England: J. Bentham.

Pickering, D. (ed.) (1765b), *The Statutes at Large from the Ninth Year of King George I to the Second Year of King George II*, vol. 15, Cambridge, England: J. Bentham.

Pickering, D. (ed.) (1787), *The Statutes at Large: From the Magna Charta, to the End of the Eleventh Parliament of Great Britain, Anno 1761* [Continued to 1807], vol. 36, Cambridge, England: John Archdeacon.

Price, R. (1772), *An Appeal to the Public on the Subject of the National Debt*, London.

Raithby, J. (ed.) (1819a), *Statutes of the Realm: 1628–80*, vol. 5, London: British History Online.

Raithby, J. (ed.) (1819b), *Statutes of the Realm: 1685–94*, vol. 6, London: British History Online.

Raithby, J. (ed.) (1820), *Statutes of the Realm: 1695–1701*, vol. 7, London: British History Online.

Raithby, J. (ed.) (1821), *Statutes of the Realm: 1702–7*, vol. 8, London: Dawsons of Pall Mall.

Raithby, J. (ed.) (1822), *Statutes of the Realm: 1708–13*, vol. 9, London: Dawsons of Pall Mall.

Records of the Exchequer of Receipt and Successors (1901), series, accessed 30 October 2021 at https://discovery.nationalarchives.gov.uk/details/r/C567.

Richards, R.D. (1930), 'The "Stop of the Exchequer"', *The Economic Journal*, 40 (Supplement 1), 45–62.

Rickards, G.K. (ed.) (1846), *The Statutes of the United Kingdom of Great Britain and Ireland*, London: Her Majesty's Statute and Law Printers.

Roseveare, H. (1969), *The Treasury: The Evolution of a British Institution*, London: Allen Lane.

Roseveare, H. (1973), *The Treasury 1660–1870: The Foundations of Control*, London: Allen & Unwin [u.a.].

Ross, E.A. (1892), 'Sinking Funds', *Publications of the American Economic Association*, 7 (4/5), 9–106.

Select Committee on Public Monies (1857), 'Report with Proceedings: 279-Sess. 2', in Reports from Committees: 30 April–28 August, vol. 9, United Kingdom: British Parliamentary Papers, pp. 495–502.

Shaw, William. A. (1906), 'The "Treasury Order Book"', *The Economic Journal*, 16 (61), 33.

Sinking Fund Act (1875), accessed 25 October 2021 at https://vlex.co.uk/vid/sinking -fund-act-1875-808431337.

The Royal Mint (2014), What Is the Trial of the Pyx? London, 3 February, accessed 15 October 2021 at https://youtu.be/UZQfA2cRHJs.

Tooze, A. (2020), 'The Death of the Central Bank Myth', accessed 22 October 2021 at https://foreignpolicy.com/2020/05/13/european-central-bank-myth-monetary -policy-german-court-ruling/.

Tucker, P. (2004), 'Reform of the Bank of England's Operations in the Sterling Money Markets', Bank of England Quarterly Bulletin, (Q2), 7 May, accessed 23 October 2021 at https://papers.ssrn.com/abstract=700164.

Tye, R. (2019), 'A History Lost – the English Tally', accessed 24 October 2021 at https://gimms.org.uk/2019/03/08/history-english-tally/.

William R. (1697), By the King. A Proclamation for Enforcing the Currency of Exchequer Bills and Notes.

3. Sovereign nations face resource constraints, not financial constraints

Yeva Nersisyan and L. Randall Wray

3.1 INTRODUCTION

This chapter begins with an overview of the foundations of MMT, demonstrating that the issue facing sovereign nations is not availability of finance in their own currency. We argue that this is true for all countries that meet our definition of a sovereign currency issuer. We respond to the claim of many critics that MMT can only apply to countries that issue one of the major international reserve currencies. We then turn to the issue of resource constraints – which are faced by sovereign currency issuers whether they are developed or developing countries. We argue that many of our critics have mistaken resource constraints for financial constraints. What small developing countries face are much more binding constraints on access to external real resources. And what MMT offers to them is an understanding of their ability to mobilize domestic resources, which can help to substitute for, and to lessen, external resource constraints.

3.2 THE AGE OF CHARTALIST MONEY

MMT follows the chartalist approach to money as developed by Knapp[1] and adopted by Keynes[2] according to which, state acceptance delineates the monetary space. This approach is opposed to what Goodhart[3] calls the 'metallist' view, in which the value of money is derived from a commodity (e.g., gold or silver) for which the currency can be redeemed. For chartalists, it is impossible to separate the theory of money from the theory of the state. According to Knapp, 'the money of a state' is that which is 'accepted at the public pay offices'. Even private bank notes, once the state accepts them, become part of the 'public pay community' – the state's pay community.[4]

> What forms part of the monetary system of the State and what does not? We must not make our definition too narrow. The criterion cannot be that the money is issued

by the State, for that would exclude kinds of money which are of the highest importance; I refer to bank-notes: they are not issued by the State, but they form a part
of its monetary system. Nor can legal tender be taken as the test, for in monetary
systems there are very frequently kinds of money which are not legal tender ... We
keep most closely to the facts if we take as our test, that the money is accepted in
payments made to the State's offices. Then all means by which a payment can be
made to the State form part of the monetary system. On this basis it is not the issue,
but the acceptation, as we call it, which is decisive. State acceptation delimits the
monetary system. By the expression 'State-acceptation' is to be understood only the
acceptance at State pay offices where the State is the recipient.[5]

Keynes distinguishes between money and the money of account, arguing: 'the
money-of-account is the description or title and the money is the thing which
answers to the description'.[6] According to Keynes, the 'money of account' is
the 'primary concept' of a theory of money, and it 'comes into existence along
with 'Debts', which are contracts for deferred payment, and 'Price-Lists',
which are offers of contracts for sale or purchase'.[7]

Money itself, namely that by delivery of which debt-contracts and price-contracts
are discharged, and in the shape of which a store of General Purchasing Power is
held, derives its character from its relationship to the Money-of-Account, since the
debts and prices must first have been expressed in terms of the latter.[8]

The state chooses the money of account as well as what 'thing' will be
accepted as money.

The State, therefore, comes in first of all as the authority of law which enforces the
payment of the thing which corresponds to the name or description in the contracts.
But it comes in doubly when, in addition, it claims the right to determine and declare
what thing corresponds to the name, and to vary its declaration from time to time –
when, that is to say, it claims the right to re-edit the dictionary. This right is claimed
by all modern states and has been so claimed for some four thousand years at least.[9]

In sum, in the '[a]ge of Chartalist or State Money' the state 'claimed the right
not only to enforce the dictionary but also to write the dictionary'.[10] Keynes
believed the 'age of State Money' to have begun 'at least' four thousand years
ago, so would apply to all the 'modern'[11] economies including those living
under the gold standard in the 19th century.

Private money, including bank money, can circulate 'side by side' with
'state money'.[12] And, similar to Knapp, Keynes argued that the state might 'use
its chartalist prerogative to declare that the [bank] debt itself is an acceptable
discharge of a liability' turning it into 'Representative Money'.[13]

At the cost of not conforming entirely with current usage, I propose to include
as State-Money not only money which is itself compulsory legal-tender but also

money which the State or the central bank undertakes to accept in payments to itself or to exchange for compulsory legal-tender money.[14]

Keynes further elaborates, 'Knapp accepts as 'Money' – rightly I think – anything which the State undertakes to accept at its pay-offices, whether or not it is declared legal-tender between citizens'.[15] Therefore, like Knapp, Keynes does not restrict 'state money' to money covered by legal tender laws, but identifies state 'acceptation' as the key to delineating the monetary space. Indeed, he argues that 'Member Bank-Money' is the primary 'thing' answering to the 'description' – money – used in private transactions (or within the 'private pay community'). When accepted in payment of taxes, it is also used in the 'public pay community' – but it is not 'definitive' money[16] from the perspective of member banks because they must deliver reserves ('Central Bank-Money') whenever taxes are paid using bank money.

In summary, according to the State Money/chartalist approach adopted by Keynes and Knapp, the state chooses the money of account and chooses what will qualify as the money 'thing' when it determines what it will accept at public pay houses. The state is free to choose a system based on a precious metal standard (gold or silver), a fiat money (floating exchange rate) or a managed money (managed exchange rate). Even if it chooses a strict gold standard, the value of the money does not really derive from gold, '[f]or Chartalism begins when the State designates the objective standard which shall correspond to the money of account'.[17] '[M]oney is the measure of value, but to regard it as having value itself is a relic of the view that the value of money is regulated by the value of the substance of which it is made, and is like confusing a theatre ticket with the performance'.[18] As it is the prerogative of the state to determine the nominal value of the things it accepts as money, it is obvious that the nominal value of a commodity money cannot be derived from the value of the objective standard since the state establishes what it will accept at public pay offices, as well as the nominal value of the thing accepted. There is then no puzzle about why 'fiat' paper money can replace a 'commodity' money (made of, or backed by, gold): the state determines the nominal value of each in acceptance of payments to itself.

3.2.1   Government Finances in the Age of Chartalist Money

MMT builds on the chartalist approach explained above to define monetary sovereignty. A nation has monetary sovereignty if the state issues a currency denominated in a money of account of its choosing, imposes taxes and other obligations (fees, fines) in its money of account and payable in its own currency, and floats its exchange rate. Further, if it issues other obligations such as treasury bonds, those are payable in its own currency. A state that enjoys monetary sovereignty is not financially constrained as it 'finances' its spending by issuing its own currency, which is 'definitive'.

Today, most treasuries make and receive payments through their central banks rather than do so directly, as in the past. Their spending takes the form of a central bank credit to a private bank's reserves, while the bank credits the deposit account of the payee. Tax payments reverse this, with both a private bank's reserve account and the taxpayers' deposit account debited. Treasuries keep deposit accounts at their central banks for these purposes, so spending leads to a deduction from the treasury's account and tax payments result in credits to those deposit accounts. Bond sales by the treasury lead to a deduction of a private bank's reserves as the central bank credits the treasury's deposit account. Once we look past intra-governmental balance sheet entries, however, it becomes clear that a currency-issuing sovereign government spends by issuing currency – in the form of central bank reserves. By their very nature, these are balance sheet entries that are potentially limitless.[19]

The MMT claim that sovereign government is not financially constrained is often distorted into a claim that governments do or can 'spend without limit', which is not the case. There are self-imposed procedural constraints, explained in the following few paragraphs, and governments also face real resource constraints, an important point that MMT economists have continuously emphasized (we address the latter in Section 3.4).

Actual government spending is always constrained by the budgeting and operating procedures adopted. A budgeting process that places limits on spending and additional constraints may be in place (such as deficit or debt limits). In the US, the appropriations process is quite complex, involving a number of committees each of which faces rigid constraints for total spending on programmes under its purview. The budgeting process is fraught with a number of impediments: there are 'pay-go' and 'scoring' rules that aim to limit budget deficits, and there are debt limits that require Congressional agreements to avoid across-the-board spending reductions. The budget approval process itself is complex as well, and in recent years agreement could not be achieved, so that appropriations required continuing resolutions that essentially limited spending to a prior year's budget.

In practice, Congress holds the key and can change or ignore these constraints. For example, in the US it is common under Republican administrations to ignore the effects on deficits (and ultimately on national debt) when enacting tax cut bills, while in times of perceived emergencies 'pay-go' rules are suspended. The pandemic response under both Presidents Trump and Biden involved spending bills that would clearly lead to huge increases to the deficit. Further, the debt ceiling is routinely raised – albeit with much political posturing nowadays.

Operationally, many nations have embraced rules that prevent overdrafts to the treasury's deposit account, and that prohibit the central bank from buying bonds directly from the treasury. At the same time, they have adopted operating procedures that ensure the treasury can always obtain credits to its deposits in a timely manner, either through credits due to tax receipts or bond sales, as necessary for clearing the debits that occur as the treasury spends. While arrangements differ, the central bank is often either under the treasury (or finance ministry) or coordinates with the treasury to facilitate payments. What is key here is the understanding, even if implicit, that the government is the only source of reserves with which taxes and bonds can be paid for. The state must provide reserves either through its treasury spending or through central bank lending or asset purchases to allow the private sector to pay taxes and buy bonds.

In the US, new bond issues are oversubscribed and there is no realistic fear that there would not be sufficient buyers (the only question is the price). Still, the Fed instructs primary dealer banks to submit bids at Treasury auctions in proportion to the size of their balance sheet. If the dealers have trouble placing the bonds, the Fed can buy them in the secondary market. From the perspective of the central bank, this is not to subvert the prohibition on overdrafts or direct 'lending' to the Treasury. Rather, as MMT scholars have shown, the Fed's focus on the smooth functioning of the payments system ensures that it cooperates with the Treasury to make sure cheques clear and to minimize the impacts on reserves from fiscal actions. Further, the Fed sees maintaining the proper functioning of the Treasury bond markets as one of its duties. All of this has been detailed in the MMT literature so we will not repeat the exposition.[20]

Central banks cannot and do not 'take away the punchbowl' to prevent treasuries from spending up to the budgeted amounts. Their response to 'out of control' spending is limited to raising the interest rate target (and, in some countries, clamping down on lending by private banks). It is often claimed that the Fed is unusually independent, privately owned by banks, and able to constrain the Treasury. Close analysis, however, shows that the Fed is a 'creature of Congress' (created by the Federal Reserve Act, with duties spelled out and occasionally changed by amendments), and really no more independent than other agencies – which while ultimately answerable to Congress, enjoy freedom from day-to-day political meddling, as does the Fed.

All of the constraints described so far are self-imposed by elected representatives – they are not imposed externally by financial markets. In spite of attempts to link spending with 'income', spending frequently exceeds tax revenue for years on end. In the US, budget deficits are the norm, and since the founding of the nation over two centuries ago, the Federal government's debt-to-GDP ratio has grown at a pace of nearly 2 per cent per year.[21] Sovereign government can always make payments on its debt – although it might miss payments due to political manoeuvring (as in occasional wrangling between Democrats and Republicans in the US over increasing the debt limit). Since all payments are made by the central bank on behalf of the Treasury, and since these payments are made by crediting bank reserves – which are simply entries representing a liability of the central bank – there is no limit to the central bank's ability to make the payments.

Some of the self-imposed constraints are necessary – the appropriation of public funds should be done through a democratic body as this enhances the chance that spending will pursue the public purpose. Others clearly stem from mainstream economics which theorizes the state as a currency user that needs to raise revenue to spend. The debt ceiling and 'pay-go' rules in the US as well as the Maastricht fiscal rules in the Eurozone are two cases in point. Rules prohibiting central bank direct purchases of government debt or direct lines of credit to the Treasury also fall in this category. To the extent that these self-imposed constraints are binding in certain nations (as mentioned, they are often ignored or sidestepped in the US), MMT leads to the conclusion that they are counterproductive and should be eliminated. This does not change the main argument that nations with sovereign currency do not face financial constraints in their own currency. Rather, it clarifies what are real and what are self-imposed constraints that can be eliminated by elected representatives.

To some degree, one could say the same thing about any private bank. It could credit any depositor's account with a keystroke of millions of dollars. By accounting convention, it would need to offset that liability with an asset, so could purchase the depositor's IOU of an equal amount. To make this profitable, the bank would charge a loan rate of interest higher than the interest rate it pays on the deposit. Bank regulators promulgate rules to determine whether the loan is performing or not. But the more immediate problem for the bank is that the depositor might withdraw funds, which then requires clearing with another bank. The important point is that the bank cannot net clear using its own liabilities[22] – rather, bank net clearing uses the liabilities of the central bank – high-powered money or currency. As Knapp put it (see above), central bank money is 'definitive'. Only the sovereign government can pay all its debts by delivering its own debt.[23]

Could a private bank behave as if it could not run out of 'money' to spend? Is there any limit? First, it faces constraints put on it by bank regulations and supervisors that assess the quality of assets, risk exposure, capital requirements and so on. Second, it faces a variety of 'market' constraints: limited ability to place its liabilities (market share, access to customers, credit ratings), limits to its ability to find qualifying assets, and limits to its capacity to make deals (staffing quality and quantity). And, finally, it faces constraints on its access to central bank money for clearing. The simple deposit multiplier story posits reserve constraints as the main limit to private money creation, but this has long been rejected by both MMT and Post Keynesians more generally – and is no longer believed by most orthodox economists. The view now is that central banks largely accommodate the demand for reserves as they target interest rates. Still, an individual bank perceives both price and quantity constraints. Borrowing reserves in the overnight interbank lending market requires interest payments (and maybe even collateral in some countries). Banks can also turn to wholesale deposits (large denomination certificates of deposit) to force reserve flows in their direction – but that is also expensive. They generally prefer to obtain reserves through demand deposits, but they face competition. Finally, they can turn to the central bank's discount window – where they pay the penalty rate and face 'frown costs'. There is thus a cost faced by banks that need reserves for net clearing – and banks that grow faster than average will incur those costs.

More important, there is a qualitative difference between a private entity's ability to service debt and the sovereign currency issuer's ability to do so. The sovereign government pays using its own IOUs, unlike all private sector entities. The holders of government bonds will be paid in government money, the final means of payment.[24] There is no day of reckoning – the payments can always be made (with a caveat that a voluntary default – such as one that would result if the US Congress could not agree to raise the debt limit, leading to prioritizing of payments the Treasury would be allowed to make – is possible). While we could quibble about what 'voluntary' or 'payments can always be made' might mean, the important difference is that a private entity cannot use its own liabilities as a final means of payment, while the sovereign routinely does so. For private entities, the typical final means of payment is a bank demand deposit, with the bank ultimately determining whether to make the payment on behalf of the customer. This could be through a loan, an overdraft facility or through pre-arranged credit lines. A private bank can 'extend and pretend' (allowing a debtor to capitalize interest payments – what Minsky[25] called a 'Ponzi' position), but a day of reckoning will arrive. Beyond some point, the bank can – and will – say no.

3.3   DOES MMT APPLY TO DEVELOPING NATIONS?

One of the long-standing criticisms of MMT is that it is US/developed nation centric. Critics claim that only the major issuers of reserve currencies can 'apply' MMT theory and policy. While a country like the US might be able to spend without financial constraints, the argument goes, developing nations do not enjoy the 'exorbitant privilege' derived from having the world's reserve currency. In developing nations, instead, MMT would inevitably lead to high budget and trade deficits, high inflation, and eventually to a currency crisis and to sovereign default. Some critics argue, therefore, that developing nations should not even attempt to use a sovereign currency – they should dollarize, peg to a currency board, or form a currency union with neighbours in similar situations.

The response to this is two-fold. First, critics confuse what are real resource constraints with balance of payments constraints. Because of balance of payments constraints, they believe, a country needs to act as if it is financially constrained, a point we address in the next subsection. MMT argues that clarifying what the actual constraints are matters for policy. Indeed, misunderstanding how sovereign currency works prevents many nations from living up to their resource capacity by adopting an unnecessarily restrictive fiscal stance while they leave domestic resources unemployed. Most nations' ability to mobilize their domestic resources using domestic currency is much greater than typically understood. Further, understanding what the actual constraints are can help governments to try to overcome them by using their domestic resources.

Second, MMT as a description of how money works and the role of the state in the monetary system (how it spends, taxes, etc.) applies to all countries that are monetarily sovereign as defined in Section 3.2 above (this is similar to how endogenous money applies in different countries; banks create money in the US just as they do elsewhere). Government spending is paid for by crediting bank accounts both in the US and elsewhere, while tax payments lead to debiting bank accounts (similar to how granting loans leads to crediting the accounts of borrowers while loan repayments lead to debits). Government spending must logically precede taxation if spending is what injects the wherewithal needed to pay taxes (again, bank loans must be granted first to create the deposits which then can be used to pay back loans). Financial markets cannot force governments with sovereign currency to default – the latter may choose to do so for a variety of reasons (some of them good), but this cannot happen due to their inability to make payments on their debt. Sovereign government can always exchange one IOU (treasury securities) for another (reserves).

The sectoral balance analysis which is an integral part of MMT also applies everywhere. Government deficits are equal to non-government sector surpluses and vice versa. If a country has a current account deficit, the government's deficit will equal the sum of the current account deficit plus the surplus (or minus the deficit) of the domestic private sector. Private sectors are almost always in surplus – net savers – so it is unlikely that a country with a current account deficit will be able to run a government balance that is not in deficit. Governments trying to balance their budgets need external surpluses unless they want their balanced stance to be achieved at the expense of the private sector. Experience shows that private sector deficits are short-lived because they are financially fragile. In that sense, the current account position constrains how much governments can restrict their fiscal positions before they throw the private sector into an unsustainable financial position. MMT thus shows what does *not* apply across time and space, and that is arbitrary debt and deficit limits. Any recommendation for a nation's development that includes or rests on such fiscal restrictions is useless, and even worse, dangerous.

3.3.1 Developing Countries and Balance of Payments Constraints

While MMT holds that sovereign governments are not financially constrained, whether developed or developing, this does not mean that they should not constrain spending. Whether or not they need to do so and to what extent depends on their internal and external resource space (the next section will discuss the importance of resource constraints). At full employment, additional spending will cause inflation and could withdraw resources from important uses (hence the MMT preference for a directed demand approach through job guarantee programmes[26] – which will automatically curtail spending as the economy approaches full employment). Even before full employment, bottlenecks could be reached, or desired private uses could be curtailed to release resources for lower priority public uses. In addition, government spending could push up against the limits of external resources accessible to a nation impacting the current account balance and affecting the domestic currency's exchange rate. This is particularly a concern for nations that peg or manage their exchange rates. In the economic literature, this has led to the notion of a balance of payments constraint – government spending (and economic growth more generally) can run up against a constraint imposed by its current account balance.

At the extreme, the idea is that increasing government spending will raise domestic demand, increasing imports relative to exports (which are largely determined by the rest of the world's income and preferences, so can be taken as more-or-less given as domestic income increases). A growing trade (and current account) deficit will depreciate the domestic currency. Beyond some point, that depreciation can reduce the value of the currency so much that in 'real' terms, net imports are not rising. This means that in real terms, the increased government spending does not actually raise income or consumption (foreign goods are so much more expensive in terms of the domestic currency that fewer are actually imported – meaning real living standards could actually decline). So while government could keep increasing its spending, the population would be worse off in real terms.

This could lead to various financial problems. The depreciation could generate a run out of the currency, generating a vicious cycle of further depreciation. Indebtedness in foreign currency would become much more burdensome. Even if the government had avoided issuing debt in foreign currency, the domestic private sectors might have done so. Defaults could generate more runs out of the currency, tightened domestic credit conditions and a financial crisis.

Obviously, if the country had been pegging or managing its currency, downward pressure on the exchange rate would be a big problem – the country could run out of foreign currency reserves needed to keep the exchange rate up. With a current account deficit, the country would likely be losing currency reserves, compounding the problem. To counter this, it might adopt austere fiscal and monetary policy. Raising interest rates might increase demand for the nation's domestic assets while also (in theory) lowering interest-elastic spending. Austere fiscal policy would lower domestic income, including spending on imports.

MMT sees these as policy choices – which does not mean they are unreasonable. The main MMT conclusion holds regardless: government still can make payments (in its own currency) as they come due and can mobilize all domestic resources using its own currency. That means it can pursue full employment, although that could be at the cost of growing current account deficits and possibly a depreciating currency. If exchange rates do fall and the Marshall–Lerner conditions[27] do not hold, total spending in domestic currency on imports will rise. Imports into domestic production become more expensive, potentially, but not necessarily, generating domestic inflation. And, as previously mentioned, debt burdens in foreign currency rise. All of this can be used as a justification for use of austerity policy – abandoning pursuit of full employment and accepting unemployed labour and other domestic resources as the cost of constraining domestic inflation and currency depreciation.

In lieu of austerity, policy could instead choose to restrict imports, perhaps prioritizing imports that are necessary for developing domestic capacity while limiting imports of luxury goods and services and those that compete with domestic production. Promoting import substitution and boosting domestic capacity to produce necessities such as food could improve prospects for development. Governments could avoid taking on foreign currency-denominated debt – both directly and indirectly (e.g., by bailing out domestic debtors who have foreign currency debt). Governments could aim to restrict the volume of imports to foreign currency earnings. All of these could be politically contentious and thus difficult policies to pursue.

A rich developed country that issues one of the international reserve currencies may well face similar political constraints that make it willing to choose austere policy over full employment. However, it can probably import more than a developing country can as it will find a greater external demand for financial assets denominated in its currency. This is why much of the 'balance of payments constraints' literature focuses on developing nations, with many critics of MMT arguing that MMT cannot apply to such nations.

The MMT approach recognizes that there are differences between reserve currency issuers and reserve currency users, but MMT identifies the source of the problem somewhat differently. Indeed, proponents believe that MMT principles apply to all nations that have their own currency – even those that manage or peg their exchange rates, although those face the possibility that they will be forced to devalue. Further, MMT thinks it is misleading to characterize the problem as one of balance of payments constraints, as the constraints are politically imposed.

Any nation that runs a trade deficit must have the means to 'pay for' it or the trade deficit would not have been incurred. The nation has either used foreign currency reserves or it has issued domestic currency debt that is willingly held. Following Minsky's classification of hedge, speculative and Ponzi positions, many developing countries get into Ponzi positions because the interest rate on their foreign-held debt exceeds the growth of capacity to service it, meaning the interest is 'capitalized' into more debt. Yet, if the debt is denominated in domestic currency, the currency issuer (the national government) can always service it. This is true of rich developed countries as well as developing nations. Private entities as currency users face constraints and may be forced to default – whether their debt is in domestic currency or foreign currency. Government debt issued in foreign currency also has default risk. All of these statements apply to both developed and developing nations.

The main difference between most developed nations (especially those that issue international reserve currencies) and most developing nations is the volume of the foreign demand for assets denominated in their currency. The demand for dollar-denominated assets is nearly insatiable, especially for those issued by the US government. This enables the US to run persistent current account deficits without downward pressure on the dollar. As such, there is little political impetus to throttle domestic demand to try to reduce the trade deficit – although it does remain a concern and leads to token policy changes, such as Trump's tariffs, that have no discernible impact on the trade deficit.

Most economists misunderstand what it takes to become the dominant reserve currency issuer – today the US dollar plays that role. Time and again we see mainstream economists like Ken Rogoff proclaiming that China is poised to displace the US. While this could happen someday, that day is far into the future. The mistake is associating the size of the economy and its importance in international trade with the use of the nation's currency as an international reserve currency. This then leads to warnings that the US dollar is in trouble because of persistent trade deficits and budget deficits (the twin deficits argument) that threaten the value of the dollar – both internally (due to inflation that supposedly results from budget deficits) and externally (trade deficits depreciate the currency). Mainstream economists (and some heterodox economists) then express dismay that the predicted fall from grace of the dollar has not already happened – but are certain it will soon.

The truth is that the international demand for the dollar is not based on trade in goods and services. As John Harvey (n.d) has conservatively calculated, financial transactions account for perhaps as much as 98.5 per cent of the dollar's use, while trade in goods and services amounts to an infinitesimal share. What this means is that the trade deficit is of very minor concern; and even inflation of goods and services prices don't matter much either. What does matter is that the dollar is supplied in sufficient quantities that it is relatively easy to obtain as required, and that the issuer's judicial system can be trusted to enforce financial contracts. The US scores well on both of those – indeed, rather than the budget and trade deficits creating a problem, they help to provide the dollar to the rest of the world. And the US courts are held in relatively high regard internationally. It also helps that the Fed demonstrated its willingness to bail out the entire world's financial system in a pinch – as it spent and lent $29 trillion in the aftermath of the Global Financial Crisis, with 40 per cent of that going to foreign central banks and a substantial chunk of the rest going to global megabanks headquartered abroad.[28]

It goes without saying that financial markets today are not ready to put their eggs into a Chinese basket. It will be many years before the Chinese judicial system and its central bank develop the kind of trust that is necessary to become one of the world's premier reserve currencies. Mainstream economists get this wrong because they focus only on trade and see the big role that China already plays as an exporter, and potentially growing role as an importer of global output. But that is not what drives demand for reserve currencies. While China is indeed important in terms of the volume of GDP and trade, and is also very important in terms of geopolitics, it is not yet financially open and global financial institutions are not ready to write a large share of their contracts in yuan and enforceable in Chinese courts. In that sense, China is still more like developing nations than like the US or the UK.

However, in terms of domestic policy, China is a sovereign currency nation and has potential domestic policy space that is similar to that of the US. In some ways, China is more willing to use that space – as evidenced by the nation's ability to achieve growth rates that are double, triple or even quadruple the rates in rich capitalist countries. On the other hand, the Chinese national government still appears to pursue small deficits – as analysed by Liu and Wray[29] – instead pushing the indebtedness on local governments and state-owned enterprises, a topic beyond the scope of this chapter.

To conclude this section, MMT does not see the position of developing nations as conflicting with the precepts of MMT, but rather, as an example of the true constraint facing the currency issuer: resource constraints. China is an example of a rapidly developing nation that has operated near its capacity (in spite of its apparent attempts to keep central government deficits small). Other developing nations that are rich in resources – Brazil and Mexico, for example – leave labour resources chronically idle, performing below potential. Some developing nations are resource poor, albeit generally with substantial quantities of underemployed labour. Critics accuse MMT of being applicable only to a small number of countries. In reality, it is the critics who use a relatively small subset of countries – those so extremely resource poor as to be largely dependent on imports for their survival – as a general case scenario suppos-edly applicable to the majority of developing nations. In truth, all nations face resource constraints and almost all fail to fully use even their domestic resources. Thus, MMT is useful for all countries that use their own currency.

3.4   SOVEREIGN NATIONS FACE RESOURCE CONSTRAINTS, NOT FINANCIAL CONSTRAINTS

In this section, we discuss the true constraint – resources – which both devel-oped and developing nations face although to different degrees. If policy pushes demand above a nation's productive capacity, it could cause inflation. There can be domestic supply constraints (lack of capital, technology, but usually not labour) and there can also be international supply constraints (inability to import what's needed). Pushing against these quantity constraints could have price effects, such as domestic price inflation or an exchange rate depreciation. Yet, in both developing and developed nations, a significant degree of unemployment is usually the norm. This state of affairs, according to MMT, indicates that a nation is not living up to its productive potential, instead choosing to let its labour and probably other resources idle. MMT argues that national government can mobilize these domestic resources to achieve full employment, and money is the tool that allows the state to do so. It is a bad policy choice to do otherwise.

It is possible for even the US to reach a state of resource scarcity although even in the best of recoveries the economy still leaves a large number of people unemployed (and capacity unutilized) – which indicates that the country is not living up to its means. Were a full-employment situation to happen, the nation might need to free up resources from certain uses to allow the government to pursue the public purpose. The Green New Deal is a case in point. Since a quick transition to green energy will require increased use of resources, we might need to find/free up resources from other uses to 'afford' it, especially as the economy nears full employment. Decreasing investment in the fossil fuel sector would, for instance, free up resources (indeed potential jobs lost in such a transition command great attention). At the same time, transitioning to a single-payer healthcare system (which is unfortunately not being currently discussed in Congress) can free up resources by cutting aggregate spending on healthcare. As we have previously argued,[30] the affordability of a compre-hensive Green New Deal depends on its net resource needs. Planning for its implementation requires sourcing the needed resources rather than matching tax revenue with government spending. Trying to 'raise revenue' by raising taxes will only help create the resource space necessary for public spending if taxes decrease the private use of resources, which is not guaranteed.

The debate around Biden's Build Back Better plan (and how to 'pay for' it) further demonstrates the usefulness of the MMT approach to 'affordability' of public spending.[31] While Congress has been handwringing over raising revenue to pay for spending to fight climate change and expand the social safety net, the real issue has always been whether the country has qualified workers and other resources required to implement these policies. As the *New York Times* reported, the shortage of skilled workers might be an impediment to the implementation of the $1 trillion infrastructure plan Congress is on track to pass.[32] Similarly, for free/subsidized access to universal pre-K or community college to become reality, we will need a sufficient number of providers and teachers/professors to accommodate the increased demand for these services. This is the real issue, which debating what kind of taxes to raise and by how much does not really solve.

Lastly, governments' response to the COVID pandemic served to further demonstrate that resources represent the true constraint to government spending. Early on, countries imposed restrictions on the exports of certain products.[33] Meanwhile, there were reports of the US diverting shipments of personal protective equipment (PPE) destined for European nations to the US.[34] While finding the goods was difficult, finding the money was not. The US government appropriated $2.2 trillion in March 2020 alone (and has since appropriated more for a total that exceeds $5 trillion) with nothing more than a Congressional decision to do so. The spending process itself occurred as it always does with the Treasury and the Fed cooperating to make sure Americans got their cheques, and businesses got their loans – while the Treasury placed its bonds without any issues. While governments were able to allocate funds to be spent with a stroke of a pen, accessing the real resources needed to fight the pandemic was not guaranteed. This proved what MMT economists had been saying all along – that the limits to spending are not financial, but real. Even as the government was not financially constrained, it could not buy what was not available for sale.[35]

It is true that a developing economy (even if monetarily sovereign) might not enjoy the same degree of access to external resources as the US since there might not be enough demand for its goods and services or its financial assets. MMT has always maintained that governments can buy whatever is for sale in *their* currency. Their ability to buy goods and services for sale in another currency, however, may be more limited. The state cannot make its currency acceptable to foreigners through taxation – the way it can for its own population. While the domestic currency is a tool for mobilizing domestic resources, its ability to mobilize foreign resources might be more constrained.

The US is in a special position because foreigners do want to export their real resources to the US in exchange for dollar-denominated assets. This expands the total real resource space available to the US by allowing Americans access to resources of the rest of the world (ROW).

MMT economists do not claim that a small developing nation's ability to access real resources will rival that of the US. Command of external resources can be limited for those that do not issue a reserve currency, and that do not have opportunities domestically for external funds. For such nations the cost of imports is closely related to their exports: they must use domestic resources to produce goods and services for exports so that they can obtain the international reserves they need to buy imports. They need to give something real to get something real since others do not want to exchange their real resources for financial claims denominated in the nation's currency. If imports are needed for development, the process of development may be constrained. It might be tempting to borrow in foreign currency to pay for imports, but this requires a commitment to make payments in the foreign currency. The interest rate on external debt usually exceeds the growth of export earnings, so these typically become Ponzi positions.[36] Some MMT economists have instead advocated for the establishment of new international institutions (to replace the current ones, like the International Monetary Fund) that would provide such nations with the necessary means to advance their development.[37]

Such nations might also be tempted to peg the currency in the belief that this stabilizes the value of the currency, eliminates exchange rate risk, and can lower borrowing costs to the interest rates near to those of the issuers of the dominant currencies. However, this comes with the risk of default, with higher default risk built into the loans, negating any advantage of lower rates due to lower exchange rate risk. At the same time, they give up domestic policy space in an attempt to reduce pressure on domestic prices and also on the exchange rate. In other words, their attempt to increase access to external resources can induce them to leave domestic resources idle.[38]

It is also possible for price pressures to emerge before a nation reaches its full potential because of bottlenecks, both domestic and imported. Bottlenecks can lead to inflation well before genuine supply constraints are hit and policy should focus on alleviating them.[39] Otherwise, countries with substantial unemployment leave potential output unproduced, while there is widespread poverty, in the name of price stability. We need to distinguish genuine resource constraints from mere bottlenecks. A targeted demand approach to fiscal policy, such as the Job Guarantee can work around bottlenecks.

Does MMT help developing economies? Critics argue that MMT does not really help developing nations because its policy proposals, whether functional finance in general or the Job Guarantee in particular, cannot be implemented there. But the usefulness of MMT for any nation, developed or developing, is not simply about certain policy prescriptions. Instead, MMT clarifies what are the true constraints on employment and growth and what are imaginary. On the latter, the recommendation is clear – imaginary constraints need to be exposed and eliminated. Governments do not necessarily need to raise taxes to spend more. Taxes need to be imposed with the goal of creating real resource space for the public sector which the latter should utilize through its spending. Arbitrary limits on deficits and debt hinder a nation's development. Austerity for the sake of balanced budgets or for the sake of preserving fiscal space for the future is counterproductive. MMT redefines the debate to clarify what is a true constraint and what is not, clearing the way for overcoming the former. What it offers to developing nations is an understanding of their ability to mobilize domestic resources, which can help to substitute for, and to lessen, external resource constraints. MMT does not necessarily have a one-size-fit-all recommendation since each country's case is different.

Lastly, what happens in the US does not stay in the US (and a similar argument can be made about other developed nations). Restrictions on trade deficits in the US lead to insufficient supply of dollars to the ROW. If the US were to pursue policy along MMT lines, it could increase the supply of dollars in the ROW by buying from other nations which could be good for developing nations. (Further, the US could lend dollars to developing nations that need them for development.) Just like trying to limit the government's deficit prevents the domestic private sector from net saving their desired amount, the same happens globally – US austerity limits the foreign sector's ability to net save their desired amount in dollars. In a dollar standard world, the dollar acts like gold in the gold standard. Limiting its quantity can have deflationary impacts both in the US but also abroad.

Developed nations, such as Germany, in the name of balancing their budgets, are trying to import demand from other nations by pursuing beggar-thy-neighbour policy, thus leading to deteriorating current account balances for others. Thus, even if MMT policies were applied only in developed nations that can do so without worrying about their current accounts and currency depreciation, it would be a service for the ROW. Rich nations could focus on boosting internal demand and could also become a net source of demand (and currency reserves) for the ROW rather than attempting to import demand from it.

3.5   CONCLUSION

MMT critics used to say MMT does not apply anywhere. It is a crazy approach that would bankrupt the nation. Then they changed their tune: maybe it applies to the US — because it has an exorbitant privilege that no other country enjoys. Now they say maybe it applies to the richest, most developed countries only.

They are special because they are rich. If the past is any guide to the future, we will soon learn that MMT applies everywhere. The new tune will be that there's nothing new in MMT – everything that MMT says was known all along by heterodox economists. As Ezra Klein[40] has recently noted, however, he never heard any of them say it.

NOTES

1. Knapp 1924 [1973].
2. Keynes 1930 [1976].
3. Goodhart 1998.
4. Knapp (1924 [1973], pp. vii–viii) does argue that even if bank notes were not accepted by the state and could not be converted on demand to the state's money, they still could be used within a 'private pay community' – that is, used by bank customers among themselves and for payments to the issuing banks.
5. Knapp 1924 [1973], p. 95.
6. Keynes 1930 [1976], pp. 3–4.
7. Keynes 1930 [1976], p. 3.
8. Keynes 1930 [1976], p. 3.
9. Keynes 1930 [1976], p. 4.
10. Keynes 1930 [1976], p. 5.
11. This is where 'modern' in Modern Money Theory comes from.
12. Keynes 1930 [1976], p. 6.
13. Keynes 1930 [1976], p. 6.
14. Keynes 1930 [1976], p. 6.
15. Keynes 1930 [1976], pp. 6–7.
16. Money is definitive if, when payment is made in it, the business is completely concluded (Knapp 1924 [1973], p. 105).
17. Keynes 1930 [1976], p. 11.
18. Keynes 1983, p. 402.
19. See Mosler 1996; Wray 1998, 2015.
20. See Bell/Kelton 2000; Tymoigne 2014, 2016; Wray 2015; see also Rezende 2009 and Teixeira 2020 for the case of Brazil.
21. Tymoigne 2019; Wray and Nersisyan 2020.
22. Banks do use one another's liabilities for clearing. For example, if Bank A has liabilities of Bank B, it can use these in payments to Bank B. But once it has exhausted all its claims against other banks, net clearing must take place in central bank liabilities. In the Circuitiste literature it is argued that no entity can use its own liabilities to settle its own liabilities, which is called seigniorage – and is ruled out by assumption (see Graziani 1989). MMT agrees that this is true for all but the sovereign currency issuer.
23. Here we are only addressing debts denominated in the domestic currency. Foreign currency debts might require obtaining foreign currency.
24. Again, here we are addressing only government debt denominated in the government's own currency.
25. Minsky 1986 [2008].
26. See Tcherneva 2020.

27. This refers to the proposition that the devaluation of a country's currency will lead to an improvement in its balance of trade with the rest of the world only if the sum of the price elasticities of its exports and imports is greater than one.
28. Felkerson 2011.
29. Liu and Wray 2014.
30. Nersisyan and Wray 2021a.
31. Nersisyan and Wray 2021b.
32. Madeleine Ngo, 'Skilled Workers Are Scarce, Posing a Challenge for Biden's Infrastructure Plan', *New York Times*, 9 September 2021. Available at: https://www.nytimes.com/2021/09/09/us/politics/biden-infrastructure-plan.html?searchResultPosition=1 (accessed 6 September 2022).
33. Ana Swanson, Zolan Kanno-Youngs and Maggie Haberman, 'Trump Seeks to Block 3M Mask Exports and Grab Masks from Its Overseas Customers', *New York Times*, 3 April 2020. Available at: https://www.nytimes.com/2020/04/03/us/politics/coronavirus-trump-3m-masks.html.
    Amie Tsang, 'E.U. Seeks Solidarity as Nations Restrict Medical Exports', *New York Times*, 7 March 2020. Available at: https://www.nytimes.com/2020/03/07/business/eu-exports-medical-equipment.html (accessed 6 September 2022).
34. Kim Willsher, Julian Borger and Oliver Holmes, 'US Accused of "Modern Piracy" after Diversion of Masks Meant for Europe', *Guardian*, 3 April 2020. Available at: https://www.theguardian.com/world/2020/apr/03/mask-wars-coronavirus-outbidding-demand (accessed 6 September 2022).
35. Productive capacity is not fixed and will eventually adjust to accommodate the increased demand. As long as there are unemployed resources (assuming they can be put to use, which may not be possible in a pandemic), demand will facilitate further supply and raise our standard of living.
36. Kregel 2004.
37. Mitchell and Fazi 2017.
38. Samba Sylla forthcoming.
39. Given the disruption to supply chains caused by the COVID pandemic, the Biden administration, for instance, is currently engaged in a comprehensive study of the US supply chain to determine where bottlenecks are and how to alleviate them.
40. *The Ezra Klein Show* (with Adam Tooze). Available at: https://www.nytimes.com/2021/09/17/opinion/ezra-klein-podcast-adam-tooze.html (accessed 6 September 2022).

REFERENCES

Bell/Kelton, Stephanie. 2000. 'Do Taxes and Bonds Finance Government Spending?', *Journal of Economic Issues*, 34(3): 603–20.
Felkerson, James. 2011. '$29,000,000,000,000: A Detailed Look at the Fed's Bailout by Funding Facility and Recipient', Levy Economics Institute Working Paper No. 698. Annandale-on-Hudson, NY: Levy Economics Institute of Bard College.
Goodhart, Charles. 1998. 'The Two Concepts of Money: Implications for the Analysis of Optimal Currency Areas', *European Journal of Political Economy*, 14: 407–32.
Graziani, Augusto. 1989. *The Theory of Monetary Circuit*, London: Thames Papers in Political Economy.

Harvey, John. Forthcoming. 'Modern Money Theory and Exchange Rates', in Y. Nersisyan and L. Randall Wray (eds), *The Elgar Companion To Modern Money Theory*, Cheltenham, UK and Northampton, MA, USA: Edward Elgar Publishing.

Keynes, John Maynard. 1930. *A Treatise on Money*, Volumes I and II, New York: Harcourt, Brace & Company. Reprinted in 1976.

Keynes, John Maynard. 1983. *The Collected Writings of John Maynard Keynes, Volume XI: Economic Articles and Correspondence; Academic*, edited by Donald Moggridge, London and Basingstoke: Macmillan/Cambridge University Press.

Knapp, George Friedrich. 1924. *The State Theory of Money*, Clifton, NY: Augustus M. Kelley. Reprinted in 1973.

Kregel, Jan A. 2004. 'Can We Create a Stable International Financial Environment That Ensures Net Resource Transfers to Developing Countries?', *Journal of Post Keynesian Economics*, 26(4): 573–90.

Liu, Xinhua and Wray, L.R. 2014. 'Options for China in a Dollar Standard World: A Sovereign Currency Approach', Levy Economics Institute Working Paper No. 783, January. Available at http://www.levyinstitute.org/publications/options-for-china-in-a-dollar-standard-world-a-sovereign-currency-approach

Minsky, Hyman. 1986. *Stabilizing an Unstable Economy*, New York: McGraw-Hill. Reprinted in 2008.

Mitchell, W. and Fazi, T. 2017. *Reclaiming the State: A Progressive Vision of Sovereignty for a Post-Neoliberal World*, London: Pluto Press.

Mosler, Warren. 1996. *Soft Currency Economics*, West Palm Beach, FL: III Finance. Updated version available at http://moslereconomics.com/wp-content/uploads/2022/08/Soft-Currency-Economics.pdf

Nersisyan, Y. and Wray, L.R. 2021a. 'Can We Afford the Green New Deal?', *Journal of Post Keynesian Economics*, 44(1): 68–88.

Nersisyan, Y. and Wray, L.R. 2021b. 'Can Biden Build Back Better? Yes, If He Abandons Fiscal "Pay Fors"', Levy Economics Institute Public Policy Brief No. 155.

Rezende, Felipe. 2009. 'The Nature of Government Finance in Brazil', *International Journal of Political Economy*, 38(1): 81–104.

Samba Sylla, Ndongo. Forthcoming. 'MMT as an Analytical Framework and a Policy Lens: An African Perspective', in Y. Nersisyan and L. Randall Wray (eds), *The Elgar Companion To Modern Money Theory*, Cheltenham, UK and Northampton, MA, USA: Edward Elgar Publishing.

Tcherneva, Pavlina. 2020. *The Case for a Job Guarantee*, Cambridge: Polity Press.

Teixeira, Jorge Caroline. 2020. 'A Critical Analysis of Brazilian Public Debt in the 2000s from an MMT Perspective', PhD Dissertation, Rio de Janeiro: Instituto de Economia, Universidade Federal do Rio de Janeiro (IE/UFRJ).

Tymoigne, Eric. 2014. 'Modern Money Theory and the Interrelation between the Treasury and the Central Bank: The Case of the United States', *Journal of Economic Issues*, 48(3): 641–62.

Tymoigne, Eric. 2016. 'Government Monetary and Fiscal Operations: Generalizing the Endogenous Money Approach', *Cambridge Journal of Economics*, 40(5): 1317–32.

Tymoigne, Eric. 2019. 'Debunking the Public Debt and Deficit Rhetoric', *Challenge*, 62(5): 281–98.

Wray, L. Randall. 1998. *Understanding Modern Money: The Key to Full Employment and Price Stability*, Cheltenham, UK and Lyme, NH, USA: Edward Elgar Publishing.

Wray, L. Randall. 2015. *Modern Money Theory: A Primer on Macroeconomics for Sovereign Monetary Systems*, New York: Palgrave Macmillan.

Wray, L.R. and Nersisyan, Y. 2020. 'Does the National Debt Matter?', *The Japanese Political Economy*, 46(4): 261–86.

4. A framework for the analysis of the price level and inflation

Warren Mosler

4.1 INTRODUCTION

The purpose of this chapter is to present a framework for the analysis of the price level and inflation. MMT (Modern Monetary Theory) is currently the only school of economic thought that, in direct contrast to other schools of thought, specifically identifies and models both the source of the price level and the dynamics behind changes in the price level. MMT offers a unique understanding of inflation, as academically defined, as part of its general framework for analysis that applies to all currency regimes.[1]

I was asked to do a chapter on 'inflation' under the textbook definition which is 'a continuous increase in the price level'. However, under close examination, this turns out to be elusive at best. At any point in time, the price level is presumably both static and quantitatively undefinable. That's why even the most sophisticated central bank research uses abstractions, the most familiar being the Consumer Price Index (CPI) which consists of selected goods and services designed to reflect the cost of living rather than 'the price level'. Nor can central banks determine a continuous rate of change of this abstraction. They can only tell you how the CPI has changed in the past, and they can attempt to forecast future changes. Even worse, they assume the source of the price level to be entirely historic, derived from an infinite regression into the past that, in theory, predates the birth of the universe.

4.2 THE MMT MONEY STORY

The MMT money story presumes a state that desires to provision itself via a monetary system sequenced as follows:

1. Imposition of coercive tax liabilities
2. State spending[2]
3. Payment of taxes and purchase of state securities.

Again, with a more extended narrative:[3]

1. The state imposes tax liabilities with penalties for non-payment. The tax credits required for the payment of taxes are units of the state's currency, issued only by the state.
2. The tax liabilities, by design, consequently, create sellers of goods and services seeking the appropriate tax credits in exchange, the latter by definition being unemployment.[4]
3. The state then provisions itself by spending its currency to purchase the goods and services it desires.
4. Taxes can then be paid and, if offered for sale by the state, state securities can then be purchased.
5. State spending in excess of tax receipts remains outstanding as the net financial assets in the economy that fulfil savings desires until used to pay taxes.

4.3   THE MMT MICRO FOUNDATION – THE CURRENCY AS A PUBLIC MONOPOLY

The MMT money story begins with the imposition of coercive tax liabilities to create a notional demand for that currency.[5] That notional demand is the sum of units of the currency needed to pay taxes and fund residual savings desires, as evidenced by what is offered for sale by agents seeking that currency in exchange for their goods and services. With today's state currencies, for example, the non-government sectors offer goods and services for sale until they have satisfied their need to pay taxes and their desires to net save.

The state monetary system is a public monopoly with the state the sole supplier of that which it requires for the payment of taxes. The state therefore necessarily dictates terms of exchange when spending to purchase goods and services, with the quantity that it can buy inversely related to the prices it pays. For example, if the tax liabilities are $100 and savings desires are $20, and the state offers to pay $1 per day for labour, the state will be able to obtain 120 days of labour. If instead the state pays $2 per day for labour, it will obtain only 60 days of labour. In both examples, the non-government sectors are selling labour at the state's price to the point where agents of those sectors have sufficient funds to comply with their tax liabilities and to net save as desired.

For a given fixed nominal tax liability and savings desire, when paying higher prices, the state both redefines the value of the currency downward and purchases less in real terms. Therefore, the state can, as a matter of arithmetic, when paying higher prices only buy more real goods and services by increasing tax liabilities or through increased savings desires. That is, to return to the prior example where tax liabilities were $100, savings desires $20, and the labour wage was increased from $1 per day to $2 per day, a tax increase to $200 or an increase of savings desires to $140 would result in the state obtaining the same 120 days of labour as it received with the $1 wage.

In the US, tax liabilities tend to increase as the US government pays higher prices due to federal, state, and local transactions taxes that are based on prices. These include income taxes where higher nominal incomes result in higher tax liabilities, and sales taxes where higher prices also result in higher tax liabilities.

Additionally, savings desires are based on real rather than nominal considerations. Retirement savings desires, for example, are based on the presumed cost of living during retirement years. As prices rise, those nominal savings desires rise accordingly. Business liquidity needs and inventory and receivables financing needs also rise as prices rise.

Therefore, in general, an economy experiencing a continuous increase in prices requires a continuous nominal increase in what is casually called 'the money supply' that constitutes the economy's net savings of financial assets. Without this increase, real savings desires cannot be achieved, as then evidenced by unemployment and excess capacity in general. This, in fact, is my narrative for the 1979 recession. Fiscal balance tightened as tax liabilities increased faster than government spending, and the real public debt growth further decelerated due to the increases in the price level, with the combination driving the economy into a severe recession.

4.4   THE SOURCE OF THE PRICE LEVEL

With the state the sole supplier of that which it demands for payment of taxes, the economy needs the state's currency and therefore state spending sets the terms of exchange; the price level is a function of prices paid by the state when it spends.

There are two primary dynamics involved in the determination of the price level. The first is the introduction of absolute value of the state's numeraire, which takes place by the prices the state pays when it spends. Moreover, the only information with regard to absolute value as measured in units of the state's currency is the information transmitted by state spending. Therefore, all nominal prices can necessarily be traced back to prices the state pays when spending its currency.

The second dynamic is the transmission of this information by markets allocating by price as they express indifference levels between buyers and sellers, and all in the context of the state's institutional structure.

The price level, therefore, consists of prices dictated by government spending policy, along with all other prices subsequently derived by market forces operating within government institutional structure.[6]

4.5   AGENTS OF THE STATE

The US Congress has designated agents to work on its behalf. These include the Federal Reserve Bank which operates the monetary system, commercial bank members of the Federal Reserve System that are federally regulated and supervised, and the US Treasury which executes purchases and sales as directed by legislation, by instructing the Federal Reserve Bank to debit or credit appropriate accounts.

Commercial bank Fed members have demand accounts at the Fed called reserve accounts. Federal tax liabilities are discharged by either the payment of Federal Reserve Notes (cash) or by the Fed debiting a member bank reserve account, and, if it is a bank client initiating the payment, by the member bank simultaneously debiting the bank account of the client making the payment. Non-bank entities can only make payments to the Fed indirectly through a Fed member bank as a correspondent, or by using cash.

Banks, as agents of the government, likewise influence the price level, as bank lending supports client borrowing to spend on goods and services. Government regulation and supervision controls the prices paid with funds borrowed from the commercial banks. And, with the unlimited liquidity inherent in a floating exchange rate policy, without regulation banks could lend without limit and without collateral requirements or other means of controlling the prices paid by borrowers, which could quickly impair the government's ability to provision itself and catastrophically devalue the currency.

4.6   THE DETERMINATION OF THE PRICE LEVEL

The state sets the terms of exchange for its currency with the prices it pays when it spends, and not per se by the quantity of currency that it spends. For example, if the state has an open-ended offer to hire soldiers at $50,000 per year, the price level as thereby defined will remain constant regardless of how many soldiers are hired and regardless of the state's total spending. The state has set the value of its numeraire exogenously, providing that information of absolute value that market forces then utilize to allocate by price with exchange values of other goods and services determined in the marketplace. Without the state-supplied information, however, there would be no expression of relative value in terms of that currency.

Should the state decide, for example, to increase the price it pays for its soldiers to $55,000 per year, it would be redefining the value of its currency downward and increasing the general price level by 10 per cent, as market forces reflect that increase in the normal course of allocating by price and determining relative value. And for as long as the state continues to pay soldiers $55,000 per year, assuming constant relative values, the price level will remain unchanged. And, for example, the state would have to continually increase the rate of pay by 10 per cent annually to support a continuous annual increase of the price level of 10 per cent.

4.7 INFLATION DYNAMICS

I begin with an academic definition of the rate of inflation: 'The continuous increase in the term structure of prices faced by economic agents today for purchases and sales for future delivery dates.'

This can also be referred to as forward pricing, and it's an expression of the policy rate of interest determined by central bank policy.

MMT makes a distinction between changes over time of the price level versus the rate of inflation which is expressed by the current term structure of prices.

The price level changes with prices paid by the state when it spends (fiscal policy) while changes in the term structure of policy interest rates (monetary policy) alter the term structure of prices. And while the term structure of prices is not a forecast of changes in the price level, that is not to say it doesn't influence the future direction of the price level.

Interest rate policy also functions as a fiscal transfer as the state is a net payer of interest to the other sectors of the economy. With public debt levels in excess of 100 per cent of GDP, for example, a 1 per cent rate hike ultimately adds interest income payments of over 1 per cent of GDP to the economy. This increase in state spending directly increases nominal incomes, and, to the extent agents receiving the interest payments increase their spending, state interest payments support sales, output, and employment.

State interest expense also reduces fiscal space as they partially satisfy the need to pay taxes and to net save created by state tax liabilities, which means there will be that many fewer goods and services offered for sale to comply with the remaining tax liabilities. This means the state's real purchases of goods and services are reduced by interest payments as per the same framework for analysis discussed in the previous examples.

Therefore, as described above, I conclude that the state's payment of interest, implemented by the state to slow the rate of growth and work to counter price increases, is far more likely to do the reverse.

Also of note is that interest payments are necessarily to those who already have money and are also paid proportionately to the amount of money one has. In prior publications, I've labelled a positive interest rate policy, 'basic income for those who already have money', which, when stated as such, has no political support whatsoever. Yet, as monetary policy that, presumably, fights inflation, central bank rate increases receive widespread support.

To summarize, I see interest rate policy as both backwards and confused. First, the rate of inflation academically defined is an expression of the central bank's policy rates, so rate hikes directly increase that measure of inflation.

Second, rate hikes constitute additional state deficit spending, which tends to also be an inflationary bias given currency institutional structure.

And third, for me, the payment of funds only to those who already have money as a cure for what's believed is inflation does not serve public purpose.

4.8   INTEREST RATES AND WAGES

An increase in the central bank's policy rate in the first instance increases state deficit spending and total income in the economy. This means wages are then a smaller percentage of total income which to some degree, depending on propensities to spend, implies that the relative value of wages has decreased.

This further implies that if wages are indexed to the general price level in the context of a positive policy interest rate, an increase in the wage will cause a larger increase in the general price level, which will then trigger a higher wage, in an accelerating spiral.

However, in the context of a 0 per cent rate policy, a wage increase would not be magnified by this process.

What I am suggesting is that this combination of wage indexation and high policy rates of interest selectively observed in nations experiencing undesired increases in the price level ironically contributes to accelerating rates of increase in the prices the interest rate policy is meant to contain.

4.9   THE HIERARCHY OF DEMAND

Demand originates with the state. Without state spending, the value of the currency is unspecified and there is no aggregate demand. Only subsequent to state spending can the currency obtain absolute value and non-government spending take place.

4.10   CONCLUSION

This chapter provides a framework for the analysis of the price level and inflation. The framework is that of the currency itself as a public monopoly, with the state setting nominal demand with its tax liabilities, as well as providing the tax credits that allow compliance with those tax liabilities.

This understanding entirely explains the source of the absolute nominal value price level over time. Also implied is the role of interest rates with regard to the academic definition of inflation and the influence of policy rates on market-determined expressions of relative value.

NOTES

1. Mosler (2020) sets out the key features of MMT.
2. Lending is the purchase of financial assets such as promissory notes, and therefore is a subset of spending in general, which includes purchases of non-financial assets.
3. Mosler (1993: 7–10, 2010: 13–30) and Forstater and Mosler (2005: 538) show the importance of developing a correct understanding of sequence when analysing the relationship between government spending, taxation, and debt sales.
4. Unemployment is defined as those seeking work in exchange for the state's currency.
5. Forstater and Mosler (1999: 166–77) provide an account of the monetary circuit focussing upon the 'central role of the State from the beginning of the analysis'.
6. By way of example, Armstrong and Mosler (2020: 19) analyse the hyperinflation period of the Weimar Republic and argue that 'the currency is a public monopoly, and monopolists are price setters. This makes the price level a function of the prices paid by the government. The Weimar inflation, as is necessarily the case, was driven by the German government's policy of paying continuously higher prices to provision itself, thus continuously redefining the value of its currency downward'.

REFERENCES

Armstrong, P. and Mosler, W. B. (2020), 'Weimar Republic Hyperinflation through a Modern Monetary Theory Lens', http://mos.lereconomics.com/wp-content/uploads/2020/11/Weimar-Republic-Hyperinflation-through-a-Modern-Monetary-Theory-Lens.pdf, accessed 28 September 2022.

Forstater, M. and Mosler, W.B. (1999), 'A General Framework for the Analysis of Currencies and Commodities', in *Full Employment and Price Stability in a Global Economy*, Cheltenham, UK and Northampton, MA, USA: Edward Elgar Publishing, Chapter 9.

Forstater, M. and Mosler, W.B. (2005), 'The Natural Rate of Interest Is Zero', *Journal of Economic Issues*, Vol. XXXIX, No. 2, June, 535–42.

Mosler, W.B. (1993), 'Soft Currency Economics', http://mos.lereconomics.com/wp-content/uploads/2022/08/Soft-Currency-Economics.pdf, accessed 28 September 2022.

Mosler, W.B. (2010), *The Seven Deadly Innocent Frauds of Economic Policy*, US Virgin Islands: Valance.

Mosler, W.B. (2020), 'MMT White Paper', http://mos.lereconomics.com/mmt-white-paper/, accessed 28 September 2022.

5. The external economy

William Mitchell

5.1 INTRODUCTION

Nations do not exist in isolation. Peoples have always roamed the globe in search of different opportunities. Nations principally trade to expand their consumption possibilities. In a world where we produce to consume, receiving goods and services is better in material terms than sending them elsewhere. Exports require the nation to incur an opportunity cost by sending real resources (embodied in final products or raw materials) to foreigners which could be used locally. Conversely, imports represent foreigners giving up their real resources (embodied in final products or raw materials), which are then enjoyed by the importing nation. Accordingly, external deficits mean that a nation enjoys a higher material living standard.

Running external surpluses (exports greater than imports) effectively means that the nation is depriving its citizens of a higher material standard of living. They are working too hard, being paid too little, and/or underconsuming. In that context, exports are a cost and imports are a benefit to a nation. People who have been conditioned to think that a nation that exports is in a stronger position than one that struggles to export goods and services, struggle to understand this fact. What we must remember is that production is not an end. The end is consumption.

Clearly, a nation that merely gives up material resources and gets nothing in return would be making itself poorer in material terms. And certainly, the history of colonial nations is riven with examples of resource plunder from colonial masters, which qualifies our statement that nations trade to expand consumption opportunities. The expansion happens but the beneficiaries may not be the nation's residents.

That exports are a 'cost' suggests the motive to export. The 'cost' is incurred to generate benefits – to enhance the material prosperity of the nation. One reason that would lead a nation to relinquish access to its own real resources would be to get other real resources that it desires from other nations through trade. Which means the export cost is best considered as an investment in generating an increased capacity to import. However, this is not to say that a nation that runs an external deficit on goods and services will not encounter issues that will be challenging. We will explore these issues in this chapter.

A nation's external link with the rest of the world is not just confined to trade in goods and services. Financial flows also cross borders and these capital flows can be significant in shaping a nation's prosperity as well as introducing instability in the value of its currency in world markets. It is thus important to consider how the two aspects of the external economy – trade and capital flows – interact.

Students in undergraduate economics programmes encounter the topic of trade in two different ways. In macroeconomics courses, they learn the role of trade in the income-expenditure framework, where exports are a source of demand for the local economy and imports represent a loss of income to the rest of the world in search of goods and services produced elsewhere. They then integrate that knowledge into an understanding of the balance of payments, which records all international transactions between a nation and other nations and consider more advanced topics such as exchange rate determination.

In courses in international economics, they begin their journey typically by learning about the motivation for trade between nations – the so-called comparative advantage framework – where the free trade approach is first outlined. Comparative advantage was first conceived as an explanation for why nations trade by the English Classical economist David Ricardo in 1817.[1] He argued that while a nation might be able to produce all goods more cheaply than any other, it was better devoting its resources to produce those goods for which it can produce relatively cheaper than another. In this case, Ricardo argued that exchanging goods between nations on this principle would make all nations better off.

While the idea of comparative advantage has been used to justify so-called 'free trade' arrangements between nations, and the ideology of the approach is often obscured to the student and they are, instead, confronted with a 'law' – the reality is that successful nations did not develop by following the principles of comparative advantage.

Initially, we introduce basic concepts that apply to any analysis of the external economy – the balance of payments, trade, capital flows, the exchange rate. Then we apply these concepts to developing an understanding of contemporary policy challenges such as industry policy, free versus fair trade agreements, currency instability, fiscal constraints arising from trade and capital controls.

5.2 THE BALANCE OF PAYMENTS

Transactions between nations involve both goods and services and financial flows. The financial transactions represent currency flows into and out of a nation and have significant implications for movements in the exchange rate and other macroeconomic aggregates, such as interest rates, the inflation rate and real GDP.

All transactions between a nation and the rest of the world are recorded in the balance of payments, which is a framework that is closely related to the national accounts.

The balance of payments and related accounts are compiled by national statistical agencies (such as the UK Office of National Statistics, the Australian Bureau of Statistics, the US Bureau of Economic Analysis) using an international standard set down in the International Monetary Fund's (IMF) Balance of Payments and International Investment Position Manual (BPM6),[2] augmented by the System of National Accounts (SNA).[3] While there are variations in terminology used by different nations, the principles are universal.

Like any accounting framework, the balance of payments is based on a double-entry debit and credit system of record. Credit entries consist of transactions where foreign residents make payments to local residents. Examples include exports of goods and services, income receivable from investments abroad, reductions in external assets or increases in external liabilities. Debit entries consist of transactions where local residents make payments to foreign residents. Examples include imports of goods and services, income payable, increases in external assets or a decrease in external liabilities.

The current account records all current transactions between a nation's residents and non-residents in goods and services, primary income and secondary income. The balance of trade records 'transactions in items that are outcomes of production activities'[4] and reflect exchanges between the local economy and the rest of the world. Primary income includes payments of wages to a resident by a non-resident or income flows associated with ownership of financial assets (for example, dividend payments). These flows add to impact on national income. Secondary income flows do not and involve redistribution of income (for example, remittances, pension payments from abroad).

Economists often emphasise the current account because the transactions it records are of direct relevance to the determination of national income.[5] While the current account of a nation tends to focus on transactions with the rest of the world, which impact on the measurement of national output and income, the capital account records the financial side of these transactions. For a nation that exports more than they import, the net outflow of goods and services would be accompanied by accumulating financial claims against the rest of the world. This is because the demand for the nation's currency to meet the payments necessary for the exports would exceed the supply of the currency to the foreign exchange market to facilitate the import expenditure.

How might this imbalance be resolved? One obvious solution would be for foreigners to issue liabilities to the domestic residents. This would lead to a net accumulation of foreign claims (assets) held by residents. This item would be recorded in the capital account as a debit because it enhances the capacity of non-residents to make transactions in the local economy. Another solution would be for non-residents to draw down local bank balances, which means that net liabilities to non-residents would be lower.

5.3 EXCHANGE RATE CONCEPTS

The exchange rate is the amount that one currency can buy of another currency in foreign exchange markets.[6] There are several different ways we can express that rate. The most obvious way is to define the *nominal exchange rate* (e), which is literally the number of units of one currency that can be purchased with one unit of another currency, the last currency being referred to as the reference currency. Consider the relationship between the Australian dollar ($A) and the British pound (£). How many Australian dollars are required to purchase one British pound? If the exchange rate is 2, then we know that it takes $A2 to buy £1. We could reverse the designated reference currency and express this exchange rate as $A1 buys £0.5. The latter quotation is the usual way we express the nominal exchange rate.

If the nominal exchange rate goes from £0.5 to £0.4 – a depreciation of the Australian dollar – then Australian residents will find all imported goods from Britain are more expensive *in Australian dollars*. Other things being equal, this should reduce the desire of Australian consumers for British goods (Australia's imports). From the perspective of British residents, the depreciation in the Australian dollar renders Australian exports cheaper in terms of sterling, and other things being equal, will stimulate demand for those exports. The opposite is the case if the Australian dollar appreciates – say from £0.5 to £0.6.

The nominal exchange rate is determined in the foreign exchange (forex) markets, where the supply of and demand for currencies are linked to trade and capital flows between countries, and as well to relative interest rates and expected changes of interest rates between countries. The determination of exchange rates is exceedingly complex, and no theory or model that has been put forward has been capable of accurately predicting exchange rate movements. Some economists consider the transactions surrounding trade dominate while others consider cross-border transactions relating to financial assets are more significant in determining exchange rate movements.

What we can say is that when the demand for a currency is stronger than its supply, then it will appreciate and vice versa. When residents of a nation buy foreign goods (imports), buy foreign assets or extend loans abroad, they need to purchase the relevant foreign currencies in which the transaction is denominated. To buy the currency they desire, they supply their currencies to the forex market in exchange. Similarly, when foreigners buy a nation's goods and services (exports) and/or its financial assets they must purchase the local currency in the forex market by supplying their own currency in exchange. This represents the demand for the local currency.

The nominal exchange rate thus shifts to balance out the demand for and supply of a particular currency against other currencies. If, for example, there is an excess supply of a nation's currency in forex markets, then, other things being equal, the currency will depreciate and vice versa.

But the real world is subject to complex lags in responses to these price signals. Economists have complex frameworks (for example, the Marshall–Lerner condition) to analyse the total impacts on a nation's imports and exports that follow from exchange rate changes, which we do not consider here.

If a nation runs a trade deficit, increasing quantities of its currency are being accumulated by foreigners. Clearly, the foreigners have allowed the nation to run a trade deficit because they preferred to accumulate financial assets denominated in its currency. The alternative would have been to spend the currency they acquired through their exports to buy the nation's imports (which would have created a bi-lateral trade balance). A trade deficit thus means that the foreigners are increasing their nominal savings in the deficit nation's currency.

While trade flows are obviously important, the capital flows on the Capital Account can also drive movements in the exchange rate, given that financial transactions are many orders of magnitude greater – at least for the world's major currencies.

The demand for a country's financial assets will play a big role in determining exchange rates. For example, most of the demand for the Australian dollar in forex markets is not for the currency, per se, but rather for Australian dollar-denominated financial and real assets. Likewise, most of the global demand for the US dollar is not for purchases of US goods and services but rather for financial assets denominated in $US that can be held as earning assets in diversified portfolios.

Further, prices in asset markets are affected by interest rates. In foreign exchange markets, participants are concerned with *relative* interest rates, that is, domestic interest rates relative to foreign interest rates, and *future* exchange rates. The decision to hold $US assets will thus be affected by current US interest rates relative to foreign interest rates, but also by expectations about the appreciation or depreciation of the US dollar relative to other currencies.

There are two rival theories concerning exchange rate determination in this regard. The mainstream approach – *purchasing power parity theorem* – focuses on trade in goods and services. The contention is that exchange rates move to equalise exchange rate-adjusted prices. In other words, whether one buys a McDonald's Big Mac sold in the US or in Australia, one should pay the same price, adjusted for exchange rates. At this point, the *purchasing power* of the two currencies would be equal (at 'parity'). Obviously, the price will deviate from this if there are differential transactions costs, including transportation costs. The important point is that this approach considers that the current account drives the exchange rate.

Keynes proposed an alternative approach – *interest rate parity theorem* – that focuses on asset markets.[7] The conjecture is that exchange rates are in equilibrium when expected returns to asset holders are equalised across exchange rates. In other words, if a portfolio holder is choosing between an Australian government bond and a US government bond, prices will tend to move to equalise total expected returns. The total return will include not only the expected interest rate paid but also the expected movement of the relative exchange rates. Purchasing power parity explanations are less capable of capturing exchange rate dynamics. By contrast, the interest rate parity theorem performs relatively well across currencies.

In terms of a nation's international competitiveness, the nominal exchange rate is only part of the story in understanding the impact of the external sector on local economic activity. The *real exchange rate* is used to measure international competitiveness and it depends on two factors: (a) movements in the nominal exchange rate, and (b) relative inflation rates (domestic and foreign).

Take a situation where the nominal exchange rate is stable but domestic prices rise faster than the foreign price level. In this case, local goods are becoming relatively dearer than foreign goods. The opposite would happen if local prices were rising more slowly than foreign prices. These movements in relative prices (domestic and foreign) are called the terms of trade and influence a nation's exports and imports.

If the real exchange rate rises, then a nation is deemed to be more competitive than before and this can arise if the nominal exchange rate increases, and/or the world price rises by more than domestic prices. Conversely, a fall in the real exchange rate indicates reduced international competitiveness and will occur if the nominal exchange rate appreciates, and/or if the domestic price level inflates faster than the foreign price level.

The solution to a declining international competitiveness is not straightforward. For example, is a declining real exchange rate driven by local prices rising faster than foreign prices, the result of, say, workers pushing wages up too quickly or firms seeking higher profit margins? During the Global Financial Crisis, mainstream economists advocated cutting wages for nations such as Greece to improve its external competitiveness, because there was no scope for adjusting its exchange rate once it entered the common currency. The problem though is that a wage-cutting exercise not only reduces aggregate spending and pushes the nation further into recession, but also is likely to undermine productivity, which further damages its international competitiveness.

In that situation, overall business investment is likely to fall in response to the extended period of recession and wage cuts, which erodes future productivity growth. Thus, there is no guarantee that this sort of strategy will lead to a significant fall in unit labour costs. The research literature is replete with evidence that nations that pay high wages and offer workers secure employment deliver superior productivity outcomes, which yield improvements in a country's international competitiveness.

5.4   THE ROLE OF TRADE IN OUTPUT AND INCOME GENERATION

In macroeconomics, students encounter the income-expenditure model early in their studies to ground their understanding of how total spending drives output, which creates incomes and employment. The income-expenditure approach is built from the basic macroeconomic rule that, subject to the existing productive capacity, total spending drives output and national income, which in turn, drives employment.[8]

Total expenditure in any period is the sum of domestic demand (household consumption, business investment and government spending) and net exports. The terminology – leakages and injections – is useful to understand how the output and income responds to changes in demand. Firms form expectations of future sales and hire productive inputs and scale production levels accordingly. Their hiring decisions generate national income (payments to inputs) and the spending that results determines how much of the production is realised in sales. If the firms overestimate spending, then the unsold inventories trigger production cuts and rising unemployment. Alternatively, if they underestimate spending, they increase output if they have productive capacity available. This dynamic process can come to rest – when expectations are realised, and total output (and national income) equals total spending. We call this an equilibrium or steady state, which just means, that at that point, there is no force present to compel firms to change production levels.

This equilibrium national output level (GDP) does not necessarily equate with the output level that would generate full employment. Keynes among others demonstrated that full employment was not guaranteed by the market system. Economies can become locked into situations where the economy is in 'equilibrium' but there is mass unemployment. This realisation motivates the role of government to use fiscal policy to act as a circuit breaker and 'shock' the economy into higher levels of output generation and employment by responding with a new injection of spending.

In relation to the external sector, net exports is the difference between an injection (exports) and a leakage (imports) from the income-expenditure stream. Expenditure on imported goods and services means that some of the national income produced in a period does not return to the local firms. We say that it has 'leaked out' of the domestic expenditure/income loop, which other things being equal, means that output will be lower than if import spending was lower. Exports are generated by external factors and comprise an outside 'injection' into the local expenditure/income loop. Exports boost local production and income and can help offset the imports leakage.

While export spending boosts national income, we consider exports to be a cost in the sense that they deprive the domestic population of the use of the real resources that are used up in the production of the goods and services sold abroad. Even though import expenditure is a leakage from the expenditure system, we consider it to provide material benefits to the domestic economy by allowing households, firms and government to enjoy access to goods and services not otherwise available or available on competitive (qualitative and/ or price) terms.

Import spending rises with national income and is also influenced, as we saw, by exchange rate movements and relative inflation rates between nations. Exports are similarly influenced by the real exchange rate as well as economic conditions in the foreign country. So as a nation's economic growth increases, it will import more goods and services. As world growth increases, exports from a nation will typically rise.

5.5   IS A CURRENT ACCOUNT DEFICIT A PROBLEM?

Modern Monetary Theory (MMT) demonstrates that spending by a currency-issuing government is only constrained by available real resources, which is contrary to the mainstream 'sound finance' assertion that growth is limited by the financial constraints that governments face. However, there is a body of literature that began with Hicks[9] and was developed by Kaldor[10] and Thirlwall[11] that considers that the true constraint on a nation's growth rate is the balance of payments. What does that mean? Mitchell[12] considers this literature in some detail. Here we present a summary of the argument.

Kaldor[13] developed a growth model where 'the general level of output at any one time is limited by available resources, and not by effective demand' and thus characterised the constraint in terms of labour scarcity. In this sense, it is uncontroversial that if the economy is operating at full capacity, then no further real output is possible.

He later departed from that view, and, instead, postulated that the growth process was constrained by export demand that a region or nation experienced.[14] His argument relied on the rather curious assumption that exports revenue was the only source of exogenous expenditure. By assuming that all domestic expenditure was purely induced by an export shock, Kaldor could show that there was a unique growth rate which created a trade balance. In other words, once domestic income was stimulated by export demand, induced import expenditure would rise and once it was equal to exports, the growth constraint was encountered. All the action is thus on the current account, with exports defining the available foreign exchange resources. The long-run constraint is binding because he thought that if the nation tried to grow at a faster rate, then it would run out of the capacity to fund its imports.

Kaldor's treatment of fiscal policy was at that time questionable. He assumed that government expenditure was limited by the endogenous taxation revenue it received. Kaldor[15] also emphasised that using fiscal policy to increase 'production and employment through a stimulus to domestic demand would ... increase imports relative to exports; this would have brought a downward pressure on sterling'. Thus, we have a very orthodox argument against discretionary fiscal interventions.

In early Keynesian growth theory,[16] investment was considered to have a dual characteristic: (a) it added to immediate aggregate demand; and (b) added to future productive capacity, which meant that future aggregate demand had to be higher again to avoid unemployment. In Kaldor's trade-driven growth approach, it is exports that take on this dichotomous role because, in addition to adding to aggregate demand, they also increase the capacity of the nation to import because of the foreign exchange they bring to the nation.

The dual nature of exports in Kaldorian growth theory spawned what has become known as the 'balance-of-payments-constrained growth' (BPCG) theory, which asserts that the long-run growth process is constrained by a nation's exports, given the assumption that there must be a balance of trade.[17] The assertion requires several assumptions to hold, including export spending is the sole autonomous demand component, the real exchange rate is stable and there is a balance of trade.

Further, the introduction of financial flows on the capital account negates the Thirlwall assumption that exports are required to pay for imported goods and services. In other words, a nation could record permanent trade deficits, without degrading its currency. In this case, the maximum BPCG output level would be below the possible output level. The question then is at what point do the net financial inflows stop. Some writers have suggested 'that the propensity of ... [net financial inflows] ... to boost growth must be regarded as a strictly short-run result ... [and] ... cannot represent the long-run equilibrium growth rate'.[18] However, that conclusion remains purely an assertion. Nations such as Australia have recorded persistent current account deficits for decades while maintaining relative currency stability.

Interestingly, later in his career, Kaldor[19] appeared to modify his position considerably 'as he applies the model to the analysis of actual processes of growth in real economies'.[20] That shift appears to have been lost on many Post Keynesians, who consider the BPCG concept to be an eternal verity.

The debate can be distilled in the following way. First, there is a difference between the overall level of foreign debt held by the private sector that a nation can bear and the ability of the national government to maintain full employment with the resources that are available to it. If there are underutilised productive resources seeking work in a nation, the currency-issuing government can always bring them back into productive use. The BPCG theory asserts that if governments persist in running fiscal deficits to achieve full employment, then eventually international financial markets will attack the currency and cause a massive depreciation with accelerating inflation coming from the rising import prices feeding into the domestic price level. The evidence is scant. There appears to be no robust statistical relationship between national fiscal dynamics and the evolution of a nation's exchange rate. It is also unlikely that import expenditure will rise dramatically because of the government supporting full employment, given most nations already have income support systems for the unemployed.

Second, an analogue of the BPCG approach is that the rise in the current account deficit (exports less than imports plus net invisibles) is interpreted as an excess of investment over saving. The claim is then that the only way a nation can counter that imbalance is through foreign investment (via an offsetting capital account surplus) which means that the net accumulation of foreign claims on the nation (via direct investment income, debt repayments or equity dividends) increases. This is the so-called 'living beyond our means' narrative and is the most popular derivative of the BPCG idea. The narrative also claims that current account deficits reduce potential growth because the increasing foreign ownership reduces profit retention and hence investment.

There are several issues. From a consumption perspective, it is undeniable that for an economy, imports represent a real benefit while exports are a real cost. Exports mean that the nation incurs an opportunity cost – the real resources embodied in the exports benefit the foreigners and locals are denied access to them. Conversely, imports represent foreigners giving the nation something real and beneficial that they could use themselves. In other words, the opportunity cost reversed. Thus, net imports means that a nation gets to enjoy a higher material living standard by consuming more goods and services than it produces for foreign consumption.

The real terms of trade for a nation are defined in terms of the relationship between exports and imports. A trade deficit is a sign that the real terms of trade are working in favour of the deficit nation.

Clearly, the motive that would lead a nation to relinquish access to its own real resources would be to get other real resources that it desires from other nations through trade. Thus, the export cost is best considered as an investment in generating an increased capacity to import beyond that allowed by net financial inflows on the capital account.

Recognising this does not mean we should disregard a current account deficit. First, it is true that foreigners (surplus nations) build up financial claims in the currency of the deficit nation. If the government allowed, they might liquidate these claims purchasing real estate (for example, Russian and Chinese property acquisitions in London), which might undermine the prosperity of the local residents (for example, through housing affordability issues). But the nation state can legislate whatever restrictions they like in this regard and prevent foreigners using the local currency, obtained through trade surpluses, to purchase strategic assets.

Second, the foreigners might liquidate their local currency holdings in forex markets. The reason that nations can run external deficits is because foreigners are willing to exchange their exports for financial claims in the local currency. That preference could change at any time. Clearly, the deficit nation gains the terms of trade benefit while the preference holds. But if the preference changed suddenly, then the deficit nation may be exposed to rather harsh adjustment costs. That possibility should always be recognised. But major sell-offs by currency holders would expose the selling parties to exchange losses if a significant exchange rate depreciation resulted.

Third, if the local currency holdings end up in the hands of speculators, which implies the motivation is different from a trading entity, the nation state can always impose capital controls to protect its currency. I will come back to capital controls later.

Fourth, more problematic is that foreign interests may seek to use their financial clout to manipulate the political system and the public through media domination. However, strict campaign funding and media ownership rules can militate against these negative consequences.

Finally, some argue that persistent external deficits accelerate the process of deindustrialisation (loss of manufacturing capacity), which reduces opportunities for high-skilled, well-paid employment, damages productivity growth and innovation, and leaves the nation reliant on imported goods and services. There are often arguments made that a nation needs to protect local manufacturing to ensure self-reliance in the event of war. However, a government can always adopt a forward-thinking industry policy to expand domestic industry, spawn innovating research and development, upskill the workforce, build export capacity and so on, as long it has available real resources or can acquire them from abroad. An MMT understanding allows us to appreciate that there would be no financial impediment for a government building national industries, funding research and development, providing first-class universities and apprenticeship training and the rest. If a nation with its own currency slides into oblivion by closing its manufacturing sector, cutting career public sector jobs and relying on low-paid and precarious service sector jobs for employment creation, then that has little to do with running external deficits, and everything to do with political choices.

Further, there are other reasons for maintaining a manufacturing sector, which include maintaining infrastructure as part of a defence strategy and building self-sufficiency in essential goods and services (such as health care products).

The conclusion here is that the BPCG literature only posits a theoretical long-run constraint based on rather restrictive assumptions. Even Kaldor recognised that in the real world, the situation is more complex and nations can indeed grow faster than the theoretical limit denoted by Thirlwall's law.

5.6 SPECULATIVE CAPITAL FLOWS AND CAPITAL CONTROLS

The balance of payments constraint literature feeds into the broader debates about whether a nation must appease the international investors or face a debilitating attack on their currency. The history of financial crises indicates that large-scale financial speculation can undermine a nation's real economy relatively quickly if the government attempts to peg its currency to another or the economy has significant foreign currency-denominated debt exposure (private or public). While the international community could agree that certain forms of speculative activity would be considered illegal, in lieu of that, the nation under attack must defend its own prosperity.

One such suggestion is to introduce capital controls, which limit the size and flexibility of international financial flows. Capital controls are policies that restrict the free movement of capital, either in terms of inflows or outflows.

There are broadly two types of capital controls used:

- Administrative or direct controls, which impose limits or bans on capital flows.
- Market-based controls, which impose extra costs on capital flows which reduce the incentives to shift funds across national borders.

A government might, for example, place limits on foreign exchange transactions, international bank transactions or bank withdrawals. Restrictions on movements of precious metals such as gold might also be considered. The aim is to limit the scope of speculative flows (in or out) to manipulate the exchange rate and relieve the strain on the central bank's foreign exchange reserves. Capital controls allow the central bank to run an autonomous monetary policy (freed from having to defend the currency parity) and the treasury to use fiscal policy to manage domestic demand in the interests of the nation.

The case for the use of capital controls is strongest for two cases: countries that desire to manage their exchange rates and nations pursuing a development strategy. As we have seen, countries that do not float their exchange rates are subject to speculative attacks. While floating rates preserve the most domestic policy space and, at the same time, remove the incentive to speculate against the currency, some countries persist in either fixing their exchange rates or in carefully managing them (sometimes within a narrow corridor). China is an example of such an exchange rate regime. In this case, the nation can guard against speculative attacks by imposing capital controls that make it difficult to exchange the currency. China has historically tightly managed the flow of capital.

A country that is pursuing a development strategy in the context of a floating exchange rate might face the prospect of strong currency appreciation. Foreigners sensing profitable opportunities in the nation might rush in with short-term investment strategies to make quick profits. However, rising exchange rates can work against the development strategy, as foreign currency prices of the nation's output rise relative to world prices. The developing nation might protect its new industries by constraining short-term capital flows to keep speculators from excessively appreciating the currency.

The case for use of capital controls by a rich, developed country on a floating exchange rate is generally weaker. However, in the absence of effective international regulation of financial practices, even such a country might need to protect itself from abusive practices by foreign financial institutions. There are notable examples in recent history.

In Europe, the short period of exchange rate stability reflected the use of capital controls, particularly by France and Italy. They prevented some of the speculative movements that would have normally destabilised the nations' exchange rates. Italy relied on capital controls extensively and only started to withdraw them in 1988 once the Single European Act banned them.[21] The Single European Act of 1986 reflected Monetarist, 'free market' notions and stipulated that all capital controls were to be abolished by 1 July 1990. Exceptions were made for Ireland and Spain (31 December 1992) and Greece and Portugal (31 December 1995).

The abolition of controls eliminated one policy tool that governments had to maintain stability, and this became evident in 1992. Eichengreen and Wyplosz,[22] among others, recognised the bind that European governments were getting themselves into when they coined the term 'The Unstable EMS'. Eichengreen and Wyplosz[23] also argued that the capital controls 'protected central banks' reserves against speculative attacks' by reducing the possibility of the exchange rate being driven below the agreed fluctuation bands (which would require central banks to sell foreign currency in return for its own). This allowed the central banks to 'retain some policy autonomy',[24] in the sense that they could pursue domestic objectives such as economic growth and low unemployment, which may have also meant that a particular nation's inflation rate was higher than its competitors. The capital controls gave them this leverage. Once capital controls were eliminated, central banks became vulnerable, as they had to focus policy on defending the nominal exchange rate parities. And with the rising instability, this vulnerability became acute.[25]

More recent examples also demonstrate that capital controls can be effective. Malaysia imposed a range of controls on capital outflows during the 1997–99 Asian financial crisis, which 'helped to stabilize the exchange rate'.[26] When the Czech and Slovak governments decided to abandon their short-lived monetary union in early 1993, cross-border currency movements were prohibited while new Slovak banknotes were issued. The old Czech banknotes were 'stamped' and were in use in Slovakia until August 1993. Capital controls were very effective in protecting the Slovak banking system. More recently, Iceland also imposed capital controls in 2008, which limited the extent of the depreciation of the currency.

While mainstream economists claim that the financial markets will always subvert capital controls, development economist Dani Rodrik[27] adopts a more realistic assessment:

> Even if true, evading the controls requires incurring additional costs to move funds in and out of a country – which is precisely what the controls aim to achieve. Otherwise, why would investors and speculators cry bloody murder whenever capital controls are mentioned as a possibility? If they really couldn't care less, then they shouldn't care at all.

In general, the balance of payments should not be an issue of concern for governments in their quest to maximise the well-being of their citizens. The reality is that all open economies are susceptible to balance of payments fluctuations. What is usually not mentioned is that these fluctuations were terminal during the fixed exchange rate system for external deficit countries because they meant the government had to permanently keep the domestic economy in a depressed state to keep the imports down so as not to run out of foreign reserves. For a flexible exchange rate economy, the exchange rate does the adjustment. There is no balance of payments constraint facing a nation in this regard.

There is also no robust evidence that nations that run continuous fiscal deficits create catastrophic exchange rate depreciation in flexible exchange rate countries. It is often overlooked that any spending growth, including private investment spending, will push up imports. For less developed nations, the necessary investment spending to promote growth is usually import-intensive because most of them must import capital equipment. However, if that investment promotes domestic capacity, then the nation can continually push against any notion that it is constrained by its external sector.

In the next section, we consider the case of a nation that must import all of its essentials to sustain life.

5.7   TRADE AND DEVELOPING COUNTRIES

A major point of difference between Post Keynesians (in the New Cambridge tradition) and MMT economists is that the latter argue that a currency-issuing government is not constrained in its capacity to generate full employment through appropriate fiscal policy settings.

Accordingly, such a government can always use its currency-issuing capacity to ensure that all available productive resources that are for sale in that currency, including all idle labour, can be productively engaged. Thus, a departure from full employment of labour is always a political choice. The capacity of a currency-issuing government, for example, to introduce a Job Guarantee is not compromised by the external status of the nation. There is no financial constraint on such a government who desires to achieve that desirable policy goal.

While that might sound salutary, it somewhat evades a further question as to whether achieving this desirable goal moves a nation out of poverty. Facing no financial constraint in its own currency does not mean that a government will be able to avoid the external factors that can constrain the advancement of material prosperity for its citizens. For less developed countries, a currency-issuing government faces different issues to that of an advanced nation, especially where essentials like food and energy must be imported. In the case of less developed countries, specific problems cannot be easily overcome by just increasing fiscal deficits.

Being able to achieve full employment doesn't mean the nation will escape material poverty. If a nation can only access limited quantities of real resources relative to its population, then no matter what capacities the government might have, that nation will, likely, remain materially poor. The ultimate constraint on material prosperity is the real resources a nation can command, which includes the skills of its people and its natural resource inventory.

Thus, even if the government productively deploys all the resources a nation has available, it will still be poor if its resource base is limited. If a nation has little that the world wants by way of its exports, and if that nation is dependent on imports for, say, food or energy, then the capacity of the currency-issuing government to alleviate poverty is limited. This is not a balance of payments constraint as it is normally considered. It is a real resource constraint arising from the unequal distribution of resources across geographic space.

Where imported food (or other essentials) dependence exists then the well-being of the citizens in that nation cannot be solved within its own borders, especially if its export potential is limited. Imposing austerity on these governments as is the standard conditionality requirements to gain access to IMF support is no solution. Typically, this undermines public infrastructure development in areas such as education and health and makes it harder for the nation to escape its poverty trap.

In these situations, the responsibility for resolving the real resource constraints that operate through the balance of payments should be shared by all nations. The multilateral institutions that were introduced in the Post World War II period to coordinate international aid – the IMF and the World Bank – have failed in their respective missions. They became agents for the 'free market' ideology and through their structural adjustment packages and related policies have made it harder for a nation to develop.

In this context, a new multilateral institution should be created to replace both the World Bank and the IMF, which is charged with the responsibility to ensure that these highly disadvantaged nations can access essential real resources such as food and not be priced out of international markets due to exchange rate fluctuations that arise from trade deficits.[28]

Other reforms are necessary. There must be international agreements to outlaw speculation by investment banks on food and other essential commodities. It makes no sense to use staple food commodities to create derivative financial assets, which rely on purchasers manipulating supply to influence world prices to maximise profits.

Relatedly, the only sustainable way to end the currency threats that weaker nations face from speculators is for nation states to come together and legislate against speculative financial flows that have no necessary relationship with improving the operation of the real economy. In the absence of such international cooperation, nations should consider imposing capital controls where they can be beneficial bulwarks against the destructive forces of speculative financial capitalism.[29]

Further, in some situations a case can be made to impose import controls on equity grounds where the export base is thin, and a nation is struggling to amass sufficient real resources to 'feed and clothe' its people. This has nothing to do with fears that speculators will damage the currency and create hyperinflation through import price acceleration. While imports are clearly a benefit and exports are clearly a cost, there are still equity implications involved in the mix of imports that a nation might enjoy.

Selective import controls targeting products that are typically consumed by the rich and that are not essential to general well-being can ensure that a nation with a limited export base can use its limited import potential to secure goods and services that meet the necessities of life.

Finally, a case can be made that there can be a global benefit arising if a nation restricts its own capacity to export. For example, it is better for coal-rich nations to avoid pursuing a growth strategy based on coal exports, given the worsening environmental problems. In those cases, a single nation should not be punished for the pattern of geographic resource distribution and a global response is needed to make sure the damage to that nation's export potential does not impair its ability to import and fight poverty.

5.8   INDUSTRY POLICY AND ECONOMIC DEVELOPMENT

The problem facing all economies and especially less developed economies is to secure a stable industrial base. Nations that trade in industrial goods face less volatile international markets than nations that rely on primary commodity exports. The latter often face large swings in their terms of trade, which impacts on their exchange rates and makes it hard to build a viable manufacturing sector. This problem was initially referred to as the Dutch Disease in an *Economist* article in 1977.

In the immediate Post World War II period, governments used planned industrial strategies as part of their policy mix to help regions maintain employment growth, encourage private investment in productive activities, and aid in the forward planning of skill development through apprenticeships and the like. These strategies were considered an essential part of the capacity to achieve and sustain full employment in most nations and to build self-sufficiency via diversity in the industrial base.

Industry policy took many forms but generally included the following elements:[30]

- Fiscal stimulus to expand production and employment by maintaining adequate spending growth.
- Import controls and other tariff-style measures.
- Price controls to stop firms exploiting the import controls and pushing higher margins.
- Compulsory planning agreements between government and multinational firms to align investment, production and employment decisions with national interest.
- Development of import-substitution strategies by government.
- Nationalisation of key firms.
- Public ownership of major banks to divert investment to advance public interest.
- Less restrictions on trade unions to advance the interests of their workers.
- Broadening of the Welfare State.
- Cuts in military spending.
- Policies to reduce wealth and income inequality.

The 'infant industry' argument justified state support for emerging industries, whereby sectors would be protected in order for them to build economies of scale that would allow them to be internationally competitive once the industry support was withdrawn. The Post World War II era – the 'Keynesian' period of full employment and strong productivity growth – saw most nations using a mixed planning, market-based system for allocating productive resources and the state was always central in setting out planning parameters, engaging in direct ownership of state enterprises, implementing comprehensive regulative frameworks and assuming responsibility as a significant employer. In terms of the major aggregates – employment, GDP and productivity growth, reduced inequality, improved scope and quality of public services (health, education, utilities etc.) – this system was very successful. Two approaches to industrialisation were taken: (a) export-oriented (for example, South Korea), and (b) import-substitution (for example, India), although in most cases, nations used both strategies. Irrespective of the approach, both involved considerable state planning and support.

The problem was that in some cases, the baby never grew up, which meant that these policies allowed corporations to profit behind 'tariff walls' and enter cosy agreements with unions to share the margins that the protectionist policies created. It was argued that protection reduced the incentive for innovation, which meant that the support had to be ongoing and ultimately self-defeating as the nation fell further behind in terms of international competitiveness.

The dawning of the Monetarist era in the late 1960s, which generalised into what we now consider to be the neoliberal period, defined by the dominance of the 'free market' orthodoxy, brought a widespread opposition towards state intervention, particularly the use of industry policies.

The conduct of the IMF and World Bank from the 1970s onwards reflects this antagonism. In its Post-Bretton Woods incarnation (post-1971), the IMF was implacably opposed to industrial policy interventions by governments. Their position became the norm among mainstream economists. It bullied governments into abandoning planning frameworks, where policy initiatives would help domestic industries grow through public subsidies, tariffs, partnerships in R&D and so on. In particular, import-substitution industrial development strategies were particularly discouraged and declined as the IMF forced governments to deregulate, privatise, impose fiscal austerity and eschew any sense of 'picking winners'.

The new emphasis was on export-bias with free flow of capital (in and out) with the requisite domination of foreign capital in local ownership. The corresponding outflows of resources and income flows to foreign owners were lauded as being the exemplar of development as health and education spending was cut and environmental degradation accelerated.

This antagonism also permeated domestic politics in many advanced nations. For example, as Britain struggled to cope with the damage caused by the OPEC oil crisis in the early 1970s, the British government Secretary for Industry, Tony Benn, proposed an alternative industrial plan to revitalise British industry in 1975. It was rejected at the time by Prime Minister Harold Wilson and Chancellor Denis Healey, who had succumbed to the Monetarist logic and were intent on imposing fiscal austerity and pursuing a deregulation agenda. They used a lie – that the government had run out of money and would have to be bailed out by the IMF – to force their Monetarist ideology onto the British Labour Party. It was no surprise that many industries went to the wall as nations abandoned fiscal support to maintain full employment, deregulated labour and financial markets, and abandoned domestic protections for their industries. The IMF claimed that this shows industry policy focused on import-substitution can never work. But the culprit was not flawed industry policy. Rather, it was the withdrawal of all the accompanying support structures that made it work, but which ran counter to the neoliberal ideology of 'free markets'.

However, the great industrial transformation stories in history were not the result of the sort of development strategies promoted by the IMF and the World Bank. For example, the state-motivated development of industry in South Korea (such as The Heavy and Chemical Industrialisation (HCI) programme), would never have occurred if self-regulating markets were prioritised. Other examples include the watchmaking industry in Switzerland.

Ha-Joon Chang[31] wrote in his masterful rejection of the neoliberal approach:

> This neo-liberal establishment would have us believe that, during its miracle years between the 1960s and the 1980s, Korea pursued a neo-liberal economic development strategy.
>
> The reality, however, was very different indeed. What Korea actually did during these decades was to nurture certain new industries, selected by the government in consultation with the private sector, through tariff protection, subsidies and other forms of government support (e.g., overseas marketing information services provided by the state export agency) until they 'grew up' enough to withstand international competition. The government owned all the banks, so it could direct the life blood of business – credit ...
>
> The Korean government also had absolute control over scarce foreign exchange (violation of foreign exchange controls could be punished with the death penalty). When combined with a carefully designed list of priorities in the use of foreign exchange, it ensured that hard-earned foreign currencies were used for importing vital machinery and industrial inputs. The Korean government heavily controlled foreign investment as well, welcoming it with open arms in certain sectors while shutting it out completely in others, according to the evolving national development plan ...
>
> The popular impression of Korea as a free-trade economy was created by its export success. But export success does not require free trade, as Japan and China

have also shown. Korean exports in the earlier period – things like simple garments and cheap electronics – were all means to earn the hard currencies needed to pay for the advanced technologies and expensive machines that were necessary for the new, more difficult industries, which were protected through tariffs and subsidies. At the same time, tariff protection and subsidies were not there to shield industries from international competition forever, but to give them the time to absorb new technologies and establish new organizational capabilities until they could compete in the world market.

The Korean economic miracle was the result of a clever and pragmatic mixture of market incentives and state direction.

As the evidence mounted that the neoliberal strategies were anti-development, even the IMF started to sing a different tune.[32] They now concede that industry policy interventions that were the basis of economic planning in the Keynesian era were highly successful and only stopped being so, in some cases, when fiscal austerity was imposed, and trade controls were abandoned in the 1970s.

It is worth reflecting on all the mistakes that were made in the 1970s and beyond that were justified by the faith in the 'market' to provide the optimal development environment. Would Tony Benn have been so easily dismissed in 1975 by the growing mainstream view that free markets were the way to go? History might have been very different if these ideologically motivated institutions had not advocated neoliberalism.

Cherif and Hasanov[33] admitted that:

> During the later period, 1980–2010, when import substitution policies were rolled back in most developing economies, the average growth rates of manufacturing production dropped significantly, and manufacturing stagnated in many economies.

The fact that the nations that chose a state-driven import-substitution approach to industrialisation grew strongly without an export-bias suggests these policies should be an important part of development strategies. The reason that growth was not sustained in many nations from the 1970s is because institutions such as the IMF and World Bank forced nations into abandoning policy support for the import-substitution strategies in return for currency support, not that such strategies failed.

Significantly, nations that pursue import-substitution strategies and increase their self-reliance are also better placed to avoid the damage from fluctuations driven by currency speculation.

5.9   FREE AND FAIR TRADE AGREEMENTS

The discussion of industry policy overlaps with the debate about free versus fair trade. Like many aspects of mainstream economic theory, 'free trade' initially sounds intuitively reasonable, but the gloss quickly fades once you understand the basis of the theory and how it derives its seemingly ideal results. In practice, the textbook 'model' is never attainable and so what goes for 'free trade' is really a stacked deck of cards that has increasingly allowed large financial capital interests to exploit workers, consumers and undermine the democratic status of elected governments.

Even within the mainstream approach the terrain has moved. The old perfectly competitive 'models' of free trade go back to the notion of comparative advantage, which was introduced by Classical economist David Ricardo,[34] and, later embodied in the Heckscher–Ohlin theorem.[35] These ideas were used to disabuse notions of government intervention in dealing with the external economy.

The idea of comparative advantage is that nations would enjoy gains from trade if they specialised in products that they can produce at the lowest relative cost even if one nation enjoyed an absolute cost advantage in the products. By trading, prices are driven down in the higher-cost nation (without the comparative advantage in that particular good) because the export inflow increases the supply of goods. Similarly, the diversion of production into export markets rather than for domestic sales reduces supply in the home market and pushes up prices. The export flows stop when the prices are equalised across countries for each good.

It is argued that trade forces specialisation and drives out higher-cost operators as productive resources are assumed to move costlessly into the production specialisation while full employment is sustained. Free trade is thus claimed to increase productive efficiency, because in each country, the respective labour forces, who are always fully employed, now produce more goods in total than before at the lowest possible cost. Further, by allowing these competitive forces to work, free trade improves the welfare of citizens in both countries, who gain access to more consumption possibilities at the lowest possible price.

The problem with the theory is that the assumptions required to generate the result that free trade is optimal never apply in the real world, including: (a) there is no unemployment and productive resources (capital and labour) are perfectly mobile between sectors and countries; (b) there is no market power to influence prices; and (c) all countries have identical production technology.

Wassily Leontief's[36] findings proved fatal for the comparative advantage model. His Leontief Paradox showed that the US, which was the nation with the most capital, was exporting goods and services that were more labour-intensive than capital-intensive, a major violation of the predictions of the Heckscher–Ohlin model. Further, the US imported more capital-intensive goods than it exported. Comparative advantage could not explain those facts. In the 1980s, the emergence of 'new trade theory' provided further argument to reject the Heckscher–Ohlin approach.[37]

Essentially, by demonstrating the underlying assumptions were invalid, these developments meant that economists could no longer argue that the results of the free trade models held. Any further claims that free trade was optimal were purely advancing vested interests and supporting ideology. New trade theory showed that government trade regulations (for example, export subsidies and/or import controls) can advance national well-being.

The ideology of advancing corporate interests at the expense of other aspirations drives the free trade mantra. The reality is that the 'free traders' do not actually believe in the textbook concept of a free market that they advance. If such a state existed, then firms would have zero market power and they would only be able to earn so-called 'normal profits', which reflect opportunity cost.

No modern corporate leader aims to achieve that state. At a minimum, they aim to manipulate the 'market' they trade into to influence prices they can get and are required to pay for inputs and end up with as big a margin on total costs as they can achieve. They aim to create a unique product and drive competitors out of business as quickly as they can. If they can take over a competitor and increase their market share, they will. They seek to manipulate consumers into believing their product is best through advertising, which uses psychological tools that go well beyond the textbook idea that such interaction with the 'market' is just to provide 'information'.

Robert Reich[38] captured this cant eloquently:

> Many of the most vocal proponents of the 'free market' – including executives of large corporations and their ubiquitous lawyers and lobbyists, denizens of Wall Street and their political lackeys, and numerous millionaires and billionaires – have for many years been actively reorganizing the market for their own benefit and would prefer these issues not be examined.

A market – any market – requires that government make and enforce the rules of the game. In most modern democracies, such rules emanate from legislatures, administrative agencies and courts. Government doesn't 'intrude' on the 'free market'. It creates the market. It is little wonder why the corporate power brokers – their lawyers and lobbyists – vehemently pursue governments to agree to pro-corporation clauses in these so-called 'free market agreements'. They know that without government support and agreement to tilt the playing field towards them and away from workers and consumers they will be forced into more equitable sharing of the national income produced in each nation.

While progressive political forces have convinced themselves that globalisation has rendered the state powerless in the face of global capital, the neoliberals worked out long ago that they had to work within the legislative environment established in each nation they wish to operate within. They sought to reconfigure the state to advance their own interests.[39] If the state was powerless, why do corporations spend billions lobbying governments to legislate in their favour?

The corporations don't seek to play by the rules. They are continually seeking to change the rules to advance their own interests, irrespective of the impact on other stakeholders (workers, consumers, local communities etc.).

We always need to remind ourselves that:[40]

> It is no accident that those with disproportionate influence over these rules, who are the largest beneficiaries of how the rules have been designed and adapted, are also among the most vehement supporters of the 'free market' and also the most ardent advocates of the relative superiority of the market over government. But the debate itself also serves their goal of distracting the public from the underlying realities of how the rules are generated and changed, their own power over this process, and the extent to which they gain from the results. In other words, not only do these 'free market' advocates want the public to agree with them about the superiority of the market but also about the central importance of this interminable debate.

In discussions about 'free trade' versus 'fair trade', the misnomer of free markets must always condition the debate.

There are now a plethora of 'free trade' agreements and national leaders make grandiose claims to their citizens about the advantages that will flow to them. One of the problems with these agreements is that they are typically shrouded in secrecy, with governments pleading 'commercial-in-confidence' as their reason for preventing a full public debate on the proposed terms and conditions.

But we know that these agreements typically give corporations priority over a state and the citizens that the state represents. A controversial aspect of these agreements which strengthen these biases are the so-called *Investor State Disputes Settlement (ISDS)* clauses, which set up mechanisms through which international corporations can take out legal action against elected governments if they believe a particular piece of legislation or a regulation undermines their opportunities for profit. It is that crude. Profit becomes prioritised over the independence of a legislature and the latter cannot compromise the former. Under these clauses, 'supra-national tribunals' which are outside any nation's judicial system, but which governments are bound to obey, are given power to adjudicate. The notion of accountability disappears.

These tribunals can declare a law enacted by a democratically elected government to be illegal and impose fines on the state for breaches. There have already been some astounding decisions in these ISDS under other agreements, which have denied governments the right to introduce policies regarding environmental protection (for example, toxic waste safeguards, forestry management processes etc.).[41]

A notable case relates to the lawsuit pursuit against the Australian government for introducing plain packaging with health warnings by an international tobacco company. The company claimed the health measures undermined its profitability. In its 2013–14 Trade and Assistance Review, the Australian Productivity Commission, which is a pro-market agency of the government, noted that:[42]

> The Australian Government continued defence of its tobacco plain packaging laws in a case brought by Philip Morris Asia in the Permanent Court of Arbitration and a number of countries in the WTO dispute settlement body. This case highlights the potential (and un-provisioned) contingent liability of Investor State Dispute Settlement (ISDS) provisions in trade and investment agreements that confer procedural rights to foreign investors not available to domestic residents. The final outcome of the case is not expected to be known for some time. The ongoing costs to Australian taxpayers of funding the preparation and defence of the tobacco plain packaging legislation, and the ultimate ruling, are unknown, unfunded and likely to be substantial.

In other words, international corporations have more rights than residents. In this case, the Australian government won the case in December 2015. Later, we learned that the court costs, of which the tobacco company was forced to pay half, summed to more than $A24 million.[43]

There is a proliferation of these cases now attacking legislation that seeks to improve health and environmental outcomes. Only advanced nations with sufficient financial resources can defend their national sovereignty in this respect from the demands of global capital. These mechanisms in the 'free trade' agreements are designed to further skew the distribution of income and wealth to the top end of the distributions and to further neuter the capacity of governments to act independently according to elected mandates. They line up with fiscal rules, independent fiscal commissions and the like as key vehicles to suppress our freedoms and choice of legislative environment in which we live.

Investor State Dispute Mechanisms are attacks on democracy. A nation state is defined by its legislature and that institution sets the legal framework in which all activity within the sovereign borders engages. Corporations have rights under that framework as do citizens. But the assumption is that the legislative framework should reflect the goals of national well-being. There is never a case that a corporation should have institutional structures available to it to usurp the checks and balances built into national legislation.

A further problem in the way 'free trade' agreements have evolved relates to the way different nations can exploit the World Trade Organization (WTO) rules. There has been an almost dichotomised development process among rich and poor nations, which goes back to the colonial era. The poorer nations (typically under colonial rule) had 'free trade' forced upon them with concomitantly poor outcomes, while the colonial powers adopted protectionist positions.[44]

Further, while tariffs have come down under successive rounds under the GATT and then the WTO, the global trading terrain has been anything but level. First, rich nations such as the US still maintain a complex array of tariffs on goods attempting to enter their borders. Japan, for example, maintains a highly protectionist stance with respect to its primary products (particularly against rice imports). These cases are generalised across most nations.

Second, the WTO maintains its view that low-wage countries attract capital because of their comparative advantage and it is this that leads to development. The evidence is not supportive of that belief.[45] The large capital interests resist any inclusion of labour standards in these 'free trade' agreements because they know they would undermine their 'race-to-the-bottom' strategy of profit capture.

Further, with organisations such as the World Bank and the IMF pushing export-led growth strategies for poorer nations, 'corporate farming' has become common. The environmental damage has been vast.

The problem is complex. The aim of economic development is to reduce (and eliminate) poverty but within an environmentally sustainable frame. However, poverty itself can undermine environmental sustainability. For example, to meet the demands of the World Bank to pay back debts, sustainable agricultural practices have been replaced by export-led farming and wide-scale deforestation in many nations (for example, Nepal).

The IMF and the World Bank have pushed massive levels of debt onto less developed nations in the name of export-led growth, which is a partner to the neoliberal 'free trade' narrative. They have also forced these nations to slash public services, privatise public assets and engage in extensive deregulation (particularly in capital flows). For example, in the 1980s, the African nation of Mali was placed under IMF and World Bank structural adjustment programmes where poverty and hardship was deliberately exacerbated by privatisation, cuts to government employment and wages, and decimation of its public education system. IMF austerity was at the forefront of years of political instability and eventually, once the IMF had a government that would do their bidding without asking questions, it was declared a model nation by the Washington organisation. Foreign investment returned to boost the cotton industry but most of the returns courtesy of the IMF privatisation policies go to foreigners and living standards remain low for the locals. More than 50 per cent of people in Mali are poor. There are gross violations of human rights and a trend over the last decades has been for people to abandon their children in the poverty-entrenched cities because they cannot care for them.[46]

The example of Mali is not isolated. It is the norm when the IMF and the World Bank are involved. The 2010 conflict in India involving the proposal to build a coal-fired power plant in Sompeta, which would have destroyed the local sustainable fishing and farming industry, is another example. The plant would have taken over valuable wetlands that is at the heart of community sustainability.[47] The OK Tedi disaster is another example of how multinational corporations, who profit from extracting resources from less developed nations, largely evade proper scrutiny of the environmental damage they create and the disruption this damage causes local communities.

It is also clear that the WTO has no coherent rules that restrict imports from nations that engage in poor environmental practices. They claim that:[48]

> ... no specific agreement dealing with the environment. However, the WTO agreements confirm governments' right to protect the environment, provided certain conditions are met, and a number of them include provisions dealing with environmental concerns.

The WTO responds to calls for trade restrictions if environmental damage is likely to result from production by claiming that:[49]

> ... measures designed to meet these objectives could hinder exports. And they agree that sustainable development depends on improved market access for developing countries' products.

They also state that 'environmental standards applied by some countries could be inappropriate', meaning that a nation does not have the right, under WTO thinking, to determine its own standards.

They have also warned against what they call 'green protectionism'.[50] They adopt the standard mainstream economics position that the solution to pollution and environmental damage is to create more growth (and damage) to generate the resources necessary to combat the damage. This view is, in part, driven by the erroneous view that the national governments are financially constrained and cannot deal with the climate change issues without raising extra tax revenue from faster economic growth.

5.10   FAIR TRADE PRINCIPLES

When we say that exports are a cost and imports are a benefit, this is referring to the opportunity cost principle adopted under a strict, other things being equal, assumption. In a material sense, with consumption as the end goal, we all typically benefit from trade, if and only if, it doesn't violate the democratic choices we make and express through national government policies in areas such as:

- Working conditions – wages and conditions, occupational safety etc.
- Rights to association and right to strike – formation of trade unions etc.
- Consumer protection – safety, ethical standards, quality of product or service etc.
- Environmental standards.

These criteria define what we call 'fair trade' and are in contradistinction to the type of trading arrangements embodied in so-called 'free trade' agreements.

Complexity arises when we try to achieve a cultural intersection as to how to define fairness in these areas. For example, the economies that avoided the plunge into high unemployment in the 1970s maintained what Paul Ormerod[51] described as a 'sector of the economy which effectively functions as an employer of last resort, which absorbs the shocks which occur from time to time, and more generally makes employment available to the less skilled, the less qualified'. Ormerod acknowledged that employment of this type may not satisfy narrow neoclassical efficiency benchmarks, but notes that societies with a high degree of social cohesion have been willing to broaden their concept of 'costs' and 'benefits' of resource usage to ensure everyone has access to paid employment opportunities. He argued that countries like Japan, Austria, Norway and Switzerland were able to maintain this capacity because each exhibited 'a high degree of shared social values, of what may be termed social cohesion, a characteristic of almost all societies in which unemployment has remained low for long periods of time'.[52] In other words, a sense of fairness (equity) was sustained by collective will to ensure political choices were made to ensure adequate levels of employment. Conversely, governments in nations such as Australia and the US have been less willing to ensure employment levels are sustained in the face of drops in economic activity.

Fair trade arrangements must therefore establish relevant labour and environmental standards to regulate trade. The WTO has had a poor record in this regard. Free trade agreements are notoriously weak in dealing with these issues. While it is recognised that nations in different periods of development will have different productive methods, working standards that are acceptable across cultures can be devised. However, within these differences, some standards remain common – the right to association, the right to adequate rest and breaks, the right to holidays, the right to fair pay, the right to strike.

While the details need to be worked out, the general principle is clear – trade should not be allowed if it violates the principles listed above.

This principle also qualifies, to some extent, the essential insight that in a materialistic sense of well-being, imports provide benefits to a nation (goods and services otherwise unattainable), while exports are a cost (real resources are sacrificed and used by foreigners rather than the nation). Adopting the view that imports are beneficial doesn't undermine our critique of 'free trade'. Indeed, it strengthens it.

Some commentators might think that this starting point then militates against the advocacy for such things as import controls. The answer is that even though, in general, exports are a cost and imports are a benefit, the framework in which we make those assessments is multidimensional and extends the concept of material progress in ways that mainstream economics typically ignores.

For example, a commercial transaction that is only considered in terms of the use value that the consumer receives may involve massive damage to the producing community. Thus, while an imported good or service might be seen in narrow terms to be a 'good' for the consumer, once we broaden our assessment of the costs and benefits of the overall chain of production and consumption a more nuanced view will emerge.

By adopting principles that allow the actual costs, including damage to the environment, destruction of local sustainable industry, damage to human dignity of unfair work practices and so on, the benefits of the import to a consumer will pale into insignificance relative to the costs of the producers. In those cases, import controls may be justified to limit the damage to the less developed nation, despite the material benefits to the more developed nation being obvious.

Further, there is a compositional aspect to the exports are a cost and imports are a benefit classification. In the case of primary commodity exporting nations such as Australia, the costs involved in mining its vast stores of iron ore may be low, given the alternative use of the resource within Australia is limited.

NOTES

1.   Ricardo, 1817.
2.   IMF, 2011.
3.   United Nations Statistical Commission, 2009.
4.   IMF, 2011: 149.
5.   See Section 5.4.
6.   A more detailed treatment of this section can be found in Mitchell et al., 2019.
7.   Keynes, 1923.
8.   See Mitchell et al., 2019 for more detail.
9.   Hicks, 1950.
10. Kaldor, 1957, 1970, 1971, 1978, 1989.
11. Thirlwall, 1979.
12. Mitchell, 2022.
13. Kaldor, 1957: 593.
14. Kaldor, 1970, 1978.

15.   Kaldor, 1971: 7.
16.   Harrod, 1939.
17.   Thirlwall, 1979.
18.   Setterfield, 2011: 408.
19.   Kaldor, 1989.
20.   Palumbo, 2009: 363.
21.   Giavazzi and Giovannini, 1989; Eichengreen and Wyplosz, 1993.
22.   Eichengreen and Wyplosz, 1993.
23.   Eichengreen and Wyplosz, 1993: 57.
24.   Eichengreen and Wyplosz, 1993: 57.
25.   For a detailed account, see Mitchell, 2015.
26.   Eichengreen, 2010: 24.
27.   Rodrik, 2010.
28.   See Mitchell and Fazi, 2017 for a more detailed development of this idea.
29.   We considered the case for capital controls in Section 5.6.
30.   Rowthorn, 1981: 4–10.
31.   Chang, 2007: xx–xxi.
32.   See Cherif and Hasanov, 2019.
33.   Cherif and Hasanov, 2019: 52.
34.   Ricardo, 1817.
35.   Heckscher, 1919; Ohlin, 1933.
36.   Leontief, 1953.
37.   Krugman, 1987.
38.   Reich, 2015: xiii.
39.   Mitchell and Fazi, 2017.
40.   Reich, 2015: 6.
41.   See UNCTAD, Investment Policy Hub, available at https://investmentpolicy .unctad.org/.
42.   Productivity Commission, 2015: 14.
43.   Ranald, 2019.
44.   Chang, 2007; Pigaud and Samba Sylla, 2020.
45.   See Chang, 2007 for case studies.
46.   Bello and Cunningham, 1994.
47.   Sarma, 2010.
48.   WTO, 2022a.
49.   WTO, 2022a.
50.   WTO, 2022b.
51.   Ormerod, 1994: 203.
52.   Ormerod, 1994: 203.

REFERENCES

Bello, W. and Cunningham, S. (1994) *Dark Victory: The US, Structural Adjustment, and Global Poverty*, London: Food First.

Chang, Ha-Joon (2007) *Bad Samaritans: The Myth of Free Trade and the Secret History of Capitalism*, London: Bloomsbury Press.

Cherif, R. and Hasanov, F. (2019) 'The Return of the Policy That Shall Not Be Named: Principles of Industrial Policy', IMF Working Paper 19/74, International Monetary Fund, Washington, DC.

Eichengreen, B.J. (2010) 'The Breakup of the Euro Area', in Alesina, A. and Giavazzi, F. (eds), *Europe and the Euro, National Bureau of Economic Research*, Chicago, IL: University of Chicago Press, pp. 11–51.

Eichengreen, B. and Wyplosz, C. (1993) 'The Unstable EMS', Brookings Papers on Economic Activity, 1, 51–143.

Giavazzi, F. and Giovannini, A. (1989) *Limiting Exchange Rate Flexibility: The European Monetary System*, Cambridge, MA: MIT Press.

Harrod, R. (1939) 'An Essay in Dynamic Theory', *The Economic Journal*, 49(193), 14–33.

Heckscher, E. (1919) 'The Effect of Foreign Trade on the Distribution of Income', *Ekonomisk Tidskrift*, 497–512.

Hicks, J.R. (1950) *A Contribution to the Theory of the Trade Cycle*, Oxford: Clarendon Press.

International Monetary Fund (IMF) (2011) Balance of Payments and International Investment Position Manual (BPM6), Washington, DC.

Kaldor, N. (1957) 'A Model of Economic Growth', *The Economic Journal*, 67(268), December, 591–624.

Kaldor, N. (1970) 'The Case for Regional Policies', *Scottish Journal of Political Economy*, 17(3), November, 337–48.

Kaldor, N. (1971) 'Conflicts in National Economic Objectives', *The Economic Journal*, 81(321), March, 1–16.

Kaldor, N. (1978) *Further Essays on Economic Theory*, London: Duckworth.

Kaldor, N. (1989) 'The Role of Effective Demand in the Short and Long-run Growth', in A. Barrére (org.), *The Foundations of Keynesian Analysis*, London: Macmillan Press.

Keynes, J.M. (1923) *A Tract on Monetary Reform*, London: Macmillan.

Krugman, P. (1987) 'Is Free Trade Passé', *The Journal of Economic Perspectives*, 1(2), 131–44.

Leontief, W. (1953) 'Domestic Production and Foreign Trade; the American Capital Position Re-examined', *Proceedings of the American Philosophical Society*, 97(4), 332–49.

Mitchell, W.F. (2015) *Eurozone Dystopia: Groupthink and Denial on a Grand Scale*, Cheltenham, UK and Northampton, MA, USA: Edward Elgar Publishing.

Mitchell, W.F. (2022) 'The Balance of Payments and Modern Monetary Theory', forthcoming.

Mitchell, W.F. and Fazi, T. (2017) *Reclaiming the State: A Progressive Vision of Sovereignty for a Post-Neoliberal World*, London: Pluto Books.

Mitchell, W.F., Wray, L.R. and Watts, M.J. (2019) *Macroeconomics*, London: Red Globe Press.

Ohlin, B. (1933) *Interregional and International Trade*, Harvard Economic Studies, Vol. 39, Cambridge, MA: Harvard University Press.

Ormerod, P. (1994) *The Death of Economics*, London: Faber and Faber.

Palumbo, A. (2009) 'Adjusting Theory to Reality: The Role of Aggregate Demand in Kaldor's Late Contributions on Economic Growth', *Review of Political Economy*, 21(3), 341–68.

Pigaud, F. and Samba Sylla, N. (2020) *Africa's Last Colonial Currency: The CFA Franc Story*, London: Pluto Press.

Productivity Commission (2015) *Trade and Assistance Review, 2013–14*, Productivity Commission Annual Report Series.

Ranald, P. (2019) 'When Even Winning Is Losing. The Surprising Cost of Defeating Philip Morris over Plain Packaging', *The Conversation*, 27 March.

Reich, R.B. (2015) *Saving Capitalism: For the Many, Not the Few*, New York: Alfred A. Knopf.

Ricardo, D. (1817) *On the Principles of Political Economy and Taxation*, London: John Murray.

Rodrik, D. (2010) 'The End of an Era in Finance', *Project Syndicate*, 11 March 2010.

Rowthorn, R. (1981) 'The Politics of the Alternative Economic Strategy', *Marxism Today*, January, 4–10.

Sarma, E.A.S. (2010) 'The Saga of Sompeta: Public Deception, Private Gains', *Economic and Political Weekly*, 45(33), August, 38–43.

Setterfield, M. (2011) 'The Remarkable Durability of Thirlwall's Law', *PSL Quarterly Review*, 64(259), 393–427.

Thirlwall, A.P. (1979) 'The Balance of Payments Constraint as an Explanation of International Growth Rate Differences', *Banca Nazionale del Lavoro Quarterly Review*, March, 32, 45–53.

United Nations Statistical Commission (2009) System of National Accounts 2008, New York.

World Trade Organization (WTO) (2022a) 'The Environment: A Specific Concern', *Understanding the WTO: Cross-cutting and New Issues*, Washington, DC.

World Trade Organization (WTO) (2022b) 'Environmental Requirements and Market Access: Preventing "Green Protectionism"', *Environment: Issues*, Washington, DC.

6. Modern Monetary Theory, the United Kingdom, and pound sterling

John T. Harvey

Among the many dire warnings from opponents of Modern Monetary Theory (MMT) is that MMT-inspired policies will cause the value of the domestic currency to collapse. However, as is the case with so many other attacks on MMT, this argument is based on economic models that do not reflect the realities of the world in which we live. In particular, it combines a theory of inflation that assumes that economies tend to operate at full employment with an explanation of exchange rate determination that ignores roughly 90 per cent of currency transactions. This chapter will expose the weaknesses of the MMT-as-currency-killer argument and then substitute for it a model that is not only firmly grounded in the real world but also shows that there is no reason to assume that MMT-inspired policies will cause a depreciation of the domestic currency. Indeed, it is more likely to cause an appreciation. Throughout, the focus will be on the UK economy and the pound sterling.

The chapter will proceed as follows. In the next section, the MMT-as-currency-killer argument is laid out in the context of the formal models used to explicitly and implicitly support it. Following that, two sections detail a more realistic vision of the operation of the domestic macroeconomy and the currency market and the questions of currency collapse and domestic price inflation are considered. A brief comment on the 1976 International Monetary Fund crisis is then made, followed by conclusions.

6.1   MMT AS CURRENCY KILLER

Attacks on MMT have been mounted by both professional and amateur economists. The former are our only concern here, of course, most of whom are from the mainstream/Neoclassical camp. Their critiques range from scathing[1] to relatively friendly.[2] The Austrians, too, have taken a turn – none of them very friendly.[3] And members of the US Congress have also been critical, even to the point of introducing legislation to block MMT from being used as a policy guide.[4]

Unfortunately, these have come from so many directions that it is difficult to generalize. Even more problematic is the fact that they generally misrepresent MMT or neglect to place individual components into a larger context. Because this chapter is concerned with exchange rates and since the MMT-as-currency-killer view typically marks inflation as the culprit, I will narrow the focus to that one particular and very common criticism: *MMT-inspired policies will cause high rates of price inflation which will, in turn, lower the international value of the domestic currency – perhaps catastrophically.*

There are a variety of models with which MMT critics implicitly and explicitly support this argument. One that is representative is the monetary model of the balance of payments. It combines the quantity theory of money with purchasing power parity and would, indeed, come to the conclusion that monetary or fiscal stimuli simply cause domestic price inflation and currency depreciation. Important premises of this approach include:

- full-employment of resources;[5]
- the demand for money is a stable function of real output and the interest rate;[6]
- the supply of money is exogenously determined;[7] and
- purchasing parity holds at all times.[8]

They justify the full-employment assumption on the grounds that the model is set in the long run. This in turn implies an unstated premise, that is, that the economy tends to, given sufficient time, "self-correct" and automatically eliminate any involuntary unemployment. This is actually a widely held belief in Neoclassicism, one shared by both right-leaning orthodox schools like Monetarism and the more left-leaning, interventionist Neoclassical Keynesians. As an example of the latter, Christina Romer, once Chair of Democratic President Barack Obama's Council of Economic Advisers, writes:

> Just as there is no regularity in the timing of business cycles, there is no reason why cycles have to occur at all. *The prevailing view among economists is that there is a level of economic activity, often referred to as full employment, at which the economy could stay forever.*[9]

This is a very revealing statement from an economist who believes that the government can legitimately play a role in determining the level of economic activity.[10]

The demand for money function can be expressed as follows (i.e., as the Cambridge Equation):

$$M^d = kPy \qquad\qquad (6.1)$$

where M^d is the demand for money, P is the domestic price level, y is real output or income (and hence Py is nominal output or income), and k is the desired ratio of nominal money balances to nominal income. That desired ratio is assumed to be inversely related to the opportunity cost of holding money, most often proxied by the rate of interest. As domestic interest rates rise, so agents would be less willing to hold unspent income as cash. For simplicity, interest rates are assumed to be constant (making k constant):

> Henceforth, the analysis will be simplified by assuming that world interest rates are constant so that the growth of demand for real balances depends only on the growth of real output (the growth of demand for nominal money balances depends of course also on the rate of change of the price level). This assumption can be justified on the grounds that real rates of return on investment are relatively stable and that money rates of interest in a longer-run growth context will be equal to real rates of return plus the (actual and expected) rate of world price inflation or minus the (actual and expected) rate of world price deflation.[11]

Given that real output, y, is also assumed to be constant at the full-employment level, this reduces the determinants of the demand for money to the price level, P.

The money supply, M^s, is determined exogenously by the monetary authority. Since in equilibrium it must be true that $M^s = M^d$, we can write:

$$M^s = kPy \tag{6.2}$$

With both k and y constant, this implies that the burden of maintaining equilibrium falls to P. P is in turn tied to conditions of international competitiveness: "domestic prices must keep in line with foreign prices".[12] Purchasing power parity creates this anchor:

$$P = SP^* \tag{6.3}$$

where P is still the domestic price level, S is domestic currency units per foreign currency unit (e.g., sterling/euro), and P* is the foreign price level.

As our ultimate goal is to examine the MMT-as-currency-killer with respect to currency prices, we need to undertake a number of adjustments. First, assume that we have a foreign equivalent of equations (6.1) (and, therefore, (6.2)), identical except for an asterisk on each variable. Now take equation (6.2) and solve for price:

$$P = M^s / ky \tag{6.2'}$$

Note that this implies that, since k and y are constant, it is changes in M^s that determine changes in P. As M^s rises, P rises, and vice versa. And in the foreign country:

$$P^* = M^{s*} / k^* y^* \qquad (6.2^{*\prime})$$

Next, solve equation (6.3) for the exchange rate:

$$S = P / P^* \qquad (6.3)$$

Substituting (6.2') and (6.2') for P and P* yields:

$$S = \left[M^s / ky \right] / \left[M^{s*} / k^* y^* \right] \qquad (6.4)$$

$$S = M^s k^* y^* / M^{s*} ky$$

Because economists are usually concerned with rates of change of these variables rather than levels, this is commonly expressed in log form (where the italicized version of a variable is its log):

$$S = M^s + k^* + y^* - M^{s*} - k - y \qquad (6.4')$$

Rearranging slightly gives:

$$S = \left(M^s - M^{s*} \right) + \left(k^* - k \right) + \left(y^* - y \right) \qquad (6.4')$$

Here we come to the core of the MMT-as-currency-killer argument. Note, first, that an expansionary MMT fiscal policy would be financed by new money creation and hence would raise M^s.[13] Recall further that S is measured as domestic currency units per foreign currency unit such that an increase in S means that the domestic currency has depreciated. Therefore, as M^s rises, so the home currency's value falls. This occurs because if k and y (and k* and y*) are constant, as they assume, then when agents spend their new income from the MMT policy, it simply bids up prices (see equation (6.2')). This makes domestic goods less competitive internationally and the consequent decline in demand for domestic currency causes it to fall in value (see equation (6.3)). The greater the increase in M^s, the higher prices rise at home and the more the currency depreciates. The story is analogous in rates of change, wherein the currency collapse would be caused by MMT-policies accelerating M^s at a significantly faster rate than M^{s*} (see equation (6.4') and recall that, as constants, the k and y variables become zero.

While this is just one version of the MMT-as-currency-killer argument, it shares a great deal with the others – including two very questionable assumptions:

1.   The economy automatically tends towards full employment;
2.   The primary determinant of currency prices is the current account.[14]

Beginning with the first, recall equation (6.2'):

$$P = M^s / ky \qquad (6.2')$$

Accepting, for the sake of argument, the assumption that the demand for money function is constant, then it is clear that if y is constant at the full-employment level (or growing at a rate consistent with that) and M^s rises (or its growth rate is higher), P must rise (or accelerate). However, not only is there no reason to believe that the market system automatically creates a job for every willing worker (more on this later), but *were we already at full employment, then no MMT policymaker would be recommending an expansionary fiscal policy in the first place.* Indeed, with something like a job guarantee, deficit spending and M^s would automatically fall as we reached full employment because it is programmed to do so.

Second, only a minority of foreign currency transactions are related to the import and export of goods and services, while the overwhelming majority are concentrated in the financial capital market where funds circulate the globe in search of the highest rate of return. This is in stark contrast to the underlying premise of the purchasing power parity equation from above:

$$P = SP^* \qquad (6.3)$$

There, the one and only factor affecting exchange rates is the competitiveness of internationally traded goods and services. This should lead to a tendency towards balanced trade and smoothly adjusting exchange rates. However, the post-Bretton Woods era has actually been witness to large and chronic trade imbalances and wildly volatile currency prices whose movements have had no correlation whatsoever with imports and exports.[15]

The reason for this is quite simple. In 2019, there was an estimated \$1650 trillion in foreign exchange market activity.[16] In that same year, world trade in goods and services was \$24.96 trillion.[17] This is 1.5 per cent of total currency market activity. Even allowing for multiple covering transactions by various parties and multiplying this by a factor of five, it still yields a total of only \$124.8 trillion, or 7.5 per cent of total foreign exchange volume. If we assumed that the appropriate factor were ten, which seems very unlikely, this does not help markedly as it only gets us to 15 per cent of the market. In other words, purchasing power parity is an explanation of currency prices that is based on something in the range of 1.5 per cent to 15 per cent of actual foreign exchange market activity.

Even supporters of purchasing power parity admit that it only holds in the long run – a period of time they say is equivalent to years or even decades. The more likely answer is that it does not hold at all. Because the factors that determine the demand for goods and services differ significantly from those that drive financial capital flows, purchasing power parity cannot possibly explain real-world currency movements. And without purchasing power parity and the full-employment assumption, the Monetary Model no longer serves as the intellectual foundation for the MMT-as-currency-killer argument.

6.2   A REALISTIC THEORY OF OUTPUT, EMPLOYMENT, AND EXCHANGE RATES

All this said, there is no guarantee that a model rejecting the full-employment and purchasing-power-parity assumptions would nevertheless come to a different conclusion. Perhaps there is another route by which MMT causes a currency crisis. To test this, a model based on more realistic assumptions will be developed below. It will be shown that not only is there no reason to expect MMT policies to cause the domestic currency to depreciate, but it is quite possible that it might actually appreciate.[18]

Because Post Keynesian economics draws its inspiration from John Maynard Keynes and as he rejected the full-employment assumption, his Z-D diagram approach will be used to explain the domestic macroeconomy (Figure 6.1). Beginning with the Z curve, it shows the number of workers (N) that firms are willing to hire at each level of expected nominal sales (Py).[19] As one would expect, these are positively related. Note, however, the fact that the Z curve becomes increasingly steep so firms must expect a larger and larger jump in sales to induce them to hire one more worker as N rises. Keynes attributes this to the fact that he is assuming all workers are paid the same wage, but that as N rises, so the marginal product of labour falls.

The D curve is aggregate demand. It, too, is positively sloped, in this instance because as employment rises, so will total incomes and, therefore, consumption spending. The intercept of the D curve represents all spending autonomous of current incomes (investment, government spending, and net exports).[20] Equilibrium employment is at the intersection of Z and D because firms are disappointed at every other point. To the right, they expected higher sales and will therefore lay off workers; to the left, they will have underestimated potential sales and will therefore add workers.

The intersection represents full employment (N_f) only by coincidence. In Keynes's world, the problem is that while firms can take actions to correct

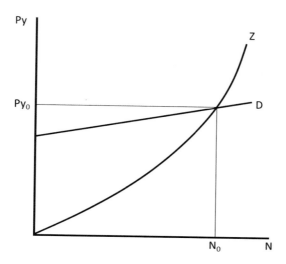

Figure 6.1   Keynes's Z-D diagram

the situation when they are disappointed (as occurs when we are not at the intersection of Z and D), workers cannot. This is in contrast to the Neoclassical view where, if there is involuntary unemployment, workers offer to work for less and this then returns us to full employment. But Post Keynesians argue that were this realistic, then we would have seen a rapid decline in unemployment during the Great Depression. There is no question that idle workers across the globe – especially because they lacked modern social support systems – were offering to work for whatever wage could be had. It was for naught, however, because *firms simply were not hiring*. It is the demand for firms' products that ultimately limits employment, not the negotiation over wages. In addition, even if wages did fall during a period of high unemployment, one must then take into consideration the fact that this also pulls the D curve down and thereby creates negative feedback. Nor is it a "solution" if workers' remuneration is pulled below a living wage. As Keynes writes, "There is, therefore, no ground for the belief that a flexible wage policy is capable of maintaining a state of continuous full employment".[21]

The Z curve is derived from the standard Neoclassical profit-maximizing point of equilibrium in the labour market:

$$W / P = MPN \tag{6.5}$$

where W is the average wage, P the price level (and hence W/P the real wage), and MPN the marginal product of labour. Over the relevant range, MPN falls as firms add more workers. If firms stop adding workers when $W / P < MPN$, then they have forgone profit opportunities – the cost of one more worker (W/P) still lies below the value of the output that worker would produce (MPN). However, if firms hire up to the point that $W / P > MPN$, then all the workers hired past $W / P = MPN$ cost more in real terms (W/P) than the real value of the output they produce (MPN).

Keynes's Z curve can be derived directly from equation (6.5) (see appendix for derivation):

$$N = Py / \left[W \left(APN / MPN \right) \right] = \left(Py / W \right) \left(MPN / APN \right) \qquad (6.6)$$

where APN is the average product of labour and all other variables are defined as above. Note how this specification explains why the Z curve becomes increasingly steep. First, equation (6.6) shows that a rise in Py – the level of nominal sales expected by firms – causes a rise in N. Second, a rise in wages (W), however, leads to a decline in N. Both of these seem perfectly reasonable. What is new is the fact that because MPN / APN will fall as N rises (since MPN will fall faster than APN), it takes an increasingly large rise in Py to induce firms to hire one more worker as N rises. This is bad news if we are hoping to reach full employment.

The D curve is:

$$Py = A + \alpha \bullet W \bullet N \qquad (6.7)$$

where A represents all forms of autonomous spending (investment, government spending, and net exports) and $\alpha \bullet W \bullet N$ is consumption (where α is the percentage of income households spend). Some versions of the D curve show α declining as N rises (on the assumption that households spend a declining percentage of income at higher income levels) and others leave it constant. We shall do the latter here for simplicity, particularly as it will not affect our conclusions.

Note that W appears in the equations for both the Z and D curves. In the former, it is a cost to firms and therefore inversely related to employment, while in the latter it is a source of demand for goods and services and therefore positively related to employment. It was already explained above that the Keynes/Post Keynesian view of the labour market rejects the Neoclassical argument that full employment is guaranteed because unemployed workers will compete among themselves, driving down wages until everyone has a job. Now here is the additional complication also referenced above: falling wages may lower costs, but they also lower sales. Which force dominates depends on the relative elasticities, but in any event, it is yet another reason to believe that a model based on more realistic premises does not come to the happy conclusion that the economy automatically tends towards full employment.

Solving equations (6.6) and (6.7) for equilibrium N yields (proof in appendix):

$$N = (Py / W)(MPN / APN) \tag{6.6}$$

$$Py = A + \alpha WN \tag{6.7}$$

$$N = (A \bullet MPN) / \left[W \bullet (APN - \alpha \bullet MPN) \right] \tag{6.8}$$

As one would expect, an increase in autonomous spending (A) unambiguously raises employment, as does an increase in the propensity to consume from current income (α). Additionally, while a high MPN makes it more likely that a worker will be hired (as she will contribute more to the firm's output and therefore be worth the cost of employing her), a higher APN lowers equilibrium employment. This is so because a higher APN means that firms can hire fewer workers to reach a given production goal. Last, the ambiguity of the effect of wages is reflected here: multiplied by APN, it is a negative, while multiplied by $\alpha \bullet MPN$ – an expression that includes the propensity to consume – it is a positive.

Before adding those elements that will allow us to discuss currency prices, it would be worthwhile to consider how MMT policies would affect equation (6.8). The primary goal, of course, is to reach full employment: if $N < N_f$, then we should engage in deficit spending until $N = N_f$. This is not accomplished, however, by the traditional Neoclassical Keynesian method of simply raising A via an increase in government spending. There are several reasons for this. First, it requires a very accurate estimate of how much the D curve needs to be shifted in order to hit N_f on the Z curve. Not only is this extremely difficult in itself, but there are myriad time lags involved in getting the information necessary to make the forecast. Second, even if all the information were available instantly, there is yet another time lag associated with passing new legislation to address problems every time they emerge. The third drawback is the fact that such ad hoc legislation is open to abuse as representatives of various constituencies work to gain a larger slice of the pie, regardless of the scope of the unemployment problem in their region. Last, it is entirely possible that the Z curve may become extremely steep or even vertical before it reaches N_f. In that event, there simply is no shift of D that will achieve full employment. Traditional Neoclassical Keynesian pump-priming cannot possibly hit the target.

For all those reasons, MMT policymakers prefer that the deficit spending comes via a job guarantee, where the government stands ready to hire any and all applicants unable to find work in the private sector. Such a system requires no careful estimate on the part of economic prognosticators because the unemployed self-identify: when there is a line outside the Job Guarantee Office, you know you need to spend more; when there is not, you do not. And once in place as a programme, there is no need for new legislation in the face of every downturn. In addition, it is more difficult to abuse if funding is directly linked to the numbers of jobless. Best of all, this policy shifts the Z curve rather than the D curve. It no longer matters if the Z curve goes vertical before N_f because we are not relying solely on what the Z curve represents, that is, private sector firms' decision to hire based on expected nominal sales. The job guarantee supplements the private sector rather than depending on it, and it also opens the possibility of creating employment opportunities aimed at solving social problems rather than simply earning a profit.[22]

Note that it is not evident thus far whether or not MMT-inspired policies might be inflationary, but that is no longer the relevant question. If exchange rates are not a function of domestic prices, as is posited in the MMT-as-currency-killer argument, then domestic price inflation is no longer going to be the causal factor in a currency collapse. We will return to the issue of domestic price inflation later; for now, however, the discussion will shift to whether or not MMT policies can cause a currency collapse via the actual driver of foreign exchange rates: the international financial market.

Andrade and Prates[23] and Kaltenbrunner[24] place currency price determination into this context by adapting Keynes's chapter 17 analysis of rates of return across asset classes, where the overall expected return is a function of an asset's own rate of return, its carrying costs, and the related liquidity premium. For the pound sterling, this could be expressed as:

$$r_£ = q_£ - c_£ + \ell_£ \qquad\qquad\qquad (6.9)$$

where $r_£$ is the total expected total return from holding sterling, $q_£$ is the own rate of return from holding sterling, $c_£$ is the associated carrying cost, and $\ell_£$ is the liquidity premium attached to sterling. Of course, strictly speaking, there is no own rate of return from holding sterling ($q_£$) – but that is precisely why financial market participants do not do that. They would instead use pounds to purchase sterling-denominated assets like a stock, stock index, bond, or interest-bearing account.[25] Because, empirically, interest rates tend to be the most important determinant of speculative financial capital flows, $q_£$ can be considered the rate of interest paid on sterling deposits.[26] The liquidity premium ($\ell_£$) would remain the convenience or security associated with the currency in question, something that would be the highest for the world reserve currency (currently the US dollar). And although in general one would expect carrying costs, per se, to be very low for a currency or related financial asset, $c_£$ could capture the effect of capital controls.[27] There is, indeed, a cost to investing in a country where the host places limits on the removal of financial assets.

Expanding this to other currencies means having a set of such equations, for example:

$$r_£ = q_£ - c_£ + \ell_£ \tag{6.9}$$

$$r_\$ = q_\$ - c_\$ + \ell_\$ \tag{6.9'}$$

$$r_€ = q_€ - c_€ + \ell_€ \tag{6.9''}$$

$$r_¥ = q_¥ - c_¥ + \ell_¥ \tag{6.9'''}$$

where each r is being driven towards equality with the others. Completing the model requires the addition of one more variable showing the expected appreciation of the currency in question relative to the base currency. The most logical base currency is the world's reserve, which today is the US dollar. This modification gives (dropping out the equations for the yen and euro for convenience – they, too, would have an "a" added to their expected return):

$$r_£ = q_£ - c_£ + \ell_£ + a_£ \tag{6.10}$$

$$r_\$ = q_\$ - c_\$ + \ell_\$ \tag{6.9'}$$

where $a_£$ is the expected appreciation of the pound relative to the US dollar. Notice that with this addition it is no longer necessary for $(q_£ - c_£ + \ell_£) = (q_\$ - c_\$ + \ell_\$)$ in order for $r_£ = r_\$$ to be true. For example, this could be an equilibrium position:

$$(q_£ - c_£ + \ell_£) > (q_\$ - c_\$ + \ell_\$)$$

if the pound were expected to depreciate relative to the dollar by the amount of the difference, such that:

$$a_£ = (q_\$ - c_\$ + \ell_\$) - (q_£ - c_£ + \ell_£)$$

In that event:

$$\left(q_\pounds - c_\pounds + \ell_\pounds + a_\pounds\right) = \left(q_\$ - c_\$ + \ell_\$\right)$$

so that $r_\pounds = r_\$$.

This is an absolutely vital point, for there is no reason to expect q, c, or ℓ to adjust in the event that one currency earns an excess return over another. Say, for example, that this situation evolved:

$$r_\pounds > r_\$$$

or, which is the equivalent:

$$\left(q_\pounds - c_\pounds + \ell_\pounds + a_\pounds\right) > \left(q_\$ - c_\$ + \ell_\$\right)$$

Now which variable will adjust as financial capital flows are being attracted to the UK? There is no reason to expect this to have a significant impact on the liquidity of either currency, so $\ell_\pounds$ and $\ell_\$$ will not change. Nor is either country likely to suddenly put up or take down capital controls – indeed, developed nations tend to have extremely low barriers in the first place. Thus, $c_\pounds$ and $c_\$$ will be unaffected. It is tempting to argue that the key lies in each country's q, or rate of interest: as capital flows into the UK, $q_\pounds$ falls, and as it flows out of the US, $q_\$$ rises. Unfortunately, while this would, indeed, return us to $r_\pounds = r_\$$, central banks tend to maintain a tight grip on interest rates. It is a simple matter for the Bank of England or the Federal Reserve to sterilize any capital flows and that would be their standard operating procedure. That leaves only $a_\pounds$ to bear the burden of adjustment, which is precisely what happens.

To see how this occurs, consider the composition of $a_\pounds$:

$$a_\pounds = \left(E^e - E^s\right)/E^s \tag{6.11}$$

where E is the dollar price of pounds and the superscripts e and s designate the expected and spot prices.[28] Now consider what happens when $r_\pounds > r_\$$ and there are net financial capital flows to the UK. As agents buy UK assets, so they will bid up the value of the pounds necessary to carry out these transactions. Because a rise in the spot price of the pound is equivalent to a rise in E^s, this lowers $a_\pounds$ and moves us back towards $r_\pounds = r_\$$. Hence, the spot exchange bears the burden of adjustment such that whenever the total expected return on a currency exceeds that of another, the spot price of the former appreciates until this is no longer true.[29]

This now gives us an operational, if simplistic, theory of exchange rate determination, and one based on the manner in which currency markets actually operate. Recall equations (6.9') and (6.10):

$$r_S = q_S - c_S + \ell_S \tag{6.9'}$$

$$r_£ = q_£ - c_£ + \ell_£ + a_£ \tag{6.10}$$

Given that, in equilibrium, $r_£ = r_S$, we can write:

$$q_S - c_S + \ell_S = q_£ - c_£ + \ell_£ + a_£$$

Solving for the expected appreciation of the pound yields:

$$a_£ = (q_S - q_£) - (c_S - c_£) + (\ell_S - \ell_£) \tag{6.11}$$

If the MMT-as-currency-killer story is true, then something about MMT-inspired policies in the UK would have to cause the spot value of the pound to fall. Given that MMT policies have no direct connection to capital flows and that developed nations do not use capital controls to any significant degree, there are only three possible avenues by which this could occur: interest rates, liquidity premiums, or exchange rate forecasts. Taking equation (6.11) and dropping out capital controls yields:

$$a_£ = (q_S - q_£) + (\ell_S - \ell_£) \tag{6.12}$$

Replacing $a_£$ with $(E^e - E^s)/E^s$ and solving for the spot pound gives (see appendix for proof):

$$E^s = E^e / (1 + q_S - q_£ + \ell_S - \ell_£) \tag{6.13}$$

If MMT-inspired policies cause catastrophic depreciations, then equation (6.13) suggests five routes by which that could occur:

- $\downarrow E^e$ (fall in the expected future value of the pound relative to the dollar)
- $\uparrow q_S$ (rise in US interest rates)
- $\downarrow q_£$ (fall in UK interest rates)
- $\uparrow \ell_S$ (rise in the liquidity premium attached to the dollar)
- $\downarrow \ell_£$ (fall in the liquidity premium attached to the pound).

As there is no direct MMT reason for either monetary authority to change their interest rate target (and certainly not enough to cause a currency collapse), that leaves either a substantial change in liquidity premiums or forecasts of future pound–dollar exchange rates. I would imagine that supporters of the MMT-as-currency-killer view would argue vehemently that both could occur. However, it is difficult to see how they could support this without either the full-employment or purchasing-power-parity assumptions behind them. If MMT combined with a job guarantee creates full employment, substantial rates of GDP growth, living wages, and an opportunity to address the many social problems that the private sector ignores (climate change being at the top of the list), then why on earth would the pound fall because either agents expected it to do ($\downarrow E^e$) so or it became less liquid ($\downarrow \ell_\pounds$)? It seems that the only possible reason would be as a result of a self-fulfilling prophecy, fuelled by detractors' own vociferous complaints about a policy they do not understand. Short of that, there is no logical reason to expect a currency collapse. Indeed, the opposite may well occur as confidence in the future growth of the UK economy rises.

6.3   MMT AND INFLATION

While the above argued that there is no reason to expect MMT-inspired policies to cause a currency collapse, the question of their inflationary impact was not addressed. This was so because, while Neoclassical economics connects the two (in the sense that inflation is the cause of the currency collapse), the Post Keynesian approach separates them on the assumption that currency prices are driven by financial capital and not trade flows. However, the question of domestic inflation is nevertheless an important one and should be addressed. In the basic macro model laid out above in equations (6.6), (6.7), and (6.8), the process by which the average price level was determined was not made explicit. To do so, I will draw on the work of another Post Keynesian scholar, Michał Kalecki.

Because when we say *inflation* we really mean *consumer price inflation* that will be this model's focus. Assume for the time being that this is a closed economy with no government sector.[30] Given that and operating with the typical Kaleckian premise that workers tend to spend all their income and capitalists none of theirs, it must be true that:[31]

$$P_C Q_C = W_C N_C + W_I N_I \tag{6.14}$$

where P_C is the average price of consumer goods, Q_C is the total quantity of goods produced and sold in the consumption-goods sector, W_C is the wage rate per worker in the consumption-goods sector, N_C is the number of workers in the consumption-goods sector, W_I is the wage rate per worker in the investment-goods sector, and N_I is the number of workers in the investment-goods sector (WN is therefore the wage bill paid by firms and total income earned by workers in the sector in question). In other words, workers in the consumption-goods and investment-goods sectors spend all their income on consumption goods, and this is the sole source of income earned by the consumption-goods sector.

The price equation can be derived from equation (6.14) by dividing through by Q_C and performing a few other simple manipulations (see appendix for proof):

$$P_C = (W_C N_C / Q_C)[1 + (W_I N_I / W_C N_C)] \tag{6.15}$$

Note that since the only cost of production at the macro level is labour cost, $W_C N_C$ represents total costs in the consumption-goods industry. Divided by Q_C this becomes average per-unit cost, which means that the core implication of equation (6.15) is that price/unit is a function of cost/unit. This is very intuitively appealing at both the macro and micro level: firms set price by first determining the cost of production.

To understand the rest of the equation, consider the following. Since profits in the consumption-goods sector (π_C) must logically be equal to:

$$\pi_C = P_C Q_C - W_C N_C \tag{6.16}$$

and since, according to equation (6.14), $P_C Q_C - W_C N_C = W_I N_I$, then it must be true that $\pi_C = W_I N_I$. In other words, the sole source of profit for consumption-goods firms are their sales to workers employed outside of their sector.[32] This makes perfect sense since selling only to your own workers simply allows you to recoup the cost of production. Revenue would equal costs and profits would be zero. Returning to the price equation (6.15), look at the result if we replace $W_I N_I$ with π_C:

$$P_C = (W_C N_C / Q_C)[1 + (\pi_C / W_C N_C)] \tag{6.17}$$

The average price of a consumer good is equal to its average cost, or $W_C N_C / Q_C$, plus the markup over cost that will generate profits: $(W_C N_C / Q_C) \bullet (\pi_C / W_C N_C)$. For example, say the following were true:

- $W_C N_C = £10 \bullet 500 = £5000$
- $Q_C = 1000$
- $\pi_C = £1000$

In that event, average cost/unit is £5000 / 1000 = £5. The final price, however, is 1.2 times that, or £6, because of the 20 per cent markup:

$$P_C = (£5000 / 1000)\left[1 + (£1000 / £5000)\right]$$

$$P_C = £5\left[1 + 0.2\right] = £5 \bullet 1.2$$

$$P_C = £6$$

Equation (6.17) implies that there are two possible sources of consumer price inflation: a rise in the average cost of production in the consumption-goods sector ($W_C N_C / Q_C$) or an increase in the markup ($\pi_C / W_C N_C$). Starting with the second, firms are limited in how much they can mark up products by, among other things, competitive conditions. Some sectors find it easier than others (and may adjust the markup in order to generate funds for investment, advertising, and other purposes).[33] Furthermore, over time it may be that industries in general become more or less oligopolistic. The argument can be made, for example, that in the post-Reagan/Thatcher era there has been a substantial decline in competition.[34] This would tend to raise the markup and, therefore, prices. The markup is also viewed by Kaleckians as an indicator of the relative power of capital versus labour. Powerful capital and weak labour, again a hallmark of the post-Reagan/Thatcher era, leads to higher markups, higher prices, and – though not directly the topic here but nevertheless extremely important – more uneven distributions of income. The last important insight to be gleaned from equation (6.17) is that increases in productivity are actually deflationary since they would lower N_C / Q_C. This means that W_C can rise and still leave prices stable if its increase is proportional to the productivity gains. Any rise in W_C greater than this will cause inflation; any lower will cause deflation.

In order to examine the question of how MMT-inspired policies would affect prices, it is necessary to add the income/wage bill generated by the job programme to the mix. This would begin with an alteration to equation (6.14):

$$P_C Q_C = W_C N_C + W_I N_I \qquad (6.14)$$

Now, with workers hired by a job programme (N_G) at a given wage (W_G), this becomes:

$$P_C Q_C = W_C N_C + W_I N_I + W_G N_G \qquad (6.18)$$

Carrying out the same derivation that yielded equation (6.17) gives (see appendix for proof):

$$P_C = \left(W_C N_C / Q_C \right) \left[1 + \left(\left(W_I N_I + W_G N_G \right) / W_C N_C \right) \right] \quad (6.19)$$

On the surface, it would appear that this most certainly implies that an MMT-inspired job guarantee would raise prices. There is little question that, *ceteris paribus*, an increase in $W_G N_G$ raises profits and, therefore, the markup. However, several other issues must be considered.

First, it is already true that government deficit spending ends up in profits (and household net saving, if the assumption that households spend all their income is relaxed), that is not new.[35] What would be new is the fact that the money would be much more directly focused on those in need of employment and training. And, ironically given MMT's position on the national government's lack of a budget constraint, it would almost certainly cost less to directly employ the unemployed than to indirectly *hope* to do so by stimulating the private sector. To give an idea of the magnitudes, in 2018, total government spending in the UK was £835 billion and the deficit was £32.3 billion. That budget left 1.175 million Britons unemployed and forced to suffer the many social ills associated with joblessness.[36] One study of the cost of a job programme in the US set it at $56,000/worker.[37] Converted to pounds at 2018's exchange rate puts that at just under £42,000/worker. Therefore, employing all of the unemployed in the UK in 2018 would have cost 1.175 million x £42,000=£49.35 billion, or just under six per cent of the entire government budget that year. This is a tiny price to be paid for the myriad benefits that would be reaped. The Labour Party's *Future Jobs Fund* has already shown how effective this can be, albeit on a much less ambitious scale.[38]

Still, if it is true that deficit spending tends to end up in profits and a job guarantee would have added £49.35 billion to that in 2018, the markup would therefore have been raised.[39] However, this may not be as problematic as it appears. To see this, first consider another of the benefits of a job guarantee: it places pressure on the private sector to offer a living wage. Indeed, minimum wage laws would no longer be necessary if workers were able to choose between a £10/hour fast food job or a government one that pays £15. This means that W_C would also rise, which increases in the denominator of the markup and thereby lowers prices. These facts, in combination with the general rejection of neoliberalism that would accompany MMT-inspired policies, mean that a job guarantee would tend to empower labour relative to capital and thereby lower rather than raise the markup.

Still, while the increase in W_C lowers the markup, it also raises the average cost of production: $W_C N_C / Q_C$. Depending on the magnitudes involved, it is possible that this increase in cost/unit could lead to a net rise in prices despite a decrease in markup. Even if this turns out to be the case, however – and I will argue below that it certainly does not have to be – this is not the same thing as saying MMT and a job guarantee impart an inflationary bias. A once-and-for-all increase in prices due to low-end workers finally seeing their wages catch up to historical productivity increases is a desired policy outcome, not something to be avoided. Thereafter, the goal would be for wages to stay roughly par with productivity, thereby creating price stability. And at any rate, inflation is a zero-sum game: there are always winners and losers, not just losers. The idea that it is only the latter has been encouraged by neoliberal scholars in order to justify policies that lead to economic contraction every time upward pressure is placed on wages by low unemployment rates. In both the US and the UK, the central bank rushes to the "rescue" by attempting to induce slowdown and recession, when in fact the only people they have rescued are owners of capital.

The above argues that there are forces pushing in both directions when it comes to the impact of MMT-inspired policies on prices. On the inflationary side are the rise in the markup caused by the increased deficit spending and the increase in cost/unit resulting from higher private sector wages. On the deflationary side is the downward pressure created by the rising power of labour versus capital, showing up especially as an increase in the denominator of the markup. While which side is stronger is an empirical question, there is evidence to suggest that any price rise would be moderate and, as mentioned above, once-and-for-all. This is so because the relative price stability of the post-Oil Shock era has been accomplished by holding wage increases below productivity gains while increasing the markup. In the US, for example, research suggests that the markup may have risen from roughly 20 per cent in 1980 to 60 per cent by 2016.[40] One of the side effects of MMT-inspired policies should be to lower that value to its pre-Reagan/Thatcher level. Reducing the markup to one-third of its current value creates substantial space for wages to rise and still leave prices stable. If this is not sufficient to address historical shortfalls between wage and productivity growth, then there may be a one-time rise in prices. There would not be a continuous trend towards inflation, however, unless those in charge of policy were trying to expand the economy past the point of full employment. That is obviously not what an MMT adviser would suggest. The job guarantee is meant to operate as a buffer stock of labour, providing a two-way price anchor on prices. It provides a floor price (the job-guarantee wage) and it dampens rises in wages in a boom as it provides a ready supply of skilled labour rather than forcing firms to compete for labour already employed in the private sector. The existence of a job guarantee does not imply zero inflation or even that zero inflation is desirable but rather that the policy itself promotes price stability – the price level will be more stable with it than without it.

6.4   1976 INTERNATIONAL MONETARY FUND STERLING CRISIS

A concern unique to the UK is the possibility of MMT-inspired policies leading to an event like the 1976 sterling crisis. While the above analysis should make it clear why any such fears are ill-founded, it would be worthwhile to say more on the topic as it has become associated with a false and dangerous myth. The conventional view is that stagflation, the rising price of oil, and the threat of sterling depreciation forced the government to approach the International Monetary Fund (IMF) for financial aid. Because IMF help comes with strings attached, these forced the UK to adopt neoliberal austerity policies even before Margaret Thatcher made this standard operating procedure. "If only," so the myth goes, "the UK had not borrowed from the IMF, the government would not have been forced down that dark path!" Chris Rogers echoes this:

> ...a substantial body of the literature argues that the Fund had a decisive influence over British economic policy making through the application of conditionality, or that crisis acted as a catalyst for policy learning by undermining the Keynesian paradigm and creating a realization among political elites that only policies of a broadly monetarist persuasion would be sufficient to sustain confidence.[41]

This is not, however, an accurate retelling. There is every indication that the Labour government already wanted to do exactly what the IMF "forced" them to do and that "in each case, the policy shift identified with the intervention of the IMF preceded the settlement of December 1976".[42] The confusion is due partly to the time lags between decisions made by the UK government (pre-IMF agreement) and their implementation (post-IMF agreement) and deliberate attempts by Labour to deflect blame.[43] In addition, there is evidence that the Treasury actually encouraged "perceptions of crisis in the foreign exchange markets despite preferences for depreciation, and that the IMF settlement was broadly in line with fiscal cuts the Treasury believed necessary".[44]

This is relevant to the current discussion not only because it is related to fears of sterling depreciation, but it points to a significant development in erstwhile populist politics in the UK.[45] This right-leaning shift in the supposedly left-leaning party emphasizes why it must be made clear that there *is* an alternative, and that alternative is Post Keynesian economics and particularly MMT and the job guarantee.

6.5   CONCLUSIONS

Those arguing from the MMT-as-currency-killer perspective understand neither how MMT and a job guarantee would operate nor how the domestic macroeconomy and exchange market work. There is absolutely no reason to expect MMT-inspired policies to cause a currency collapse and if there is an adjustment in prices, it would be one-time and intentional. This is all quite clear when placed into the context of economic models with more realistic premises. In addition, a job guarantee would allow us to reduce the many social costs associated with involuntary unemployment and to address critical concerns, like climate change, that the private sector ignores. MMT and a job guarantee do not replace the market system, they actually strengthen, support, and supplement it while creating a minimum standard of living for workers commensurate with what our technology and resources can provide.

NOTES

1. Krugman 2019, Rogoff 2019, Summers 2019.
2. Mankiw 2020.
3. Brady 2020, Newman 2020, Skousen 2020.
4. Dabney 2021.
5. Johnson 1972, p. 1571. This is one of the classic, early iterations of the model.
6. Johnson 1972, p. 1563.
7. Were we studying a fixed exchange rate regime, which was the original version of the model, it would also be necessary to specify the fact that money supplies have a domestic and foreign component.
8. Johnson 1972, p. 1571.
9. Romer 2008, emphasis added.
10. Of course, the full-employment assumption places this model in an entirely different universe than MMT, wherein unemployment is considered to be the default situation and the overriding goal of policy is to eliminate it.
11. Johnson 1972, p. 1564.
12. Johnson 1972, p. 1570.
13. The story usually told with equation (6.4') concerns monetary policy and how when a central bank raises the supply of money, this causes inflation. However, it is premised on the assumption that the central bank can force unwanted cash on people and/or raise people's incomes. It can do neither. But, as it is a fair description of the effect of an expansionary MMT policy (i.e., it will create new income), I will not take issue with that here.
14. One could also add k being constant, but that would not substantially affect the argument here.
15. Harvey 2012.
16. Bank for International Settlements 2019, p. 3. Based on the bank's report of daily turnover being $6.6 trillion/day. This was multiplied by the approximate number of working days in a year, 250.
17. World Trade Organization 2020, p. 17.
18. Not that this should necessarily be a policy goal.
19. Keynes used nominal as opposed to real sales because he believed that this was the world in which business enterprises existed, particularly in the short run. Their contracts are in nominal terms, their sales are in nominal terms, they pay workers in nominal terms, etc. Over the course of decades, it may become neces-

sary to focus more on real values as price levels vary, but not, argued Keynes, in general.

20. Keynes actually allows for some forms of consumption to be autonomous and some forms of investment, etc., to be affected by changes in employment. However, none of that would change the conclusions here.
21. Keynes 1936, p. 267.
22. Note that a job guarantee would also increase A, or the intercept of the D curve. This may appear to then create the same problems the Neoclassical Keynesians have in trying to estimate the required A to hit full employment, but it does not. Even if the rise in the D curve creates jobs in the private sector and, therefore, outside the job guarantee, that simply shortens the line outside the Job Guarantee Office. The policy target remains simple and straightforward: how many willing workers are unemployed? We still do not have to try to guess the possible impact of A.
23. Andrade and Prates 2013.
24. Kaltenbrunner 2015.
25. Or they would purchase spot and forward contracts or currency swaps with mismatched maturity dates, which incorporates interest differentials.
26. See, for example, Cheung and Chinn 2000, Harvey 2004, 2005, Kim and Park 2020.
27. Andrade and Prates 2013.
28. Note that E is the inverse of the S used earlier in the chapter.
29. Note that this is primarily true in the developed world. In the case of a developing nation's currency, one is more likely to see at least some adjustment in q or c.
30. For sake of argument, assume that the government does supply currency and creates a base value for it by taxing. What we are really trying to omit here is direct government employment, which will be key to explaining the job guarantee.
31. Given data on consumption from income by quintile in the US, the former is not a bad approximation. If we can assume that the bottom 80 per cent of income earners tend to be workers, they do, in fact, spend in the range of 100 per cent of their income. On the other hand, if the top 20 per cent are capitalists, then the assumption that they spend none of their income is not well supported (the actual number is around 60 per cent). However, a more complex model that includes capitalist consumption would not change our results here.
32. Assuming that workers do not spend credit money created endogenously by the private sector banking system. However, relaxing that will not change the conclusions here.
33. See Eichner 1976 for an alternate microeconomics from the Post Keynesian perspective.
34. Bajgar et al. 2019.
35. Tcherneva 2012.
36. Tcherneva 2017.
37. Which resulted in a $32,500/worker income; see Paul, Darity and Hamilton 2018.
38. Trades Union Congress 2020.
39. Of course, this would also raise government revenues and lower other social welfare costs, thus reducing the impact of the increased spending. However, I will ignore that here so as to err on the side of caution in creating these estimates.

40. De Loecker, Eeckhout and Unger 2020.
41. Rogers 2009, p. 974.
42. Ludlam 1992, p. 716.
43. Ludlam 1992, Rogers 2009.
44. Rogers 2009, p. 972.
45. Ludlam 1992, p. 727.

REFERENCES

Andrade, Rogerio P. and Prates, Daniela Magalhães, 2013. "Exchange rate dynamics in a peripheral monetary economy", *Journal of Post Keynesian Economics*, 35(3), 399–416.

Bajgar, M., Berlingieri, G., Calligaris, S., Criscuolo, C. and Timmis, J., 2019. "Industry concentration in Europe and North America", OECD Productivity Working Papers, No. 18, OECD Publishing, Paris, https://doi.org/10.1787/2ff98246-en

Bank for International Settlements, 2019. *Triennial Central Bank Survey: Foreign Exchange Turnover in April 2019*, Basel: Bank for International Settlements, accessed 6 December 2020 at https://www.bis.org/statistics/rpfx19_fx.pdf

Brady, G.L., 2020. "Modern monetary theory: Some additional dimensions", *Atlantic Economic Journal*, 48(1), 1–9.

Cheung, Y. and Chinn, M.D., 2000. "Currency traders and exchange rate dynamics:

A Survey of the U.S. market", *Journal of International Money and Finance*,

20 (2001), 439–471, accessed 28 September 2022 at https://www.ssc.wisc.edu/~mchinn/cheung_chinn_JIMF.pdf

Dabney, Miranda, 2021. "Hern, Braun introduce resolution condemning Modern Monetary Theory", Press release, US Representative Kevin Hern, accessed 22 April 2021 at https://hern.house.gov/news/documentsingle.aspx?DocumentID=315

De Loecker, J., Eeckhout, J. and Unger, G., 2020. "The rise of market power and the macroeconomic implications", *The Quarterly Journal of Economics*, 135(2), 561–644.

Eichner, A., 1976. *The Megacorp and Oligopoly*, Cambridge: Cambridge University Press.

Harvey, J.T., 2004. "Deviations from uncovered interest rate parity: A Post Keynesian explanation", *Journal of Post Keynesian Economics*, 27(1), 19–35.

Harvey, J.T., 2005. "Post Keynesian versus neoclassical explanations of exchange rate movements: A short look at the long run", *Journal of Post Keynesian Economics*, 28(2), 161–79.

Harvey, John T., 2012. "Exchange rate behavior during the Great Recession", *Journal of Economic Issues*, 46(2), 313–22.

Johnson, H.G., 1972. "The monetary approach to balance-of-payments theory", *Journal of Financial and Quantitative Analysis*, 1555–72.

Kaltenbrunner, Annina, 2015. "A post Keynesian framework of exchange rate determination: A Minskyan approach", *Journal of Post Keynesian Economics*, 38(3), 426–48.

Keynes, J.M., 1936. *The General Theory of Employment, Interest and Money*, San Diego, CA: Harcourt Brace Jovanovich.

Kim, Y. and Park, C., 2020. "Are exchange rates disconnected from macroeconomic variables? Evidence from the factor approach", *Empirical Economics*, 58(4), 1713–47.

Krugman, P., 2019. "Running on MMT (Wonkish)", *The New York Times*, 25 February.

Ludlam, S., 1992. "The gnomes of Washington: Four myths of the 1976 IMF crisis", *Political Studies*, 40(4), 713–27.

Mankiw, N.G., 2020. "A skeptic's guide to Modern Monetary Theory", *AEA Papers and Proceedings*, 110, 141–4.

Newman, P., 2020. "Modern Monetary Theory: An Austrian interprevtation of recrudescent Keynesianism", *Atlantic Economic Journal*, 48(1), 23–31.

Paul, M., Darity Jr, W. and Hamilton, D., 2018. "The federal job guarantee: A policy to achieve permanent full employment", Center on Budget and Policy Priorities.

Rogers, C., 2009. "The politics of economic policy making in Britain: A reassessment of the 1976 IMF crisis", *Politics & Policy*, 37(5), 971–94.

Rogoff, K., 2019. "Modern monetary nonsense", *Project Syndicate*, 4(3).

Romer, Christina D., 2008. "Business Cycles." In *The Concise Encyclopedia of Economics*, ed. David R. Henderson, Indianapolis, IN: Liberty Fund, accessed 26 July 2020 at http://www.econlib.org/library/Enc/BusinessCycles.html

Skousen, M., 2020. "There's much ruin in a nation: An analysis of Modern Monetary Theory", *Atlantic Economic Journal*, 48(1), 11–21.

Summers, L.H., 2019. "The left's embrace of modern monetary theory is a recipe for disaster", *Washington Post*, 4 March.

Tcherneva, P.R., 2012. "Inflationary and distributional effects of alternative fiscal policies: An augmented Minskyan–Kaleckian model", Levy Economics Institute Working Paper No. 706, accessed 22 April 2021 at http://www.levyinstitute.org/pubs/wp_706.pdf

Tcherneva, P.R., 2017. "Unemployment: The silent epidemic", Levy Economics Institute, Working Papers Series, No. 895.

Trades Union Congress, 2020. "A new plan for jobs – why we need a new jobs guarantee", Research report released 4 May 2020 at https://www.tuc.org.uk/research-analysis/reports/new-plan-jobs-why-we-need-new-jobs-guarantee

World Trade Organization, 2020. *World Trade Statistical Review 2020*, Geneva: WTO, accessed 6 December 2020 at https://www.wto.org/english/res_e/statis_e/wts2020_e/wts2020_e.pdf

APPENDIX

6.A1   Deriving Keynes's Z Curve from the Neoclassical Labour Market Equilibrium Condition:

$$W / P = MPN \tag{6.5}$$

$$W / MPN = P$$

$$\left(W / MPN\right) y = Py$$

$$\left(W / MPN\right) y \left(N / N\right) = Py$$

$$\left(W / MPN\right) \left(y / N\right) N = Py$$

$$\left(W / MPN\right) APN \bullet N = Py$$

$$\left[\left(W \bullet APN\right) / MPN\right] N = Py$$

$$\left[W \left(APN / MPN\right)\right] N = Py$$

$$N = Py / \left[W \left(APN / MPN\right)\right] = \left(Py / W\right)\left(MPN / APN\right) \tag{6.6}$$

6.A2   Solving for N in Keynes's Z-D System:

$$N = (Py / W)(MPN / APN)$$
(6.6)

$$Py = A + \alpha \bullet W \bullet N$$
(6.7)

$$N = \left[(A + \alpha \bullet W \bullet N) / W \right](MPN / APN)$$

$$N = (A \bullet MPN + \alpha \bullet W \bullet N \bullet MPN) / (W \bullet APN)$$

$$N = (A \bullet MPN) / (W \bullet APN) + (\alpha \bullet W \bullet N \bullet MPN) / (W \bullet APN)$$

$$N - (\alpha \bullet W \bullet N \bullet MPN) / (W \bullet APN) = (A \bullet MPN) / (W \bullet APN)$$

$$N \left[1 - (\alpha \bullet W \bullet MPN) / (W \bullet APN) \right] = (A \bullet MPN) / (W \bullet APN)$$

$$N \left[1 - (\alpha \bullet MPN) / (APN) \right] = (A \bullet MPN) / (W \bullet APN)$$

$$N \left[(APN / APN) - (\alpha \bullet MPN) / (APN) \right] = (A \bullet MPN) / (W \bullet APN)$$

$$N \left[(APN - \alpha \bullet MPN) / (APN) \right] = (A \bullet MPN) / (W \bullet APN)$$

$$N = (A \bullet MPN) / (W \bullet APN) \left[APN / (APN - \alpha \bullet MPN) \right]$$

$$N = (A \bullet MPN \bullet APN) / \left[(W \bullet APN^2 - W \bullet APN \bullet \alpha \bullet MPN) \right]$$

$$N = (A \bullet MPN) / \left[(W \bullet APN - W \bullet \alpha \bullet MPN) \right]$$

$$N = \frac{A \bullet MPN}{\left[W \bullet (APN - \alpha \bullet MPN) \right]}$$
(6.8)

6.A3   Solving for the Spot Pound:

$$a_\pounds = \left(q_\$ - q_\pounds\right) + \left(\ell_\$ - \ell_\pounds\right) \tag{6.12}$$

$$\left(E^e - E^s\right)/E^s = \left(q_\$ - q_\pounds\right) + \left(\ell_\$ - \ell_\pounds\right)$$

$$\left(E^e - E^s\right) = \left[\left(q_\$ - q_\pounds\right) + \left(\ell_\$ - \ell_\pounds\right)\right]E^s$$

$$-E^s = \left[\left(q_\$ - q_\pounds\right) + \left(\ell_\$ - \ell_\pounds\right)\right]E^s - E^e$$

$$E^s = E^e - \left[\left(q_\$ - q_\pounds\right) + \left(\ell_\$ - \ell_\pounds\right)\right]E^s$$

$$E^s + \left[\left(q_\$ - q_\pounds\right) + \left(\ell_\$ - \ell_\pounds\right)\right]E^s = E^e$$

$$E^s\left[\left(1 + \left(q_\$ - q_\pounds\right) + \left(\ell_\$ - \ell_\pounds\right)\right)\right] = E^e$$

$$E^s = E^e / \left(1 + q_\$ - q_\pounds + \ell_\$ - \ell_\pounds\right) \tag{6.13}$$

6.A4   Deriving Kalecki's Price Equation:

$$P_C Q_C = W_C N_C + W_I N_I \tag{6.14}$$

$$P_C = W_C N_C / Q_C + W_I N_I / Q_C$$

$$P_C = W_C N_C / Q_C + \left(W_I N_I / Q_C\right)\left(W_C N_C / W_C N_C\right)$$

$$P_C = W_C N_C / Q_C + \left(W_C N_C / Q_C\right)\left(W_I N_I / W_C N_C\right)$$

$$P_C = \left(W_C N_C / Q_C\right)\left[1 + \left(W_I N_I / W_C N_C\right)\right] \tag{6.15}$$

6.A5   Deriving Kalecki's Price Equation with a Job Programme:

$$P_C Q_C = W_C N_C + W_I N_I + W_G N_G \tag{6.18}$$

$$P_C = W_C N_C / Q_C + W_I N_I / Q_C + W_G N_G / Q_C$$

$$P_C = W_C N_C / Q_C + (W_I N_I / Q_C)(W_C N_C / W_C N_C) + (W_G N_G / Q_C)(W_C N_C / W_C N_C)$$

$$P_C = W_C N_C / Q_C + (W_C N_C / Q_C)(W_I N_I / W_C N_C) + (W_C N_C / Q_C)(W_G N_G / W_C N_C)$$

$$P_C = (W_C N_C / Q_C)\left[1 + (W_I N_I / W_C N_C) + (W_G N_G / W_C N_C)\right]$$

$$P_C = (W_C N_C / Q_C)\left[1 + ((W_I N_I + W_G N_G) / W_C N_C)\right] \tag{6.19}$$

7.   The Eurozone and Brexit

Stuart Medina Miltimore and William Mitchell

7.1   INTRODUCTION

In this chapter, we explore the evolution of the Economic and Monetary Union (EMU) and argue that there was little possibility that an effective currency union could be achieved given the economic, historical and cultural differences between the nations involved and the influence of the emerging neoliberal ideology in the 1980s, which created a dysfunctional architecture that appeased those differences.

We also consider where the more recent decision by the British government, following their June 2016 Referendum, to leave membership of the European Union fits into this narrative.

Initially, we take an historical approach to understand the difficulties that nations with very different economic structures and a lack of cultural solidarity face when they try to fix exchange rates and adopt a common currency. This approach also allows us to understand how the growing dominance of neoliberal economics in the 1970s and 1980s intersected with post-World War II Franco-German rivalry to create the EMU, which we argue has undermined prosperity, denies reality, and rejects viable solutions, thus exposing the Member States to a state of ongoing crisis and stagnation.

The great European political leaders in the immediate post-World War II period were not motivated to put the European economies into a straitjacket of austerity and hardship. Their aspiration was to achieve peacetime prosperity and they devised the 'European Project' as an ambitious plan for European integration. Their goal was to ensure that there were no more large-scale military conflicts fought on continental European soil and they broadly embraced a Keynesian economic policy consensus with governments committed to sustaining full employment and reducing inequality.

Politicians learned from the Great Depression that without major government intervention, capitalism creates periodic crises with elevated and persistent mass unemployment. The Keynesian era of macroeconomic policy that followed World War II saw governments using deficits to supplement private spending to ensure there were sufficient jobs for all those who wanted to work. Governments around the world found the recipe for sustained material prosperity for their citizens. This consensus started to break down in the mid-1970s.

Within this broad policy consensus, it was Franco-German rivalry that conditioned the process of integration. France's aim was to stop Germany from ever invading it again. It considered an integrated Europe to be the means for it to consolidate its dominant position in European affairs but wanted to surrender as little national sovereignty as possible. On the other hand, Germany was a pariah and sought a restoration of national pride through economic success. The 'European Project' offered the Germans a way back as a world citizen. The problem was that their obsessive fear of inflation, stemming from the 1920s, meant that negotiations over the new Europe would be conditioned by Bundesbank culture. This contrast in ambitions constrained the process of integration until the 1980s.

In the 1960s and 1970s, the European leaders commissioned studies into what structures are required for federations to function effectively. Economists studied Australia, Canada and the United States (US) and concluded that such a federation would require a strong fiscal function at the federal level, integrated closely with the central banking function, and both embedded into a federal parliament system to provide democratic legitimacy. Such a fiscal function would stand ready to make permanent transfers between the geographic units within the federation to resolve asymmetric shocks which threaten convergence. The studies uniformly concluded that the historical, cultural and political situation within the European Community would make it unlikely that such a structure could be successfully agreed upon. In particular, France and Germany were reluctant to surrender their sovereignty on terms that would be acceptable to the other.

The situation changed in the 1980s with the advent of Monetarist economic thinking emerging as the dominant school of thought in macroeconomic policymaking. France was emboldened to pursue a 'fort franc' policy that brought it closer to the Bundesbank culture, which reflected an obsessive fear of inflation and a willingness to embrace fiscal rectitude. Once that change in geopolitical relations occurred, it was a small step for Jacques Delors to take to produce the monetary architecture that was laid at Maastricht.

Europe embraced neoliberalism and embedded the ideology in the very legal structure that binds the Member States. This ideology led to a certain homogeneity among the different political parties with respect to macroeconomic policy, which made it easy for the then European Commission to introduce the fiscal rules known as the Stability and Growth Pact (SGP). The culture of austerity was then prominent in Europe and the consequences have been stagnating growth, elevated levels of unemployment with very high levels of youth joblessness, cuts in services, wages, pensions and increasing divergence. The very opposite to what the European elites promised the citizens of Europe.

Many progressive thinkers seem to think the problems can be resolved within the structure of the EMU, with tweaks such as the introduction of a Europe-wide unemployment scheme. Our contention is that the euro is the problem. The problems are embedded in the architecture of the Union defined by the Treaties which are almost impossible to reform.

We argue that it is better for the Treaties to be dissolved and the Member States of the EMU to restore their currency sovereignty. They are then able to negotiate mutually agreeable arrangements in the form of intergovernmental agreements rather than tie themselves in a neoliberal straitjacket within the Treaty system.

We also consider the exit by the United Kingdom (UK) from the European Union, noting that the EMU is separate from the Union. We construct that discussion within the context of the European Union as exemplifying the most advanced form of neoliberalism known and the need for the British people to reassert their democratic voice.

7.2   WHY A SINGLE CURRENCY?

At the end of World War II, most of the world nations entered the Bretton Woods agreement to fix their exchange rates and tie them to the value of gold via the US dollar. The latter was convertible into gold at a fixed price and so the designers of the system considered this would maintain global financial stability. The use of the US dollar as a reserve currency exposed the instability of the Bretton Woods system early on. Economist Robert Triffin warned in the early 1960s that the system required the US to run balance of payments deficits so that other nations, who used the US dollar as the dominant currency in international transactions, were able to acquire them. By the 1960s, nations started to worry about the value of their growing US dollar reserve holdings and whether the US would continue to maintain gold convertibility. These fears led nations to increasingly exercise their right to convert their US dollar holdings into gold, which significantly reduced the stock of US-held gold reserves. The so-called Triffin paradox was that the Bretton Woods system required the expansion of US dollars into world markets, which also undermined confidence in the dollar's value and led to increased demands for convertibility back into gold. The loss of gold reserves further reinforced the view that the US dollar was overvalued and, eventually, the system would come unstuck.[1]

Realising the system was unviable, the US President abandoned convertibility in August 1971. For the next two years, under the guise of the Smithsonian Agreement, there were attempts to reform the fixed exchange rate system. But inevitably, it collapsed and by the mid-1970s, most nations adopted floating exchange rates, which hailed the advent of the fiat currency era.

However, the European Economic Community (EEC) nations adopted their own variants, first, 'le serpent l'intérieur du tunnel', then just the snake, and when those systems failed, they introduced the European Monetary System in 1978 to maintain currency stability across a membership that was disparate in terms of economic structure and trade strength.

The problem for the EEC nations was that the first major initiative of the newly formed EEC in 1962 created the Common Agricultural Policy (CAP), which was motivated by the French desire to protect its farmers and gain subsidies from Germany, and the German desire to expand its industrial export market. However, the administrative complexity of the scheme forced the Member States to maintain fixed exchange rates. The goal was currency stability to support the CAP, but that aim proved impossible to achieve, as the course of history over the next several decades demonstrated. Even in the 1960s, as the mark strengthened in value and became dominant, France and Italy had to endure regular currency crises and suppress domestic economic activity to maintain the agreed parities.

All the pre-EMU currency arrangements were dominated by the German mark, in recognition of the strength of its export machine and the other nations were then forced to maintain domestic policy to continually defend their vulnerable currencies. The resulting bias towards high levels of unemployment and high interest rates proved to be politically difficult. The experience should have taught the European nations that entering a currency union would be a fraught exercise.

Which raises the question: why would the European nations choose to surrender their currencies altogether and adopt the euro? To answer this question, we need to explore the ideological underpinnings that established the European Union (EU) as a neoliberal project. The euro can be best understood as another cog in the wheel driving the process of depoliticisation of European democracies – the creation of institutions that are irresponsive to popular demands such as an independent central bank or complex legislative processes estranged from the citizen. The single currency illustrates how limitations to monetary sovereignty not only constrain the space available for economic policy but also define boundaries for a popular democracy.

The series of European treaties signed in the 1950s – the European Coal and Steel Community, the Treaties of Rome establishing the EEC and Euratom – were drawn in the spirit of overcoming nearly a century of Franco-German enmity and avoiding a repetition of the great wars that had wreaked havoc on the continent for more than a century. While the Treaty of Rome (1957) was designed to establish a spirit of trust and cooperation amongst European countries through trade and economic integration, the leaders in the 1960s and 1970s were more ambitious and sought to further the process of monetary integration.

The pro-European proponents wanted more than a regime of pegged exchange rates. The euro was touted as a symbol that would bring together Europeans in a shared identity. As former European Commission (EC) President Jean-Claude Juncker remarked, once citizens held the new notes and coins in their hands at the start of 2002, 'a new we-feeling would develop: we Europeans'.[2]

But we need to take a step back to understand how the great European rivals – France and Germany – agreed to surrender their own currencies and enter an arrangement that constrained the democratic choices of each.

The Treaty of Rome formalised the 'European Project' – which was a plan for increased European integration – to accomplish the goal of lasting peace. But the process of integration was dominated by Franco-German rivalry with France seeking 'European-level' structures that they could dominate, which would stop any further German military aggression. Their aim included maintaining as much national sovereignty as was possible and created integrated initiatives as intergovernmental agreements. Germany's motivation was to salvage its national pride by repairing its damaged economy. They saw the 'European Project' as a way back as a world citizen. But their inflation angst, which arose from their experience in the 1920s, was ever-present and any negotiations with France on economic integration reflected the stern culture of the Bundesbank. Up until the 1980s, it was these factors that constrained any significant movements towards a monetary union.

The 1970 Werner Report[3] and the 1975 study by the MacDougall Committee[4] both sought to outline the requirements for the creation of a full economic and monetary union. After studying successful federations such as Australia, Canada and the US, both reports concluded that an effective economic and monetary union would require a strong fiscal presence at the federal level that had political legitimacy through a European-level parliament. The latter study concluded that 'It is most unlikely that the Community will be anything like so fully integrated in the field of public finance for many years to come as the existing economic unions we have studied.'[5] As a result, there was little progress towards a monetary union during this period because neither France nor Germany could agree to cede sovereignty, such were their suspicions of each other.

In the 1980s, the situation changed markedly, not because there was any shift in the long-standing Franco-German rivalry nor any cultural enlightenment, but, rather, because the Monetarist surge within the academy in the 1970s spread into central banking and treasury departments. The idea of a single currency seemed advantageous from the German perspective because they could preserve German competitiveness from the periodic revaluations that the Deutschmark experienced. They knew, however, that this would require significant changes to domestic policy, to reduce unit costs. However, it was other EEC Member States such as France and Italy who pushed for monetary integration. Both countries were fed up with the hard-currency interest policy of the Bundesbank, which, given the premise of the free movement of capital in a financialising common market, had become the de facto central bank of Europe. They were also irked, the French above all, by the periodic necessity of devaluing their currency vis-à-vis the Deutschmark to maintain their competitiveness.[6]

For the first time, the old Keynesian planning ministry in France was overtaken in policy influence by an increasingly Monetarist-influenced finance ministry. The Barre Plan in 1976 effectively abandoned the Gaullist 'Keynesian' influence, and, later, Delors pursued a 'fort franc' policy under Mitterand's famous 'tournant de la rigueur' in 1983. At this time, Franco-German rivalry morphed into a Monetarist consensus, Bundesbank-style between the two nations. Across Europe, unemployment became a policy tool aimed at maintaining price stability rather than a policy target, as it had been during the Keynesian era up until the mid-1970s.

The Delors Report[7] ignored the findings of the Werner and MacDougall Reports and, instead, embraced the new neoliberal orthodoxy, which channelled the Monetarist disdain for government intervention by designing the EMU architecture to deliberately suppress the capacity of national fiscal policy to maintain low unemployment. Delors appeased the French by maintaining economic policymaking at the national level and the Germans with the accompanying harsh fiscal rules.

The reunification of Germany also created anxiety in the UK and France. For the French, a 'federal' Europe could help curb a reunified Germany within the principle of 'not a German Europe, but a European Germany'. The Germans were initially not enthusiastic about monetary union, but Chancellor Kohl gave way for fear of losing support for German reunification. When major allies in Kohl's political camp threatened to rebel, he overcame their resistance by ensuring that the common monetary regime would follow the German model, with the European Central Bank as a copy of the Bundesbank writ large.[8]

Beyond European powers jockeying for position, the economics profession also provided an ideological underpinning for the euro. The economists that had informed the Werner and MacDougall enquiries were of a Keynesian orientation, which ran counter with the emerging Monetarism that became the dominant voice in the Delors Committee. Further, the so-called theory of Optimal Currency Areas (OCA), which defined the conditions that were essential for nations to share a single currency,[9] predicated against the European states joining in such a union.[10]

The EMU proponents in the late 1980s largely ignored the requirements set out in the OCA literature to be significant for their plans. Wyplosz[11] said that the EC 'officials did not waste much time on the issue, which they saw as mainly political'. The Maastricht Treaty was more about making progress towards the adoption of the single currency and the requisite institutional changes that would be required to accommodate this process rather than a deep analysis of whether it would be optimal. But the declaration that the OCA literature was irrelevant went much deeper than that.

In the 1990 *One Market, One Money* publication by the European Commission[12] concluded that the OCA literature provided a 'rather limited framework whose adequacy for today's analysis is questionable'. They claimed that the 'whole approach ignores policy credibility issues which have been stressed by recent macroeconomic theory' (p. 46), which was code for OCA being associated with the Keynesian view that fiscal policy provides an effective means of stabilising economies hit with private spending fluctuations. The 'policy credibility issues' related to the unproven Monetarist assertions that fiscal policy was ineffective and caused inflation, which can only be controlled with tight monetary policy.

Any serious application of the OCA theory would have been highly inconvenient to the proponents of the EMU. Of the conditions necessary to satisfy the existence of an OCA, only those relating to openness of trade between the nations could be reasonably met. The other conditions were not satisfied. The Treaty deliberately negated the capacity for a federal fiscal capacity to redress regional unemployment and there was no sense that labour was mobile. Eichengreen[13] cautioned that while capital movements would be unimpeded in the EMU, a depressed region could hardly expect job saving capital inflow, and that regional disparities brought about by movements in the economic cycle are resolved more effectively by fiscal transfers rather than labour or capital movement. De Grauwe[14] argued that the EMU proponents were ideologically selective in their use of the prevailing knowledge.

Whichever way you wish to interpret the OCA theory, it is obvious that the group of nations that entered the EMU did not remotely satisfy the conditions required to ensure that the adoption of a common currency would be beneficial overall. The result was that the only adjustments open to them once a major private spending collapse occurred would be very costly, a point ignored by the EMU proponents.

Europe was to understand that folly more clearly with the onset of the Global Financial Crisis (GFC).

7.3   A DYSFUNCTIONAL UNION CREATED

British economist Wynne Godley wrote a short but prescient essay in 1992 on the Maastricht Treaty, which laid out the architecture for the EMU in that year. He opined:

> The central idea of the Maastricht Treaty is that the EEC countries should move towards an economic and monetary union, with a single currency managed by an independent central bank. But how is the rest of economic policy to be run? As the treaty proposes no new institutions other than a European bank, its sponsors must suppose that nothing more is needed. But this could only be correct if modern economies were self-adjusting systems that didn't need any management at all.[15]

The original sin of the EMU was that it was concocted during the neoliberal era which saw the abandonment of Keynesian fiscal policy dominance as a means of sustaining full employment. The mainstream economists engendered a disdain for discretionary fiscal policy being used to smooth out fluctuations in private spending and maintain low levels of unemployment. To politically justify this paradigm shift, the economists claimed that, in fact, the full employment level of unemployment had shifted upwards and only structural reforms, such as cutting welfare payments, lowering the minimum wage and the like, could reduce it. The policymakers shifted from seeing unemployment as a policy target to using it as a policy tool to discipline any inflationary pressures. In terms of macroeconomic policy assignment, fiscal policy was subjugated to a renewed emphasis on monetary policy aimed at keeping inflation stable and low. It was claimed that if this goal was attained, the economy would naturally equilibrate at full employment.[16]

Italian economist Franco Modigliani, who was one of the economists who coined the term Non-Accelerating Inflation Rate of Unemployment (NAIRU), which drove the bias towards monetary policy dominance over fiscal policy, reflected on his legacy during a lecture he gave in Freiburg on 6 April 2000:

> Unemployment is primarily due to lack of aggregate demand. This is mainly the outcome of erroneous macroeconomic policies ... [the decisions of Central Banks] ... inspired by an obsessive fear of inflation ... coupled with a benign neglect for unemployment ... have resulted in systematically over-tight monetary policy decisions, apparently based on an objectionable use of the so-called NAIRU approach. The contractive effects of these policies have been reinforced by common, very tight fiscal policies.

The European Treaties pursued this subjugation of fiscal policy to the extreme by declining to establish a European-level fiscal function, while at the same time, designing the Stability and Growth Pact (SGP) to ensure minimal flexibility existed for Member States to use their retained fiscal functions. Their fiscal capacity was limited by layered rules for deficit (less than 3 per cent of GDP), spending increases (limited by changes in GDP) and public debt rules (less than 60 per cent of GDP). The EMU had a single currency and a single monetary policy, and, in theory, each country would be allowed to operate independent fiscal policies. But, in effect, lacking the support of a central bank that could finance deficits or purchase treasuries when needed, and bound by the Maastricht criteria, government spending would be limited by tax receipts and borrowing in the open market in competition with the private sector.[17] Surrendering their currencies meant that they became dependent on private bond investors to run fiscal deficits, and, during the GFC that became unworkable.

In federations like the US or Canada, central governments are currency issuers and spending logically precedes taxation. Taxes drive money and central banks carry out monetary operations to set the interest rates. In the EMU this sequence is reversed. Member States are reduced to the status of currency users, much like municipalities or regional governments, and they need to raise taxes or borrow money before spending. Interest rates on their bond issues are determined by the market.[18]

The austerity bias became apparent even before the euro was introduced. Strict convergence criteria imposed by the Maastricht Treaty forced many European economies to cut government spending and increase taxes in order to meet the final transition stage criteria for entry to the EMU in the late 1990s. Consequently, GDP growth rates were suppressed, and unemployment remained at elevated levels. The European debates about how the common currency would work were dominated by German concerns about inflation and their distrust of Southern Europeans, who were suspected of not taking the convergence criteria seriously. These suspicions had two major consequences. First, it meant that the new union would have no integrated fiscal and monetary function. Second, given the fiscal tools were left at the Member State level, the Germans insisted that tight constraints be placed on the Member States to stop them abusing the common currency. The level of distrust was so high that the Member States should have realised then that it would be difficult to work together to make the common currency deliver prosperity for all the European nations that joined.

The SGP included a 'preventative arm' and 'reinforced surveillance of budgetary positions and the coordination of economic policies'. This was completed with a 'corrective arm' which outlined a process for the elimination of so-called 'excessive deficits'.[19] Although some deficit leeway above 3 per cent for nations that were enduring major recessions was provided, it would soon be seen that the SGP undermined the capacity of the national governments to respond to recessions with increased discretionary spending.[20]

The arbitrary 3 per cent limit to fiscal deficits condemned governments to compensate the effect of automatic stabilisers, which increased fiscal deficits, with contractions in discretionary spending if they wanted to avoid fines and other corrective actions from the EC. The damage goes beyond the inability to manage the economic cycle. Austerity policies pursued after the GFC have permanently depressed public investment for most countries. Underinvestment has compromised public services, education, healthcare, public infrastructures and research and development. These are spending items that not only provide wellbeing for current generations but are also critical for improved productivity in the long run.

The fiscal rules are also reinforced by surveillance through the Excessive Deficit Mechanism. The system allows EC technocrats to overrule fiscal decisions of elected governments in the Member States. The arrangements revealed a blind belief that constraints on fiscal policy would allow the central banks to maintain price stability and that the operation of 'automatic stabilisers' that are built into national government fiscal positions would be sufficient to restore growth during recessions.

The Treaties also established the System of European Central Banks (ESCB) with the former national central banks integrated with the newly created European Central Bank (ECB), which had charge of monetary policy. Consistent with the developments in the economics profession, the ECB was declared independent from the political process and charged with maintaining price stability in the monetary union.

Article 123 of the Treaty on the Functioning of the European Union (TFEU) – the so-called no 'bailout' clause – banned overdrafts or any other type of credit facility with the ECB or with the national central banks in favour of Union institutions, bodies, offices or agencies, central governments, regional, local or other public authorities, other bodies governed by public law, or public undertakings of Member States, as well as the purchase directly from them by the ECB or national central banks of debt instruments.

Together with the SGP rules, the no bailout clause was intended to force fiscal discipline on the Member State governments. The intent was to force the Member States to 'obey' the dictates of the private bond investors, who knew that the government debt carried credit risk because the Member States had surrendered their currency sovereignty. It was argued that this external discipline would ensure that deficits remained within the fiscal limits.

As we will see in Section 7.4, the hopes for the system were far-fetched and the defects in the monetary architecture manifest very early in the monetary union's history.

7.4   THE CRACKS APPEAR IMMEDIATELY AND WIDEN AS TIME PASSES

Ironically, soon after the adoption of the common currency, it would be Germany, followed by France, who would first trespass beyond the SGP limits during the 2003 recession. The transgression had little consequence for both countries and no action was taken after a stand-off between the European Council and the Commission, and some rule changes demanded by Germany. In the aftermath, Germany implemented the 2004 Hartz reforms which would enhance its economy's competitiveness by disciplining its labour force through cutbacks in the welfare state and deregulation of the job market which created the Mini-job era, a diminished form of employment with pay and conditions stripped back significantly. The reforms ensured that Germany's export-led growth model, which relied on repressing domestic demand and keeping unit costs relatively low, could continue after the nation lost its ability to manipulate the mark exchange rate. Germany effectively undermined the stability of the EMU by adopting a model which, given the dominance of intra-EU trade, relied on its currency partners running large external deficits, while it suppressed its own imports. German unit labour costs were persistently lower than the other Member States.[21] Germany has regularly posted external trade surpluses between 6 and 8 per cent of GDP in the following years. In effect, Germany learned that a managed process of 'internal devaluation' pursued alone would improve German exports at the expense of its EMU partners.

There were two negative consequences of this growing imbalance in an environment where the ECB ran a one-size-fits-all interest rate regime. First, the less competitive Member States, which were now unable to enjoy the benefits of any exchange rate flexibility within the Eurozone, were forced to run burgeoning trade deficits by Germany's mercantilist strategy. That, alone, was unsustainable. Second, the massive trade surpluses that Germany was running could not find a reasonable return in the German markets and, consequently, investors exported the capital to the other Member States. The ECB had set interest rates to suit the recessed German economy (2003) at a time when the Southern states were growing. The uniform interest rate was clearly not suitable for a geographic area as large as the EMU where the economies were of vastly different industrial structures. The combination of low rates and a flood of capital into the 'periphery' fuelled the massive rise in private sector indebtedness in nations where real estate bubbles such as in Spain, Ireland and the UK developed in the lead-up to the GFC.

The introduction of the euro created an asymmetry in adjustment that is like that observed under the gold standard where increases in the amount of money requires that countries previously increase their gold reserves. But higher reserves do not imply an automatic expansion of spending and money supply since excess gold was frequently sterilised. Similarly, in the EMU, debtor countries are forced to reduce their deficits, prices and wages. However, creditor countries, which are accumulating balances in euros, are not required to adopt expansionary measures. When peripheral nations were forced to adjust through an internal devaluation process, Germany imposed additional costs on them by failing to take expansionary measures and not allowing increases in its imports.[22]

There was a misplaced confidence in the stability of the system leading into the GFC. Basking in smug complacency, the European elites presented the euro as a resounding success and waxed lyrical about the macroeconomic stability of the area with the low inflation rates presented as evidence of success.[23]

But history soon overtook this hubris and the disruption in financial markets that became the GFC exposed the dysfunctional euro architecture. On a global basis, the GFC exposed the fragility of a deregulated global financial system built on financial securitisation, shadow banking, lax prudential oversight, which had delivered relatively modest GDP growth rates, declining productivity (less investment in capital formation) and massive, unsustainable real estate bubbles. Despite the warnings of heterodox economists, governments, which had become captive to the financial speculators, overlooked the growing vulnerability of the overleveraged private sector balance sheets while celebrating their fiscal surpluses. These surpluses were only possible because the private credit binge allowed spending growth to be maintained in the face of the massive fiscal withdrawals. But predictably, the fiscal surpluses combined with burgeoning trade deficits generated record private sector deficits, creating an increasingly unsustainable debt burden.[24]

For the euro nations, the GFC quickly exposed the lack of a federal authority as a serious flaw in the design of the Union. What started as a private debt crisis soon morphed into a public debt crisis. The GFC laid bare the rashness of the decision by Member States to roll their central banks into the euro system, which meant they no longer had a lender of last resort that they could rely on. Upon relinquishing their own currencies, the 19 Member States began issuing debt in a foreign currency, which immediately introduced the problem of credit risk. These nations were from that point on beholden to the bond market investors if they were spending more than their tax revenue. Countries that had joined the EMU with a legacy of high public debt, such as Italy or Greece, found themselves in a predicament. The crisis quickly entangled nations, such as Ireland or Spain, which had fostered massive real estate bubbles and financial speculation during the previous decade, in a doom-loop scenario. Although they had not been running large fiscal deficits before the crisis, the GFC pushed their deficits out, which increased the risk of default. The bond investors also understood that a two-way dependency between banks and their sovereigns existed. Bank resolution was still the responsibility of Member States but, without the issuing capacity of a central bank, rescuing a financial institution would lead to even larger public debt burdens. A real risk of default of the peripheral nations prompted a large-scale flight-to-safety to German and other Northern European bonds. By 2010, investors were demanding increasingly higher yields for Southern European treasuries which compromised the solvency of those states.[25]

Mainstream economists constructed the GFC as signalling a global problem of excessive fiscal deficits and public debt without differentiating between the currency-issuing states, which were having no problems maintaining low yields on the debt, and the EMU states that had surrendered their currency sovereignty. Harvard economist Roberto Alesina coined the term 'expansive austerity' and convinced European policymakers that large discretionary reductions in their fiscal deficits would be successful in overcoming the crisis without causing recessions.[26] The International Monetary Fund (IMF) started talking about 'growth-friendly austerity', which of course is a misnomer. European institutions pressed Member States to embark on fiscal consolidations and doubled down on their commitment to fiscal rectitude. The EC proposed the so-called Six-Pack, a new 'Macroeconomic Imbalance Procedure', with a 'new surveillance and enforcement mechanism' and harsher sanctions for compliance failure and the obligation to reduce the 'gap between its debt level and the 60 per cent reference'.[27]

Two infamous letters sent in 2011 by ECB president Jean Claude Trichet to Spanish and Italian Premiers Zapatero[28] and Berlusconi,[29] conditioning the support of the ECB to structural reforms in the labour and other markets, caused the downfall of the latter and led the Spanish Social-Democratic premier to introduce a golden rule amendment to the Constitution and abandon discretionary stimulus packages. Greece, Portugal, Cyprus, Ireland and Spain were bailed out through the European Stability Mechanism (ESM), an agreement outside of the EU Treaties, which created a €700 billion loan facility lent by Eurozone Member States. The rescue effectively placed those countries under the supervision of the EC, the ECB and the IMF, the so-called *Troika*. The 'democratic deficit' widened.

The crisis also revealed that European solidarity was in short supply. Southern nations were accused of profligacy and former Eurogroup President Jeroen Dijsselbloem irked public opinion in those countries by condemning them for wanting to spend 'all the money on spirits and women and then ask for help'.[30] The results of the austerity were predictable with endemic stagnation and persistently high unemployment becoming the norm in the post GFC period.[31] Some refer to this decade as creating a 'lost generation', given the sustained high youth unemployment rates.

While the introduction of the ESM was constructed by the European elites as a success, the only way the monetary union has survived, and Member States have remained solvent, is because the ECB has effectively defied the no bailout restriction and funded the fiscal deficits of the Member States through its bond-buying programmes. Almost all the debt being issued by governments in the monetary union over the last several years has been purchased by the ECB.

The necessity for the ECB to engage in this way can be traced back to the initial decision by Member States to surrender their currency sovereignty, but at the same time, continue to accept the primary fiscal policy responsibility. In the early days of the GFC, bond yields rose rapidly for the Member States most impacted (Spain, Italy, Portugal etc.) and the ECB had little choice other than to suppress the discretion of the private bond markets to set yields for fear that the already recessed nations would find it difficult rolling over funding for the deficits that the recessions had created. In May 2010, the ECB introduced the Securities Markets Programme, which was the first of several large-scale government bond purchasing programmes that persist today. These programmes purchased large quantities of government debt in secondary markets and effectively took away the credit risk facing private dealers. They allowed the Member States to continue to issue debt into the primary markets and fund their deficits. Without these ongoing ECB purchases, several Member States, including Italy, would have become insolvent during the GFC and beyond.

The ECB justified the bond-buying programmes as being necessary to ensure 'a functioning monetary policy transmission mechanism by promoting the functioning of certain key government and private bond segments'[32] – that is, as a legitimate monetary policy operation. However, the reality is that they have been buying government bonds in the secondary markets in exchange for euros, which the ECB creates out of 'thin air', in quantities far beyond anything that would be required for purely operational reasons. The purpose has been to lower yields on government bonds as bond investors knew they could offload securities from distressed states onto the ECB. The ECB has been effectively funding the Member State deficits and acting contrary to the spirit, at least, of the no bailout clause in the TFEU.

The problem with that policy is not the fact that the ECB has been funding the deficits, despite the misgivings the mainstream economists might have about that practice. Rather, the problem has been that up until the pandemic, the purchases were conditional on Member States obeying the fiscal dictates of the EC and, in that vein, while they avoided the collapse of the Eurozone, they also perpetuated the austerity bias.[33]

But it is ironic that despite all the efforts of Delors and those that followed to limit the fiscal function in the EMU and impose no bailout restrictions on the ECB, the central bank they created has effectively been maintaining a type of fiscal function which fills the void left by the Treaties and maintains the solvency of the Member States. This irony exemplifies the poorly contrived architecture that the Maastricht process pushed onto the European nations.

7.5   THE NEW FISCAL POLICY DOMINANCE – TEMPORARY OR A PATH TO REFORM?

More than 12 years after the GFC there is growing awareness that the dominant New Keynesian economics paradigm has become degenerative in the Lakatosian sense. It is full of internal theoretical inconsistencies and lacks empirical veracity. In practical terms, it failed to anticipate the crisis, believing that financial markets were efficient and would not fail in the way they did. Efficient market theory was used as the authority for governments around the world to deregulate financial markets and relax prudential oversight, which, in turn, created the conditions for the crisis. Further, mainstream economists then constructed the problem that they had helped to create as one of excessive fiscal deficits and pressured governments to implement austerity remedies that prolonged the crisis unnecessarily. The fiscal positions were largely just a response to the non-government spending collapse, which should have been the policy focus.

To maintain reputation, debates amongst mainstream economists are now revolving around a temporary return to fiscal dominance within the neoclassical framework. Former IMF chief economist Olivier Blanchard 'argued that public debt may have no fiscal cost' since the 'safe rate' was historically low. Although he claimed that 'public debt reduces capital accumulation and may therefore have welfare costs' these costs could 'be smaller than typically assumed'.[34]

This sort of erroneous reasoning is now commonplace among mainstream economists, who claim they have changed their views because monetary policy has, for now, hit the so-called 'zero bound limit' rendering monetary policy momentarily ineffective. In a 2020 speech Isabel Schnabel, Member of the Executive Board of the ECB, recognised that

> The first consequence is that fiscal policy has become more important as a macroeconomic stabilisation tool. When natural rates are low and policy rates are constrained by the lower bound, a more accommodative fiscal policy is needed to lift the economy out of a low-growth, low-inflation trap ... Fiscal expansion is indispensable at the current juncture to sustain demand and mitigate the long-term costs of the crisis.[35]

The ad hoc nature of the mainstream response to their past failures is breathtaking.

While world economies were struggling before the Covid pandemic, it is now clear that the old narrative about sound finance and a reliance on private markets to solve the economic problems is discredited. The insights provided by Modern Monetary Theory (MMT) are to the fore. Not only do governments have to deal with the ongoing costs of the pandemic, but they must also face the climate crisis, which will require a substantial role for fiscal policy over an extended period. The mainstream view that there is only a temporary need for expanded fiscal support, until monetary policy normalises again, indicates that they have not learned any lessons from the last few decades, which have been marked by poorly performing economies and rising inequality.

The problem in Europe is magnified given the flawed architecture of the EMU and the bias towards austerity embedded in the legal framework. In the face of the severest downturn in economic activity since World War II, the European Council agreed in April 2020 to activate an 'escape clause' in the SGP to allow Member States to increase spending beyond deficit limits. In tandem, the ECB announced an additional bond purchasing programme – the Pandemic Emergency Purchase Programme (PEPP) – which supplemented the already significant Asset Purchasing Programmes. For the mainstream economists, this temporary suspension of rules is conditioned on the perpetuation of a low interest rate environment without any recognition that central banks can sustain zero interest rates in perpetuity.

Despite the current suspension of fiscal rules, it is hard to teach an old dog a new trick. Except for Germany, whose government deemed that it was in a fiscal position to invest heavily in economic recovery, Member States remain coy about taking advantage of the increased flexibility. An IMF review showed that, amongst developed economies, Eurozone countries were less willing to implement direct fiscal impulse measures (additional spending or forgone revenue), opting instead for equity, loans and guarantees which have a smaller fiscal multiplier effect since the aid needs to be repaid or may never even produce a cash flow into the economy.[36] Whether this reluctance is a product of an entrenched austerity bias, conditioned on years of hectoring from the EC, or whether it reflects a fear that they will have to pay a greater price in terms of fiscal cuts when the Commission resumes the Excessive Deficit Mechanism is a matter of conjecture.

But rather than risk increased deficits, the prime ministers of Italy and Spain promoted the idea of a rescue package known as Next Generation EU (NGEU) with a budget of €750 billion. NGEU gives the EC authorisation to issue debt that would be paid back in seven years after 2027 with increased national contributions to the EU Budget.[37] The package was finally approved by the Council in July 2020 following acrimonious discussions. The so-called 'Frugal Four' (Austria, Denmark, the Netherlands and Sweden), who had the sympathy of Germany in their fiscally conservative ambitions, refused to concede on the issue of permanent transfers and blamed Southern Europeans for not having done enough previously to create the necessary 'fiscal space' and fund their own recoveries.[38] Eventually, the group acquiesced to NGEU after securing rebates in their contribution to the EU budget.[39] The proposal stimulus was inadequate in quantum, given the crisis, and the delays in implementation meant that the damage has been severe. Further, it mostly took the form of loans rather than grants, as a result of an unwillingness of the Northern nations to allow permanent transfers within the Union.

Disbursement of the funds did not begin until a year later after the EC placed two bond tranches totalling €15 billion in the market[40] and approved the structural reforms plans submitted by Member States.[41] For most countries, annual transfers will not exceed 1.6 per cent of gross national income and most of the disbursement will be happening between 2022 and 2024.[42] Neither the size nor the timing of the disbursements will be sufficient to bring the nations most afflicted by the pandemic out of the recession. Also, supposedly inclusive energy transition goals of the NGEU programme are questioned by environmentalist and progressive movements who caution that funds will be hoarded by large companies[43] and invested in large-scale infrastructure projects,[44] while direct job creation and upgrading of neglected public infrastructure after decades of underinvestment will get symbolic support only. NGEU is a manifestation of the austerity bias and the continued hollowing out of the state that pervades the neoliberal coteries ruling Europe.

7.6   CAN THE EUROZONE BE FIXED?

Suboptimal outcomes in the Eurozone are the result of the institutional arrangements limiting the fiscal capacity of the Member States. There are three options as a way forward: (a) Continue as before with ongoing stagnation and growing social instability; (b) Address the dysfunctional architecture by creating a meaningful federal fiscal capacity closely linked with the central bank capacity – as in the functioning federations such as Canada and Australia. Within this context, we suggest overt monetary financing (OMF) of the Member States by the ECB become normalised practice to eliminate the reliance on private debt markets;[45] and (c) Break-up the Union, restore currency sovereignty to the Member States and engage in European agreements, where appropriate, on an intergovernmental basis, rather than a binding Treaty.

The first option does not appear to be attractive. Several ad hoc proposals have been made to work 'within' the current system, for example, the expansion of a European unemployment insurance capacity, but all fall short of dealing with the basic architectural shortcomings of the system.

Several authors have explored a federal solution with a European Fiscal Authority and European Treasury which could resort to OMF and have the capacity to issue debt.[46] The essential philosophy underpinning such a move would be that the Member States would subjugate their fiscal autonomy to a federal authority, which to gain legitimacy would be embedded in a democratically elected European government. Essentially, this is what the Werner and MacDougall committees determined would be required. This would require an acceptance that permanent transfers would be made within the federation to address asymmetrical spending shocks. The federal authority would commit its treasury and central bank resources to maintain full employment and price stability, with a Job Guarantee programme, introduced to bolster the safety net and strengthen the automatic stabilisers in the face of fluctuating non-government spending.

We do not consider the move to a truly federal Europe to be politically possible within the modern European context. In the first place, it would require major modifications to the European Treaties and thus require the assent of all EU Member States and a lengthy process of change. It is also highly unlikely that Germany or the 'Frugal Four' would ever agree to this sort of structural shift. The cultural obstacles persist against arrangements that would imply net transfers from the wealthier export economies of Northern European to Southern countries. Germany has shown an unwillingness to engage as a Member State in a true federal system where permanent transfers between states are commonplace. This reluctance is evidenced in survey data where German residents exhibited a 'low willingness to accept fiscal risk-sharing through common unemployment insurance, while a sovereign insolvency procedure aimed at strengthening market discipline is supported by a majority of the survey participants'.[47]

The paradox of the European Project is that divergence rather than the aspired convergence has become the norm.[48] Europe is split by an imaginary line that separates Northern creditor nations from Southern debtor nations. The latter have borne the brunt of the adjustment based on fiscal consolidation and internal devaluation to correct trade imbalances that both sides contributed to create. The cultural and economic fault lines in the EU help us understand why the most likely fix for the single currency will neither be a federal government nor a system of fiscal transfers.

The most likely scenario is that nations will be forced into unilateral exit, driven by social instability arising from persistent crises. Nations such as Italy have still not recovered from the GFC as a result of the austerity bias imposed. While there are strong pressures to sustain the common currency and institutional blockages exist to discourage exit, the long-term decline in material prosperity will eat away at social harmony and shift the political focus towards new arrangements.

7.7   DEMOCRACY AT STAKE

It has been argued that the evolution of the EU towards increasing power in Brussels and the imposition of technical fiscal and other rules has created a 'democratic deficit' within the Member States, where unelected Commission technocrats can impose harsh austerity settings on elected governments against their will. The experience of Greece during the GFC was an extreme example of this phenomenon. The role of the ECB in the Greek stand-off in June 2015 was particularly illuminating in this respect.

The role of the ECB since the GFC in sustaining the currency through its large-scale bond-buying programmes, yet participating in the imposition of deep austerity policies (and being a partner in the Troika) reinforces the deterioration in the quality of democracy in the deficit nations. By threatening to shut down Greece's banking system in 2015, the ECB demonstrated clearly that it had the power to cause the downfall of an elected government or to force them to adopt policies that they lacked a popular mandate for.

Further, Streeck[49] argues that all emergency relief to Member States that are in crisis are always conditional on the technocratic surveillance mechanisms introduced by the Commission, which have the capacity to override the discretion of the elected government. The peripheral nations have now entered a sort of neocolonial relationship with the Union, where some of the leading nations and EU institutions have discretion over them and their parliaments.[50] This was graphically depicted by former Spanish Premier Zapatero, who recalls how, in one of the summits dedicated to the Greek crisis, the 'text was forged in closed meetings in which usually Germany, Greece, France, the EC, the President of the Council, and, on occasions, the president of the ECB were represented. The bulk of the Governments patiently awaited the results of this peculiar work method ... before the formal council meetings.'[51] A more recent example of this phenomenon was the downfall of the Five Star and Lega Nord coalition in Italy and its replacement by Mario Draghi.[52]

The EU is far from being a true federation. The German Constitutional Court (*Bundesverfassungsgericht*) defines the EU as a 'Staatenverbund'; a special type of multilateral organisation that ties the Member States through strict legal and administrative structures, but maintains their territorial sovereignty.[53] The Constitutional Court, in a landmark ruling regarding the compatibility of the Treaty of Lisbon with Germany's basic law, made some clarifying statements.

> The extent of the Union's freedom of action has steadily and considerably increased, not least by the Treaty of Lisbon, so that meanwhile in some fields of policy, the European Union has a shape that corresponds to that of a federal state, i.e. is analogous to that of a state. In contrast, the internal decision-making and appointment

procedures remain predominantly committed to the pattern of an international organisation, i.e. are analogous to international law; as before, the structure of the European Union essentially follows the principle of the equality of states.[54]

In a federation, the central government is democratically elected, and its parliament is empowered by a constitutional process (formally or otherwise). It controls the national fiscal function and monetary policy. It is accountable to the voters for the consequences of that policy, which gives the national government democratic legitimacy. Further, it has the capacity to make permanent fiscal transfers to the states that are part of the federation. There is a sense of nation defining the way these Member States participate within the federal system.

It could be posited that the European Parliament provides the sort of democratic legitimacy that other EU governance institutions lack, but the German Constitutional Court clarifies that neither

as regards its composition nor its position in the European competence structure is the European Parliament sufficiently prepared to take representative and assignable majority decisions as uniform decisions on political direction. Measured against requirements placed on democracy in states, its election does not take due account of equality, and it is not competent to take authoritative decisions on political direction in the context of the supranational balancing of interests between the states.[55]

The important point is that the fiscal and monetary functions that normally reside in the national government (through its treasury and central bank) are severed in the EU, even though the Member States retained both fiscal policy functions and their central banks. However, monetary policy is determined by the ECB Governing Council, and transmitted through the European System of Central Banks. There is no democratic accountability in this process, although the individual Member State central banks are members of the System and the ECB has to appear before the European Parliament regularly.

Further, while the Member States retained their fiscal functions, the EU Treaties place significant constraints on the discretion of any government through the various fiscal rules and surveillance mechanisms.

A true understanding of democracy implies that it relies on institutions capable of managing the inherent conflicts present in any society between social classes and territories and within the capitalist class. It is unlikely that such clashes between interest groups can be managed without effective monetary and fiscal sovereignty or through multilateral organisations such as the EU. Without European-level political parties, trade unions, media and civic organisations, real democracy at the EU level can only be an illusion.

A restoration of currency sovereignty for the Member States in the Eurozone would enable more scope for *repoliticisation* of the economic governance

of European Member States.[56] The accountability for economic policy performance would be again closely integrated with the election process. In the
EMU, the neoliberalism has been embedded in the very structure of the legal
framework – the Treaties. That makes it very hard for an alternative political
perspective – such as socialism or social-democratic values – to thrive because
the neoliberal constraints are always in play. The restoration of Member State
sovereignty means that rival ideologies can once again contest the political
terrain and the government can then better reflect the will of the people. We
saw in 2015 how quickly the European institutions trampled the elected government of Greece, which had just been endorsed by the people via a referendum to reject neoliberal austerity.

There is still a rationale for Europe-level institutions based on intergovernmental agreements, which would pursue activities that are best achieved
through international cooperation, either because the challenges exceed
a nation's border or its resources are insufficient to execute them in isolation.
Examples include agreements on reduction of greenhouse gas emissions,
human rights and migration, and similar. But trying to force all the Member
States of the EMU to share a common currency has not proven to be successful.

7.8   THE ROAD TO BREXIT

Each step taken in the process of European integration made it increasingly
difficult to reverse. The fact that the common currency and the rules surrounding it are embedded in the very legal structure of the EU (the Treaties) means
that there is a high degree of rigidity in the arrangements because it is very hard
to change the Treaties. It is not as though a change of government will bring
a new ideological focus to policy.

The theorists of European integration speak of a functionalist approach that
was well summarised by Jean Monnet, considered one of the founding fathers
of the EEC: every decision should create a problem that would oblige leaders
to take another decision always in the right direction towards a more perfect
union.[57]

But the momentum for integration observed in the 1980s and 1990s seems
to have ground to a halt as a result of a series of crises and a heightened sense
of dysfunction in the basic architecture of the EMU. Several countries such as
Denmark, Sweden, Poland, Hungary and the Czech Republic have declined to
adopt the euro. Poland and Hungary, governed by right-leaning governments,
have clashed regularly with the EC regarding the protection of LGBTI rights[58]
and the rule of law requirements to gain access to the NGEU funds.[59] At no
point since the end of World War II have Europe's Member States confronted
each other with so much discord and hostility, nor the concept of European
unification been so imperilled. For the first time since inception, we have seen

a Member State, the UK, exit the Union after its historic Brexit referendum of June 2016.

Brexit terminated Britain's awkward membership in the European Project. Brexit became a Conservative Party project, while the Labour Party largely assumed a Remain stance, which was one of the contributing factors in its December 2019 General Election loss. Such positions were not always so. The UK entered the EEC in 1973 under the Conservative government of Edward Heath. The left-wing branch of the Labour Party, under the leadership of Michael Foot and Tony Benn, had opposed entry into the EEC precisely on the grounds that they understood that it made a socialist programme unfeasible. Leading into the first 1974 General Election, Labour promised that there would be a referendum to determine Britain's ongoing membership of the EEC. The referendum, which was held in June 1975, split the Labour Party, with its more conservative leadership, who had come under the influence of Milton Friedman's Monetarism, using it as a wedge to reduce the influence of the left wing in the Party. The referendum 'provided the opportunity for the leadership to inflict a comprehensive and decisive defeat on the Left'.[60]

The Conservatives, who were initially pro-Europe, increasingly became Eurosceptic, under the leadership of Margaret Thatcher, who perceived the EEC as promoting excessive bureaucracy, statism and interference in the market and opposed to the laissez-faire policies she preferred. She vehemently opposed the Maastricht Treaty and saw the process of integration as a betrayal to the original project of a loosely regulated association of states set up to facilitate free trade, moving towards a bureaucratic form of federalism under the control of the Franco-German axis.

In 1990, Thatcher was also opposed to joining the European Exchange Rate Mechanism (ERM), the system which established narrow fluctuation bands around a central exchange rate for each European currency and was designed to address the failures of previous exchange rate fixing mechanisms in Europe. Thatcher was aghast that the Chancellor of the Exchequer, John Major, whom she saw as falling prey to a pro-European lobby, was becoming increasingly excited about integration within the ERM and Delors's monetary union plans. The issue, ultimately, forced the resignation of Thatcher, and, her successor, Major pressed ahead with participation in the ERM.[61] However, when George Soros's Quantum Fund began a speculative attack against the pound and other European currencies on 16 September 1992, an episode known as 'Black Wednesday', the Bank of England struggled to support the exchange rate after spending more than £10 billion of its foreign reserves. Germany, responsible for triggering the episode by raising interest rates to counteract the perceived risk of inflation arising from the annexation of the German Democratic Republic, was not supportive of the beleaguered currencies. The Bundesbank refused to prop up those currencies or lower interest rates. Ultimately the

Bank of England let the pound float and depreciate by 13 per cent and never joined a European exchange rate regime again. For many, 'Black Wednesday' became 'White Wednesday' because it was the day Britain regained its policy independence.[62]

Growing Euroscepticism amongst the ranks of the Conservative Party was catalysed by the creation of Nigel Farage's Eurosceptic party UKIP, which made a dent in Conservative Party support. The UKIP threat seems to have tipped the balance in favour of Prime Minister Cameron's decision to hold a referendum which he hoped would validate Britain's membership in the EU.[63]

The 2016 Brexit referendum and its aftermath have proven to be extremely divisive. Both sides have made acrimonious accusations of lying about the issues. The Leave campaign referendum's victory was represented by Europhiles, either as the result of xenophobic deceits encouraged by the Eurosceptic press or as a populist reaction to the government's fiscal austerity policies and general discontent about the economy. On the other side 'Remainers' were reproached for using 'Project Fear', which attempted to raise anxiety about the future of the UK outside the EU, using so-called independent economic reports that were sensationalist in their predictions of doom. None of the predictions subsequently transpired.

The 'Leavers' were strongly associated with the population that had endured significant material losses as a result of globalisation and the neoliberal overlay. They had seen their communities fractured through high unemployment, loss of government services and declining public infrastructure. The issue of migration was a significant determinant of the decision to vote Leave, but these concerns are always accentuated when there is persistent mass unemployment and economic hardship.

However, opposition to EU membership was always high in the UK and support for exiting the EU never fell below 30 per cent, with a minimum in the late 1980s, polling consistently above 40 per cent thereafter.[64] Nearly two-thirds of Britons do not identify as European, one of the lowest percentages in Europe. Further, the EU barometer showed that mistrust of the EU was among the highest in the British population.[65] A survey conducted on participants in the referendum showed that the Leave vote won by wide margins in the older cohorts; the unemployed; the retirees especially those on a public pension; council and housing association tenants; those with secondary education or less; and whites. In contrast, 'the AB social group (broadly speaking, professionals and managers) were the only social group among whom a majority voted to remain (57 per cent). C1s divided fairly evenly; nearly two-thirds of C2DEs (64 per cent) voted to leave the EU.'[66]

It was clear that the hollowing out of the regions caused by neoliberal economic policies in an increasingly global world had created divisions within

British society, with the high-income urbanites predominantly supporting the Remain position and the regions, who had been left behind, supporting the Leave vote. Many of the latter had historically voted Labour, and while most Labour voters were in the former camp, the majority of Labour MPs were elected in constituencies that had voted to Leave. That point was ignored by the Labour leadership going into the 2019 General Election and was a decisive factor in their eventual loss.

We consider Brexit is better seen as an indictment of neoliberalism as represented by the EU than as an expression of 'small England' nationalism, even though the latter was clearly of influence in the outcome.

7.9   AFTERMATH OF BREXIT; OPPORTUNITY

It is still too early to assess the consequences of Britain's decision to exit the EU. It will ultimately depend on the ongoing policy response of the British government and early announcements indicated that they were aware that they would have to address the hollowing out of the Midlands and the North of England as a matter of urgency (the so-called 'levelling out' storyline).

However, the onset of the pandemic has complicated any straightforward analysis and we will have to wait some time before the impacts of Brexit, separate from the pandemic, are able to be fully appreciated.

What we know to date, however, is that the aftermath of the Brexit referendum saw a badly handled withdrawal agreement negotiation that was extended beyond the two-year period mandated by the EU Treaties and twice voted down by the House of Commons in unprecedented defeats that led to the resignation of the Theresa May cabinet.[67] The 2019 General Election called by Boris Johnson, in effect, became a second Brexit referendum and returned him to power with a 'get Brexit done' mandate and the poorest electoral turnout for the Labour Party since 1935.[68] Jeremy Corbyn's ambivalent stance, driven by deep divisions within the Labour Party, turned away many Labour voters.

The final withdrawal agreement was signed with minor changes to the Theresa May agreement regarding the more contentious issues such as the Northern Ireland backstop and fishing rights.

More than a year later the predictions of collapse of the British economy by the Remain camp have failed to materialise. While growth in the UK has been lacklustre the Eurozone has not fared any better, especially during the pandemic. But the bitterness and rancour rage on. Any piece of bad news will likely be attributed to Brexit by Europhiles. A drop in foreign trade figures observed in January 2021 was construed as the forecasted doom augured by 'Remainers'[69] but the Office of National Statistics (ONS) made it clear that as the economy adjusted to the changed circumstances, volatility was to be expected. Indeed, foreign trade experienced a robust rebound in April 2021 and monthly imports from non-EU countries were the highest since records began in January 1997. Clearly, some trade partner substitution has been observed. Factors such as stockpiling before the country departed from the customs union and fallout from the pandemic also distorted the trade figures.[70]

Analyst Wolfgang Münchau has decried that the 'forecasts of unmitigated gloom, however, have been wrong and deceitful. When economists failed to predict the global financial crisis, they did not [do] so out of malice or political bias. But their Brexit forecasts were not an innocent mistake – nor will they be remembered as such.'[71]

What should we make then of Brexit? Clearly, a nation can prosper and trade outside the aegis of the EU. Whether Britain prospers in the post-Brexit era will depend largely on the decisions taken by the British government in relation to domestic spending and taxation. If it truly pursues a nation-building exercise (including its 'levelling up' promises), invests in revitalising public infrastructure, strengthens regulative frameworks in relation to the major services (energy, transport, water etc.), preferably reversing the damaging privatisations, improves funding to local council authorities and targets job creation, then the prospects are that Brexit will not hold back the material progress of the economy. But if the government reverts to the neoliberal austerity mindset that has marked most of its current tenure (since 2010), then it is likely that Brexit will compound the damage already caused.

With the pandemic blurring the situation since Britain formally left the EU, it is hard to clearly separate out the impacts of Brexit and we will have to wait for some time to fully appreciate the costs and benefits. The ONS has tentatively concluded at the time of writing that the government seems to be acting with more flexibility than the Member States of the EU. The general government deficit (or net borrowing) was £65.3 billion during the December-quarter 2020, equivalent to 11.9 per cent of GDP; this is 4.9 percentage points above the average of the 27 EU Member States for the same period.[72]

Brexit has created an opportunity to depart from the neoliberal policies that have dominated the country since the Thatcher era. Exit from the EU was necessary but not sufficient for the implementation of a more progressive agenda. As a monetary sovereign, the UK can now decide how it utilises its resources and has the potential to secure levels of prosperity beyond reach for many of the EU's peripheral nations. EU fiscal deficit rules embedded in Treaties such as the SGP may be ignored, even though it is true that the EC had no real disciplinary mechanism available had Britain defied the rules while a Member State. Further, it is also true that the British government had been a major influence on the neoliberal direction that the Commission has taken over the last several decades. But now, Commission preapproval of general fiscal settings in Britain is a thing of the past and the European Court of Justice is no longer able to overrule legislation introduced within the British parliamentary system.

The ball is now in the British government's court, and it can no longer claim it is constrained in its policy settings by EU membership. That freedom provides more scope for progressive parties to articulate a path forward in terms of dealing with climate change, the pandemic and restoring the scope and quality of public services.

NOTES

1. Triffin, 1960.
2. Streeck, 2015: 11.
3. European Commission, 1970.
4. European Commission, 1977.
5. MacDougall Report, 1977: 11.
6. Streeck, 2015: 16.
7. European Commission, 1989a, 1989b.
8. Streeck, 2015: 17.
9. Mundell, 1961.
10. See Mitchell, 2015 for an in-depth discussion.
11. Wyplosz, 2006: 212.
12. European Commission, 1990: 46.
13. Eichengreen, 1992.
14. De Grauwe, 2006.
15. Godley, 1992.
16. Mitchell, 2015.
17. Wray, 1998: 91–3.
18. Godley, 1997; Wray, 1998.
19. European Council, 1997.
20. Mitchell, 2015.
21. Bibow, 2019.
22. Esteve et al., 2017.
23. Buti and Gaspar, 2008.
24. Godley and Wray, 1999.
25. Mitchell, 2015; Bibow, 2019.
26. Alesina, 2010.
27. Mitchell, 2015.
28. Trichet and Fernández Ordóñez, 2011.
29. Trichet and Draghi, 2011.
30. Bertrand, 2017.
31. Mitchell, 2015.
32. González-Páramo, 2011.
33. Mitchell, 2015.
34. Blanchard, 2019.
35. Schnabel, 2020.
36. IMF, 2021.
37. General Secretariat of the Council, 2020.
38. Khan, 2020.
39. Khan and Peel, 2020.
40. European Commission, 2021.

41. Euronews, 2021.
42. Red MMT, 2021; see also Darvas, 2020.
43. Dombey, 2020.
44. Scherer et al., 2021.
45. Mitchell, 2015.
46. For example, Mitchell, 2015; Cruz Hidalgo et al., 2019.
47. Dolls and Wehrhöfer, 2021 (quote from abstract).
48. Streeck, 2015: 13.
49. Streeck, 2015.
50. Alonso González, 2011.
51. Rodríguez Zapatero, 2013: 224.
52. Fazi, 2021.
53. Medina Ortega, 2014: 58–62.
54. Bundesverfassungsgericht, 2009.
55. Bundesverfassungsgericht, 2009.
56. Mitchell and Fazi, 2017.
57. Estella de Noriega, 2014.
58. Than and Baczynska, 2021.
59. BBC News, 2020a.
60. Mitchell and Fazi, 2017: 65.
61. Thatcher, 1993.
62. Mitchell, 2015.
63. Mason, 2016.
64. Ipsos Mori, 2014.
65. Dennison and Carl, 2016.
66. Ashcroft, 2016.
67. BBC News, 2020b.
68. BBC News, 2019.
69. Inman, 2021.
70. Office for National Statistics, 2021a.
71. Münchau, 2021.
72. Office for National Statistics, 2021b.

REFERENCES

Alesina, A. (2010) 'Fiscal adjustments: Lessons from recent history', Prepared for Ecofin meeting in Madrid, 15 April 2010.

Alonso González, L. (2011) 'Puede sobrevivir el euro?', *Informes de la Fundación 1º de Mayo*, Madrid, June.

Ashcroft, L. (2016) 'How the United Kingdom voted on Thursday … and why', *Lord Ashcroft Polls*, 24 June.

BBC News (2019) 'Election results 2019: Boris Johnson returns to power with big majority', 13 December.

BBC News (2020a) 'EU budget blocked by Hungary and Poland over rule of law issue', 16 November.

BBC News (2020b) 'Brexit: Theresa May's deal is voted down in historic Commons defeat', 15 January.

Bertrand, P. (2017) 'Calls for Eurogroup President to resign after "drinks and women" outrage', *Euronews*, 23 March.

Bibow, G. (2019) '20 years of the German euro are enough', *Revista de Economía Crítica*, Primer Semestre, 27, 32–46.

Blanchard, O. (2019) 'Public debt and low interest rates', *American Economic Review*, 109(4), 1197 –229.

Bundesverfassungsgericht (2009) *Act Approving the Treaty of Lisbon compatible with the Basic Law; accompanying law unconstitutional to the extent that legislative bodies have not been accorded sufficient rights of participation*, 30 June.

Buti, M., and Gaspar, V. (2008) 'The first ten years of the euro', *VoxEU*, 24 December.

Cruz Hidalgo, E., Tcherneva, P.R., and Ehnts, D. (2019) 'Completing the Euro: The Euro Treasury and the Job Guarantee', *Revista de Ecobnomía Crítica*, 27, 20.

Darvas, Zsolt (2020) 'Next generation EU payments across countries and years', 12 November, https://www.bruegel.org/blog-post/next-generation-eu-payments-across-countries-and-years (accessed September 2022).

De Grauwe, P. (2006) 'What Have We Learnt About Monetary Integration Since the Maastricht Treaty?', *Journal of Common Market Studies*, 44(4), 711–30.

Delors Report (1989) See European Commission (1989a and 1989b).

Dennison, J., and Carl, N. (2016) *The Ultimate Causes of Brexit: History, Culture and Geography*. [Online]. https://blogs.lse.ac.uk/politicsandpolicy/explaining-brexit/ (accessed 2 August 2021).

Dolls, M., and Wehrhöfer, N. (2021) 'Attitudes towards euro area reforms: Evidence from a randomized survey experiment', *European Journal of Political Economy*, 67, March, 101971.

Dombey, D. (2020) 'Spanish companies jostle for EU recovery fund billions', *Financial Times*, 16 December.

Eichengreen, B.J. (1992) 'Should the Maastricht Treaty be saved?', *Princeton Studies in International Finance*, 74, December, 24–5.

Estella de Noriega, A. (2014) *España y Europa. Hacia una nueva relación*, Tirant lo Blanch, Madrid.

Esteve, V., Navarro-Ibáñez, M., and Prats, M.A. (2017) 'The gold standard and the euro: A reflection from a reading of *A Tract on Monetary Reform*', *Cuadernos de Economía*, 40(114), 247–55.

Euronews (2021) 'Hungary left waiting as 12 EU states have spending plans for COVID recovery approved', 13 July.

European Commission (1970) *Report to the Council and the Commission on the realization by stages of economic and monetary union in the Community*, Luxembourg, 8 October 1970, also known as the Werner Report.

European Commission (1977) *Report of the Study Group on the Role of Public Finance in European Integration*, Volume 1: General Report, Brussels, April, also known as the MacDougall Report.

European Commission (1989a) *Report on economic and monetary union in the European Community*, Brussels, 17 April 1989, also known as the Delors Report.

European Commission (1989b) *Collection of papers submitted to the Committee for the Study of Economic and Monetary Union*, 17 April 1989, also known as the Delors Report Appendix.

European Commission (1990) 'One market, one money. An evaluation of the potential benefits and costs of forming an economic and monetary union', *European Economy*, 44, October.

European Commission (2021) 'NextGenerationEU: European Commission raises further €10 billion in a successful third bond to support Europe's recovery', Brussels, 13 July.

European Council (1997) 'Council Regulation (EC) No. 1466/97 on the strengthening of the surveillance of budgetary positions and the surveillance and coordination of economic policies', 7 July.

Fazi, T. (2021) 'Mario Draghi is the problem, not the solution', *Brave New Europe*, 19 February.

General Secretariat of the Council (2020) Special meeting of the European Council (17, 18, 19, 20 and 21 July 2020) – Conclusions, Brussels.

Godley, W. (1992) 'Maastricht and all that', *London Review of Books*, 14(19), October.

Godley, W. (1997) 'Curried EMU – the meal that fails to nourish', *Observer*, 31 August, 24.

Godley, W., and Wray, L.R. (1999) 'Can Goldilocks survive?', *Levy Institute Policy Note 1999/4*.

González-Páramo, J.M. (2011) 'The ECB's monetary policy during the crisis', Closing speech at the Tenth Economic Policy Conference, Málaga, 21 October 2011.

Inman, P. (2021) 'It's not Covid that's damaging British trade. It's Brexit', *Guardian*, 20 July.

International Monetary Fund (IMF) (2021) *Fiscal Monitor Database of Country Fiscal Measures in Response to the COVID-19 Pandemic*, IMF Fiscal Affairs Department, Washington, DC.

Ipsos Mori (2014) 'European Union membership – trends', 15 June.

Khan, M. (2020) 'Frugal four' chief Mark Rutte leads opposition to EU recovery plan', *Financial Times*, 18 June.

Khan, M., and Peel, M. (2020) '"Frugal four" fight to protect EU budget rebates', *Financial Times*, 18 August.

MacDougall Report (1977) See European Commission (1977).

Mason, R. (2016) 'How did UK end up voting to leave the European Union?', *Guardian*, 24 June.

Medina Ortega, M. (2014) *El derecho de secesión en la Unión Europea*, Marcial Pons, Madrid.

Mitchell, W.F. (2015) *Eurozone Dystopia: Groupthink and Denial on a Grand Scale*, Edward Elgar Publishing, Cheltenham, UK and Northampton, MA, USA.

Mitchell, W.F., and Fazi, T. (2017) *Reclaiming the State. A Progressive Vision of Sovereignty for Post-Neoliberal World*, Pluto Press, London.

Münchau, W. (2021) 'So much for the Brexit scare stories', *Euro Intelligence*, 16 April.

Mundell, R.A. (1961) 'A theory of optimum currency areas', *American Economic Review*, 51, 657–65.

Office for National Statistics (2021a) 'UK Trade: April 2021', 11 June.

Office for National Statistics (2021b) 'UK government debt and deficit: December 2020', 30 April.

Red MMT (2021) http://www.redmmt.es/2-a-cuanto-ascenderan-las-ayudas-que-recibiran-los-estados-europeos-por-los-fondos-next-generation-eu-a-lo-largo-de-la-vida-del-programa/ (accessed September 2022).

Rodríguez Zapatero, J. (2013) *El Dilema. 600 días de vertigo*, Planeta, Barcelona.

Scherer, N., González Briz, E., and Blázquez Sánchez, N. (2021) 'Guide to NextGenerationEU: Doing more harm than good', *Observatori del Deute en la Globalització*.

Schnabel, I. (2020) 'The shadow of fiscal dominance: Misconceptions, perceptions and perspectives', European Central Bank, 11 September.

Streeck, W. (2015) 'Why the euro divides Europe', *New Left Review*, 5–26.

Than, K., and Baczynska, G. (2021) 'Hungary's clash with EU over LGBT rights deepens', Reuters, 8 July.

Thatcher, M. (1993) *The Downing Street Years*, Harper Collins Publishers, London.

Trichet, J.-C., and Draghi, M. (2011) *Letter to Prime Minister Silvio Berlusconi*, 5 August.

Trichet, J-C., and Fernández Ordóñez, M. (2011) *Letter to Mr. Rodríguez Zapatero*, 5 August.

Triffin, R. (1960) *Gold and the Dollar Crisis. The Future of Convertibility*, Oxford University Press, London.

Werner Report (1970) See European Commission (1970).

Wray, L.R. (1998) *Understanding Modern Money*, Edward Elgar Publishing, Cheltenham, UK and Lyme, NH, USA.

Wyplosz, C. (2006) 'European Monetary Union: The dark sides of a major success', *Economic Policy*, 21(46), April, 207–47.

8. Modern Monetary Theory as post-neoliberal economics: the role of methodology–philosophy

Phil Armstrong and Jamie Morgan

8.1 INTRODUCTION

In this chapter, we set out how methodology and philosophy provide a strand of argument which can be used to support the Modern Monetary Theory (MMT) project within broader heterodox understandings of the nature of economics. Given that other chapters in this volume explore MMT in detail, our chapter is weighted towards a more general situating argument. We begin with some preliminaries that set out the meaning, scope and role of methodology informed by philosophy, we then set out one of the more prominent varieties of methodological–philosophical interventions, critical realism, and finally we draw links between realist argument and MMT. MMT's relevance rests on claims regarding the status of sovereign currency issuers.[1] Advocates argue that mainstream economists misunderstand the nature and significance of this status. According to proponents of MMT, mainstream economists mis-specify how currency issuance operates to provide financing and the nature of the economic constraints this occurs under and the powers it provides. Mainstream economists thus fail to adequately specify the potentials of this mechanism. MMT theorists provide an alternative explanation of this mechanism which simultaneously contests the practices internalised with mainstream misunderstanding. They thus combine a different understanding of current systemically significant structures, organisations and institutions with advocacy of a different way of *developing* and *directing* them. In so doing, MMT theorists recognise that while status as a currency issuer has generalisable potentials, this is different than claiming that status is universally the case or that all currency issuers have equal degrees of freedom, or that they need to be committed to the same set of subsequent policy foci using available financing potentials (though clearly there have been preferred associated goals). We argue that when considered along these lines, MMT constitutes a form of contingent 'depth-realist' theory of historically produced open systems and that it has various features that might be derived from and explored in terms of exploratory practices, identifying 'demi-regularity' and using 'contrast explanation' and 'retroduction'.

To be clear, MMT does not stand or fall on the basis of methodology–philosophy. Methodology–philosophy may add additional warrant to MMT, but cannot make it explanatorily complete, empirically vindicated or infallible – merely provisionally methodologically–philosophically plausible. Suggesting that MMT is a variant of open systems theory does, however, speak to James K. Galbraith's claim that 'useful economists' understand that human institutions are man-made, mutable and potentially subject to democratic control.[2] Still, it is also important to pay due attention to the embedded nature of an economy, i.e., basic biophysical limits and we conclude with some comment on this. Human institutions may be man-made, and we may be able to direct and democratically control financing in order to achieve socio-economic goals, but it is important not to neglect the material limits over which we have little or no *ultimate* control.

8.2   SOME INITIAL SIGNIFICANT CONTEXT-SETTING POINTS, ILLUSTRATED USING JAMES K. GALBRAITH

As the other chapters in this volume make clear, MMT is an important contribution both to economic theory and practical policy. While being mainly associated today with the work of Warren Mosler, Bill Mitchell, L. Randall Wray, Stephanie Kelton, Pavlina Tcherneva, Fadhel Kaboub and others (many of whom contribute to this volume), historically it draws on various aspects of the work of Abba Lerner, Wynne Godley, Hyman Minsky, Georg Friedrich Knapp, Alfred Mitchell-Innes, John Maynard Keynes and a host of others. Creative use of antecedents, of course, leads to some dispute regarding genealogy and authority within the history of economic thought. MMT, however, is typically categorised as post-Keynesian, though this too is not without disagreement.[3] In any case, MMT is, broadly speaking, considered heterodox and as such is positioned as oppositional to the current core of mainstream economics. This invokes various issues shared with the rest of heterodoxy, not least of which is, what is it that differentiates heterodox economics from the current mainstream?

In a recent essay, Galbraith articulates the difference.[4] He refers to the current mainstream as theory that does not begin from practical questions of how the social world is, or real-world problems of policy. Rather, particularly in its originating forms, it begins from highly unrealistic first principles or axioms from which mathematical systems are derived that create ideal model worlds. Over the years, this has involved use of rational self-interest, representative agents (deforming overly generalised concepts of firms, households etc.), neutral money, natural rates of interest and unemployment and so on. In terms of internal critique of axioms and concepts and models, the main concession has been to 'relax restrictive assumptions', but this is heavily influenced by the point of departure.[5] For Galbraith, mainstream economics claims to 'model the system' but does so in distorted ways that cannot cope with the actual nature of an economy. Its models cannot cope adequately with observable real-time features of an evolving economy: complex non-linearity, irreversibility, contingent cumulative development, intrinsic instability and ultimately degrees and types of uncertainty, particularly fundamental uncertainty. As such, it offers little in the way of constructive engagement with practical policy issues of how to structure an economy and its sectors in terms of the conventions, regulations, institutions etc. that create and facilitate the functioning of real-world economic mechanisms.[6]

Instead, the core of the mainstream restricts policy to advocating versions of a world that does not exist in search of a classical Newtonian physics-influenced concept of equilibrium buffeted by 'shocks', a terminology that renders real-world events exogenous, possibly random and, in some ways, anomalous; becoming interference in an otherwise smoothly functioning system of market clearing price signalling at the micro level, aggregated at the macro level and with the understanding that the whole has an internal dynamism leading to continuous growth within a circular flow of income. Furthermore, mainstream theory typically presupposes this leads to maximum social welfare through, as far as possible, self-regulating markets. The economist's main task then becomes to identify distortions and externalities and offer means to ease or remove these to correct price signalling systems and restore imagined efficient outcomes – whether that be micro or macro, modelled at different scales using dynamic stochastic general equilibrium (DSGE) etc.[7] In the meantime, the real economy experiences hidden unemployment, cumulative problems of inequality, financial instability and ultimately environmental carnage. The mainstream is thus real-world affecting, policy powerful and yet simultaneously banal, anodyne and falsely posed.

Galbraith contrasts the current mainstream with what he terms 'the useful economist', those who start from recognised economic problems and understand that human institutions are man-made, mutable and potentially subject to democratic control – albeit within basic biophysical limits as described via Georgescu-Roegen and subsequent thinkers (and this is something we will return to). For Galbraith, Keynesians, original institutionalists and various fellow travellers are 'useful economists' – and in particular, he draws attention to the work of his father, the British Cambridge economists and American post-Keynesians, including the main proponents of MMT.[8] For Galbraith, these are not just united in their difference to the current mainstream by critique of its specific theory, but rather by rejection of its form and purpose.

Mainstream and especially neoclassical economics, by contrast, involves a kind of theory–practice contradiction – it self-identifies as objective science (conflated with its formally derived 'proofs') as though it were descriptive of immutable, timeless and universal economic laws (even if the term law has fallen out of favour) and yet has also been a key strand in the neoliberal project that has advocated given policies that *produce* one version of a possible world.[9] While neoliberalism does not reduce to economic theory only, mainstream formulations, omissions and legitimations have been a key strand in neoliberalism – not least the call to remove distortions, which has in reality, and amongst other things, amounted to disempowerment of labour and empowerment of corporations. The point we want to draw attention to here is that Galbraith's essay highlights – a point he is not alone in making – that non-mainstream economics (heterodox economics etc.) shares a difference with the mainstream in terms of how theory is framed and directed. This brings us to an important question that shapes this chapter – what does it mean to claim commonality across diversity and how does one make the case for any *given* approach within economics that recognises that social science both seeks to explain and advocate in order to produce a possible world? We would argue that methodology and philosophy play a useful subordinate role.

Clearly, no policy-relevant real-world economics stands or falls on methodology or philosophy alone. Empirically adequate theory explains how things are, what is possible based on how things are and helps us achieve desired goals. As Galbraith illustrates, there are basic features of theorising, of policy, its practice and orientation and ultimately of sociology of knowledge of economics (i.e., what is accepted as what economists might spend their time thinking and working on) which can undermine a discipline and its parts. Engaging with these issues brings methodology and philosophy into the remit of economics and while methodological and philosophical exploration and argument do not make you a 'useful economist', ignorance of them may help to inadvertently make you a 'useless' one.[10] This is something that *all* the great economists over the years have at least implicitly recognised, since each has spent some time ruminating on the nature of economics, its scope, limits and potentials.

8.3   THE ROLE OF METHODOLOGY AND PHILOSOPHY

Perhaps the most prominent post-Keynesian to work on methodology is Sheila Dow. She places methodology in the context of schools of thought, distinguishes methodology from mere use of methods and highlights that schools involve shared commitments (a framework of concepts and perspectives) and a 'mode of reasoning':

> A school of thought refers to its technical procedures, i.e., to its modelling techniques, its choices of categories, and its preferred testing procedures. But these in turn derive from an underlying conceptualisation of reality and preferred modes of reasoning. We use the term 'methodology' to encompass both the methods actually employed within a school of thought and the underlying world view or vision, which generated them.[11]

For Dow, methodology is influenced by one of two 'modes of thought'. First, a Cartesian/Euclidean mode, and this is typical of the core of the mainstream. In a similar vein to Galbraith, she associates the mainstream with building models from first principles and axioms but emphasises that it usually involves deductive logical forms and a classically geometric mathematical perspective (albeit with subsequent innovations). This approach places great value on clarity, concision, certainty, rigour, elegance and predictive power and considers these hallmarks of economics as a quantitative science. However, Dow argues little is done to demonstrate the relevance of the mathematics or develop explanations of real-world phenomena – the assumptions of theory and models come first, and the world is fitted to them. Drawing on Keynes, she contrasts this with a second or Babylonian mode which has no *a priori* commitment to a single form of reasoning, exploration, explanation type or method, but rather accommodates to the 'problem at hand'. This Babylonian-situated procedure, however, does not imply a lack of structure, coherence or direction of investigation, but rather willingness to explore multiple evidence sources and engage in open-minded learning to develop theory that fits contexts – cumulatively or *a posteriori*, leading to a sense of acquired confidence that work is currently, in the philosophical sense, 'justified' in and of its context.

One does not need to be a proponent of Dow's categorisation of modes of thought to appreciate the underlying claim that methodology matters, because it is here that orientations to what theory is, and how one analyses, are shaped. And, as reference to Keynes indicates, economics has a long history of methodological rumination and this has been a primary constituent in the clarification and formulation of different approaches, whether the term has been used or not – Chapter 1 of Jevons's *Theory of Political Economy*, Book 1 and the appendices of Marshall's *Principles of Economics*, the *Methodenstreit*, various interventions of original institutionalists, Harcourt's *Some Cambridge Controversies in the Theory of Capital* etc. Methodologically informed works are numerous and no list can be exhaustive these days, but a list can illustrate that while diverse, such works are often purposive state of the field surveys and analyses. For example, Shackle's *The Years of High Theory,* Robbins's *Essay on the Nature and Significance of Economic Science,* and more latterly within and without the mainstream, Ferber and Nelson's *Beyond Economic Man*, Lee and Cronin's *Handbook of Research Methods and Applications in Heterodox Economics* and Rodrik's *Economics Rules*.

It is also worth noting that methodological inquiry has been assimilated into and influenced by the growing scholastic division of labour created by the modern higher education system, with its disciplines, its tendency to foster sub-disciplines and its penchant for varieties of inter-disciplinary crossover. Methodological inquiry has been professionalised and specialised and over the last 40 years, this has resulted in contributions from scholars whose emphasis one might describe as more towards economists as philosophers (e.g., Mark Blaug, Daniel Hausman, Roger Backhouse, Bruce Caldwell, Lawrence Boland etc.) and ones whose emphasis is more as philosophers venturing into the field of economics (Nancy Cartwright via John Davis, John O'Neill, Uskali Mäki etc.).[12] To refer to a previous comment, this work parallels and over-laps with that of economists with more of a specific theory-shaping point to make – in MMT circles Wray's *Modern Money Theory*, Kelton's more public understanding-oriented and recent *The Deficit Myth*, and more broadly across post-Keynesianism, Minsky's collected *Can It Happen Again?*, some of the work of Jan Kregel, Victoria Chick and so on.

To be clear, mentioning the range of works we have in the last two para-graphs is more than a name-checking exercise. As any reasonably informed reader will be aware, the professionalisation of economics and the develop-ment of sub-disciplines has produced numerous effects, and these too have become a subject of critique regarding the state of the field. While it is clear that methodology matters to economics as it does to any field of inquiry, there have been various claims and counterclaims made regarding the necessity of an additional specialism and regarding the efficacy of work from that specialism.

Since contributors to schools tend to draw on and creatively develop the work of antecedents who themselves write on the nature and scope of eco-nomics, it is sometimes argued that methodology is superfluous discussion of what is already available in more theory-specific works within a given school or approach. Furthermore, and this is more of a critique common to the non-mainstream, it is sometimes argued that the development of a sub-discipline of methodology and philosophy of economics (as well as history of economic thought) has observably been part of a deselection of these from the economics education of most economists, since as sub-disciplines they have been deemed non-essential. As such, their sub-disciplinary status has been conducive to hiving off history of thought *and* more diverse approaches to economics as well as fundamental reflection on the state of the field and ultimately critique to 'electives', which not all departments offer and few students choose, since these electives appear to have little immediate bearing on a career, given the direction of travel of the field and expectations of the skillset.

As various commentators note, the sociology of knowledge of economics seems to operate according to adverse *processes* that actively work against diversity. This is not to suggest the mainstream lacks different foci, theory and claims or dispute regarding the adequacy of methods, but rather that this is highly restricted to 'loosening', as Galbraith suggests, and to dispute regarding relative technical merits of similarly posed models, within a 'Cartesian/ Euclidean' frame, as Dow intimates. As such, the development of the field continues to suppress pluralism of perspective, theory, skills and methods, particularly those which offer fundamental critical reflection and interchange. Somewhat ironically then, methodology has become a strand in this broader process of selection. Put another way, the actual positive impact of methodology has been questioned at the same time as works on methodology have accumulated and proliferated and the underlying significance of methodology has been highlighted. However, this is not an unrecognised contradiction, but rather has become part of, over the years, the methodological critique of the mainstream – insofar as the emphasis of methodology has undergone something of a change in relation to philosophy.

8.4   PHILOSOPHY AS UNDERLABOURER

As reference to the work of various 'economists as philosophers' in the previous section might indicate to some readers, for much of the twentieth century, the assessment of economics tended to explore the mainstream in terms of its own claims to be a science according to dominant theory and criteria of what constitutes a science. Works like Blaug's *The Methodology of Economics* and Caldwell's *Beyond Positivism* thus set out the various threads or development of philosophy of science that seemed to have most relevance for economics – matching economics' claim to be a body of quantitative theory and models using applied analytical statistical techniques to test hypotheses etc., to different generalised conceptions of what this involves.[13] The frame of reference was, therefore, empiricism, positivism/logical positivism and subsequent variations – and thus the focus was whether economics did or could verify, confirm or falsify its claims according to the law-like status of those claims. Interested economists were required to master a new field, beginning with the unified science project of the logical positivists (published initially primarily via the *Minnesota Studies in Philosophy of Science*) with its 'hypothetico-deductive' model of scientific explanation and 'deductive-nomological' and 'inductive-probabilistic' 'covering laws', but quickly taking in the various critiques of the adequacy of these – leading to familiarity with Popper's *Logic*, his *Conjectures* and his 'three worlds', and the various conditions under which advancement in knowledge occurs or is resisted – Kuhnian 'paradigm shifts' and Lakatosian degenerating 'scientific research programmes' where a community grimly hangs onto an unfalsifiable 'core' etc.

To be clear, one need not have a ready grasp of these works for brief reference to them to be relevant here – the list provides a flavour of the subject and the ultimate point is that each speaks to the same general implication. Methodology initially took the mainstream on its own terms as a scientific project for which a dominant set of concerns in philosophy of science already existed. Scholars such as Blaug and Caldwell were, however, critical of the degree to which economics was successful in this project – hence the combination of concern with testing and the problem of how a field of inquiry responds. But this tended to mask a significant point. The philosophy of science approach was focused on *epistemic* adequacy, i.e., refining a theory of knowledge that best expressed the capacity of any discipline to pursue scientific theorisation and research. Any critique of this kind, however, presupposes that economics *could* be a science along the lines stated in the received philosophy of science and that this *was* an adequate account of both science and of the world.

There is space here then for a different line of inquiry and this began first in philosophy of science in the 1970s, notably with Rom Harré and Roy Bhaskar, which suggested that positivism and variants were *not* an adequate account of science, before transitioning to critique of the influence of positivism etc. on the social sciences in the 1980s, a line of reasoning with obvious appeal in economics, which was experiencing both a development of 'formalism' and a reaction against this into and through the 1990s. This different line of inquiry and critique was more 'metaphysical', returning to issues that analytical philosophy had eschewed for much of the twentieth century; it asked a deceptively simple question: what must be the case for given theory and/or methods to be applicable and adequate? As such, it focused on what 'must' be presupposed about the nature of reality.

To be clear, however, the use of 'must' is highly conditional – it is about implications, which are then subject to critique in terms of plausibility and consistency. Moreover, the initial role of philosophy here is not to assert in isolation or *a priori* what reality 'is' as though we had some unmediated access to reality – since this would substitute philosophy for science, and assumptions and assertions for evidence and focused empirical research, pre-empting the development of theory and applications in any given disciplinary domain, while committing variants on well-recognised problems of 'rationalism' and 'foundationalism' in philosophy. Rather, the point is to suggest that *all* theory, methods and applications and their goals presuppose some kind of reality that makes sense of their approach (giving focus, purpose and justification to the interrogation), and as such, they have a metaphysic or 'ontology', i.e., a 'theory of being', which parallels a theory of knowledge. In this sense, all theory is 'realist' insofar as it makes claims beyond itself and which only make sense if the world is 'such and such'.

To reiterate, while the claim is that all theory etc. presuppose some conception of reality, the initial point is that methodological and philosophical reflection can help us explore these – it is not a claim that one particular set of theories of the nature of reality are and must be correct – any warrantable claims only follow from additional argument in dialogue with, and complementary to, further theory and empirical investigation and thus argumentation and evidence. A focus on ontology thus speaks to Galbraith's 'useful economist' and Dow's 'Babylonian' mode of thought. Proponents of 'realism' and in particular 'critical realism' have been the main advocates of this shift in emphasis in the role of methodology and philosophy over the last half-century, and especially so in economics, but it is important not to conflate the specifics of what the accounts of reality realists in general, and critical realists in particular, offer and the value of methodological–philosophical reflection that they use to make a space for their *specific* claims. The introduction of metaphysics or ontology opens up rather than closes down a set of debates about what 'must' be the case – and this applies also to scientific realism and to more hermeneutic and phenomenological approaches which have quite different things to say about the difference between natural and social science than positivism, as well as to more radical constructivist and post-structuralist approaches that question the very nature of knowledge, truth and reality; if one moves beyond the focus of methodology and philosophy that has dominated in economics.

In any case, if we accept that all approaches have an 'ontology', then a space is opened up for exploration and clarification of that ontology – making explicit what may have been implicit and here, philosophy can (using a phrase appropriated from Locke) serve an 'underlabouring' function. Philosophy does not replace theory or empirical research, but rather provides a domain of argument in which assumptions, formulations and implications of approaches to theory and research are explored and the goals, justifications and consequences are assessed. As such, it is not foundationalist 'news from nowhere', but rather a way of exploring frameworks of theory and empirical research from a different point of view, typically in terms of the continual problems that arise and persist – the omissions, failures, tensions, puzzles or aporia etc.

A focus on ontology can provide *one* (not the only) way to explore the commonalities and differences between the primary works of schools or approaches, it can provide *a* useful perspective when considering the consistency of attempts to build on work within those schools, it can provide *a* basis to consider possible ways to resolve any conceptual impasse for long-standing problems commonly identified across a discipline (what is termed 'immanent critique'), and, if we return to the final comment in the previous section, it can orient on or identify characteristics of adverse selection criteria which form part of the sociology of knowledge of a discipline. As such, ontology has offered the prospect of more wide-ranging and flexible methodological–philosophical investigation than the previously dominant focus on epistemic adequacy issues.

Again, this turn to ontology started to gain a foothold in philosophy of science in the 1970s, spread through the social sciences in the 1980s and started to come to the fore in economics in the 1990s (one of the few places it has not been in competition with post-structuralism). To some twenty-first-century readers, for whom the twentieth century is someone else's past rather than lived experience, this may seem like 'ancient history', but as Galbraith's recent comments regarding the contrast in form and purpose between the mainstream and 'useful economists' indicate, ontologically significant problematic differences persist.

Contemporary economics includes a wide array of different approaches to realism – for example, informing Geoff Hodgson's work on Original Institutionalism and, as should be clear from her Cartesian/Euclidean-Babylonian distinction, Sheila Dow's work,[14] but perhaps the best-known 'ontologist' and 'realist' is Tony Lawson whose *Economics & Reality*[15] and *Reorienting Economics*[16] have been standard reference points while the Cambridge Realist Workshop and Cambridge Social Ontology Group have been focal points for discussion and dissemination of ideas, notably via *Cambridge Journal of Economics* and Routledge's *Economics as Social Theory* (EAST) book series. Lawson himself is something of a controversial figure due to his trenchant and uncompromising critique of mathematical modelling and because of his comments that such modelling continues to undermine non-mainstream economics. At the same time, however, a set of underlying critiques of the ontology of mainstream economics have become widespread in heterodox economics, as have arguments in favour of an alternative ontology, and these are as relevant to MMT as any other heterodox or non-mainstream variant.

8.5   THE MAINSTREAM ONTOLOGY

If we begin from the 'deceptively simple question' at the heart of the 'ontological turn' in methodology–philosophy in economics, it is possible to reconstruct a fairly generic set of 'realist' claims, characteristics, concepts and arguments. To be clear, there is considerable nuance and some degree of discussion, disagreement and variation regarding the substance and significance of aspects of the whole, but our purpose here is to highlight commonality rather than difference. Recall that the orienting question is: 'what "must" be the case for given theory and/or methods to be applicable and adequate?'[17]

If we recall Galbraith's comments on the form and purpose of mainstream economics and Dow's 'Cartesian/Euclidean' mode of thought, both emphasise that the mainstream begins from axiomatic first principles and tries to fit the world to these. As readers are no doubt aware, however, mainstream economics has tried to justify this procedure by circumscribing the 'economy' as a domain that has different potentials than other aspects of society – a problem, for example, that conflicted Marshall. Economics has access to a vast array of recorded and publicly available quantitative data on all aspects of economic activity (prices, costs, inflation, unemployment etc.) and concerns itself with publicly observable behaviours. First principles reduce, essentialise and universalise this behaviour and do so according to a narrowed inference that an overwhelmingly transactional frame of reference is matched to a very narrow concept of instrumental, individual (entity) self-interested rational action. The result is unrealistic axiom idealisation rather than more or less focus on some realistically premised aspect of the whole – and this, of course, has led to numerous lines of defence, most notoriously from Friedman. But the net effect has been to translate an interest in patterns into an assumption of stable situations or outcomes where the overwhelming emphasis is on the 'regularity' of the outcome – a focus that reflects the legacy of positivism and a long-standing aspiration to emulate its vision of natural science; despite that, few mainstream economists today would self-identify as positivists or typically find themselves required to reflect on its legacy or their attitudes towards the nature of science; and albeit today 'regularity' need not mean absence of variation, but rather highly sophisticated stochastics, cycles, convergences or 'normal'.

In any case, formal mathematical theorems or proofs and modelled applications assume 'regularity' to be what lies beneath the froth of observable variation and presume that identifying fundamental principles and regularised quantified outcomes is what economic science offers (and as Galbraith notes, any failure is a failure of the world requiring policy to remove 'distortions', 'frictions' etc.).[18] For realists and notably critical realists, such theory and method rely on two 'closure' conditions and a further condition or procedure that facilitates these in any given theorisation or application. The closure conditions are most clearly set out by Lawson:[19]

1. Extrinsic closure: the theory or application has no unelaborated/identified (even if some elements are allowed for via error terms in some approaches) conditions or influences, the theorised situation or system contains all relevant variables and is closed off from interference i.e., is isolated.
2. Intrinsic closure: the isolated situation or system behaves consistently in its internal state; behaviour is coherent and repeats.

As any mathematically competent person will recognise, 'intrinsic closure' is most easily expressed mathematically if behaviours are individuated or isolated, so the separation of the situation or system from others (the extrinsic closure) is typically matched with an 'atomistic' separation and subsequent summation of the individual parts (via intrinsic closure). However, given that the point of theory and method is to express and then demonstrate or test a set of enduring relationships, it must also be assumed that the combined aspects of the situation or system of atomistic parts do in fact sum in some consistent and coherent sense, i.e., that they are determinate, repeated or reproduced to some given end. So, a further condition is required to produce order and expedite standard mathematical or symbolic logical expression:

3. The aggregation condition: a set of restrictions that manipulate the composition of parts such that summation has significance according to some guiding concept.

Hence the assumption of equilibrium and the many 'fixes' needed to *impose* equilibrium on mathematical theorems (the problem of which has been recognised since at least Walras but is perhaps best known in the mainstream from the Sonnenschein–Mantel–Debreu theorem debacle regarding uniqueness and shape of demand functions etc.) and hence the standard procedures required to make a DSGE work, or in order to claim 'well-behaved' data, internal and external validity in standard econometric models and tests etc.

It should be clear then that the implicit ontology of the mainstream resonates with heterodox critiques of the form and purpose of mainstream theory. Mainstream economics works with a notoriously impoverished concept of human being (the economic agent) and a concomitantly poor conception of time or rather what human being enables us to do through and in time. Time becomes stylised mechanistic periodisation and what we do and how we do it becomes a matter of mere measurement, rather than meaning that produces activity which can *sometimes* be measured. This oddly dehumanised reality sits awkwardly with what we observe around us and this ontology is quite different than the features of economies that non-mainstream economists orient on and attempt to address in a host of different ways. From a what 'must' be the case point of view, a shorthand for the sense made of this is 'historic open systems'.[20]

8.6 (CRITICAL) REALISM AND THE CASE FOR HISTORIC OPEN SYSTEMS

In an underlabouring sense, various realists and critical realists have synthesised an ontology intended to reflect, support and inform more adequate ways of theorising and researching an economy.[21] Rather than start from known fictions, this ontology seeks to express widely acknowledged aspects of activity that have otherwise proved problematic within the mainstream ontology.

However, to make sense of the realist case we need to introduce some prior standard terminology.[22]

In general, realists argue that the success of the natural sciences and the manifest capacity of an intelligent species such as our own to create societies provide grounds for us to infer that reality is 'stratified', 'emergent' and complexly ordered. In the natural sciences, realists argue that it typically requires laboratory conditions to *produce* observable event regularities and this implies that scientists are isolating the powers or capacities of structured entities which exhibit causal effects.[23] As such, reality *in general* appears to have 'depth': entities have powers deriving from their structure or organisation, these are active in reality producing events and these in turn can be experienced. There is, therefore, a distinction between the existence of continual sources of possible events, the events that actually occur and the empirical sense made of some subset of events. Moreover, when we consider the world around us it is clear that events vary and so we infer that the actual, as a series of events, is dependent on the powers and capacities of a complex mix of structured entities. Reality is thus ordered yet contingent and it becomes, as we have previously suggested, an error to conflate order with event regularity, since this places the emphasis on seeking regularity rather than focusing on how structured entities lead to causal powers and how combinations give rise to series of events, i.e., how and what makes things happen.

Furthermore, since series of events exhibit patterns and order to different degrees over different timescales and spatial extents, it follows that structured entities are only relatively stable in their mixes and only relatively enduring in their characteristics. There is thus a dynamic to reality, even if there are seemingly fundamental features such as gravitational shaping of space–time or quantum effects that give order to the elements of the periodic table. Concomitantly, there is no reason to think physics is fully or exhaustively explanatory of reality. Rather there seem to be grounds to argue reality has 'strata' that also imbue it with order: the activity we describe as physics makes possible the characteristics of atoms and molecules, but chemistry does not reduce to physics any more than biology reduces to chemistry or society reduces to biology. Reality exhibits 'emergence', i.e., organisation leads to properties that arise because of organisation and are thus irreducible to parts in isolation. With emergence comes new powers or potentials, the existence of which do not 'violate' what is made possible in the order of reality, but rather add novelty as reality unfolds. Organic life is one such novelty and a conscious self-aware and intelligent species is another. With intelligence comes curiosity, meaning and directed intention, leading to two mutually related developments. First, the capacity to interrogate and manipulate the world around us. This is activity of an emergent structured entity working back on a material reality in which it is embedded. Second, the capacity to produce new emergent entities whose existence depends on 'us', i.e., society and its subsets produced through the concatenation of our activity. Our very idea of economy cuts across both of these and this brings us to historic 'open systems'.

Historic open systems start from what we actually observe around us, which is that economies develop as socially specific and culturally influenced *temporal* systems. They are a complex combination of what 'we' (our species and where some because of their positions have more influence than others) in part and whole seek to create and the unintended consequences of the activity through which 'we' seek to get things done. As a species we do not passively experience the transition from one moment to the next, we plan, organise, intend and anticipate because our intelligence makes possible a connection from the past to the present to possible futures. That connection is grounded in what is classically termed an agent–structure dynamic – and different strands of heterodox theory approach this in different ways to different ends, but with (arguably) a common underlying recognition.[24] For example, as Karl Polanyi, Galbraith senior and numerous Original Institutionalists remind us, a system of markets is an *institutional* arrangement conceived to achieve some purpose according to some contingent set of *historic* arrangements. This is a reminder that at the most general level, complexity and contingency arise because the organisation of society leads to sources of habit, conventions, rules, regulation, law etc. and these precede and provide context for activity, grounding powers or capacities for *meaningful* social action. For a realist, these highlight the importance of social relationality and of institution-building to create economic mechanisms and outcomes and these are core (though not the only) areas of investigation for any adequate economics. For social theorists, they invoke the way any subset of social reality involves an agent–structure issue of 'enablement' and 'constraint', which shapes conduct. And for a critical realist, this is suggestive of the complex *temporal* interplay of structured entities, which imbue the 'depth' of social reality with characteristics particular to an intelligent species.

There is not the space here to explore what is 'particular' to social reality in any detail, but consider an issue that has troubled social theorists through the years – the issue of interpretation (hermeneutics) and the apparent capacity of our species to add meaningful components to the world (the order created by our ways of organising ourselves) and infuse meaning into the world (the 'phenomenological' significance that arises with a first-person perspective) – all attributes that mainstream economics barbarises. With these in mind, at first sight it may seem odd to distinguish a complex mix of structured entities from events and (empirical) experience when considering social reality, since as agents we are used to thinking of our sense of what we are doing and why as coinciding with what we are doing. Obviously in order to be a competent agent, one must have *some* grasp (intuitive or explicit) of how to

proceed appropriately in any given situation. But it is important to make the
depth-realist distinction for two reasons. First, without it, an adequate understanding becomes conceptualised as a complete understanding of the conditions that create the grounds of activity and the consequences of it (as events)
and there is no reason why this should be so and many reasons why it is rarely
if ever the case. Second, social scientists are a further step removed from the
activity and if we did not distinguish interpretation from events etc. it would
be impossible for social scientists to be wrong, and by inference, mainstream
economics could not be in error and it would make little sense to argue that the
sources of our activity can be misunderstood, can be worked upon and can be
developed to some purpose.[25]

Yet as a practical matter things can usually be 'otherwise'. We influence the
world around us reproducing or changing the various contextualising aspects
that enable and constrain our activity and this imbues social reality with temporal characteristics of process – an open system quite unlike the ontology
characteristic of the mainstream.[26] So while the social world, including the
economy, exhibits order and periods of relative stability, not least because
that is one of the main purposes of civilisation, it equally exhibits variation,
difference or diversity, as well as change-transition-transformation observable
at different scales and to different degrees. As such, it is a peculiar feature of
our existence that we produce a social reality that tends to exceed our given
understanding and yet our intelligent interrogation of what we have wrought is
one of the main ways in which things become otherwise – a point that evokes
James K. Galbraith's claim that 'useful economists' understand that human
institutions are man-made, mutable and potentially subject to democratic
control. This brings us finally to MMT, which we suggested in the introduction
constitutes a form of contingent 'depth-realist' theory of historically produced
open systems and that it has various features that might be derived from and
explored in terms of exploratory practices such as 'demi-regularity', 'contrast
explanation' and retroduction.

8.7   MMT AS OPEN SYSTEMS THEORY: 'DEMI-REGULARITY', 'CONTRAST EXPLANATION' AND RETRODUCTION

Some of the previous section may seem far removed from the specifics of
economic theory and research. However, remember what the purpose of
methodology–philosophy is: underlabouring to clarify and support the work
of economists. Here we argue that there are various exploratory practices
available that are consistent with a realist social ontology and which can help

situate MMT within an open systems approach. A useful concept here is that of demi-regularity:

> Over restricted regions of time–space certain mechanisms may come to dominate others and/or shine through: non-spurious rough and ready, partial regularities may be observed. Although the social world is open, dynamic and changing, certain mechanisms may, over regions of time–space, be reproduced continuously and come to be (occasionally) apparent in their effects at the level of actual phenomena, giving rise to rough and ready generalities or partial regularities, holding to such a degree that *prima facie* an explanation is called for.[27]

A concept of demi-regularity helps us make sense of the structuring of events. It is one useful way to begin the process of exploring and explaining how things happen, since it can be used to orient concern with the 'generative mechanisms' through which things happen. Unlike the mainstream, as a starting point it does not require us to commit the error of seeking significance in an atomistic or refined version of the regularity itself. It does not encourage the error of 'looking through' the complex mix of conditions to explain order as regularity, based on some model that strips out the significance of contingency for the *degrees* of order to be found in economic activity based on its social relations, institutions etc. It encourages us to think more consistently about temporality while also providing a hook for meaningful investigation. Here a sensitivity to 'contrasts' can also be a useful way to initiate investigation.[28] Lawson, for example, argues that a researcher who has acquired sufficient familiarity with their area of study is liable to have their curiosity piqued and this can take a variety of contrastive forms: the endurance of a pattern, its breaking down, the failure of anticipations or of familiar explanations or one of a host of other sources of 'surprise'. Within these possibilities one can have in combination a 'contrastive demi-reg' that invites explanation.[29]

A contrastive demi-reg investigation has previously been undertaken for MMT based on Organisation for Economic Co-operation and Development (OECD) data.[30] Notably, in the period immediately preceding and following the Global Financial Crisis (GFC), the expectation of mainstream economists that expanding government deficits as a percentage of GDP tends to cause increased long-term interest rates on government debt *is not borne out*. This is insofar as countries issue their own sovereign currency and operate under floating exchange rates. In fact, in numerous cases, the general trend of rising deficits is accompanied by falling, rather than rising, long-term interest rates in the period under consideration, while in others there is no clear relationship. Eurozone members, meanwhile, are not sovereign currency issuers and their experience has been somewhat different. For France, Germany, Italy and the Netherlands there was no apparent significant relationship between deficit size as a percentage of GDP and long-term interest rates. However, for Greece,

Ireland, Portugal and Spain, higher deficits were accompanied by higher long-term interest rates.

Clearly, these groupings invite different explanations based on different 'demi-regs' and there are at least two contrasts that might immediately be invoked. First, what one might anticipate based on mainstream explanations and second, between one place and another. Both speak to diverse temporal processes, institutional arrangements, other economic characteristics, contingency and the scope to use financing differently – where this latter point includes a failure to distinguish economic constraints because a country is not a sovereign currency issuer from misunderstandings of the potential of a country that is a sovereign currency issuer (e.g., induced by socialisation exercised through theory and convention that assumes a state is equivalent to a household, that taxation must ultimately finance government spending, that bond 'vigilantes' have the upper hand etc.), from counterproductive institutional arrangements that prevent the state making use of its scope for financing economic activity insofar as it *is* a sovereign currency issuer (e.g., budget rules that constrain the US Senate), and from the other contextualising factors that may limit the degree of freedom any given sovereign currency issuer may exercise (since countries are subject to power and influence from multiple sources).

It should then be clear that contrastive demi-regs invite context-sensitive explanation of the mechanisms in play and, inter alia, critique of received forms of theory that are unable to make adequate sense of the mechanisms.[31] Other chapters in this volume provide greater detail regarding features of MMT and it is to these one might look for more or less persuasive accounts of and evidence for the mechanisms. However, it should be clear that much of what we have discussed in this chapter resonates with MMT's concerns. Furthermore, one might also note that a demi-regs investigation requires one to take seriously the difference between sources of events, events themselves and the concatenation of interpretations of the sources of events, i.e., it invokes a depth-realist account of historic process, and arguably this sits comfortably with the underlying theory and intent of MMT as set out in the other chapters. Illustrating this, moreover, brings us to another relevant exploratory practice, 'retroduction'.

Social science employs several different modes of 'inference' and these provide logical forms for different ways of structuring theory and investigation, as well as different grounds for legitimation of theory and investigation (in turn affecting 'justification' procedures for 'argumentation' schemes). The most familiar of these modes of inference in economics are deduction and induction – and we referred to the former of these briefly in previous sections. Deduction has a logical structure where the conclusion is entailed or follows necessarily from the premises and the conclusion does not exceed what the premises allow (in philosophy the structure is 'non-ampliative' and if valid has a 'truth-transmission' characteristic, which should not be confused with an evidential claim or with the claim that a 'true' statement is also a statement of something that is real). This, in principle, leads to theory first, followed by hypothesis tests and confirmations, but has created all of the problems philosophy of science has discussed in previous decades (what it means to verify, confirm or falsify theory). Induction reverses deduction by starting from some observations and builds theory more tentatively as forms of generalisations, which can exceed in some sense what the premises allow (it is 'ampliative'). Deduction has dominated theory and model construction in economics, though induction tends to be invoked (following Marshall) as a break on theory – on the understanding that empirical investigation leads to theory and model reconstruction or modification – but this interplay – formal deductive constructs informed by induction – has been highly restricted, with heavy emphasis on econometrics and thus analytical statistical methods with little thought for the ontological mismatch this tends to involve (and in practice little attempt to apply scientific method through replication of findings etc.). Social science, however, offers a range of other 'ampliative' modes of inference and these are more or less creative and encouraging of the use of diverse methods.

Retroduction is inference from effects to generative mechanisms. Retroduction, however, is sensitised to, rather than tries to assume away, the complexity of social reality: the contingency and variability of events, the difficulty of making sense of the role of theory and interpretations in influencing events and how we view events, and the complex mix of mechanisms that *may* occur differently in different places and times. As such, retroduction starts from the premise that methods of inquiry ought to fit the problem or issue under scrutiny, but that the nature of that problem allows for innovative use of multiple methods. For example, Danermark et al. (2019) suggest: comparative study, study of extreme and/or pathological cases, counterfactual thinking and social experiment, while Wendy Olsen makes creative use of combinations of qualitative and quantitative techniques. This to be clear is different than a primitive pragmatism that amounts to instrumentalism or 'anything goes', and it does not discount simplification, abstraction or any other procedure. Retroduction does, however, tend to invite a practice of 'retrodiction' or iterative engagement for theory-building and evidence use, and this sits comfortably with Dow's 'Babylonian' mode of thought drawn for Keynes.

One might then argue that MMT provides a more plausible explanation of the contrasting mechanisms that apply in Euro-using nations and those with their own sovereign, non-convertible currencies under floating exchange rates and that these mechanisms can be retroduced.[32] MMT distinguishes clearly between sovereign currency issuers and nations using the Euro. Euro-using nations have ceded their money-issuing power to another entity, the European

Central Bank. Each nation's government is forced to act as a 'currency user' (rather reminiscent of US states). As such, taxes do fund spending, borrowing from private sector Euro holders may be necessary to fund spending, default is technically possible and, in the absence of European Central Bank (ECB) assistance, the need to sell debt on bond markets may drive yields to very high levels. In the case of nations such as Ireland, Greece and Portugal, where default risk has periodically seemed significantly heightened, we might expect bond yields to rise. In contrast, in countries such as Germany, the Netherlands and France, where default risk has been perceived as being very low, demand for bonds remained high. In fact, given fears about the future value of private financial assets and expectations of relatively low short-term interest rate policy settings by the ECB, bond yields for these countries actually fell despite significantly higher public sector deficits in the period 2007–2011.

If we look to countries that are sovereign currency issuers and operate under floating exchange rates, 'borrowing' by the state is not operationally required and even if the state decided to borrow, there would not be any straightforward correlation between increased deficits and rising long-term rates.[33] The government spends first and creates reserves, *ex nihilo*. It is never revenue-constrained as a currency user might be. The so-called 'borrowing' operation which removes the reserves is, rather, voluntary.[34] A currency issuer could allow any untaxed spending to remain in the system. However, such a policy would result in the overnight rate falling to zero (if no other action was taken, such as the central bank agreeing to pay interest on excess reserves).

We could go on, but the previous ought to be sufficient to establish that various exploratory approaches drawn from methodology and philosophy may support and inform MMT and how these in turn situate MMT as part of a depth-realist historic open systems ontology, an ontology that provides an additional strand of argument for MMT and thus justification of it – though there are numerous other issues arising and we briefly note these in concluding.

8.8   CONCLUSION: MMT AND POST-NEOLIBERAL ECONOMICS

Early on, we suggested Galbraith's comments on differences in form and purpose in economics invoke an important question, what does it mean to claim commonality across diversity and how does one make the case for any *given* approach within economics that recognises that social science both seeks to explain and advocate in order to produce a possible world? By way of conclusion, we can decompose this question into two parts. If we ask, 'what does it mean to claim commonality across diversity?', then it ought to be clear that methodology and philosophy allow us to think in terms of different ontologies and their relative plausibility, consistency and insight. On this basis,

MMT seems quite different than mainstream economics and seems far more compatible with a depth-realist historic open systems approach; advocates of this ontology, in turn, have variously argued its merits for heterodox economics.[35] This underlabouring function, of course, does not prevent continuing disagreement – Lawson, for example, in addition to his many contributions to general matters of social ontology, suggests that MMT would be improved if it adopted his 'social positioning theory' of money, which distinguishes what money *is* from how and what it is created *for*.[36]

Second, if we consider 'how does one make the case for any *given* approach within economics that recognises that social science both seeks to explain and advocate in order to produce a possible world?', then clearly MMT sits comfortably within Galbraith's category of 'useful economists' who understand that human institutions are man-made, mutable and potentially subject to democratic control. Different places have adopted different institutions and have over time created conditions that constrain and enable them.[37] As we briefly suggested in the introduction and as the other chapters in this volume more clearly establish, MMT provides a different understanding of current systemically significant structures, organisations and institutions and combines this with advocacy of a different way of *developing* and *directing* them.[38] MMT is a source of new explanations and insight and as Roy Bhaskar once noted, these often come from those conversant with but not over-socialised by the issues of some field of inquiry – an observation that does not negate the merits of a Babylonian mode of thought – Warren Mosler notably works in finance rather than in academic economics.

As readers are no doubt aware, advocates of MMT around the world have been at the forefront of 'progressive' movements to make use of state financing to address the many pathologies and problems of the neoliberal era: investment to provide secure well-paid employment, Job Guarantee schemes, renewal of infrastructure, spending to improve access to and standards of well-being enhancing services (social care, medical care, education etc.), and most recently, financing for transformations to economy and society to address the increasingly urgent conjoint crises of climate change and ecological breakdown. It is in terms of climate change and ecological breakdown, however, that MMT faces perhaps its most important challenge, since any adequate post-neoliberal economics must be reconciled to these. This too is an area where ontology can offer underlabouring insight albeit in the form of basic common sense (which mainstream economics has worked hard to suppress even as it has developed environmental economics).

Social reality may be emergent, but it does not float free, if reality is stratified. Institutions may be man-made and economic mechanisms may be biddable, but an economy is a material process on a finite planet. The dilemma for MMT is that financing is not just a possible source of investment for solutions to climate and ecological breakdown, it is an invitation to act at scale, which might prove incompatible with actually solving climate and ecological breakdown. It is one thing, for example, to suggest that in functional finance the limit on financing is full use of available resources without inducement of inflation, but another to suggest this level of economic activity will not eventually set the planet on fire, even if factories are busily spitting out solar panels and electric cars.

To be clear, the dilemma is not 'news from nowhere' to post-Keynesians, it forms the basis of Galbraith's recent essay following on from his book *The End of Normal* and to their credit post-Keynesians in general have engaged in dialogue with ecological economists on this point.[39] Nor is it news to advocates of MMT who have worked on Green New Deals.[40] Nor is it an argument *against* MMT, since MMT offers one of the more promising avenues by which financing might be secured and directed to achieve some of what the world now urgently requires – public interest directed investment for a *global* emergency – but it is an indication that advocates of MMT need to start thinking creatively about how to achieve different ways of living, how to connect together activity occurring within different countries and what 'enough' means on a finite planet.

NOTES

1. For background material on MMT, see Armstrong, 2015, 2018a, 2018b, 2019a, 2019b, 2020a; Kelton, 2020; Mitchell et al., 2019; Mosler, 2010, 2012; Wray, 1998, 2012.
2. Galbraith, 2021.
3. See Armstrong, 2018a, 2020b; Fullbrook and Morgan, 2020.
4. Galbraith, 2021.
5. Infecting game theory, behavioural economics, formalised network approaches, experimental economics and so on.
6. Though the full argument requires more nuance since mainstream economics advocates some kinds of rule use – such as a Taylor Rule to set interest rates in relation to inflationary effects – the point though is that these begin with false premises and conflate limited statistical associations with adequate explanation of real-world relations.
7. Hence, the problem of points of departure and loosening; in behavioural economics this becomes a curious language where how people really act (rather than the standards defined by model entities that have never existed) becomes forms of bias and irrationality rather than situated reasoned conduct.
8. British Cambridge refers to the place (distinguished from Cambridge, Massachusetts) not the nationality of those involved. Again, see Armstrong, 2018a, 2020b for a discussion of the commonalities and distinctions between MMT and other heterodox schools, in particular, post-Keynesianism.
9. Note that 'possible world' is not being used here in the strict sense as formulated by David Lewis in relation to counterfactuals in analytical philosophy, but rather in the ordinary language sense of a real possibility that can be produced (since

Lewis's work is critiqued for its conflation of conceivable and possible and for empty sets of infinite non-demonstrable unformed possibilities etc. – see the work of Nicholas Rescher and others).

10. While Galbraith orients on 'useful economists' with the implication that some economists are 'useless', in political discourse a 'useful idiot' is one who propagandises for a cause without comprehending the full implications of their position and its consequences – so there is perhaps a different way of putting this.

11. Dow, 1996: 2.

12. And there is, of course, notable overlap with sociology – for example, Max Weber in the past and Geoffrey Ingham and Andrew Sayer today.

13. As the title of Blaug's work suggests, methodology has not always clearly meant fundamental framing in the sense used by Dow, it is often conflated with or reduced to mere collection of common methods. Dow's use is the more insightful.

14. See also Chick and Dow, 2005; Dow, 2012; Fleetwood, 2017.

15. Lawson, 1997.

16. Lawson, 2003.

17. The following discussion draws on Lawson, 1997, 2003; Lawson and Morgan, 2021.

18. There is a further tension here worth noting. We have emphasised the aspect of Dow and Galbraith's work that focuses on axioms and their effects on models but there is greater range to the exploration of philosophy of science credentials of economics. Axiom-based modelling tends to be deductive in its logical form and positivist in its construction and claims, and this sits awkwardly with an empiricist strand in economics, which tends to be more inductive in its approach, for example, building econometric tests that eschew formal theory but work on the basis of an empiricist 'naïve objectivism'. Both have been influential.

19. Lawson, 1997: 77–81.

20. See Armstrong, 2020b: 393–5.

21. See, for example, Lawson, 2003 and the reference lists of Lawson and Morgan, 2021; Morgan, 2016a, 2016b.

22. For fuller accounts of this standard terminology and its derivation, see Bhaskar, 1975 [2008], 1978 [2015]; Buch-Hansen and Nielsen, 2020; Collier, 1994; Danermark et al., 2019; Sayer, 1992. In addition, critical realism typically argues for a triad of: ontological realism, epistemological relativism and judgmental rationalism.

23. Failing this natural science often relies on 'natural experiment' situations where some situation or unusual event allows an underlying principle to be tested (an eclipse allows the effect of gravity on light to be tested). In natural science, especially physics, one also has the concept of fields that are part of the structured way in which things can happen.

24. The most well-known argument to this effect is Lawson, 2006.

25. The standard argumentation scheme for this draws on the terminology of 'epistemic fallacy' – the reduction of what is to what is known; and the distinction between how we conceive, study and model reality – the 'transitive' resources of our thought – and the 'intransitive' aspects of reality we apply them to (even if those intransitive aspects can be in some cases products of our activity, i.e., components of social reality).

26. Note that 'process' is typically contrasted with 'substance' in philosophy – a storm is a process not a thing you can hold in your hand. Perhaps the

best-known survey of the concept of process and attempt to reconcile it with the temporal flow of materiality and entities is Rescher, 1996.

27. Lawson, 1997: 204.
28. Morgan and Patomäki, 2017.
29. Lawson, 2003: 107, 1997: 209.
30. Armstrong, 2018b. Source: *OECD Stat* data 2007–2011. We would point out that this data predates the introduction of the Outright Monetary Transactions programme (which allowed the ECB to purchase government bonds in secondary markets) in 2012. The adoption of this programme dampened perceived default risk and was followed by reduced government bond spreads, an observation consistent with the expectations of MMT.
31. However, we would note that attempts to do the same have been notably absent in the case of the mainstream. Faced with trying to explain the fact that, say, Japan has very low interest rates on government debt despite its relatively high debt to GDP ratio compared to say, Greece, which has a much lower ratio, they rely on an ad hoc explanation par excellence – that the assumed higher net savings desires of the Japanese domestic private sector and their supposed willingness to lend at lower interest rates than overseas investors provides the explanation. However, mainstream economists are also keen to suggest that this situation may end 'soon' – without specifying when. They continue with the same contention that, *ceteris paribus*, a positive causal relationship exists between heightened government deficits as a percentage of GDP and increased long-term interest rates on government debt, using the cases of Eurozone countries (where nations must act as currency users in the manner of US states and perceived heightened default risk would be expected to raise bond yields, for example, Greece and Portugal) to support their contention but either ignoring data or producing ad hoc modifications (such as that used to 'explain' the apparent 'anomaly' of Japan) when faced with the mass of contradictory data from currency-issuing nations outside the Eurozone. See Armstrong, 2018b.
32. Armstrong, 2018b.
33. Armstrong, 2018b.
34. Mosler, 2012.
35. Armstrong, 2020b.
36. Lawson, 2019.
37. MMT contains an explicit recognition of how institutional change impacts on the real mechanisms present in an economy. For example, MMT stresses that the social structures and institutions extant under the Gold Standard – those necessary for its survival – determined the actual behaviour of the authorities observed by economists as policy outcomes or 'events' (Armstrong, 2015; Mosler, 2012). MMT highlights the contrast between these Gold Standard institutions and the nature of contemporary institutions and mechanisms at work in monetary systems when a nation issues its own non-convertible currency where state and central bank must work hand-in-hand on a daily basis. From an MMT perspective, membership of the Gold Standard involved the adoption of structures and required certain behaviours on the part of the state when they became part of social reality (Armstrong, 2015; Mosler, 2012). However, social realities fundamentally changed in 1971 and new structures, mechanisms and rules apply for nations with their own sovereign currencies operating under floating exchange rates.
38. See also Armstrong, 2015.
39. Galbraith, 2020; Holt et al., 2009.
40. For example, Nersisyan and Wray, 2020.

REFERENCES

Armstrong, P. (2015) 'Heterodox theories of Money and Modern Monetary Theory (MMT)', accessed 21 July 2021 at https://mosJereconomics.com/wp-content/uploads/2007/12/Money-and-MMT.pdf

Armstrong, P. (2018a) 'Keynes's view of deficits and functional finance; a Modern Monetary Theory perspective', *International Review of Applied Economics*, 32(6): 241–53.

Armstrong, P. (2018b) 'MMT and an alternative heterodox paradigm', Gower Initiative for Modern Money Studies, accessed 21 July 2021 at https://gimms.org.uk/2018/12/26/mmt-heterodox-alternative-paradigm/

Armstrong, P. (2019a) 'All MMT advocates recognise that constraints exist', *Financial Times*, 10 May, accessed 21 July 2021 at https://www.ft.com/content/ba269e50-7016-11e9-bf5c-6eeb837566c5

Armstrong, P. (2019b) 'A simple MMT advocate's response to the Gavyn Davies article "What you need to know about modern monetary theory"', Gower Initiative for Modern Money Studies, 27 May, accessed 21 July 2021 at https://gimms.org.uk/2019/05/27/phil-armstrong-gavyn-davies-response/

Armstrong, P. (2020a) 'An MMT perspective on macroeconomic policy space', in E. Fullbrook and J. Morgan (eds), *Modern Monetary Theory and Its Critics*, Bristol: Real World Economics Books, pp. 67–96.

Armstrong, P. (2020b) *Can Heterodox Economics Make a Difference?: Conversations with Key Thinkers*, Cheltenham, UK and Northampton, MA, USA: Edward Elgar.

Bhaskar, R. (1975) *A Realist Theory of Science*, London: Routledge. Reprinted in 2008.

Bhaskar, R. (1978) *The Possibility of Naturalism*, London: Routledge. Reprinted in 2015.

Buch-Hansen, H. and Nielsen, P. (2020) *Critical Realism: Basics and Beyond*, London: Macmillan.

Chick, V. and Dow, S.C. (2005) 'The meaning of open systems', *Journal of Economic Methodology*, 12(3): 361–81.

Collier, A. (1994) *Critical Realism*, London: Verso.

Danermark, B., Ekstrom, M., Jakobsen, L. and Karlsson, J. (2019) *Explaining Society*, second edn, London: Routledge.

Dow, S.C. (1996) *The Methodology of Macroeconomic Thought*, second edn, Cheltenham, UK and Brookfield, VT, USA: Edward Elgar Publishing.

Dow, S.C. (2012) *Foundations for New Economic Thinking*, Basingstoke: Palgrave Macmillan.

Fleetwood, S. (2017) 'The critical realist conception of open and closed systems', *Journal of Economic Methodology*, 24(1): 41–68.

Fullbrook, E. and Morgan, J. (eds) (2020) *Modern Monetary Theory and its Critics*, Bristol: Real World Economics Books.

Galbraith, J. (2020) 'Economics and the climate catastrophe', *Globalizations*, 18(7): 1117-22.

Galbraith, J. (2021) 'What is economics? A policy discipline for the real world', *Real-World Economics Review*, 96: 67-81.

Holt, R., Pressman, P. and Spash, C. (eds) (2009) *Post Keynesian and Ecological Economics*, Cheltenham, UK and Northampton, MA, USA: Edward Elgar Publishing.

Kelton, S. (2020) *The Deficit Myth*, London: John Murray.

Lawson, T. (1997) *Economics and Reality*, London: Routledge.

Lawson, T. (2003) *Reorienting Economics*, London: Routledge.

Lawson, T. (2006) 'The nature of heterodox economics', *Cambridge Journal of Economics*, 30(3): 947–83.

Lawson, T. (2019) 'Money's relation to debt: Some problems with MMT's conception of money', *Real-World Economics Review*, 89: 109–28.

Lawson, T. and Morgan, J. (2021) 'Cambridge social ontology, the philosophical critique of modern economics and social positioning theory: An interview with Tony Lawson, part 1', *Journal of Critical Realism*, 20(1): 72–97.

Mitchell, W.F., Wray, L.R. and Watts, M.J. (2019) *Macroeconomics*, London: Red Globe Press.

Morgan, J. (2016a) 'The contemporary relevance of a Cambridge tradition: Economics as political economy, political economy as social theory and ethical theory', *Cambridge Journal of Economics*, 40(2): 663–700.

Morgan, J. (2016b) 'Critical realism as a social ontology for economics' in Fred Lee and Bruce Cronin (eds), *Handbook of Research Methods and Applications in Heterodox Economics*, Cheltenham, UK and Northampton, MA, USA: Edward Elgar Publishing, pp. 15–34.

Morgan, J. and Patomäki, H. (2017) 'Contrast explanation in economics: Its context, meaning, and potential', *Cambridge Journal of Economics*, 41(5): 1391–418.

Mosler, W. (2010) *The Seven Deadly Innocent Frauds of Economic Policy*, US Virgin Islands: Valance.

Mosler, W. (2012) *Soft Currency Economics II*, US Virgin Islands: Valance.

Nersisyan, Y. and Wray, L.R. (2020) 'Can we afford the Green New Deal?', Levy Economics Institute, Public Policy Brief No. 148.

Rescher, N. (1996) *Process Metaphysics*, New York: State University of New York Press.

Sayer, A. (1992) *Method in Social Science*, second edn, London: Routledge.

Wray, L.R. (1998) *Understanding Modern Money*, Cheltenham, UK and Lyme, NH, USA: Edward Elgar Publishing.

Wray, L.R. (2012) *Modern Monetary Theory*, Basingstoke: Palgrave Macmillan.

9. Tax as a hygiene factor: setting UK taxation policy using Modern Monetary Theory

Neil Wilson

Taxes are dull. They are boring. Nobody wants to think about them; fewer want to have to pay them. However, like the sewage system, we must have effective taxation or unpleasantness ensues.

MMT makes the case that taxes drive currency.[1] A sovereign nation like the UK[2] does not need tax revenue per se, but instead imposes taxes in its jurisdiction for other purposes. This chapter explains why the UK imposes taxation, analyses the current approach, and restructures the UK tax system using the MMT lens.

9.1 WHY TAX?

If the nation does not need your taxes, why tax at all?

9.1.1 Driving the Denomination

Taxes drive money. Without the obligation, currency acceptance becomes a Greater Fool contest where 'confidence' reigns.[3] However, once a nation starts to tax, it can provision itself without the explicit use of force.[4] What is less frequently understood about this process is that it is expectational in nature. If a person expects to suffer a tax liability and knows that the nation has the capacity and capability to enforce it upon them, then they are likely to seek to obtain the denomination[5] necessary to extinguish their expected liability whether they are confident in that denomination or not. Not a penny of tax has to be paid over for the process to work. It works via fear of future consequences, which is why it can be used, if required, as a 'starter motor' to force a particular denomination to circulate.

9.1.2   Releasing the Resources

Taxes reduce the demand for physical resources from the non-government sectors. Resources which then become available for purchase by the government in pursuit of the socio-economic programme it was elected to provide. You will note the order here. Resources have to be available[6] for the government to purchase *before* the government can purchase them.[7] In essence, the government can only purchase that which is unemployed and unencumbered. If what it physically needs isn't available, then it has to make it available by reducing demand sufficiently to release what is required. Taxation is the main way of doing that.[8]

These are the two, and only two, economic reasons for taxation in a sovereign nation, where that nation wishes to exploit the advantage of its currency, drive its output to the higher level MMT shows is available and distribute that output fairly across its population.

9.2   POLITICAL TAXES IN THE UK

Taxation is an intensely political concept and there are many other political reasons put forward for depriving people of their money. Since most of the taxation analysis from MMT economists has been focused on the USA, these reasons get called 'taxes' in the literature. However, in the UK we generally have different names for such charges: Levies, Duties, Revenues, Excise, Tariffs, Tolls or Fees.

For example, Tobacco Duty is an attempt to reduce the consumption of tobacco, Fuel Duty supposedly reduces the consumption of carbon-based fuels, Air Passenger Duty purports to reduce the number of flights. If the ultimate purpose of these duties is achieved, then the money raised from them drops to zero. As you can see, this is a different purpose to a general tax which has to constantly release a resource for the public use regardless of economic conditions or alterations in behaviour.

TV licence fee receipts are a hypothecated charge that closely matches the amount paid by the UK government to fund the BBC. The two are linked in the minds of taxpayers to the extent that the licence fee is seen as a service charge that pays for the BBC, even though it is imposed on anybody in the UK watching TV broadcast streams from any source, including those on platforms such as YouTube or Twitch.[9] If the BBC were to be abolished, then the public would expect the licence fee to disappear too.

Although most tithes were abolished by the Tithe Act 1936,[10] a remnant still exists in the form of the Chancel Repair Liability, which is the right of a church to impose a charge on certain property within England and Wales for the upkeep of the parish buildings. Several rents of this character persist in

British land law, from ground rents charged because your property is 'lease-hold' rather than 'freehold', to the newer 'maintenance' rent charges included as covenants in 'freehold' deeds.[11] All these arise because you cannot own land outright in England and Wales, only an interest in land. Taxing land is very popular amongst many political operators, even though an MMT analysis shows that it serves little or no purpose.[12] The public sector generally has a surplus of land assets, so from an MMT perspective, a land tax does not directly free up any useful resources.

Much of the politics of the last 30 years or so has been an attempt, on all sides of the political spectrum, to make taxes more important than they are, whether that is cutting taxes in the naive belief that eliminating the correspond-ing government spending will not affect aggregate demand, or imposing taxes in the naive belief that they will magically alter behaviour in some specified way without material side effects. The MMT analysis shows that neither of those things is economically useful, although, of course, they may be polit-ically expedient. MMT suggests that economic management is best done on the spend side, via direct grants, purchases and improved automatic stabilisers.

The result of political interference and using the taxation side of the economy for management, forced in part by the limitation on state aid that came from the UK's membership of the European Union (EU), has caused an explosion in the size of the UK tax code. This unnecessary complication has increased the opportunities for tax avoidance, which has brought with it even more legislation to try to deal with the problem.

The increased bureaucracy of tax compliance was recognised in 2010 and addressed in the traditional British fashion, by adding further bureaucracy in the form of the Office of Tax Simplification (OTS).[13] The OTS purports 'to offer recommendations and advice to the Chancellor about how to make the UK tax system simpler, not least for individuals and smaller businesses', but since it operates in a traditional paradigm, it can only really tinker around the edges.

By looking through the MMT lens, we can strip away all these political complications and get back to the root function of the UK taxation system which all shades of political colour can use to achieve their ends. This results in a level of simplification that the OTS, trapped by the false paradigm of financing fiscal flows, can never manage.

9.3   TAXATION PRINCIPLES

Now we have the two economic reasons for taxation: Driving the Denomination and Releasing the Resources, we can draw from these some principles which a functional tax system will need to adhere to if it is to fulfil its economic purpose.

9.3.1   Tax Costs, Not Profits

Releasing the Resources simply means entities in the economy must purchase fewer things of particular types. A sure-fire way of doing that is to make them more expensive to buy. Costs are a matter of fact. An entity has definitely contracted to receive them. An amount has definitely been transferred to settle the bill. The payee is very unlikely to take less just to reduce the tax bill of the payer. If an entity can reduce their costs, then they are doing more with less, which is what we want to drive forward productivity. Therefore, it makes far more sense for taxes to apply to costs, not profits. Tax due then becomes a matter of transaction fact rather than accounting opinion.

This implies that tax is imposed on a cash basis, not an accrual basis. Again, this makes sense. If somebody is building a factory, they are using a lot of manpower that is no longer available to the public sector to use to build a school. Amortising tax payments over 20 years makes no sense from a functional viewpoint. It's the resources being used now that matter.

9.3.2   Keep Tax Simple

Tax avoidance is nature's way of telling you your tax code is too complicated. Simplify the code and the problem will go away.

At root, tax avoidance comes from a political difference of opinion on the application of a statute. Since tax is about Releasing the Resources, you can't have that difference of opinion. Tax law must be clear, it must be black and white, and it must be easily understood. Nobody can believe they have more purchasing power than they should have or, as with evasion, inflation could result.

Multiple allowances and offsets, complicated tables and rates, arguments over what is a cake and what is a biscuit[14] or the esoteric difference between 'necessary' and 'necessarily'[15] confuse the best minds, never mind Bob the Builder trying to work out what he owes on the back of his packet of Regals.

Compliance with tax law should be straightforward and not require a veritable army of our best and brightest working to provide what are essentially legalese translation services. Simplification frees up highly skilled individuals, who would otherwise be engaged in the business of compliance, to work in more productive endeavours.

9.3.3   Never Pay Your Own Tax

There are three steps to taxation. There is a liability imposed on a person, there is an assessment of that liability, and then there is a payment in settlement of the assessment. The worst collection rates arise when the person with the liability is responsible for the assessment and the payment of the tax. Tax should be assessed and paid by a third party, preferably one that owes a debt to the tax liability holder rather than receiving from them. Nobody likes paying tax and entities settling their own bill will try to minimise it. However, when you are paying other people's taxes, and are liable for any mistakes in doing so, you will strive to get the right amount.[16]

9.3.4   Value All Transactions

One of the concerns with transaction taxes is how they get started. If nobody ever exchanges in your denomination, then why would anybody take it? The way around that is to value all transactions within your jurisdiction in the prescribed denomination. Even if you pay for other people's time using physical assets or foreign currency, then that exchange or distribution is valued as though it had been paid in the denomination and tax demanded in that denomination.[17]

In the same way that a set of accounts has a reporting currency into which all transactions are translated, tax should have a calculation denomination into which all transactions are translated. That doesn't have to be limited to transactions within the country's borders, it can apply to a country's citizens worldwide.[18]

9.3.5   Be Seen to Be Fair

A tax system has to be perceived as fair by the people it is imposed upon if it is to have a chance of operating successfully. People are not the rational actors of theory and myth. Stories matter because people believe them, not because they are true. In the realm of taxation, that means political taxes applied for social reasons, not economic ones. Not just to deal with society's ills via 'sin' taxes, but to satisfy the population's sense of fairness, however skewed from physical reality that may be. In an MMT-inspired economy, that can lead to more people on the Job Guarantee than is ideal,[19] even though economic output will still be greater taking the functional approach than the fiscal approach.

9.3.6   Evaders Must Be Jailed

Certain offences are of a higher category of harm than others and always warrant a custodial sentence. Some, like murder, are obvious, others less so. Contempt of Court, for example, 'is not a wrong done to another party to the litigation. It is an affront to the rule of law itself and to the court'.[20] Counterfeiting the currency is a serious offence: 'It is a trite observation made in these cases, but nevertheless correct, that the issue of counterfeit notes undermines the whole economy of the country … It follows therefore that this type of offence is one which inevitably in nearly every case, would require a custodial sentence.'[21] The evasion of tax must fall into this category. Neither fines, nor confiscation of property, is sufficient recompense for tax evasion. Liberty must be lost. It seems that the 'de minimis' by which tax evasion results in a jail sentence gets ever higher.[22] That must stop. Tax evasion must be treated with the same seriousness as counterfeiting the currency, and for the same reasons.

Strong enforcement is important for two main reasons. First, the acceptance of the currency across the nation's jurisdiction depends upon the expectations that the denomination will be demanded in all corners. The UK has only one land border in Northern Ireland and the sharpness of the currency border at that point depends upon the denomination everybody expects to have to pay to settle their liabilities.[23] If tax liability enforcement is weak, then the stronger currency will come to dominate.[24] That leads to a reduction in the number of people prepared to work for the nation's denomination to provide public services.

Second, tax evasion provides somebody with more purchasing power than they should have, which means that the resources that the public sector expected to have available won't be there or, worse, those hired by the public sector will have to pay more for the resources they need to live, resulting in inflation.

Robust prosecution of tax laws is the indispensable foundation for both Driving the Denomination and Releasing the Resources. The reputation of His Majesty's Inspectors of Taxes for getting blood out of a stone must be maintained.

9.4   TAX INCIDENCE

Tax incidence distinguishes between the entities who ultimately bear the tax burden and those on whom tax is initially imposed. There is much theoretical matter in the mainstream literature, but all of it is couched in financial terms. The functional approach of MMT requires that tax incidence is judged on the basis that it Releases the Resources that the public sector wants to purchase and that it avoids inflation pressure. The mainstream approach considers a tax to be 'efficient' if it can collect revenue while leaving production and consumption decisions relatively unchanged.[25] 'Efficient' taxes are unlikely to work from the functional viewpoint, which requires 'effective' taxation instead. Therefore, the theoretical work from the mainstream is likely of little relevance,[26] but the empirical studies may hold some useful information if analysed carefully. What we want to discover is how tightly a tax binds to those it is imposed upon, and how easily they can move that cost to another person. Does the tax achieve its goal of reducing the demand for the items the government wishes to buy? We also want the tax to be consistent in effect and symmetrical so that raising a tax rate has the same incidence as lowering it.

Benzarti and Carloni looked into the incidence of VAT in France[27] and concluded:

> Because prices tend not to adjust downwards, our analysis suggests that VAT cuts are not an effective measure to stimulate consumer demand. In contrast, our evidence shows that VAT cuts are desirable if the goal is to stimulate supply by increasing profits of business owners. In addition, our findings imply that temporary VAT cuts that are reversed by equally large VAT increases can result in higher equilibrium prices that harm consumers. Finally, reduced VAT rates often apply to commodities that are necessities (such as food and medication) and are therefore consumed disproportionally more by low-income households. The evidence we provide suggests that if VAT rates were reduced to benefit those households, this goal is not likely to be achieved, because of the limited pass-through to prices.

Velasquez and Vtyurina[28] examined the effect of taxes on labour supply in EU New Member States:

> The second objective of our econometric analysis is to shed some light on the effects of different taxes on different margins of hours. This allows us to quantify the approximate deadweight loss of taxation at a more granular level and to quantify potential gains from policy actions. First, we estimate the elasticity of aggregate hours with respect to consumption, personal income, and social security tax rates. We find that social security contributions deter hours the most, followed by consumption taxes and, to a lesser extent, personal income taxes. We also show that these taxes have heterogeneous effects on hours along the intensive (hours per worker) and extensive margin (employment rate). Consumption and personal income taxes are found to affect hours per worker, but not employment rates. On the other hand, social security contributions are negatively associated with employment rates, but do not seem to affect hours per worker.

Adam et al. undertook a panel analysis of 35 years of National Insurance data in the UK[29] from which they concluded:

> Our estimates suggest that responses to employee and employer NICs differ significantly. We find that reductions in marginal rates of employee NICs have positive and statistically significant effects on labor cost, operating via hours of work. We also find that labor cost falls more than one-for-one when average employer NICs rates are reduced, but by much less when employee NICs rates are reduced, with most of the effect (and nearly all of the difference) operating via hourly labor cost. These findings are robust across specifications based on different instruments, different sub-periods of analysis, and different sub-groups of employees.
> We interpret this as evidence that employees change their hours in response to NICs, but that in the short- to medium-run at least, the formal incidence of NICs matters for their behavioral impacts and economic incidence. If employers

respond to changes in marginal employer NICs rates at all, they do so by adjusting the number of employees they hire and/or how they compensate their employees (things we cannot observe in our data), rather than by adjusting the hours offered to individual employees.

Lane and Wray[30] analysed corporation taxes and where the incidence falls:

> It might seem silly to ask the question, but who really pays those corporate taxes? While it would appear that corporate taxes fall on shareholders through reduced profits, this is only true in the short run. In order to remain viable investments for current and potential shareholders, in the long run corporations strive to maintain and improve their profit margins – and do so by raising prices and/or cutting costs, including wage and benefit costs. Consequently, the burden of an increase in corporate taxes is ultimately shared by consumers and the factors of production, including labor.

Goodman[31] asked the question directly, 'Who Pays the Corporate Income Tax'?

> ... let's turn to the corporate income tax. Who pays it? When all adjustments are said and done there are several candidates, including consumers, workers and stockholders. How is the burden distributed among those three groups?
> The surprising answer is that economists don't know.

Wray[32] refers to the famous paper by Ruml[33] and to Minsky[34] in his disdain of the corporate income tax.

> However, much of the corporate tax is passed backwards to employees (in the form of lower wages and salaries, and benefits) and forward to consumers in the form of higher prices. Again, we do not know exactly how much of the tax is paid by employees and consumers ...
> Ruml argued that corporate taxes distort decision making – to take actions to minimize taxes rather than those that would otherwise make the best business sense ...
> Minsky agrees with Ruml: the corporation tax encourages debt as well as spending on advertising, marketing and perks for executives since these can be written off taxes ...
> Whenever I am asked at conferences 'what should we do about corporations moving offshore to evade taxes', I say 'eliminate the corporate income tax'. When someone then asks 'but how will we afford programs to help the poor?', I respond, as Ruml, Chairman of the Federal Reserve Bank of New York did, 'Taxes for revenue are obsolete'.

Tax incidence is further complicated by the notion of tax salience,[35] which is the idea that people respond to factors other than the net tax liability, such as the way that taxes are displayed and the tax payment mechanism. Chetty et al.[36] found that posting sales tax-inclusive prices on price labels altered consumption rates, whereas sales taxes calculated at the register did not.[37] The perception of the level of taxes by individuals varies due to a number of factors. Fochmann and Wiemann[38] found that:

> Subjects perceive a too high net wage because they underestimate the tax. We conjecture that tax perception depends on the tax rate, the presentation of the tax and the experience subjects have with taxation. These conjectures are confirmed in four further treatments employing a direct and an indirect progressive tax scale. It turns out that simple taxes are particularly prone to being misperceived because their simplicity reduces the tax salience.

However, it is the impact of salience on tax payment mechanisms that is most illuminating. Finkelstein[39] notes:

> For every dollar of revenue raised by the US income tax system, taxpayers incur about 10 cents in private compliance costs associated with record keeping and tax filing. These compliance costs impose a dead-weight burden on society. Yet policies that would reduce these costs are frequently opposed by policy-makers and economists who believe that compliance costs play an important role in keeping taxes visible and salient to the electorate, who then serve as an important check on attempts to raise the scale of government activity beyond what an informed citizenry would want.
>
> The idea that a less visible tax system may fuel the growth of government can be traced back at least to John Stuart Mill's 1848 *Principles of Political Economy*. It has its modern roots in the public choice tradition of 'fiscal illusion'. In a series of influential books and articles, James Buchanan and co-authors have argued that citizens systematically under-estimate the tax price of public sector activities, and that government in turn exploits this misperception to allow it to reach a size that is larger than an informed citizenry would want.

Information on the effect of tax salience remains hard to come by:[40]

> Empirical evidence of the impact of tax salience on tax rates, however, has proved extremely elusive. Most of the evidence comes from cross sectional studies of the relationship between the size of government and the visibility of the tax system, where the direction of causality is far from clear. Moreover, the sign of any effect of tax salience on tax rates is theoretically ambiguous. The link between tax salience and tax rates is therefore an open empirical question.

What work there has been on tax salience has been directed at individuals, usually as earners or consumers. There is a total lack of empirical data about the impact of tax salience upon corporations and the consequent effect upon the incidence of taxes paid by firms.

9.5   THE FUNGIBILITY FALLACY

If you talk about tax in fiscal terms, it makes tax a fungible concept. One £10 note is the same as any other.[41] From that point of view, raising taxes in one part of the economy or from one set of people is just the same as raising it anywhere else.

However, when you start to talk about tax in terms of Releasing the Resources, this is no longer the case. All of a sudden skill, aptitude and experience start to play a part. Not everybody can become a brain surgeon no matter how much training you apply, and it takes many years to produce one in any case. Moving manpower between areas of the economy is not instant, and may not even be possible. People are not fungible; they are very much individuals.

Taxation policy has to be framed with the end goal in mind, which is to release real resources the public sector wishes to buy in the current period. Almost certainly that means permanent workers with high skill, aptitude and experience.[42]

This implies that taxation must be targeted and progressive. It must be targeted to release the right sort of resources. A surplus of dockers is no good when you want doctors. It must be progressive so that the tax binds tighter on those who are paid more. Almost by definition, those who are paid more are more likely to have the scarce skills and experience the public sector requires. Naturally, the private sector will fight to retain its skilled resources and the tax may have to be quite fierce to force the private sector to release them.[43]

Nevertheless, it is important not to overstate the case. Adding complexity in an attempt to micromanage the labour market is unlikely to work. The interaction between tax incidence and resource fungibility is not easy to predict with certainty. Therefore, simplicity should trump other issues where there is a conflict. However, the relative lack of fungibility amongst the resources required by the government does call into question flat tax, wealth tax and land tax proposals, which need to demonstrate how they would work to free up real resources to give the real space for governments to spend.

9.6   A MODEST PROPOSAL

Functional analysis of the taxation mechanisms via the MMT lens leads to a fundamentally different view of taxation. The primary purpose is to Release the Resources the public sector requires to fulfil the democratic mandate of the elected government. The limitations of fungibility require that the tax is specific and detailed. Yet the secondary purpose of Driving the Denomination and the anti-avoidance and anti-evasion powers of simplicity requires tax that is general and broad-based. This is the engineering trade-off at the heart of the tax system.

Furthermore, we have the main insight of MMT – that the money system and the real production system are at best inductively connected. A change in the flow of money isn't necessarily going to translate one-to-one into changes in the production system.

On top of all this, we have people's perception. Tax salience matters. People believe taxes pay for things. People have certain views about certain taxes: income tax is a drain, but National Insurance goes in a pot. Finally, the elephant in the room: people would much rather that somebody else paid tax and they kept their money.

We mustn't forget fairness. The UK population has an innate sense of fairness, and it is one of the main drivers of political direction in the country. Everybody must pay their fair share of tax, as the saying goes. The problem is that each person's definition of what is fair differs and it moves over time.

The MMT literature doesn't give much direction as there is little consensus on any particular tax mechanism and the broader tax literature is crippled by both political bias and an outdated revenue-raising viewpoint.

A way through this minefield is to separate the required taxation from the political taxation. What approach would deliver the outcomes required whatever political stripe happens to be in favour at the time? Space doesn't permit a detailed design, so what follows is an overview proposal.

A look at the tax collection data gives a clear steer. The UK's PAYE (Paye as You Earn) system is by far the most effective tax collection mechanism. Tax is assessed on the individual and then collected and paid by the entity operating the PAYE system, usually the employer or the trust paying the pension. This goes to the principle of payment by third parties, ease of enforcement and the impact of tax salience.

However, nobody would suggest that operating a PAYE system is easy to understand. It needs to be vastly simplified and the warts it has grown over the years stripped away. We can do this by getting rid of the various construction schemes, student loan payments, the classes of National Insurance and the peculiar bandings, allowances and offsets of income tax. This goes to the principle of simplicity.

National Insurance has been called in the past a 'tax on jobs'.[44] Yet tax is there to reduce jobs in the private sector so that replacement jobs can be created in the public sector. If 'business leaders' complain that National Insurance will lead to them employing fewer people, then that is exactly what is required. The small amount of evidence about tax incidence backs this up. Employer's National Insurance is the form of taxation where the economic incidence most closely matches the legal incidence. Firms respond to changes in it symmetrically by hiring more or fewer workers. It is imposed on the individual but paid by the employer – which means the individual's wage doesn't change, just the chance of the job existing in the first place.

The existing nature of National Insurance helps. It is non-cumulative and applies on a payment-by-payment basis. Of all the taxes it is a tax on 'now' that is collected early, on a cash basis with no offset. This ensures that resources are released 'now' for government use. It is a tax on the primary cost of doing business, giving an added incentive to replace labour with automation, and thereby driving forward productivity.[45]

Taxation should be shifted towards Employer's National Insurance and away from the other taxes. However, leaving the tax as is would not be sufficient. Its scope must be widened, the cap removed and more rate bands introduced. If and when it replaces income tax, it has to be applied to pensions in payment. Banded taxation allows the government to roughly target skill levels. This will help release the type of people required by the public sector. And since that naturally leads to a progressive taxation structure, it would be seen as fair.

PAYE would need to be extended. The current regime for unincorporated businesses should end and all businesses should be treated as separate entities from their owners. All value transferred to worker/owners should be channelled via a third-party-operated PAYE scheme, and subject to the National Insurance charge.[46] It could, and perhaps should, replace corporation tax, income tax, even VAT, as the primary means by which business is taxed – at source, immediately, based upon expenditure on labour, not profits.

We are lucky in the UK that the PAYE system is so well established as the primary method by which people pay their taxes. This proposal extends and substantially simplifies the mechanism, and which, if taken to its logical conclusion, would remove deductions from wages and make tax disappear completely for the majority of voters, passing the responsibility onto third-party employers and pension providers. A transformation of Employer's National Insurance into the primary tax collection mechanism will Release the Resources necessary for the government to fulfil its democratic mandate and is sufficiently broad-based to Drive the Denomination. It is a fair tax, and recent National Insurance increases have been accepted by the wider population.

Perhaps most importantly it need not be an aggressive change. The system already exists. It would be a journey towards an end goal that can be done in baby steps. A penny change here, a simplification there, followed by a cut in some other tax to compensate.

9.7   CONCLUSIONS

The few pages written by MMT economists do little more than lay out the main theoretical drivers for taxation.[47] This is largely because taxation is a secondary consideration,[48] behind reinvigorating the spend-side automatic stabilisers and putting the banks, particularly central banks, back into their proper place in the order of things. To abuse Herzberg,[49] the Job Guarantee, the true nature of government financing and the hierarchy of money are the intrinsic motivators of MMT, whereas taxation is merely a 'hygiene factor' – the monetary equivalent of managing the flush.

In this chapter, we have derived the general principles a taxation system needs to exhibit and proposed a major simplification to the UK tax regime based upon those principles. This will both Drive the Denomination and Release the Resources.

We argue that these two principal reasons for taxation lead to the conclusion that we should tax costs not profits. We show that the functional justification for progressive taxation is that skilled people tend to be more expensive and taxation needs to release some of them for public use.

We argue that 'political taxes' are required to ensure the tax system is perceived to be fair, and show that the UK has a tradition of giving political taxes different names (duties, levies, etc.) which helps separate the required 'operational taxation' from those achieving a political end. This means the regime proposed will support any UK government that chooses to take the MMT functional approach, whatever their political stripe.

Taxes do indeed drive money, but it is the efficient and effective spending of money by both public and private entities that drives the economy.

NOTES

1. Wray 2015, p. 137; Mitchell et al. 2019, p. 323.
2. A sovereign nation is one that issues its own currency without a promise to convert at a fixed value to gold or foreign currency.
3. Currencies may still circulate and can circulate for a long time via other means. Taxation is only a sufficient, not a necessary, condition for circulation of a denomination. See Deficit Owls 2016.
4. Kelton 2020.
5. By offering goods and services for sale in that denomination.
6. Availability can be capacity to produce. The bread doesn't have to be on the shelf, but sufficient capacity within the bread production system does.
7. This is the 'halting condition' that automatically shuts off government spending. Once the government runs out of things that are available for sale in exchange for its currency at a price worth paying, spending stops.
8. Government can use non-fiscal powers. See Kelton 2020, note 20, p. 272.
9. Communications Act 2003, s365(7) states '... sums received by the BBC by virtue of any regulations under this section must be paid into the Consolidated Fund'. The BBC is just the nominated tax collector.
10. Tithe Act 1936.
11. Permitted by Rentcharges Act 1977, s2 which abolished feudal rent charges.
12. Mitchell 2015a, 2015b.

13. Office of Tax Simplification n.d.
14. HM Revenue & Customs 2016.
15. HM Revenue & Customs 2014.
16. In effect this leverages the agency problem for the public good.
17. This resolves the bootstrap dilemma in Wray 2015, p. 150.
18. UK tax is resolved based upon residence and domicile, whereas US tax is based around citizenship.
19. Where political taxation is excessive and ends up dampening effective demand.
20. *Commissioners for Her Majesty's Revenue and Customs v. Munir* [2015] EWHC 1366 (Ch) at [9(i)].
21. *R v Howard* (1985) 7 Cr.App.R.(S) 320 at p. 322.
22. At the time of writing, it is £12,500. See Revenue Fraud – Sentencing 2014.
23. Which tend to be transitively driven by the taxation denomination.
24. As we see in 'dollarised' nations.
25. Varela 2016.
26. No change there then.
27. Quoted from Benzarti and Carloni 2017; see also Benzarti and Carloni 2019.
28. Velasquez and Vtyurina 2019, p. 6.
29. Adam et al. 2019, p. 41.
30. Lane and Wray 2020.
31. Goodman 2021.
32. Wray 2015, pp. 154–6.
33. Ruml 1946.
34. Minsky 2008.
35. Varela 2016.
36. Chetty et al. 2009.
37. This corresponds to inc. VAT and ex. VAT pricing in the UK.
38. Fochmann and Weimann 2011.
39. Finkelstein 2009, pp. 969–70.
40. Finkelstein 2009, p. 970.
41. Ignoring the serial number obviously.
42. It already has access to general, unskilled, casual labour via the Job Guarantee. You cannot run required public services with such labour as the private sector will poach it during a boom.
43. To the extent that taxation may not be sufficient, and private involvement may have to be excluded by law.
44. The Yorkshire Post 2010.
45. Which may mean fewer people are employed. Since that then makes them available for the public sector to use, there will be less need to tax. The MMT view shows how more automation can mean lower taxes for the size of government required.
46. Eliminating the Construction Industry Scheme and the Off-Payroll Working Rules.
47. See Wilson 2021 for an overview.
48. 'MMT is agnostic about where the tax revenue comes from' in Mitchell 2021.
49. Herzberg 1993.
50. Remember that these tables are drawn up in the paradigm of raising finance and therefore include duties and levies. See HM Revenue & Customs 2021.
51. Earnings are 'anything that constitutes an emolument of the employment'.

52. There is a once a quarter option if your PAYE tax payment is less than £1500 per month.
53. The new year starts on 'Lady Day' in the Julian Calendar. At the time of writing, the UK tax year still starts on that date – even though we've been using the Gregorian Calendar since 1752. The OTS has put forward proposals to move it to a more rational end date. See Office of Tax Simplification 2021.
54. Keep 2021.

REFERENCES

Adam, S., D. Phillips and B. Roantree (2019), '35 years of reforms: A panel analysis of the incidence of, and employee and employer responses to, social security contributions in the UK', *Journal of Public Economics*, 171, 29–50.
Benzarti, Y. and D. Carloni (2017), 'Assessing the incidence of value-added taxes', accessed 28 September 2022 at https://cepr.org/voxeu/columns/assessing-incidence-value-added-taxes.
Benzarti, Y. and D. Carloni (2019), 'Who really benefits from consumption tax cuts? Evidence from a large VAT reform in France', *American Economic Journal: Economic Policy*, 11 (1), 38–63.
Chetty, R., A. Looney and K. Kroft (2009), 'Salience and taxation: Theory and evidence', *American Economic Review*, 99 (4), 1145–77.
Communications Act (2003), accessed 1 August 2021 at https://www.legislation.gov.uk/ukpga/2003/21/section/365.
Deficit Owls (2016), 'MMT: Taxes are sufficient but not necessary to drive a currency', 23 August, accessed 31 July 2021 at https://www.youtube.com/watch?v=0C0_XUuQaRU.
Finkelstein, A. (2009), 'E-ztax: Tax salience and tax rates*', *The Quarterly Journal of Economics*, 124 (3), 969–1010.
Fochmann, M. and J. Weimann (2011), 'The effects of tax salience and tax experience on individual work efforts in a framed field experiment', *FinanzArchiv*, 69, https://doi.org/10.1628/001522113X675692.
Goodman, J.C. (2021), 'Who pays the corporate income tax?', accessed 17 July 2021 at https://www.forbes.com/sites/johngoodman/2021/04/02/who-pays-the-corporate-income-tax/.
Herzberg, F. (1993), *Motivation to Work*, 1st edn, New Brunswick, NJ: Transaction Publishers.
HM Revenue & Customs (2014), EIM31645 – Employment Income Manual – HMRC Internal Manual, accessed 9 January 2022 at https://www.gov.uk/hmrc-internal-manuals/employment-income-manual/eim31645.
HM Revenue & Customs (2016), VFOOD6260 – VAT Food – HMRC Internal Manual, accessed 9 January 2022 at https://www.gov.uk/hmrc-internal-manuals/vat-food/vfood6260.
HM Revenue & Customs (2020), 'Measuring tax gaps', accessed 8 January 2022 at https://webarchive.nationalarchives.gov.uk/ukgwa/20200806185314mp_/https://assets.publishing.service.gov.uk/government/uploads/system/uploads/attachment_data/file/907122/Measuring_tax_gaps_2020_edition.pdf.
HM Revenue & Customs (2021), 'Measuring tax gaps', accessed 9 January 2022 at https://www.gov.uk/government/statistics/measuring-tax-gaps/measuring-tax-gaps-2021-edition-tax-gap-estimates-for-2019-to-2020.

Keep, M. (2021), 'Tax statistics: An overview', accessed 18 July 2021 at https://commonslibrary.parliament.uk/research-briefings/cbp-8513/.

Kelton, S. (2020), *The Deficit Myth: Modern Monetary Theory and How to Build a Better Economy*, London: John Murray.

Lane, E. and L.R. Wray (2020), 'Is it time to eliminate federal corporate income taxes?', *SSRN Electronic Journal*, https://doi.org/10.2139/ssrn.3734445.

Minsky, H.P. (2008), *Stabilizing an Unstable Economy*, vol. 1, New York: McGraw-Hill.

Mitchell, W. (2015a), 'Henry George and MMT – Part 1', accessed 30 June 2021 at http://bilbo.economicoutlook.net/blog/?p=30215.

Mitchell, W. (2015b), 'Henry George and MMT – Part 2', accessed 30 June 2021 at http://bilbo.economicoutlook.net/blog/?p=30219.

Mitchell, W. (2021), 'Booming growth in Britain (Brexit?) but child poverty rises (austerity)', accessed 31 July 2021 at http://bilbo.economicoutlook.net/blog/?p=47987.

Mitchell, W., L.R. Wray and M. Watts (2019), *Macroeconomics*, London: Macmillan Education UK.

Office of Tax Simplification (2021), 'Exploring a change to the UK tax year end date', 15 September, accessed 9 January 2022 at https://assets.publishing.service.gov.uk/government/uploads/system/uploads/attachment_data/file/1016718/Tax_year_end_date_report___web_copy_.pdf.

Office of Tax Simplification (n.d.), 'Office of Tax Simplification – about us', accessed 30 June 2021 at https://www.gov.uk/government/organisations/office-of-tax-simplification/about.

Rentcharges Act (1977), accessed 9 January 2022 at https://www.legislation.gov.uk/ukpga/1977/30/introduction.

Revenue Fraud – Sentencing (2014), accessed 3 July 2021 at https://www.sentencingcouncil.org.uk/offences/magistrates-court/item/revenue-fraud/.

Ruml, B. (1946), 'Taxes for revenue are obsolete', *American Affairs*, 8 (1), 35–9.

The Yorkshire Post (2010), 'No time for a tax on jobs', 1 April, accessed 21 July 2021 at https://www.yorkshirepost.co.uk/news/opinion/columnists/no-time-tax-jobs-1980006.

Tithe Act (1936), accessed 9 January 2022 at https://www.legislation.gov.uk/ukpga/Geo5and1Edw8/26/43/introduction.

Varela, P. (2016), 'What is tax salience?', https://apo.org.au/node/67651.

Velasquez, A. and S. Vtyurina (2019), 'How does taxation affect hours worked in EU New Member States?', IMF Working Papers, 19 (130), 1.

Wilson, N. (2021), 'MMT economists on taxation', accessed 31 July 2021 at https://new-wayland.com/blog/mmt-economists-on-taxation/.

Wray, L.R. (2015), *Modern Money Theory: A Primer on Macroeconomics for Sovereign Monetary Systems*, 2nd edn, Houndmills, Basingstoke and New York: Palgrave Macmillan.

APPENDIX: UK TAX COLLECTION EVIDENCE

Every year HMRC produces a document describing the 'tax gap' for each major type of tax in the UK. This is the difference between the theoretical liability and the amount collected. The latest figures are below.[50]

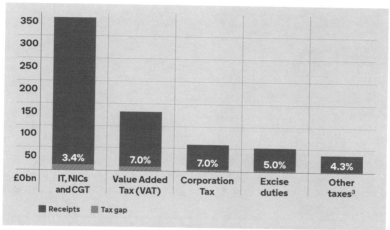

Source: HM Revenue & Customs (2020), 'Measuring tax gaps', accessed 8 January 2022 at https://webarchive.nationalarchives.gov.uk/ukgwa/20200807090250mp_/https://assets .publishing.service.gov.uk/government/uploads/system/uploads/attachment_data/file/907122/ Measuring_tax_gaps_2020_edition.pdf. Contains public sector information licensed under the Open Government Licence v3.0.

Figure 9.A1   Tax gap by type of tax – value and share of total theoretical liabilities 2018–19

VAT is the UK's consumption tax, and has the worst percentage tax gap of all the main taxes, closely followed by business profit taxation – both corporation tax and 'self-assessment' which is largely self-employed businesses.

The best collection percentage is via the UK's Pay as You Earn system (PAYE), which is how the majority of people pay their direct taxes. The system raises some £300 billion of taxation with a shortfall of £3 billion, whereas the £50 billion or so raised outside PAYE in self-assessment is short by £6.5 billion.

PAYE is a charge on earnings[51] and consists of a cumulative progressive income tax charge, and a non-cumulative National Insurance charge that are both deducted from earnings, plus a non-cumulative National Insurance charge

Tax	Type	2005-06		2013-14	2014-15	2015-16	2016-17	2017-18	2018-19
							Percentage tax gap[2,3]		
Value Added Tax	Total VAT	14.0%		11.9%	10.4%	8.6%	8.9%	8.6%	7.0%
Excise duties	Tobacco duties	21.7%		16.5%	12.8%	16.4%	17.8%	13.7%	14.0%
	Alcohol duties[4]	9.8%		11.1%	14.7%	10.1%	9.4%	8.1%	7.5%
	Hydrocarbon oils duties	2.8%		0.1%	0.1%	0.1%	0.5%	0.5%	0.5%
	Other excise duties[5]	6.3%		10.0%	12.1%	8.8%	8.4%	6.7%	6.3%
	Total excise duties	8.4%		6.5%	6.4%	6.1%	6.3%	5.0%	5.0%
Income Tax, National Insurance contributions and Capital Gains Tax	Self Assessment	16.7%		24.7%	22.9%	16.2%	12.6%	13.0%	12.9%
	PAYE	1.5%		1.7%	1.3%	1.3%	1.1%	0.9%	1.0%
	Avoidance[6]	n/a		n/a	n/a	n/a	n/a	n/a	n/a
	Hidden economy[6]	n/a		n/a	n/a	n/a	n/a	n/a	n/a
	Total personal income taxes	4.5%		5.6%	5.3%	4.1%	3.5%	3.3%	3.4%
Corporation Tax	Small businesses	19.1%		13.0%	14.9%	14.7%	13.6%	13.6%	14.4%
	Mid-sized businesses	13.5%		9.7%	12.1%	9.2%	6.6%	6.4%	6.8%
	Large businesses	8.8%		4.0%	4.3%	4.6%	3.2%	3.2%	2.9%
	Total Corporation Tax	11.3%		7.8%	9.1%	8.8%	7.0%	6.8%	7.0%
Other taxes[7]	Stamp duties	2.5%		1.3%	1.4%	1.2%	1.1%	1.0%	1.3%
	Other direct taxes[8]	3.1%		8.6%	8.4%	7.8%	7.7%	8.6%	8.6%
	Other indirect taxes	7.5%		6.1%	6.1%	6.3%	6.6%	4.7%	5.5%
	Total other taxes	4.3%		4.5%	4.3%	4.3%	4.4%	3.7%	4.3%
Total tax gap		7.5%		7.2%	6.8%	5.8%	5.3%	5.0%	4.7%

1 Figures for previous years have been revised.
2 Estimates are rounded to nearest 0.1%.
3 The percentage tax gap for tax types may differ between Chapter 1 and subsequent chapters. We use published receipts figures in Chapter 1 as liability figures are not available at the level required across all tax heads. Read the published receipts figures used in Chapter 1 on GOV.UK:
    www.gov.uk/government/statistics/hmrc-tax-and-nics-receipts-for-the-uk
4 The total alcohol duties figure excludes wine. as wine is now included in 'Other excise duties' in this edition. We explain this further in Chapter 3.
5 'Other excise duties' includes betting and gaming duties, cider and perry duties, spirit-based ready-to-drink duties and wine duties.
6 Percentage tax gap estimates for avoidance and the hidden economy are not shown as tax receipts cannot be calculated.
7 The petroleum tax gap is not calculated from tax year 2015 to 2016 as Petroleum Revenue Tax was permanently zero-rated from 1 January 2016.
8 'Other taxes' includes indirect taxes (Aggregates Levy, Air Passenger Duty, Customs Duty, Climate Change Levy, Insurance Premium Tax, Landfill Tax, Soft Drinks Industry Levy) and direct taxes (Stamp duties, Inheritance Tax and Petroleum Revenue Tax for years prior to 2015 to 2016).

Source: HM Revenue & Customs (2020), 'Measuring tax gaps', accessed 8 January 2022 at https://webarchive.nationalarchives.gov.uk/ukgwa/20200807090250mp_/https://assets .publishing.service.gov.uk/government/uploads/system/uploads/attachment_data/file/907122/ Measuring_tax_gaps_2020_edition.pdf. Contains public sector information licensed under the Open Government Licence v3.0.

Figure 9.A2   Percentage tax gap by type of tax

to the employer based on the total earnings. Tax is collected by the employer when the earnings are paid, and transferred to the exchequer once a month.[52]

VAT is a charge on the supply of goods and services. It is imposed on the seller, a return filed once a quarter and the tax transferred to the exchequer a month later. Corporation tax is a tax on corporate profits, and self-assessed. Both the return and payment are due nine months and one day after the end of the company year.

The traditional tax return is an increasingly rare sight in the UK and is filed largely by those operating as sole traders and unincorporated partnerships. The self-assessed returns are drawn up to the tax year end date of 5 April[53] with both the return and the tax payment due by 31 January the following year.

Both corporations and individuals may have to pay tax early on account depending upon various parameters.

Keep[54] produced an overview of the statistics of the main UK taxes for Parliament in February 2021.

10. Checklist of an employment guarantee programme: the Plan Jefes de Hogar from Argentina revisited 20 years later[1]

Daniel Kostzer

10.1 INTRODUCTION

Twenty years ago, Argentina was the "poster-child" of the Washington Consensus. Its accelerated and radical process of deregulation, privatization, internationalization (or financialization) of the economy could be widely observed. These actions followed from an acceptance of the illusion that "free markets" would lead the country to be a relevant cog in the "first world economic mechanism".

At the 1998 Annual Meeting of the International Monetary Fund (IMF) and the World Bank, the Argentinian President at the time, Carlos Menem, invited President Clinton to join him on stage and then said, *"What we are dealing with, then, is a moral issue, one which we must address if we are to muster political support for a global economy based on market forces"*,[2] receiving a standing ovation from the crowd of dark-suited participants.

Here we present a response from the public sector, set against the canonical wisdom. It included a massive – almost universal – employment guarantee or public employment programme (PEP) aiming to face the multiplicity of difficulties and problems that Argentina was confronting as a result of the long period of financial valorization and secular "structural adjustment" policies.[3] The lessons learned, which shed light upon both how to contextualize such a programme and the elements to be considered in its implementation, will be outlined in a checklist below.

10.2 HOW DID ARGENTINA GET THERE?

The architect of the orthodox economic policies of the 1990s, President Carlos Menem (1989–99) would have liked to continue his leadership, but could not retain power owing to the constitution, which restricted presidents to only two periods in office. The opposition won the general election, but the main message, despite the socio-economic indicators and the desire for change by the population, was to maintain the currency board that pegged the peso to the dollar, and all the institutions reshaped during the 1990s. On top of that, the new administration insisted upon dismantling the few strong labour market regulations that were still in place, with a "Labour Reform" law, associated with the suspicion of corrupt practices at the parliament.[4]

During 2000 and mid-2001, the course of the government was the same as before: adjustment over adjustment. The tightening of the fiscal policies was evident in all the jurisdictions of the federal government. At the same time, the unemployment rate, closure of enterprises, and poverty were going up significantly.

The new administration had been having discussions about how to solve these problems since June 2000. An influential group of economists, mainly from the Ministry of Finance, considered that the problem was a "matching between supply and demand in the labor market", because those unemployed were low-skilled workers, youngsters, and at the bottom categories of employment and, at the same time, the average wages were increasing steadily.

They ignored something that is quite frequently observed in recessionary labour markets: the "composition effect". When the economy slows down, firms engage in "labour hoarding" which means that they keep those workers with higher skills or whose work is more central to the production process, since it would be cheaper to keep them than to fire them, recruit again, and retrain new staff to restore capacity utilization when the demand requires it. Of course, this phenomenon does not apply to those unskilled workers that can rejoin the organization at a very low – or no – cost. The composition effect is what makes the average wage of higher-skilled workers increase relative to that of low-skilled workers, even if it falls in real terms or if the total wage-bill is contracting.

By the end of the 1990s, it seemed clear that the existing arrangements, including pegging the currency to the US dollar by law, limiting money printing (and therefore, fiscal deficits to the reserves in the central bank), which survived in the midst of the recession and concurrent indebtedness of the private and public sector, would be insufficient to deal with the effect on Argentina of the shock waves caused by multiple crises of the late 1990s (the 1997 Asia crisis, further exacerbated in 1998 by the Russian crisis and in 1999 by the Brazilian crisis).

Another measure implemented during 2000 (more stringently than in the previous period of the 1990s) was the reduction in the employers' contributions to social security. This approach led to a decrease in contributions to half the previous level and was based upon the idea that elevated contributions could have been a cause of lack of employment generation (contributions were conceptualized as "non-wage labour costs"). Such measures proved to be ineffective. The government introduced many short-lived measures during 2000 and 2001. The most extreme example was the designation of a Minister of the Economy, Ricardo López Murphy, whose appointment lasted only two weeks,[5] after voices, some from the opposition but mainly inside the governing alliance, rejected his plan.

The government called upon Domingo Cavallo, architect of the "convertibility plan" (1991). He was sworn in on 1 March 2001 as Minister of the Economy. The syllogism was quite simple: "if he invented the convertibility, and inventors are best placed to use their own inventions, he can be the only one that will know how to get us out of trouble". The result was more adjustment, a further reduction of salaries of civil servants by 13 per cent, zero deficit laws, and the request for assistance to the "always ready for more adjustments" IMF, which – in perfect harmony with the international banks – organized the so-called "mega-exchange" in order to guarantee the dollars that would allow the repatriation of funds to large investors.

By the first week of December 2001, the government was forced to impose a control on bank withdrawals by the public. Massive protests erupted, not only by unemployed people – the so-called *piqueteros* – that had been quite frequent in most of the major cities of Argentina since 1996, but also by middle classes banging cooking pans at the entrance of banks, demanding their savings.

By 19 and 20 December 2001, the cities of Argentina witnessed confrontations between the police and protestors that ended in dozens of dead and hundreds of wounded. On that final evening President de la Rua resigned, opening two weeks of uncertainty with five different presidents, until the former Governor of the Province of Buenos Aires, and defeated presidential candidate in the 1999 elections, Eduardo Duhalde, was chosen by the Parliament on 2 January 2002 to finish the mandate in 2003.[6]

By the first quarter of 2002, the unemployment rate was around 25 per cent of the active population, the poverty rate peaked at 56 per cent and, tragically, people were starving in a country that has agricultural exports that can feed 400 million (or ten times its population).

10.3   THE JEFES DE HOGAR PROGRAMME: FROM SCRATCH TO MASSIVE IMPLEMENTATION IN NO TIME

The new president called on non-governmental organizations (NGOs), churches, trade unions, and employers' associations to join a large series of initiatives, much closer to charity than a state policy, while outside the *piqueteros* and *caceroleros* brought cities into chaos.

After a couple of months of drifting among different initiatives that never flourished, a new programme based on providing employment to all those that were willing to devote 20 hours per week in exchange for a salary set at 75 per cent of the statutory minimum wage was put in place. This was the Plan Jefes de Hogar Desempleados (Unemployed head of households).

This plan required an important effort of coordination among different areas of the federal government, plus coordination with the provincial and municipal governments,[7] from the governmental side, and NGOs,[8] worker's unions, grassroots and social movements on the community front. A new form of private–public partnership emerged in Argentina: a new "social pact".

The functioning of the programme was quite intricate but, nevertheless, it was introduced quickly. The different organizations (local governments, NGOs, trade unions, etc.) presented their projects to the national authorities, according to a set of predefined typologies, with all the technical details on the number of potential workers, main activities, contributions by the local communities (materials, tools, places to work), and the expected results. These required the previous endorsement of the local authorities, then the Ministry of Labour at the national level would approve and "trigger" the order to pay the beneficiaries after the month of work. The National Administration for Social Security (ANSES) oversaw sending the payments to the ad hoc bank accounts of the beneficiaries.

The "Consejos Consultivos Locales" (local consultative councils) were introduced in a number of municipalities. They supported the oversight of the projects and the evolution of the programme, helping with the adaptation of typologies and other administrative details.

This gigantic operation went smoothly, with just a small number of complaints and few allegations of corruption; these were channelled to a special fiscal attorney, who would investigate them.

The projects consisted of a number of typologies: community kitchens and canteen services in schools, cleaning of parks, schools, and hospitals, community environmental improvements, gardening and farming, bricks and tiles production, communal bakeries, self-construction, sidewalk repair, irrigation schemes, etc. Later, this list would include the return to school for those that didn't finish school, as well as vocational training and skills development.

At its peak, the Jefes Plan occupied 2.4 million workers, a figure which decreased as the private labour market recovered and provided new jobs. By 2009 there was a smaller number of beneficiaries, mainly women with more than two children, remaining in the Jefes. Later, the scheme was replaced by the new universal programme of child allowance: AUH (Asignacion Universal por Hijo).[9]

From the gender perspective, the transition of the Plan Jefes was quite interesting and an idiosyncratic reflection of society. In principle, the beneficiaries included a similar number of men and women but, as the economy started to recover, the men either found a job or – since more opportunities were on the horizon – went to look for jobs in traditional activities. The positions left by the men in the programme were often occupied by women from the same household. This tendency increased to the point that by 2004 more than two-thirds of the beneficiaries of the Jefes were women.

There are a number of *ex post* evaluations of the Plan Jefes, and I will not replicate them here. The contribution in these pages will be to develop a checklist of the main questions that should be answered when implementing a PEP like the Jefes de Hogar. Some of these questions were part of the preparation for the Jefes, while others are the result of the experience and reflect insights in relation to best practice.[10, 11]

Public employment programmes (PEPs) have a general macroeconomic and monetary theoretical foundation showing their applicability in situations of high unemployment and recession (considered by other authors in this volume), but the peculiarities of the different contexts require us to answer additional questions, particularly in relation to specific labour markets and their functioning. In the text below, we consider the characteristics of a PEP in a multi-dimensional way and relate these features to the Jefes programme.

10.4 INTRODUCTION TO PUBLIC EMPLOYMENT PROGRAMMES (PEP)[12]

10.4.1 Conceptual Framework to Understand Employment Programmes in Crisis Context

Within the universe of public policies, "safety nets" include those interventions aimed at vulnerable populations in the face of economic shocks and are designed to promote more inclusive growth.[13] These are interventions that protect households from falling into poverty in the short run, and/or providing the instruments to support the planning and future decisions of their members. They refer to income transfer programmes (cash, in-kind transfer programmes such as the provision of food, subsidies for essential goods and services), and PEPs, also known as workfare programmes, programmes of employer of last resort, or employment guarantee programmes. The main difference is in the conditionality imposed in each case. In the case of the PEP, the availability to work for a certain time is a key feature.[14]

The conditions that need to be satisfied in order to gain access to these interventions bind different groups of beneficiaries and influence the expected (or desired) impacts, which is why more than one type of scheme tends to coexist in adverse contexts. Access is conditional on an income below the poverty line in some programmes; for others, it depends on the existence of unemployed members, the presence of children in the household, etc., or a combination of the above.[15]

Additionally, in the case of some of these interventions, beneficiaries must meet certain participation requirements to continue receiving benefits. Such is the case of conditional cash transfers (CCTs) where the receipt of the benefit is subject to compliance with activities related to the child members of the household, such as vaccination and education requirements, or health supervision of pregnant women.

In the case of PEP, the requirements consist of time availability for labour activities generally linked to the production of public goods and services, and/ or participation in training and education. However, it should be noted that PEPs also tend to incorporate the typical conditionalities of CCTs' design when they define the household rather than the worker as the beneficiary unit.[16]

Conditionality seeks to extend the impacts of the programme beyond the short-term effects generated. On top of the creation of temporary jobs that provide income, the participation of the vulnerable population in the labour force aims to prevent future unemployment by reducing the dependence of the beneficiary – linking with the labour market, or deepening/updating skills – thus promoting their inclusion to the formal market in times of economic recovery.

The use of a PEP as a tool has been extensive, both temporally and regionally. PEPs are exemplified by the New Deal measures during the Great Depression.[17] Then they spread to other developed and underdeveloped countries, but when countries have had almost full employment, they have been used as targeted and localized schemes, focused upon special economic and promotional zones, rather than as a universal approach.

In response to the financial crisis starting in 2008/9, in middle-income countries, PEPs represented the fourth most widely used labour market policy, after training, entrepreneurship incentives, and assistance in job search.[18]

Evidence from industrialized countries, and that collected in transition and developing countries, suggests that in their recent history PEPs have proved as effective as anti-poverty programmes but have generally not led their beneficiaries to better employment or income opportunities.[19, 20]

10.4.2 The Benefits of the Public Employment Programmes

Within the institutional framework provided by social protection, PEPs are emerging as interventions with desirable characteristics for policymakers. On the one hand, they are outside the charity sector, since they demand work in exchange for money transfer, and if it is extended in time, given the voluntary nature of access, it can constitute a "rights-based intervention" marking a change in the conceptualization of the policy. In this respect, PEPs are aligned with the third principle of the International Labour Organization's (ILO) Recommendation 202[21] on Social Protection Floors, which states "basic income security for persons in active age who are unable to earn sufficient income, in particular in cases of sickness, unemployment, maternity and disability".[22]

On the other hand, the participation in community activities and the monitoring of the beneficiaries – inherent to the design – enhances individual and local (regional) growth, facilitating the integration of vulnerable groups into the community, maximizing support for the programme and reveals valuable information for other interventions within the domain of social protection.

Likewise, they can facilitate citizens' auditing and verification of actions, which allows the implementation of measures and is consistent with a goal of transparency.

10.4.3   Social Benefits of PEPs

Here is a list of the potential benefits of PEPs in the social sphere.

- *They solve problems related to basic household needs.* Many of the households with unemployed members have insufficient income, exposing other indicators of unfulfilled basic needs, such as dropping out of school, precarious housing and overcrowding, higher infant or maternal mortality rate, lack of water and sanitation, etc. The provision of a basic income through employment helps to improve this situation.
- *They improve human capital at the individual, regional, and aggregate level.* It is recognized that the probability that an unemployed person will get a job falls as the period of unemployment grows, so that a programme that contains either skills development and/or "on-the-job training", as a constituent part, constitutes a way to avoid the diminishing of skills. This effect is increased if there are complementary tasks to perform which enhance future employability.
- *They involve beneficiaries in collective projects.* In general, crises have an initial effect of dismantling solidarity networks, generating individual or family behaviours and strategies. There is a tendency to blame the unemployed as an individual, further eroding self-confidence. This type of programme involves them in collective projects, many of them designed from the grassroots, based on the real needs of the community, restoring solidarity chains and social networks. In general, they reinforce the willingness and the perceived value of participating in a common project, with benefits to the overall community, besides those enrolled in the PEP.

- *They reduce pressures on unprotected or informal labour markets.* Many unemployed people enter the market in sectors of lower relative productivity and without protection, competing with other individuals in the same or similar situation (often slightly less poor), which can reduce the remuneration received. The presence of a labour opportunity with compensation that guarantees a minimum floor for pay and conditions increases the bargaining power of the workers, hence, the possibility of improving working conditions in these markets.

10.4.4 Benefits to the Local Economy

- *They are basically counter-cyclical initiatives.* A PEP's main function is to reduce the impact of shocks that affect the economy, as well as reducing the impact of cyclical effects at the local level. A PEP aims to mitigate the effects upon vulnerable social sectors. These programmes compensate for the drop in employment in low periods, while releasing workers to the private sector when its demands require it. They can be counter-cyclical, seasonal, or long term.[23]
- *They make it possible to improve basic infrastructure and social and local services.* The beneficiaries are mainly involved in community projects that allow the improvement of basic infrastructure (streets, parks, schools, drains, sanitation, housing, etc.) in the regions where they live, as well as in services that are relied upon by the community such as childcare, school support, health assistants, among others.[24]
- *They generate multiplier effects locally.* When the projects operate at a reasonable scale, they support increases in local demand, they restore credit for consumption – entrepreneurs know that they are more likely to obtain a stable and secure income – and this effect is greater the more important the "impulse" is relative to income added to the area. They can restore the sectoral production chains that may have been interrupted by the drop in demand for certain goods and services.
- *They induce the creation of quality and stable jobs through their relationship to the productive/private sectors.* If domestic demand is induced and some of the activities developed within the framework of the PEP can be oriented to improve the productivity of the region, it is much more likely that local companies will be able to appropriate the gains, in terms of human capacities, improved infrastructure, etc. and become more competitive.

10.5   THE CHECKLIST FOR THE FEASIBILITY ANALYSIS OF PEPS

10.5.1   The Context: Which Are the Variables That Suggest the Relevance or Not of an Employment Programme?

The labour market is the transmission mechanism that links the economy as a whole, as a structure and systemically, in a recursive way, with the well-being of households in the material dimension. From these dynamics, the levels of equity and poverty that condition the growth pattern of the economy show through and occur within a set of institutions, public and private, and laws and regulations.

The "forces" that create or destroy jobs may have various origins that must be considered:

Is the current situation a result of a lack of accumulation in the capital stock to generate jobs? Or, is there idle installed capacity and the problem is the lack of aggregate demand that sets that capital stock into production?

This must be the first question to be answered from the political point of view when considering the instrument to face the crisis. In other words, Are we suffering from so-called "Marxian" or "Keynesian" unemployment?

It may happen that when an economy faces a macroeconomic shock, the country has already experienced several years of recession, and on some levels has exhausted its resources and mechanisms for adapting consumption to current income. Many income support strategies under the control of the household may have already been used, such as savings, available indebtedness, the entry of additional members into the workforce, or the sale of productive assets. Even when some households still have one or more of these strategies available, in the face of a severe economic shock the value of assets decreases, as well as the probability of profitable employment and self-employment, and consequently their potential to become effective safety nets falls.[25] This is where the intervention in the form of PEPs plays a key role by compensating for the fall in the demand for labour.

10.5.2   Analysis from the Supply and Demand Side of the Labour Market

10.5.2.1 Decline in real wages

In some countries, the interaction between the shock and wages is the dominant effect of the crisis. In this case, macro volatility is transmitted and amplified to wages in a general way. The role of a PEP is to function as insurance, allowing the smoothing of household consumption.

The increase in the labour supply during the crisis reinforces the fall in wages. And, due to the decline in demand, workers are unable to maintain the salary level or the working time (overtime) to protect their incomes.

10.5.2.2 Increased job supply

The labour supply is more elastic for the so-called secondary[26] workers – women and younger household members – than for men in adulthood, hence, a greater response is expected from these groups.[27] Newcomers to the workforce face lower chances of getting a job, or at least a competitive remuneration. Additionally, participation in the workforce by secondary workers induces changes and adjustments within the household, with potential long-term implications (school abandonment, care activities, etc.).

A PEP has the potential to become a functional employment alternative (through the same programme or with complementary programmes/actions) to the new structure of the household and contribute to the stabilization of income in the family.

10.5.2.3 Job losses

Job loss has been the most recurrent effect of the shocks experienced in Latin America[28] with the exception of Mexico. In fact, in most countries, unemployment rates have remained higher than pre-crisis levels.[29] In the absence of widespread unemployment insurance, a PEP can fill that role. However, it is important to establish the nature of unemployment prior to designing a PEP.

If unemployment is structural, that is, it is produced by changes in technology, which determine an oversupply of labour with particular skills or in particular places, or by decline or secular absence in investment, a PEP can be valuable in changing the skills profile of the unemployed – through its training – so that the mismatch of skills between workers and the needs of industry can be alleviated.

If unemployment is of a "Keynesian" nature, that is, it originates from the insufficiency of aggregate demand, a fall in wages, instead of driving growth in the demand for labour, reduces it even more because it decreases workers' expenditures. Here, the selection of projects in the PEP with a large multiplier effect would promote the recovery of aggregate demand.

10.5.2.4 Changes in the composition of employment

"Small changes in unemployment rate can hide large changes in employment."[30]

There are difficulties in replacing the jobs lost from a contracting sector by job creation in an expanding one, especially if the losses originated in changes of the relative prices in the tradable and non-tradable sectors, following shifts in the pattern of demand. The transition of workers between sectors can be facilitated by the design of a PEP, where training activities accelerate the reskilling of workers and reduce the amplitude of the unemployment cycle.

Another possible change in patterns of employment is characterized by movements of workers from jobs protected by social security (formalized wage earners) to non-protected jobs (underemployment and informality), generating a mass of workers without the benefits of social protection. In this case, a PEP can become an "occupation of choice" by offering better wages and working conditions than the informal jobs market. It sets the "de facto minimum wage" for the informal economy.

Finally, transitions can be generated between occupational categories, from the "wage earner" to self-employed, and to unemployed. Here a PEP could enhance the asset and human capital formation of the self-employed and contribute to more sustainable income generation, in addition to improving access to the formal labour market during the upturn.

Long-term impacts (not only transitory effects on income) tend to emerge after crises. If they affect the capacities of household members, they can lead to persistent poverty and unemployment and contribute to its intergenerational transmission.

In general, poverty does not fall quickly to pre-crisis levels. This can affect the health of the community, school attendance, in turn, promoting unfavourable biases in the population with impacts on inequality. A PEP could prevent or mitigate these effects by devising protection mechanisms through the provision of current income and the means to promote the accumulation of human capital at home.

10.6   THE GOAL OF THE PEP

10.6.1   Job Promotion or Anti-poverty Programme?

The diagnosis of the importance of contextually determined variables is very important since such an analysis informs the design of PEP. A programme can be configured to fulfil multiple roles. The priority will be derived from the poverty and employment composition of the vulnerable population.

As mentioned above, although income is an attribute of individuals transferred to households, poverty, measured with any of the conventional methods, is an attribute of households or the family. An awareness of this differentiation is central if design problems that might have unfavourable consequences in the solution of the problems are to be avoided. Here are some of the issues and how to address them by defining the characteristics of the beneficiaries.

10.6.2 Profile of Poverty

Determining the composition of poverty according to the inactive–active population ratio, household structure (headship, presence of children and the elderly, household dependency rate), geographic concentration and living conditions is a crucial precursor to programme design. Producing a taxonomy based upon income (current or short-term poverty) or unsatisfied basic needs (structural poverty) is crucial to a programme designer if she wishes to appreciate its profile and trajectory (Katzman Matrix).[31]

10.6.3 Workforce Profile

It is important to determine both the duration of unemployment, previous experience, achievements in formal education, and professional training for the unemployed members of the community and the composition of the employed population by salaried and self-employed occupational categories, by hours worked (underemployment), as well as degree of labour protection (informal jobs).

A researcher would also determine the economic sectors where recruitment was occurring and those that were shedding jobs.

The analysis overall would be designed to provide the means to deal with the effects of the shock to employment and answer the following questions:

- Who will receive the benefit and the work?
- Will the intervention unit be the individual or the household?
- Is it necessary to provide training (and of what type) or short-term work producing goods and services of value to the community?

10.7 EXPECTED RESULTS

10.7.1 What Are the Expected Impacts on Beneficiaries, Communes, and Macro Level

The exercise of determining the potential impacts of a PEP that does not yet exist calls for strong assumptions. In the absence of information to assess the change in the status quo when executing a PEP, the construction of a counterfactual is required. The role of the assumptions is to establish the mechanisms that would affect the response of the agents (not just the beneficiaries[32]) to the programme. Since a transfer to a PEP is expected to have a strong correlation with household labour supply, behavioural effects are likely.

The *ex ante* evaluation, despite its limitations, makes it possible to make explicit the channels by which the PEP is expected to act in the presence of a macroeconomic shock: employment, prices (consumption, production, wages), access to goods and services (through improvement in the provision), assets (social, human, financial) and transfers.

The previous steps make it possible to gather information on the context in which the PEP will work and the drivers or agents of change, the interaction of both promoted by the PEP will give rise to different scenarios. The expected impacts should be specified in the following dimensions:

- Beneficiary: estimates on the reduction of indigence and poverty, inequality, change in the workforce, fall in unemployment.
- Community: expansions and/or improvements of local infrastructure, provision of local services, expected reduction of regional disparities, strengthened capacities in local governments.
- Aggregate stability: recovery of aggregate demand, social stability.

10.7.2 The Financial Support

10.7.2.1 How to maximize it?
As mentioned, PEPs can elicit general political support by satisfying the ethical principle that beneficiaries receive the transfer in exchange for working in the production of goods and services. However, political acceptance is strengthened by transmitting the PEP as a measure of last resort, and one way to sustain it is to launch other complementary labour market policies at the same time.[33]

More importantly, the expected impacts are mediated by institutions, and PEPs can alter the roles, rules, and incentives of some organizations, as well as incentives in the marketplace. The analysis of the interests of the actors with the capacity to influence is critical to determining the support and assessing the emerging difficulties which may arise in the formulation and implementation of a PEP.[34]

Therefore, the identification of groups and organizations that are relevant for a PEP is obtained by analysing not only those directly involved in the programme, but also those affected by its implementation, analysing what may happen in the short term and the long term:

- Actors who channel the demands of the population potentially benefiting from the PEP.
- Actors who compete for the attention of the population potentially.
- Beneficiaries of the PEP: other levels of government, third sector, unions.
- Actors that may be indirectly affected by the potential PEP: private sector and employers' representatives, trade unions, beneficiaries of other programmes.

Once the affected groups have been identified, an assessment of their influence on decision-makers can be made, with a focus upon the deepening of tensions existing in the short term and insights into how to think about their improvement in the long term.

From this, one can investigate the possibility of mutually beneficial partnerships within the framework of the PEP:

• Making the PEP meet their demands and involving them in the process.
• Making the services provided via the PEP benefit and complement others.
• Instituting prevention mechanisms to contain or mitigate the distortions generated in the labour market or on prices through other public interventions or exceptions.
• Planning communication and dissemination strategies.

10.7.3   Targeting

10.7.3.1 To whom?

Once the significance of a PEP as a means to serve the vulnerable population has been determined, one of the next steps is the selection of the method for identifying beneficiaries, focusing the programme on those who need it is the way to maximize its impact. The justification of a PEP requires it to identify the "ideal" beneficiaries who would receive the major benefit from the programme, but it is also required to distinguish them from the rest of the total population.

In theory, a PEP in its role of providing an employment guarantee is synonymous with universal coverage and self-selection. In practice, based on budget constraints, it is restricted to subgroups.

Some selection methods involve "individual/household assessment" such as means tests (direct or proxy) and community targeting. A second group of methods such as geographical targeting and demographic targeting relies on the evaluation of a specific variable highly correlated with poverty or unemployment that the PEP aims to mitigate. Finally, the "self-selection method" proposes the use of incentives instead of restrictions on access to the programme. These methods have been used individually or in combination to improve results. Below is a brief description of each method.

• Means tests. Eligibility is based on comparison of the applicant's household/individual's income to some threshold set by the PEP. Verification of the information provided on income is based on documentation by the beneficiary himself, external sources, or evaluation interviews.
• Proxy means tests. A score is generated for applicants based on a set of easily observable characteristics (geographic location, household structure,

assets ownership, educational level, adult occupations, among others) and it is compared with the cut-off point established for determining eligible applicants for the PEP.

- Community focus. The leaders or members of community groups (religious institutions, NGOs, representations of unemployed workers) guide the selection of beneficiaries based on their comparative advantages in identifying the needs of their populations. They can be existing or purposely formed with the function of determining who meets the PEP access requirements.[35]
- Geographic targeting. Those eligible are those who reside in the prioritized areas according to poverty or unemployment maps. There are marginalized areas where the phenomenon is spatially concentrated. The limitation is to attend to areas with high social heterogeneity.
- Demographic targeting. A single (categorical) variable such as age, gender, or ethnicity determines the applicant's eligibility. This works very well for young people or ethnic groups.
- Self-selection. The level of benefit that PEP provides is often used as a tool to encourage participation by those who need it and discourage participation by those who do not.[36]

Targeting faces imperfect information, the eligibility of beneficiaries is subject to error. Non-vulnerable individuals or households that identify themselves as vulnerable (inclusion error) can enter the PEP, or populations that are vulnerable might be identified as not vulnerable and thus deprive them of access to PEP (exclusion error).

An inclusion error generates some inefficiency, wasting programme resources by leaving less in the budget for those who need it the most or demanding more budget to achieve the same impact on results. On the other hand, an exclusion error generates ineffectiveness, leaving the individual and their home without the benefits associated with the PEP and reducing the expected impact. The latter is significantly more damaging than the former error.

Considering that the programme can generate changes in behaviour and effects, and that the collection of information is not cost-free, to a greater or lesser extent, all these methods face a trade-off between errors of inclusion and exclusion, as well as between levels, precision, and cost.

While means tests and proxy means tests are more extensive in terms of information requirements, categorical methods and self-selection are less demanding.

The administrative costs involved in the targeting stage should be analysed in terms of the size of the transfer and its complementarity with the cost of registering applicants for admission – and may be relatively low. Also, the existence of proxy means tests used for other programmes can allow cost savings.

Applicants' verified income level, score, or reservation salary need to be parameters for the targeting method to work. If they change too much, the assessment based on the time of the survey will not be representative of the applicant's evaluation at the time of determining their eligibility.

Although community targeting has low information costs, it can be vulnerable to favouritism or lack of transparency.

The presence of a large number of potential beneficiaries can generate incentives to develop power relations and political patronage. Also, the delegation of the targeting power can encourage local actors to magnify the needs to oversize the PEP and thus gain greater prominence or even prestige on the political scene.

Means tests, community and demographic targeting can lead to stigmatization of beneficiaries, promoting exclusion errors. If stigmatization has a high probability and there are no effective mitigation mechanisms, other methods such as geographic targeting are more appropriate.

Difficult-to-grasp work arrangements can constitute a significant unobserved component that amplifies inclusion and exclusion errors in means tests, proxy means, and self-selection. The impossibility of verifying these work arrangements makes it problematic to evaluate changes in the behaviour of the beneficiaries in view of the PEP and to design mechanisms suited for this purpose. In order to meet the requirements, workers employed in the informal sector, underemployed or self-employed can simulate being unemployed; or, due to high transaction costs, they may choose not to participate in the programme despite having poverty wages. On the other hand, inactive workers who do not face transaction costs would be incentivized to participate, increasing the workforce under the plan but not returning to their previous condition once it is finished.

Excessive demands for information can discourage participation. Excessive documentation requirements for the assessment of applicants may generate higher costs in provision than the potential gains from the application of the information. Thus, while seeking to reduce inclusion errors, exclusion errors can be amplified.

Finally, an important result of the targeting process, in addition to the identification of the beneficiary population of the PEP, is the detection of excluded groups that require complementary actions from the state. These "at risk" populations may not meet all the requirements to participate in a PEP but nevertheless face income gaps and find themselves on the margins of other public interventions; they may even be adversely affected by the implementation of the PEP in terms of their relative position in society.

10.7.4 The Work Commitment

10.7.4.1 What to do? The same to all?
In addition to acting as unemployment insurance through the provision of a transfer, the central characteristic of a PEP is that beneficiaries can participate in public infrastructure development activities, community services or in training and education activities to promote their development and integration into the labour market. PEPs can differ fundamentally in their approach to selecting activities, broadly based upon the rationale that the need to enhance participation of beneficiaries determines the type of work provided and its level of intensity.

10.7.4.2 Development of infrastructure and public services
The allocation of resources to areas of high unemployment and the creation or maintenance of the infrastructure and public services network that indirectly benefit the most vulnerable groups is consistent with an underlying aim of maximizing the redistributive impact of the PEP. To do this, a survey of local needs makes it possible to identify which projects would enhance the benefits for the affected community. Even at the local level, there may be a portfolio of projects which the PEP can carry out jointly with local organizations and government.

The type of projects selected result from the choice of those that make use of labour more intensively, are cost-effective, respond to local needs and have a greater multiplier effect. In general, the labour cost of PEP projects represents from 30–40 per cent to 80 per cent of the total cost, depending on their nature.[37]

They range from road construction and maintenance projects, sewers, sanitation and running water, afforestation, irrigation, maintenance of buildings and public spaces, social services in charitable and public institutions to the provision of personal services such as care for children, the elderly or people with disabilities. Projects can also be developed based on "green jobs" utilizing highly labour-intensive methods such as waste treatment, recycling, or related to renewable energy generation.[38, 39, 40]

The choice of labour-intensive projects implies that the largest proportion of costs involved in funding the programme will be composed of benefit payments (salaries). In projects where other inputs are required, these should be taken into account when budgeting the PEP. When projects involve equipment and materials, new cost elements enter into planning the implementation.

When there is local ownership of PEP projects or a PEP complements local projects, the costs can be shared with local actors. The programme can provide labour resources, share the cost of other necessary inputs, or even make use of existing management schemes.

Finally, in addition to what has been previously stated, two other elements play an important role in the selection of the type of projects. On the one hand, the profile of the beneficiary population defines what types of projects would constitute an adequate employment opportunity. On the other, the need to rapidly scale up the programme influences the selection. Services projects can be implemented faster than infrastructure development projects, or if the latter is chosen, the quality of the assets generated can be affected, potentially undermining political support and impact.

10.7.4.3 Training and skills development

The projects for the development of social infrastructure generate a large proportion of low-skilled employment, and they may ignore certain characteristics – such as human capital – of those who participate or potentially may take part. The learning of professional practices, training, formal education for adults and specializations are instruments designed to increase the future income generation capacity of the current beneficiaries, favouring their emancipation from the programme. To fully take account of this, it is also necessary to identify the potential labour supply, the profiles demanded, and the ways to fill that potential "gap".

The human capital gap arises from the diagnostic process and may generate demand for:

- "Back to school", formal education at basic levels (adult education) or higher (tertiary and university levels)
- Specializations, or apprenticeships and professional practice
- Certification of occupations
- On-the-job training and internships.

After the preceding identification, different alternatives arise for its development, with diverse budgetary implications, implementation time and management of the programme. If it is a question of basic education, the public education system can be used; in the case of specializations and certifications, agreements can be established with existing teaching institutions or ad hoc training can be formulated jointly with trade unions and employers' associations. Lastly, on-the-job training requires articulation with firms and organizations, and specific conditions of cooperation.

The alternatives are not necessarily mutually exclusive. Qualifications can be obtained by the beneficiaries in parallel to employment, sequentially (training them in specific capacities for the development of a project) or be differentiated according to beneficiary profiles.

There may be impediments to individual and household compliance. Compliance with the conditionality, whether training or employment, may be influenced by the presence of children, the elderly, and people with disabilities in the household under the beneficiary's care, as well as the difficulties and costs of accessing transport to attend the projects. The removal of these barriers can be achieved by coordinating the PEP with other existing programmes (nurseries, subsidies) or by adding a "flexibility" consideration in terms of proximity, flexible hours, and nature of the activity.

10.8   THE LENGTH OF THE PEP

10.8.1   For How Long Should the Programme Be in Place?

The optimal duration of PEP is tied to meeting the objectives. If it has functioned as an effective safety net by lifting individuals and their families out of poverty and into the job market, the mission of the PEP has been carried out. In the same way, when the PEP is conceived as a means to alleviate the suffering of families in the face of seasonality in the demand, it can be viewed as achieving its aims when its participants are all re-employed in the public or private sector.

However, this process may take longer than economic recovery for many beneficiaries and may exceed the completion time for social infrastructure development projects and training activities.

There are several types of alternatives in terms of duration:

- Unlimited: free entry and exit of beneficiaries, according to compliance with the requirements for access to the programme. The risks of this modality are the possibility of dependence of the beneficiaries (disincentives to seek or stay in a job) and the incorporation into regular activities in unfavourable conditions with respect to the staff who perform these tasks.
- Limited: in time (months of duration) or in number of times that the beneficiary can participate in the programme (number of entries and exits according to their opportunities in the labour market). This is the case of temporary employment programmes fundamentally linked to the seasonality of economic activity, and emergency programmes due to natural disasters.

The presence of beneficiaries in the programme even at the end of the projects indicates the need to continue granting safety nets, but perhaps the profile of the beneficiaries who have not been able to leave the PEP demands more specific interventions. Such is the case of the persistence of women with children or in charge of other members of the household, since in general, they have the burden of these tasks. Also, for a population with the characteristics of structural and persistent poverty, workers living in dispersed geographical areas, ethnic group diversity others, the exit from the PEP may well require a new intervention or coordination with existing programmes.

10.9 COORDINATION WITH OTHER INITIATIVES

10.9.1 Is the PEP a "Silver Bullet"? One Size Fits All?

A PEP targets a population that many other interventions do not serve (except other active labour market policies), and these are households with at least one member in the workforce. The breadth of this condition also gives rise to a potentially heterogeneous beneficiary population where profiles typically of wage earners coexist with those of inactive population in its broadest sense (students, housewives, elderly people without pensions).

In effect, this heterogeneity in the face of a shock may deepen the existing differences in the vulnerable population, and possibly a PEP, however broadly it may be defined, may not address very specific problems, not directly linked to the lack of employment, for example, advocates of the Job Guarantee (JG) are careful to point out that a JG scheme only *directly* benefits those ready, willing and able to work but without a job.[41] As a result, they are in favour of a basic income payable to those unable or unwilling to work. The income received would, in broad terms, be set at a lower level than the JG but would be sufficient to allow the recipient to live a dignified and fulfilling life. However, it is important to stress that although the "base" level of a basic income might be lower than the income a JG recipient might be expected to earn, the basic income reflects the individual needs of the recipient and would be expected to rise in line with recipient needs. The benefits of a JG combined with a basic income in this way are stressed by the advocates of Modern Monetary Theory (MMT), who reject the contention that a Universal Basic Income is preferable to a JG scheme.[42]

The vulnerable population subject to a potential PEP may also qualify to participate in some of the existing social protection programmes, or even be a current beneficiary of one of them. The aforementioned programmes can address specific problems of the population such as old age, food and mal-nourishment, interruptions in the accumulation of human capital, community isolation through various interventions such as pensions for the elderly without coverage of the social security system, food assistance to poor families, schol-arships to children from low-income families, participation in community activities, and also some seasonal employment programmes.

The effectiveness in the design and monitoring of a PEP is more complex in the presence of the proliferation of other programmes. The comparison of the universe of existing programmes with the needs faced allows to minimize the distortion in a potential PEP, bearing in mind, a priori, the following challenges:

- The reinforcement of existing programmes, such as those that serve the elderly, young and school-age children.
- The introduction of changes (if necessary) in the access requirements of these programmes that make it possible to gain homogeneity and fairness.
- Coordination with these programmes, sharing information and establishing bridges to promote access, compensation, and entry and exits to and from the PEP.
- Strong and effective institutional dialogue with the managers of the different programmes.

Regarding employment programmes already in operation, the existence of a new PEP may raise the need for synergies (training programmes, seasonal employment), a participation option (sector employment programmes), or eventually integration that involves the transfer of the mandatory beneficiary (to similar employment programmes).

Finally, we might stress that a PEP, specifically a JG, is a key MMT-informed policy. MMT suggests the policy should be permanent, giving a "floor" to pay and working conditions, thus making firms compete for workers, not the reverse. MMT authors show how the JG provides a buffer stock of employed labour and that this acts as both a price anchor and an automatic stabilizer, providing a counter-inflationary policy superior to orthodox monetary policy.[43]

10.10 CONCLUSIONS

The Jefes programme in Argentina started to fade away after 2004/05, when the bulk of the so-called "core workers" (e.g., heads of household between 24 and 59 years old) found jobs in the private or public sector, and the new entrants to the labour market found jobs directly. This left a group of workers that were unable to find jobs due to many reasons. Most of them were women with small children, or who were in charge of other adults in the household, that independent of the wage they would receive in the private sector, wouldn't have the chance to leave their home for 8–10 or more hours, without hiring somebody to do the work.

However, the programme maintained a significant number (a little less than a million workers), until 2009, when the AUH (Universal Child Allowance) was introduced, that is paid to every child under 18 years old, independent of the working condition of the mother. This was a universal policy that is maintained until today, and a significant support for vulnerable households.

One recurrent question relates to the conditions required to make governments implement an employment guarantee programme? How high would the unemployment rate have to be? How high would poverty have to be? And the answer in Argentina: until the protests were unbearable! When this happened, policymakers worked with real urgency to solve the problem.

So far at least, PEPs have largely been seen as programmes for macroeconomic emergencies; however, it should be highlighted that unemployment, at the individual, human level, is an "emergency". Unemployment is not merely a cause of macroeconomic "negative externalities", but families suffer from it, not only in terms of income, but also in a wide range of ways including harm to the self-esteem of the women or men suffering from it.

In these pages, and from the perspective of a practitioner, we have tried to show not only the advantages of employment guarantee or PEP, where the state plays the role of employer of last resort (ELR), but also the important steps and considerations that have to be taken into account for its successful implementation. We argue that if the relevant authorities start with a low-scale scheme, and develop from that base, some of the potential hazards in implementation can be easily avoided and the "scale-up" can occur when needed. But this requires programmes to begin before unemployment increases, when the economic and social impacts are still relatively low.

In contrast to seeing a PEP or JG as a crisis measure, for the reasons outlined above, for an MMT advocate, an employment guarantee should be a permanent feature of the economy, providing the opportunity for everybody ready and willing to work, but unable to find suitable employment, with the opportunity to contribute meaningfully to the quality of life for the community. The experience of Argentina confirms the feasibility of implementing a successful PEP or JG. The insights of MMT show why it is not just possible to introduce a JG in a monetary production economy, it is, indeed, essential.

NOTES

1. My sincere acknowledgement to Evelyn Vezza who participated in the original operationalization of the ideas developed here.
2. IMF Boards of Governors Annual General Meeting (1998), Statement by the Hon. Carlos Saul Menem.
3. We use the term "structural adjustment" to refer to the concept coined by Williamson in 1989, explicit in John Williamson, 1990.
4. That parliamentary bill included an extension of the trial period, reduction of social security contributions, and other traditional flexibilization initiatives that didn't pass. However, it brought the governing coalition into the crisis that ended with the resignation of the Vice President Carlos Alvarez.
5. Ricardo López Murphy, University of Chicago graduate, announced the ultra-orthodox set of measures that included reduction of wages and pensions,

expenditure cuts, and the imposition of fees upon students in the historically free Argentinean public university system.

6.   It is very interesting to see the resilience of the democratic institutions in a country that in the past saw so many interruptions by the military.

7.   The political system in Argentina is a federal one, the result of an agreement from the provinces in 1853, with a central government, 24 provinces, and municipalities with high levels of autonomy, which was strengthened in the Constitutional Reform of 1994, when the decentralization recommendations from the Washington Consensus were in fashion.

8.   These were foundations, associations linked to religions, school groups, cooperatives, sports clubs, neighbours' groups, etc. Some of them could be described as a legal entity, while others just required formal registration in order to present projects to the programme. Many of the presently active social movements of Argentina were created in light of the Jefes.

9.   In Argentina every worker registered to the social security system was entitled to child allowance, but this didn't apply to self-employed or non-registered (informal) workers.

10.   Galasso and Ravallion, 2004.

11.   Tcherneva, 2013.

12.   A revision of public works schemas and employment programmes can be found in Lal et al., 2010.

13.   Inclusive growth is the pattern of GDP or economic growth that aims to increase incomes as well as improving income distribution. The World Bank uses as indicators for its so-called "twin goals" the reduction of extreme poverty and the increase of the GDP appropriation by the bottom 40 per cent of the income distribution.

14.   The experience of the NREGA (National Rural Employment Guarantee Act) in India is very interesting. The rural population can request that up to a maximum number of workdays be provided by the local authorities, in order to cover the off-season in agricultural production.

15.   Given that sometimes these interventions are budget constrained, rather than limited by objective indicators, there are combinations that require specific interventions designed to reduce the number of those that could be on the fringes of the programme. It should be noted that in the case of these interventions it is certainly worse to accidentally exclude somebody that needs the benefit than to include somebody that is near – but outside – the boundaries.

16.   This happens when vaccination, school attendance, health controls, pregnancy check-ups, training and skills development for teenagers, and other conditionalities for the children are incorporated such as was the case of the Jefes Programme in Argentina.

17.   Forstater, 1999.

18.   Cazes, Verick, and Heuer, 2009.

19.   Constructing a counterfactual is a difficult task, but nevertheless we argue that, in general, the main problem has been the scope and time limitations of these programmes.

20.   Betcherman, Olivas, and Dar, 2004.

21.   International Labour Organization, 2012b.

22.   International Labour Organization, 2012b.

23.   This brings to the fore the discussion concerning when to start to implement PEPs. Even if they are greatly enhanced when a crisis erupts, the beneficial effect

of a "buffer-stock" policy would be much greater if it operated in normal periods. If a PEP is permanent, then less administrative pressure emerges in a crisis when the programme has to be dramatically upscaled.

24. Many of these valuable services don't have a market price due to the lack of income of the residents in the areas with high unemployment, but the need for them is present.

25. McKenzie, 2004.

26. Workers employed in the secondary segment or submarket are distinguished from those employed in the primary segment in dual labour market theory (Reich, Gordon, and Edwards, 1973). See also the International Labour Organization, 2012a.

27. Secondary workers are those that when the main income recipient of the household loses part or the totality of the income, or even has uncertainty on the perception of the future income, join the labour market looking for a job.

28. Lustig, 2000.

29. Rodrik, 2001.

30. Fallon and Lucas, 2002.

31. Rubén Kaztman (1995): The Katzman Matrix is the result of combining the direct and the indirect method of measurement of poverty (unsatisfied basic needs and incomes) in order to characterize poverty as "structural poverty", where both levels aren't achieved; "inertial poverty", when there are universal basic necessities (UBN), even if the income is above the poverty line; "new poor" when the basic needs are covered, but the income is below the poverty line; and "non-poor" when both are fulfilled.

32. There are other dimensions that should be considered there, including the absorption of workers from temporary activities, such as agricultural workers, which, in the case of the Jefes Programme, required an additional rule, to allow them to work at the farms during the high seasons without losing the benefit during the downturn.

33. Lal et al., 2010.

34. These influences may come from employers' organizations, trade unions, and local governments that see their interests affected by the introduction of the PEP.

35. School teachers can be an important source of information, since they often understand the reality of the households where their students live. However, it must be acknowledged that using teachers as an information conduit would impose an additional burden upon them.

36. This point involves the moral issue of how much should a beneficiary, and the family, be able to do with the benefit. It is important that judgement is based on objective indicators of purchasing power in terms of necessities at a minimum socially accepted, not just symbolic, amount.

37. Subbarao et al., 2013.

38. Evans-Clock et al., 2009.

39. Tcherneva, 2020.

40. Global Institute for Sustainable Prosperity Working Papers.

41. It is important to stress that access to a JG scheme is *entirely voluntary*. Workers are "taken as they are" (indeed if a person wishes to work but needs support to do so, the "support workers" would also be able to access JG employment). There is no compulsion involved with a JG and the importance of not conflating a JG, in any way, with so-called "Workfare" schemes (where individuals who are categorized as "able to work" are required to work or face losing benefit)

cannot be overestimated. If an individual does not wish to access the JG scheme, that remains entirely their choice and their access to basic income remains unaffected. The costs of "fitness for work" assessments are thus avoided and the well-documented cases of clearly mentally or physically incapable individuals being expected to work have no opportunity of being repeated here.

42.   The Gower Initiative for Modern Money Studies (n.d. a) set out the case for the JG, and also explain why a JG is a superior policy option to the Universal Basic Income (n.d. b).

43.   Wray, 1998; Mitchell, 2013; Tcherneva, 2013, 2020; Mosler and Silipo, 2016; Armstrong, 2020.

REFERENCES

Armstrong, P. (2020), "Modern Monetary Theory and Its Relationship to Heterodox Economics", Solent University https://pure.solent.ac.uk/ws/portalfiles/portal/26193370/Full_Thesis_and_Appendices_1_4_post_viva_FINAL.pdf (accessed 28 September 2022).

Betcherman, G., Olivas, C. and Dar, A. (2004), "Impacts of Active Labor Market Programs: New Evidence from Evaluations with Particular Attention to Developing and Transition Countries", Social Protection Discussion Papers No. 0402, The World Bank, January.

Cazes, S., Verick, S. and Heuer, C. (2009), "Labor Market Policies in Times of Crises", Employment Working Paper No. 35, International Labour Office.

Evans-Clock, C., Poschen, P., Sanchez, A. and Hoffman, C. (2009), "ILO International Initiatives on Future Skill Needs for the Green Economy", Presentation and Paper on Future Skills Needs for the Green Economy, Research Paper, European Centre for the Development of Vocational Training.

Fallon, P. and Lucas, R. (2002), "The Impact of Financial Crisis on Labor Markets, Household Incomes, and Poverty: A Review of Evidence", *The World Bank Research Observer*, 17(1).

Forstater, M. (1999), "Public Employment and Economic Flexibility: The Job Opportunity Approach to Full Employment", https://www.econstor.eu/bitstream/10419/54324/1/676511341.pdf (accessed August 2021).

Galasso, E. and Ravallion, M. (2004), "Social Protection in a Crisis: Argentina's Plan Jefes y Jefas", *World Bank Economic Review*, 18(3): 367–99 https://openknowledge.worldbank.org/handle/10986/17165 (accessed August 2021).

Global Institute for Sustainable Prosperity, http://www.global-isp.org/working-papers/ (accessed August 2021).

Gower Initiative for Modern Money Studies (n.d. a), "Job Guarantee", https://gimms.org.uk/fact-sheets/universal-basic-income/ (accessed 19 October 2021).

Gower Initiative for Modern Money Studies, (n.d. b), "Universal Basic Income or Job Guarantee?", https://gimms.org.uk/fact-sheets/universal-basic-income/ (accessed 19 October 2021).

IMF Boards of Governors Annual General Meeting (1998), Statement by the Hon. Carlos Saul Menem, President of the Republic of Argentina, at the Annual Meetings of the Boards of Governors of the International Monetary Fund and the World Bank

Group, Washington, DC, Press Release No. 5, 6–8 October, https://www.imf.org/external/am/1998/speeches/pr05e.pdf (accessed August 2021).

International Labour Organization (2012a), "Labour Market Segmentation", https://www.ilo.org/global/topics/employment-security/labour-market-segmentation/lang--en/index.htm (accessed 19 October 2021).

International Labour Organization (2012b), "The ILO Social Protection Floor Recommendation (2012)", International Labour Organization, No. 202, https://www.ilo.org/secsoc/areas-of-work/legal-advice/WCMS_205341/lang--en/index.htm (accessed August 2021).

Kaztman, R. (1995), "La Medición de las Necesidades Básicas Insatisfechas en los Censos de Población", Comisión Económica para América Latina y el Caribe (CEPAL), Oficina de Montevideo, https://www.cepal.org/es/publicaciones/34702-la-medicion-necesidades-basicas-insatisfechas-censos-poblacion (accessed August 2021).

Lal, K., Miller, S., Lieuw-Kie-Song, M. and Kostzer, D. (2010), "Public Works and Employment Programs: Towards a Long-Term Development Approach", UNDP-IPC, Brasilia, https://ipcig.org/pub/IPCWorkingPaper66.pdf (accessed August 2021).

Lustig, N. (2000), "Crises and the Poor: Socially Responsible Macroeconomics", *Sustainable Development Department Technical Papers Series*, IADB, February.

McKenzie, S. (2004), "Social Sustainability: Towards Some Definitions", *Hawke Research Institute Working Paper Series*, No. 27, https://www.semanticscholar.org/paper/Social-sustainability%3A-towards-some-definitions-Mckenzie/7a7ec41a3d0c0fb4f9099db456b32166b25275c9 (accessed August 2021).

Mitchell, W. (2013), "What Is Job Guarantee – Bill Mitchell – Modern Monetary Theory", 4 May, http://bilbo.economicoutlook.net/blog/?p=23719 (accessed 19 October 2021).

Mosler, W. and Silipo, D. (2016), "Maximising Price Stability in a Monetary Economy", Levy Economics Institute, Working Paper No. 864, April.

Reich, M., Gordon, D. and Edwards, R. (1973), "A Theory of Labor Market Segmentation", *The American Economic Review*, 63(2): 359–65.

Rodrik, D. (2001), "Why Is There So Much Economic Insecurity in Latin America?" *CEPAL Review* No. 73.

Subbarao, K., del Ninno, C., Andrews, C. and Rodriguez, C. (2013), "Public Works as a Safety Net: Design, Evidence, and Implementation", World Bank, https://openknowledge.worldbank.org/handle/10986/11882 (accessed 28 September 2022).

Tcherneva, P. (2013), "Beyond Full Employment: What Argentina's Plan Jefes Can Teach Us about the Employer of Last Resort", in M.J. Murray and M. Forstater (eds), *Employment Guarantee Schemes*, New York: Palgrave Macmillan, https://link.springer.com/chapter/10.1057/9781137313997_4 (accessed August 2021).

Tcherneva, P. (2020), "The Case for a Job Guarantee", http://pavlina-tcherneva.net/job-guarantee-faq/ (accessed 19 October 2021).

Williamson, J. (1990), "Latin American Adjustment: How Much Has Happened?", Washington, DC: Institute for International Economics, described in Daniel Kostzer and Carla Gras, "Impactos del ajuste estructural en los sectores más vulnerables de

Argentina", in *Cuadernos de Geografía*, No. 3, España, Universidad de Cádiz, 1992, https://rodin.uca.es/xmlui/bitstream/handle/10498/14101/18387597.pdf?sequence= 1&isAllowed=y (accessed August 2021).

Wray, L.R. (1998), *Understanding Modern Money,* Cheltenham, UK and Lyme, NH, USA: Edward Elgar Publishing.

11. Three lessons from government spending and the post-pandemic recovery

Pavlina R. Tcherneva

The central lesson of the COVID-19 fiscal response is that money is not scarce. Without delay, governments around the world appropriated budgets that dwarfed any other post-war crisis policy. In 2020, Japan passed a stimulus package equal to 54.8 per cent of GDP, while in the US, it was equivalent to 26.9 per cent and in Canada to 20.1 per cent. Italy, France, and Germany spent 10.1, 10.4, and 10.7 per cent of GDP, respectively.[1]

11.1 LESSON 1: THE FUNDING IS ALWAYS THERE

These governments budgeted anywhere from one-tenth to more than one-half of their economies to fight the pandemic. No taxpayers were called upon to foot the bill, no creditors were asked to lend them money. Governments voted for the budgets they considered to be necessary and their central banks made the payments. The size of the response was all the evidence one needed to grasp the monetary reality. Governments which issue and control their own currencies face no financing constraints and no threat of insolvency or default. They use their fiscal and monetary institutions (Ministries of Finance, Treasuries, Exchequers, and Central Banks) to make all necessary payments. Whatever policy priority a monetarily sovereign government has, the funding is always there.

Governments which do not have monetary sovereignty tried to recreate it. The Eurozone, which was designed to restrict government spending, broke its own rules. Countries were allowed to breach the Maastricht debt and deficit limits and, more importantly, there was no possibility of default on pandemic bonds because the European Central Bank guaranteed them through the Pandemic Emergency Guarantee Programme.

Modern Money Theory (MMT) focuses on the undertheorized aspects of the currency as a public monopoly and its implications for public finance.[2] It studies the financial architecture of different policy regimes to understand the available policy space for tackling urgent economic concerns, such as financial crises, climate disasters, unemployment, and poverty, among others. When the world faced the mother of all crises, none of the institutional intricacies of public finance presented an obstacle to funding the pandemic response.

MMT recognizes that finance is not a limited resource. It is manufactured and created in the act of spending. In the modern world, the exclusive monopoly to issue the currency endows governments with unparalleled spending power. For MMT, that the issuer can spend without technical constraints is a rather trivial observation. What MMT stresses is that taxes and borrowing cannot pre-fund the issuer of the currency, as the currency must be provided *before* it can be used for tax collections or bond purchases. The substantive question for MMT then is how to deploy this spending power for achieving the two central macroeconomic goals: full employment and price stability.

The pandemic offered some insights here too. While funding was rapidly mobilized across the globe, the way these large budgets were spent differed greatly. In many European countries, governments offered to pay a portion of the salaries of affected workers, with wage replacement rates ranging from 50 per cent to 90 per cent. In Denmark, for example, the government covered 75 per cent of the earnings of salaried workers and 90 per cent of wage workers who were impacted by the pandemic. Germany's social insurance policy, Kurzarbeit, paid 60 per cent of wages for any hours that were cut due to the pandemic.[3]

Scandinavian countries used another policy to support labour markets. Governments participated in tripartite negotiations with firms and unions, working to minimize the number of layoffs and offering to pay the wages of those workers whose jobs would have been eliminated, thus effectively becoming the employer of last resort (ELR). Such tripartite negotiations had been used in the past to maintain long-run full employment, and in countries like Sweden for example, until the early 1990s, the government had played the ELR role by directly employing the unemployed.

By contrast, the US offered weak and provisional salary support in 2020. The government provided business loans to firms, which could be forgiven if used to pay wages, but many small businesses could not access the lending programmes and even those who could ended up slashing employment. The countries that protected payrolls directly, saw a smaller increase in the unemployment rate. In Germany, unemployment rose from 5 per cent in March 2020 to 5.9 per cent in April 2020, while in the US, it soared from 4.4 per cent to 14.7 per cent during the same period. It was the highest jump in unemployment among all of the above-mentioned countries, even though the US had passed one of the largest fiscal packages.

Funding was not the issue. The initial $2.2 trillion CARES Act was large enough to pay every single wage in the US for three months, with funding to spare that could have employed every unemployed person at a living wage.[4] Had the US attempted a direct payroll subsidy, like those in Europe, and the government paid a portion of the wages, the budget could have protected jobs through the end of 2020, and likely even longer. Another sizable budget ($900 billion) followed later in 2020 and, still, the US experienced its worst labour market shock in post-war history.

In the first month and a half of the pandemic, the US lost 22 million jobs, or the equivalent of all jobs created in the previous 11 years of recovery after the 2008 Great Recession. At the time, the Federal Reserve had forecast that unemployment could exceed Great Depression levels if the government failed to act swiftly.[5] Fortunately, unlike after the Great Recession, the government response was immediate and large: income bounced back to its previous trend (Figure 11.1) and the economy experienced its shortest-lived post-war recession.

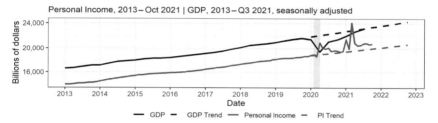

Source: U.S. BLS, retrieved from FRED, Federal Reserve Bank of St. Louis.

Figure 11.1   Personal income and GDP

Government expanded unemployment insurance and provided additional cash assistance, keeping many families out of poverty and helping reduce child poverty by 50 per cent. The eviction moratoria helped prevent a spike in homelessness. What this fiscal support did not achieve, however, was a return to pre-pandemic employment levels (Figure 11.2).

While the unemployment rate fell quickly as the economy 'reopened', largely due to a collapse in the labour force participation rate (Figure 11.3), it has become typical for companies to complain of labour shortages. Yet, as of October 2021, total non-farm employment is still 4.2 million jobs short of its pre-pandemic high.

Meanwhile, evidence suggests that firms which are able to offer good pay with benefits do not face the same difficulties finding workers.[6] What the pandemic has revealed is that there is an acute shortage, not of workers, but of well-paying jobs.[7]

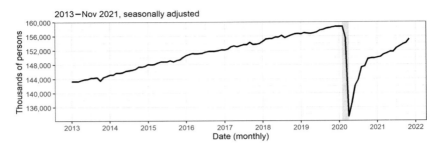

Source: U.S. BLS, retrieved from FRED, Federal Reserve Bank of St. Louis.

Figure 11.2   Employment level

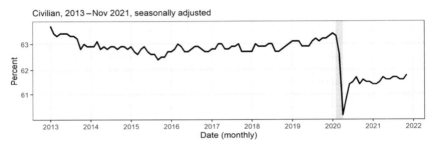

Source: U.S. BLS, retrieved from FRED, Federal Reserve Bank of St. Louis.

Figure 11.3   Labour force participation rate

The conservative argument that government pandemic payments discouraged people from working is also not supported by the evidence. A recent survey shows that the vast majority (60–70 per cent) of jobseekers during the summer 2021 months were ready to take employment immediately. The main reasons why the rest delayed returning to work were: (1) having a financial cushion or a working spouse, (2) COVID fears and (3) having care responsibilities.[8] Unemployment insurance payments were the *least* important factor for not seeking work straight away, accounting for a negligible 6 per cent of jobseekers in September 2021.

11.2   LESSON 2: UNEMPLOYMENT IS A POLICY CHOICE

Given the differences in pandemic-related job losses across the globe, the second lesson of the pandemic was that unemployment is a policy choice. Many governments appropriated budgets that were large enough to protect jobs and employ the unemployed, yet all came out with elevated levels of unemployment. Countries which offered direct salary support experienced smaller spikes in unemployment, while the US allowed mass unemployment to develop. None pursued aggressive ELR policies to eliminate unemployment altogether. The sole exception was China, which provided unconditional wage guarantees to all workers,[9] effectively becoming the employer of *first* resort.

From a macro perspective, in a market-based economy, the policymaker faces two options: either close the output gap or close the employment gap. These are distinct outcomes that do not usually coincide, even though economists often mistake one for the other. Aggregate demand management typically pushes growth to potential output around some 'acceptable' level of unemployment (the so-called NAIRU), which amounts to supporting jobless recoveries.[10] Often the output gap is closed, not because growth has returned to the previous trend, but because of hysteresis effects that push potential output below its previous highs, and in either case it is not the result of closing the jobs gap. And as noted, in the US, that has also meant a steady decline in the labour force participation rate during the last three recessions.

The second policy option is to focus on the employment (or labour demand) gap and close it via direct employment of the unemployed. This can be accomplished via programmes that provide public service employment options to all jobseekers on an as-needed basis, including mass mobilization, large-scale public investment, ELR, and job guarantee (JG) policies.

The modern money approach emphasizes that these are structural macroeconomic stabilization responses, not just job creation programmes, and are superior to conventional stimulus methods.[11] Mass mobilization is a critical intervention in times of crises, but it is not a guarantee of tight full employment. ELR and JG can accomplish this task, though they are somewhat separate, even if related, policies.

With ELR programmes, the government could temporarily and partially nationalize the payroll (as European nations did during the pandemic), but typically ELR is a government policy that provides employment to those who have not found private sector employment. In the literature, ELR and JG are often used interchangeably and share many common characteristics. The 'last resort' in the ELR name suggests, however, that public employment would be offered when all other options have been exhausted. If the available private sector opportunities are punitive or pay poverty wages, the ELR would surely not be an adequate solution. The JG by contrast is an explicit alternative to them. It is also often motivated by a human-rights claim to decent employment for all. It is available to all jobseekers wanting to take the living wage-benefit job offer in the Job Guarantee. While both the JG and ELR could serve as transitional employment offers for the unemployed, the ELR implies a conditionality, whereas the JG is a public option and an assurance (it provides a choice among alternatives and a guarantee of an 'opt-out' from bad jobs). The ELR offer of public employment is provided when and if the individual has been unsuccessful in securing (usually) private sector employment. ELR could also mean a subsidy to private firms to retain workers, which is why the policy is typically associated with the tripartite negotiation model of Scandinavian countries, and Sweden in particular. ELR had worked reasonably well there, as the country had comparatively stronger labour laws that regulate private sector employment.

Countries like the US, however, where the labour market is more precarious and unequal, could benefit from a more robust labour policy such as the JG. Unlike the Scandinavian model, the JG is an explicit public employment option for any jobseeker. Participation in the JG is not conditional on one's inability to secure a private sector employment offer. The JG offers a minimum living wage and is an alternative to 'bad' jobs. While it may be more 'disruptive' to the private sector than the ELR, it does exert pressure on firms to match the pay and benefits offered by the JG, thus establishing an effective wage floor for the economy as a whole, and strengthening the bargaining power of the most vulnerable workers.

Faced with the need to restore jobs quickly after the pandemic, the newly elected US government has begun pursuing large-scale public investment programmes (i.e., President Biden's Infrastructure and Build Back Better bills). While this approach would help improve the labour market further, creating quality jobs across the wage spectrum, it is not a policy that would benefit all last-in-first-out workers, or those with systematic barriers to employment. Therefore, a comprehensive job preservation and job creation strategy would consist of mass mobilization, ELR, and JG, because only the latter can secure enough employment opportunities for all workers in every community. Furthermore, the JG and ELR proposals explicitly aim to provide on-the-job training and assistance with transitioning to other employment opportunities.

As MMT stresses, only the JG and ELR would vary with changes in economic conditions, thus offering a more robust automatic stabilizer than the conventional approach.[12] Standard policy uses unemployment and income transfers as economic stabilizers, allowing them to expand in downturns and shrink in expansion, providing a floor to collapsing aggregate demand. This is not a very robust stabilizer, as mass layoffs create the very conditions that discourage hiring and prolong the downturn. By contrast, the JG sustains jobs at living incomes, allowing spending, profits, business sentiment, and consumer expectations to recover faster. Put simply, an automatic *unemployment* stabilizer is weaker than an automatic *employment* stabilizer.

For MMT, the latter is the preferred policy option for several reasons. First, the government helps create monetary unemployment[13] and is thus responsible for eliminating it. Second, the unemployed are already part of the public sector and the government is already responsible for addressing the associated real social costs. Third, as the single supplier of currency, it can choose the manner in which it spends. By employing the unemployed, it can establish the effective minimum wage in the economy, stabilizing one systemically important price – the base wage.[14] Fourth, by doing so, the JG raises the wage floor by establishing a labour standard for pay and working conditions for all jobs. Fifth, it is a policy that provides an alternative to precarious and poorly paid work and increases competition in the labour market for workers. As an alternative to the most precarious private sector work, the JG pressures firms to improve their pay and benefits if they wish to retain and attract employees. Many private sector workers will get a pay raise, which in turn will boost spending, growth, and firm profits. The JG makes the poverty-paying business model unworkable. Sixth, the JG removes the 'threat of the sack' from employment practices that often create difficult working conditions and labour market pathologies (wage theft, discrimination, harassment). Seventh, while the JG gives workers the power to say 'no' to abusive employers, it also serves as a more robust transitional programme for people seeking employment. It is a stepping stone for young people entering the labour market, an employment opportunity for caregivers who wish to return to paid work, and a bridge to civilian employment for former inmates and veterans.

Payroll protection can effectively prevent mass layoffs in a pandemic, but without a JG, it is inadequate for combating unemployment and poorly paid employment. Nevertheless, because the government was essentially bankrolling private firms through large firm subsidies and pandemic lending programmes, it had the full prerogative to extract other demands in exchange: hazard pay for workers, guaranteed paid leave, and an increase in the minimum wage to $15/hour, thus helping ongoing local legislative efforts to raise the minimum wage. In the US, nearly half of all workers earn below $10.22/hour,[15] which is below the poverty level for a family of three. Such conditionalities would have had the effect of fortifying working conditions across large swaths of the labour market during the pandemic and beyond.

11.3   LESSON 3: LARGE GOVERNMENT SPENDING IS NOT THE INEVITABLE SOURCE OF INFLATION

The third lesson of the pandemic is that despite the large-scale fiscal support, inflation was not a consequence of the unprecedented fiscal budgets. When private activity stopped, governments supported incomes and maintained purchasing power, preventing the deflation that would have occurred otherwise. While aggregate demand received much-needed life support, as of November 2021, there was no evidence of demand-pull inflation. All evidence indicates that current price pressures are due to widespread global disruptions on the supply side: shutting down of factories, transportation routes, and ports; a slow resumption of production and working through backlogs in the supply chain; a shift in the structure of private demand away from services to goods; and price setting in the energy sector by OPEC. Price increases came from bottlenecks, logistical challenges, oil cartel production and pricing decisions, not from government spending beyond full employment. At the micro level, some firms exploited their market power (and media-stoked inflation worries) to raise prices, not only to cover rising costs, but also to pad profits, emboldened by the fact that customers had already begun to perceive price increases as 'unavoidable'.[16] In just Q2 and Q3 of 2021, US non-financial corporations posted the largest profit margins since 1950, up 37 per cent year-over-year, compared to the 12 per cent increase in total compensation during the period.[17] Further, the global benchmark Brent Crude oil had risen 38 per cent in 2021, propped up by curtailed production from the OPEC+ group of producers. Despite global calls to alleviate rising oil prices, as of November 2021, OPEC has declined to revise production quotas. Price-setting power of monopsonies, near-monopolies, and cartels, supply chain bottlenecks, lower level of production and structural shifts in private demand have so far been responsible for the observable price increases, not government spending.

As MMT stresses, inflation is often a supply-side phenomenon with multiple causes.[18] Inflation generated by strong aggregate demand beyond full employment is rarely observed, apart from the immediate post-World War II (WWII) period. The pandemic experience so far seems to bear this out. As new variants of the coronavirus continue to impact production in different parts of the globe, it is unclear how long it will take for the supply-side challenges to resolve. This will also determine if inflation remains transitory or becomes entrenched. And if it does become entrenched, MMT would not advise raising interest rates to fight it. On the contrary, MMT argues that the standard inflation-fighting tool (raising rates) likely has the reverse effect.[19] What would raising interest rates do today to stop the inflation processes described thus far? Would raising rates alleviate problems emerging from the supply chain, firm pricing power, OPEC decisions, or the shortage of truck drivers? Clearly not. If anything, raising interest rates would *increase* the cost of production further, thus feeding the inflationary process. As it was the case under Volker, rates and inflation kept rising lockstep for years, until double-digit rates eventually plunged the economy into a recession. MMT rejects the conventional view that an economic slowdown, a reduction in wages, and unemployment are 'solutions' to inflationary pressures. There are multiple ways to tackle a sustained increase in the price level, including investments that can alleviate bottlenecks or shortages on the supply side (which means more, not less, government spending), while maintaining full employment through an anti-cyclical employment stabilizer like the JG.

The pandemic necessitated a fiscal response that was not seen since WWII. It revealed many fault lines in the economy: poorly paid and vulnerable essential workers, an integrated global supply chain that can lock up, low levels of public health preparedness, and inadequate mobilization. But it also revealed some possibilities by corroborating some key MMT tenets: (1) money is not scarce, (2) unemployment is a policy choice, and (3) inflation is not inevitably the result of large government spending. This suggests concrete steps for rethinking policy, since the question is clearly not whether we can financially afford to act, but how. MMT insists that full employment need not be sacrificed for price stability and that there are many tools available to the policymaker to start thinking about the things that matter – not budgets and accounting ratios, but public health, jobs, and the environment. To tackle these, we would do well to heed the lessons of the pandemic.

NOTES

1. Dziedzicki et al. 2021.
2. Wray 2012.
3. By contrast, the Chinese government provided a full and unconditional wage guarantee for all workers.
4. Tcherneva 2020a.
5. Bullard 2020.
6. Black 2021.
7. Shierholz 2021.
8. Bunker 2021.
9. Dziedzicki et al. 2021.
10. Tcherneva 2014.
11. Tcherneva 2020b.
12. Tcherneva 2020b.
13. Mosler and Silipo 2017.
14. Tcherneva 2002.
15. Ross and Bateman 2019.
16. Terlep 2021.
17. Boesler et al. 2021.

18.   Fullwiler et al. 2019.
19.   Mosler and Armstrong 2019.

REFERENCES

Black, T. 2021. 'Highly paid union workers give UPS a surprise win in delivery war', *Bloomberg*, 4 November.

Boesler, M., Deaux, J. and Dimitrieva, K. 2021. 'Fattest profits since 1950s debunk wage-inflation story of CEOs', *Bloomberg*, 30 November.

Bullard, J. 2020. 'Assessing second-quarter unemployment amid the pandemic', *Federal Reserve Bank of St. Louis*, 28 May.

Bunker, N. 2021. 'Indeed Job Search Survey September 2021: Job search stays stagnant', *Indeed Hiring Lab*, 21 October.

Dziedzicki, K., Drame, I. and Gevorkyan, A. 2021. 'COVID-19 economic response packages – a cross national comparison', Henry George School of Social Science Dynamic Tracker, https://www.hgsss.org/covid-19-economic-news/ (accessed 30 August 2022).

Fullwiler, S., Grey, R. and Tankus, N. 2019. 'An MMT response on what causes inflation', *Financial Times*, 1 March.

Mosler, W. and Armstrong, P. 2019. 'A discussion of central bank operations and interest rate policy,' GIMMS Working Paper, The Gower Initiative for Modern Money Studies.

Mosler, W. and Silipo, D. 2017. 'Maximizing price stability in a monetary economy', *Journal of Policy Modeling*, 39 (2): 272–89.

Ross, M. and Bateman, N. 2019. 'Low-wage work is more pervasive than you think, and there aren't enough "good jobs" to go around', Metropolitan Policy Program, Brookings Institute, Washington, DC, November.

Shierholz, H. 2021. 'U.S. labor shortage? Unlikely. Here's why', Economic Policy Institute, 4 May.

Tcherneva, P.R. 2002. 'Monopoly money: The State as a price setter', *Oeconomicus*, Winter: 124–43.

Tcherneva, P.R. 2014. 'Reorienting fiscal policy: A bottom-up approach', *Journal of Post Keynesian Economics*, 37 (1): 43–66.

Tcherneva, P.R. 2020a. 'What if we nationalized payroll?', Levy Economics Institute, 30 March.

Tcherneva, P.R. 2020b. *The Case for a Job Guarantee*, Cambridge, UK: Polity Press.

Terlep, S. 2021. 'U.S. corporate giants bet shoppers will keep paying higher prices', *Wall Street Journal*, 24 October.

Wray, L.R. 2012. *Modern Money Theory: A Primer on Macroeconomics for Sovereign Monetary Systems*, New York: Palgrave Macmillan.

12. Modern Monetary Theory and public policy in the United Kingdom

Deborah Harrington and Jessica Ormerod

Anything we can do, we can afford ... We are immeasurably richer than our predeces-sors. Is it not evident that some sophistry, some fallacy, governs our collective action if we are forced to be so much meaner than they in the embellishments of life? ... Yet these must be only the trimmings on the more solid, urgent, and necessary outgoings on housing the people, on reconstructing industry and transport and on replanning the environment of our everyday life.

John Maynard Keynes[1]

The first part of this book deals with Modern Monetary Theory macroeconom-ics, the 'envelope' in which all economic activity takes place. It looks amongst other concerns at the mechanics of state finance; inflation; trade flows; unem-ployment and the Job Guarantee. At the heart of MMT is a description of how money creation works. This part of the equation is missing from classical economic thinking, leaving it disconnected from the real world.

This chapter gives an overview on the UK government's funding of its social programme and explores the exceptionality of some elements of the Welfare State created post-1945 by Clement Attlee's Labour government. It looks at the enduring quality of the work of William Beveridge in 1942 in detailing the responsibilities of a modern government in caring for the welfare of its people. Beveridge was a Liberal politician and director of the London School of Economics (LSE) from 1919 to 1937.[2] Hayek, a contemporary of Beveridge at the LSE, responded to Beveridge's proposals with his book *The Road to Serfdom*.

Keynes called economics a 'moral science' and the positions provided by these two major publications effectively set out the key opposing moral and philosophical grounds of the economic discourse examined here. These translate into real-world policies and events that have a profound impact on the public wellbeing.

The chapter considers key UK government departments' contemporary delivery of the main socio-economic determinants of health, particularly income security. In Beveridge's language, the state needed to slay the Five Giants of Want, Disease, Ignorance, Squalor, and Idleness on its road to post-war reconstruction and social security, health, education, housing and full employment were its weapons. Perhaps a category for the protection of the environment should be added, though it does not fall within this chapter's scope: its giant might be named Greed. Ownership and disposal of the public estate and the effect of global political and policy pressures also play a significant role in public finance.

The MMT lens applied in this chapter takes as its fundamental realities:

- That the UK government, in common with other countries which have their own currency, their own central bank, a floating exchange rate, and no foreign currency debt, faces no financial budget constraint at all.
- That consequently the UK cannot run out of pounds sterling. But the availability of resources, domestic or imported, whether people, skills, technology, infrastructure, natural or ecological, do constrain its ability to spend without unbalancing the economy or creating additional inflationary pressure.
- That the balance of the economy is of far greater importance than balancing the budget. This re-frames our understanding of deficit spending to be a measure of how well the government has tackled inequalities and poverty, involuntary unemployment, the quality of and access to public services such as health and education, the availability and quality of housing and the speed of its implementation of environmental improvements.
- That the government as currency issuer and tax authority creates net financial assets for the non-governmental sector through deficit spending. If the non-governmental sector wants to net save in sterling, then the government has to be in deficit. An insufficient deficit level forces the non-governmental sector to fund its spending by increasing private debt.

Recognising the existence and importance of public money provides a different lens on public policy and the spending that directly affects our everyday life from cradle to the grave: the services which support our basic needs. It allows different questions to be asked about the policy realm for government beyond or, perhaps more accurately, within the envelope of the macro.

In the UK the sets of conventions and rules which have been applied down the last few decades, particularly since 1976,[3] have, to a greater or lesser extent, obscured the monetary realities of public finance. These conventions insist that public spending must be paid for through taxation, the government sale of assets or 'selling off the family silver', as Harold MacMillan[4] put it, or borrowing money now at interest (via gilts) which will have to be repaid in the future. This borrowing is presumed to create additional taxation for future generations, which is always characterised as a 'burden'.

The language used around public spending is framed to contrast it with the private sector, using both sectors as if they were respectively the debit and credit sides of the government's household budget. Under these conditions healthcare is market 'demand' rather than clinical need, libraries are seen as luxuries which can be dispensed with in hard times.[5] In total, services are considered only in terms of being a drain on a financially constrained purse for which the private citizen as taxpayer carries the burden. Keynes described this as 'the vile doctrine of the nineteenth century that every enterprise must justify itself in pounds, shillings and pence of cash income ...'[6]

The government's first objective must therefore be to reduce the burden of those taxes, spend responsibly, and make hard choices so it can live within its means, balance the books and pay down the debt. Public services and the health of the nation effectively become discretionary spending for the state, with philanthropy or the private individual's purse left to make up the shortfall.

Under these conditions, inequality has grown to such an extent that Professor Philip Alston, United Nations Special Rapporteur on extreme poverty and human rights, reported in November 2018 on the UK that it

> ... is obvious to anyone who opens their eyes to see the immense growth in foodbanks and the queues waiting outside them, the people sleeping rough in the streets, the growth of homelessness, the sense of deep despair that leads even the Government to appoint a Minister for suicide prevention and civil society, to report in depth on unheard of levels of loneliness and isolation.[7]

As this is being written, the country and the world is coming to terms with the aftermath of the 2020–21 Covid-19 pandemic and the acceptance of new endemic disease. This period together with government support for the banks after the financial crash of 2008 have involved a scale of spending possibly unprecedented outside of wartime, in parallel with the deepening of financial insecurity for many people. This has not yet changed the economic discourse, although as Beveridge wrote in 1942, 'Now, when the war is abolishing landmarks of every kind, is the opportunity for using experience in a clear field. A revolutionary moment in the world's history is a time for revolutions, not for patching.'[8] This may not be a time of war, but both political and economic landmarks are surely shifting significantly.

The very ancient principles of care for the poor and the health of the nation which establish the obligations of society are largely uncontested in mainstream political ideology. But the moral and political stances which are applied to those obligations, and consequent outcomes such as those described by Alston, are mediated through the assumptions made about the effect of public spending on the economy and the question of who pays for it and how. The arguments about paying for our obligations are altered when seen through an MMT lens, which assumes the affordability to be answered within the constraints listed above, when the government is the currency issuer. This still leaves the question of who pays, but it becomes explicitly political rather than being framed as financial necessity. It also foregrounds resources rather than finance.

Central to Beveridge's work was the idea that by guaranteeing that no member of society at any age would fall into poverty, people would be set free by an absence of worry about how to maintain the basics of life. It is a principle echoed ten years later in Aneurin Bevan's collection of essays *In Place of Fear*.[9] Bevan was Minister of Health and Housing (1945–51) and had battles with his own government as well as the Conservative Opposition over the cost of Britain's National Health Service (NHS),[10] but for him it was foremost a moral obligation.

He wrote,

> The collective principle asserts that the resources of medical skills and the apparatus of healing shall be placed at the disposal of the patient, without charge, when he or she needs them; that medical treatment and care should be a communal responsibility; that they should be made available to rich and poor alike in accordance with medical need and by no other criteria. It claims that financial anxiety in times of sickness is a serious hindrance to recovery, apart from its unnecessary cruelty. It insists that no society can legitimately call itself civilised if a sick person is denied medical aid because of lack of means.[11]

In 1945 Winston Churchill, wartime Prime Minister and leader of the Conservative Party (1940–55), read *The Road to Serfdom* and wanted part of the party's valuable paper ration to be used to print abridged copies to use as election material. And it was another of Hayek's books, *The Constitution of Liberty*, which Margaret Thatcher was reputed to have brought to her first Shadow Cabinet meeting in 1975 as leader of the party, saying 'This is what we believe.'

The principles she brought to public policy have superseded Beveridge's and have dominated policy and practice for longer. US economist Milton Friedman was adviser to both Thatcher and Ronald Reagan who became President of the US two years after Thatcher became Prime Minister in the UK. Friedman was a co-founder, with Hayek, of the Mont Pelerin Society, an organisation formed to promote the free-market values they believed were under threat from the kind of state planning which was being developed in the UK and elsewhere. Thatcher's association with Friedman and Reagan broke the post-war consensus on the provision of public services in the UK and started in earnest the long-term dismantling of the Beveridge-inspired Welfare State. Thatcher famously said in 1979 at her first Conservative Party

Conference as Prime Minister, 'The Government have no money on their own. There is only taxpayer's money.'[12]

Friedman expresses the desirability of private charity, describing how the laissez-faire attitudes of the 19th century grew private wealth, thereby creating the conditions for a proliferation of charities. He laments the growth of government welfare activities as driving out charitable activities. He says poverty is distressing and should be relieved, but he frames charity as an act concerned with the need of individual recipients rather than a characteristic of groups.[13]

His concern is that to tackle poverty by setting a minimum standard or floor for everyone distorts the efficient and effective functioning of the market, ultimately impeding the growth of private wealth. In Friedman's terms, poverty can be recognised and quantified at an individual level, but to address it at state level with such devices as minimum or living wages or by universal health services, child or pension benefit is to disrupt the action of wealth-creating individuals by the imposition of collective action.

These positions involve diametrically opposed concepts of the freedom of the individual. For Beveridge and Attlee's government, meaningful freedom for the individual could not be achieved unless basic needs were assured. They saw the state's role as ensuring a safety net for 'the means of healthy existence' through work and income. Beveridge's report was drawn up after widespread analysis of the poverty existing in the UK at that time including a survey commissioned just before the outbreak of war by the Unemployment Assistance Board.[14]

Day[15] details part of a description from the survey, based on interviews with the unemployed in several different towns, which gives an insight into the weekly cycle of impoverished life, centred around the day when unemployment assistance is doled out – of one or two proper meals a week followed only by tea and bread, trips back and forth to the pawn shop – a cycle where 'there are not a few pennies left over at the end of the week, but a few pennies short'. It includes descriptions of families of four or five people living in one dirty room surrounded by filthy linen and its indescribably horrible smell. There are details of the physical and mental effects of chronic unemployment – malnourished men and women rendered listless and depressed by their enforced idleness.

Although written in 1936, it is a description which is recognisably reflected in Alston's report for the United Nations in 2018.[16]

The concept of freedom as seen by Hayek and Friedman was very different. 'The key component of their respective concept of freedom was labelled negative freedom (or "freedom from") by Sir Isaiah Berlin in his *Four Essays on Liberty*.'[17] Primarily focused on the 'free' market economy, these freedoms are based on theoretical concepts rather than the empirical research which Beveridge used. In a free market where both buyer and seller are willing participants, businesses only create products that customers need, and customers are in the position of deciding the success or failure of products by evaluating their features and price. In their model, the government would have a minimal role and would regulate activity only in cases of absolute necessity. This self-regulating market 'free from' government interference will provide superior products and meet all needs. Government spending and functions which restrict the market's operations should be minimised.

Kelton[18] points out that these restrictions placed on public spending, which are clearly self-imposed once the MMT realities are understood, only ever apply to peacetime spending, and disappear in times of war. Thatcher herself said, regarding her government's expenditure on the Falklands War in 1982, that 'The War Cabinet was never tempted to compromise the security of our troops for financial reasons. Everything we did was governed by military necessity.'[19]

12.1   GOLD STANDARD THINKING IN A FIAT CURRENCY WORLD

The MMT lens can be applied to social policy questions in any economic system, as it looks at what the currency constraints are to assess the potential for and consequences of government action or inaction. The real resource and monetary position post-1945 did not affect the government's commitment to a Beveridge-style Welfare State but it financially constrained it.

While this programme of social reform may have come from the experiences the country had lived through in the previous 30 years – two world wars, the Depression, a flu pandemic which had killed many[20] and left many more impoverished – the thinking behind it was not new. In mid-19th-century Germany, Virchow had drawn connections between poverty and living conditions, and illness. He stated that 'medicine is social science and politics nothing but medicine on a grand scale'.[21]

It is a recurrent theme in political philosophy. As Tudor Hart states, 'Since (the 17th Century) objective analysis of social health and health care has endured repeated cycles of birth, decline and rediscovery, always related to contemporary political and economic climates of democratic advance or oligarchic retreat.'[22]

1945 was not a time of fiat currency and the government faced both severe real resource constraints, a prospective deficit in its US$ balance of payments and a US$ denominated debt to both the US and Canada. The US loan created additional pressures as it was made on conditions of convertibility to the US$ which drained the government's dollar reserves.

The Cabinet papers of 1947[23] outline the reductions which would be necessary in overseas expenditure and in the import programme. Serious issues under consideration included the impact of nutritional and other consequences of proposed food cuts. Nonetheless, even under these pressures, it took three years before the commitment to the raft of new social policies began to be eroded.

In 1951, Bevan became Minister for Labour and National Service but resigned from the Cabinet when a decision was taken to bring in charges for certain NHS services. He did not contest the constraints on fiscal policy but asked about the likely effects of the proposed spending and cuts programme on employment and inflation. In his resignation speech to Parliament he said,

> The fact of the matter is, as everybody knows, that the extent to which stockpiling has already taken place, the extent to which the civil economy is being turned over to defence purposes in other parts of the world is dragging prices up everywhere … raw materials, machine tools and components are not forthcoming in sufficient quantity … we should not put figures on account of defence expenditure which would not be realised, and if they tried to be realised would have the result of inflating prices in this country and all over the world.[24]

He said that the consequences of increased defence spending, which was already accelerating unsustainably in the US, would be to create mass unemployment in addition to the underemployment the country was already experiencing. He objected to the defence programme being funded to the detriment of people's daily lives and to the maintenance of the social programme. He claimed inflation would immediately begin to take away from pensioners 'the few shillings' they had received in the Budget.

He further advised that economists be removed from the Treasury because they knew nothing of real planning. He added that they had an additional misfortune because the Chancellor was an economist. In respect of the NHS, he objected to the artificial ceiling on its budget, saying it would not allow for rising prices. 'This is the beginning of the end. Once you start this there is no logical stopping point.'[25]

The political framework has changed over the last few decades and with it not only the economic understanding, but the approach government takes to its social programmes. Mitchell et al. point out the 'deep gulf' between the current orthodoxy and an analysis based on MMT's more heterodox approach.[26] The dominant question has become one of overall cost to the State which underpins arguments for an austerity programme to reduce the budgets for social programmes, combined with a push to transfer expenditure off its books. 'Overall, NHS organisational decisions have shifted in character from being clinically based to economics based.'[27] This is not the same as Bevan's critique, which would be consistent with the MMT analysis, where one element of spending is examined for its potential impact on other departments' ability to provide employment, social security and health, under severe monetary and resource constraints.

The creation of the NHS and the Welfare State marked the UK out as an anomaly compared with other wealthy industrialised nations with the extent of its state-provided services and non-contributory benefits. Uniquely the NHS had no eligibility rules at all. A tourist or newly arrived immigrant was as entitled to all its services as any British citizen.[28]

Although the Welfare State was a Labour achievement, built on the work of Beveridge who was a Liberal, its policies were so successful, they were broadly continued for 30 years, regardless of who was in government. The economic perspective which has superseded it has been used as a tool to drive a specific narrative about the role of the state as a provider of services. First, the idea that a budget deficit is a bad thing and cutting the deficit is a hard but necessary choice which responsible politicians will shoulder, even though it means cutting services. Second, the idea that society operates better free of the intervention of government as far as practicably possible.

These ideas are encapsulated in one of David Cameron's earliest speeches as Prime Minister in the Conservative–Liberal Democrat Coalition of 2010–15. He said:[29]

> There are the things you do because it's your duty. Sometimes unpopular – but you do them because it is in the national interest. And yes, cutting the deficit falls into that camp. But there are the things you do because it's your passion ... And my great passion is building the Big Society.

Cameron goes on to elaborate that the Big Society is

> Where people, in their everyday lives, in their homes, in their neighbourhoods, in their workplace don't always turn to officials, local authorities or central government for answers to the problems they face but instead feel both free and powerful enough to help themselves and their own communities. It's about people setting up great new schools. Businesses helping people getting trained for work. Charities working to rehabilitate offenders ... For years, there was the basic assumption at the heart of government that the way to improve things in society was to micromanage from the centre, from Westminster. But this just doesn't work. We've got the biggest budget deficit in the G20. And over the past decade, many of our most pressing social problems got worse, not better.

Mitchell et al. state that

> In a market economy where goods and services are exchanged for money, the non-government sector's capability to command goods and services depends not only on availability but on the sector's capacity to finance purchases. For the government sector the ability to command goods and services which are for sale in the currency that it issues depends only on the availability of those resources

as illustrated by the post-war choices over food and imports discussed in this chapter.

> This is a fundamental difference, which should inform our understanding of ... the major deep debates in macroeconomics because of its implications for physical policy choices.[30]

From 1976 onwards, the UK's state apparatus has been dismantled to bring it more into line with other countries. That is private sector provision of services, conditionality for state benefits and a gradual transfer of financial responsibilities from the public purse to private pockets. Within this framework, state mechanisms are seen as 'interventions' in the workings of the market which is portrayed as both the natural state of things and as the proper determinant of resource allocation.

This is not a simple question of the two main political parties representing different political arguments. The policies of this period, based on New Public Management,[31] 'living within our means'[32] and social capital[33] have acquired over time a de-politicised 'neutral' quality, adopted by all political parties.

This theoretical decoupling of politics from economic decisions was expressed in 1997 by the Labour government's Chancellor, Gordon Brown, by granting the Bank of England operational responsibility for setting the short-term policy interest rate, with a view to achieving an inflation target. As Ian McCafferty, an external member of the Bank's Monetary Policy Committee stated on the 20th anniversary of its creation, '"Operational" in the sense that the Bank is responsible for the delivery of the inflation target, and for designing and operating the tools to do so, but the choice of that target remains with the Government, and the Bank is required to explain and justify its decisions to Parliament.'[34]

In 2010, George Osborne, Chancellor for the Coalition government, announced the creation of the Office of Budget Responsibility (OBR), another notionally independent body to monitor the government's fiscal plans in line with their commitment to balance the books. 'If we don't get on top of our debt, every family in Britain will be poorer and the dreams of millions of young people will be dashed. Mortgages will be higher; businesses will go bust and debt interest will become one of the largest items of government spending.'

The government's press notice stated that the new OBR Chief Secretary would meet with members of the Cabinet to plan £6 billion of cuts to services, 'to make an immediate start on tackling the UK's unprecedented £163 billion deficit, boosting credibility and helping keep interest rates lower for longer'.[35]

The trade journal for the health service, the *Health Service Journal* (HSJ), commented in an editorial that it expected the OBR's de-politicisation of public finance forecasts to be welcomed 'because it helps keep the government on track to meet its fundamental commitment to eradicating the deficit'. But it noted in respect of the NHS that its power to appeal to the Treasury for more funds would be weakened on the grounds that healthcare provision would otherwise suffer, 'when the Chancellor can use the OBR's cold and compelling logic as a political buffer'.[36]

If the objective of public policy is to provide a well-educated and healthy population, political choices will be the arbiter of how that is defined. Abba Lerner, whose Functional Finance principles form part of the core thinking of MMT, described the relationship between the government and non-government sectors in a simple but radical way.[37] He said only government can undertake the responsibility for fiscal spending. And the first objective of that spending is to keep the total rate of spending at a level that means all current goods and services produced can be bought at whatever the current prices are which would buy them all. If it allows too much to be spent there will be inflation. If too little is spent there will be unemployment. The government uses a combination of taxes and spending to achieve its objectives. Taxation removes spending power from the non-government sector which could be applied to cool an overheating economy or to allow government to spend on its priorities without creating too much overall demand.

De-politicisation can therefore be in name only. The Treasury is the arbiter of spending decisions: that responsibility cannot be given away. The Treasury owns the Bank of England, and the Bank creates funds on the Treasury's authority (Berkeley, Tye and Wilson, this volume). As McCafferty stated, 'the choice of that target remains with the Government'. Fiscal policy remains the responsibility of Parliament. A government which believes in free trade and the state as a funding stream, not a provider of services, will have a different set of public policy objectives from a statist one, or one which believes in devolving power from the centre. Yet all use the same levers to direct spending.

12.2   THE EFFECT OF AN AGEING POPULATION ON PUBLIC SPENDING

One of the challenges through the ages has been how to ensure the welfare of those with no form of independent income. This is the main subject of Beveridge's 1942 Report.[38] Beveridge analysed the complex web of contributory insurance-based pensions and benefits and means-tested relief for destitution. This encompassed the Poor Law, which dates from 1501, all schemes following the Workmen's Compensation Act, 1897, and special provisions, for example for disability (including industrial injury), special services for children, medical and funeral expenses. The provisions he reviewed were made up of a range of social, mutual benefit and private insurances.

In his report he finds some elements which are seriously deficient but overall states that otherwise 'British provision for security, in adequacy of amount and in comprehensiveness, will stand comparison with that of any other country; few countries will stand comparison with Britain.'

MMT shows that there is a direct relationship between public spending and the amount of private debt or savings in the economy. The Department for Work and Pensions (DWP) has the largest budget of any UK government department.[39] It is unique among the departments in that it provides direct cash transfers from the government to qualifying citizens rather than providing or paying for the delivery of services in kind.

In 2020–21, £123.5 billion, around 58 per cent of the DWP's budget, was spent on benefits to pensioners, including the State Pension and disability benefits. Benefits to working-age people and children, of which the largest were Universal Credit and disability benefits, amounted to £88.6 billion.

For a government whose overriding objective is to balance the budget, the cost of pensions and benefits is their biggest problem. Through the MMT lens, the most important considerations are: available resources; the productive capacity to match spending; and the impact of spending on distribution and inequalities.

Between 1946 and 1964 there was a significant expansion in the birth rate, creating a demographic bulge known as 'the baby boom'. The cost of providing services to this group has been the highest as it has passed through its various life stages. They have benefitted from the NHS and the Welfare State for their whole lives. New schools had to be built to accommodate them. They spent more years in education than earlier generations, their tuition fees were paid and means-tested grants were available to help them with their living costs at university. The 1991 to 1992 Health Survey for England found that most people (71 per cent) in their 70s at that time, that is, born in the 1920s in the post-WWI boom, had no qualifications and only 10 per cent had an A-level (qualifications at age 18) or higher. By 2015 less than half (47 per cent) had no qualifications, and the proportion educated to at least A-level had trebled to 31 per cent.[40]

In 1979 around 32 per cent of all homes in the UK were council-owned, housing 42 per cent of the population. In 1980 Thatcher's government expanded the council house Right to Buy scheme which offered discounts on asking prices substantially below the private market, to council tenants depending on their length of tenure. Home ownership increased as a result from 55 per cent in 1979 to over 70 per cent in the early 2000s.[41]

The oldest of that generation are now 75 and the youngest 57. Now they have a need for the care services of the state, whether health or social.

Mitchell et al.[42] note that

> The ageing society debate is at the forefront of calls to reduce government deficits. The proposition is that national governments will not be able to afford to maintain the spending necessary to support the growing demands for medical care and pension support as their population ages. At some point, the argument goes, governments will run out of money and other public spending programs will become heavily compromised.

Pensions and social security benefits exist when there is sufficient capacity in the economy to provide the material goods to support more people than are involved in the production of those goods. Those benefits can be assessed in terms of their ability to provide the recipients with access to that surplus production, sufficient as Beveridge said to provide a healthy life. They can also be assessed in terms of aggregate income and the effect on demand.

Mitchell et al.[43] discuss what ratios between working and non-working age groups are used by economists to determine whether the cost of benefits is sustainable. They look at the total, age and child dependency ratios. This divides the population by age: child is below 15, working age from 15 to 65, and retirement post-65. The figures are taken from those typical in most countries which have universal education and retirement provision.

The baby boom years are an example of those ratios. High fertility rates post-war gave a high child dependency ratio: a high number of children relative to the working-age population required high investment in maternity services and schools. As that generation grew up, fertility rates dropped and the 'bulge' in the population was in the working-age group. Now they are transferring into retirement the age dependency ratio is rising.

MMT economists have developed the alternative concept of an effective dependency ratio, arguing that the classical definitions are too broad and flawed. The economic contribution of housework and childrearing, which are mainly women's activities, are ignored in conventional frameworks. In retirement, older people may take care of grandchildren, participate in charitable activities, continue to work either full- or part-time. In the working-age group, there is a cohort who may never work through sickness or disability, full- and part-time students and the unemployed. There are the underemployed and the hidden unemployed to be taken into consideration. The standard framework would assume that the solution to a high age dependency ratio would be to raise the pension age. The effective dependency ratio shows that fully utilising the unemployed and underemployed would be more effective.[44]

The change in the prevailing attitudes to state benefits is the area where the moral and political divide is most evident. For Beveridge, people were seen as being subject to social conditions over which they have no or limited control. This can lead to periods of low income and provide little opportunity to save or insure against poverty. The policy response was a collective one, providing a flat rate universal state pension combined with means-tested income support providing a base level for everyone and extra help for those that needed it most (for example for high rents or disability). The contemporary view which foregrounds personal freedom to make choices implies that a lack of financial planning underlies poverty whether during working age or retirement. People may be seen as feckless, making poor life choices, having saved insufficiently through their working lives or not having any foresight. The policy response is to create savings schemes which are either mandatory or offer significant tax incentives.

Tax advantageous savings schemes have been designed for both pensions and for those on working-age income support.

The latest release on pension wealth in Great Britain[45] shows that total private pension wealth in Great Britain was £6.1 trillion in April 2016 to March 2018 (42 per cent of total wealth), up from £3.6 trillion (34 per cent of total wealth) in July 2006 to June 2008, after adjusting for inflation. Pension wealth exceeded private property wealth.

In 2010, 43 per cent of people had made or were making contributions to a private pension scheme. By 2018 that had increased to 53 per cent, partly because of the introduction of an automatic payroll enrolment scheme being set up by the government. Men below pension age are more likely to have active pension schemes than women (56 per cent compared with 51 per cent) and men have higher pension wealth than women (£25,300 compared with £20,000). The 47 per cent with no private pension will be more likely to be wholly dependent on state pension provision. They may be self-employed, unemployed or economically inactive.

There are severe inequalities between the richest and poorest pensioners, some inequality between men and women in the pension holders' group and inequalities between the North and South of England in part due to differences in property prices. Household median wealth in the Southeast was £503,400, up 43 per cent between 2006 and 2018 and lowest in the Northeast at £168,500.

In 2021–22 the weekly basic statutory state pension (SP) for someone with full entitlement is £137.60.[46] Unlike Beveridge's assumption that this is the benefit that should provide the base income, this falls below the level the government calculates is needed for subsistence. Those who have no other income and savings and investments lower than £10,000 can apply for means-tested Pension Credit which raises the pension to £177.10. A new basic level was introduced in 2016. At £179.60 it is marginally higher than Pension Credit. For those claiming Pension Credit who have more than £10,000 savings, every additional £500 is counted as £1 of income, even if no such income is derived from it.[47] Pension Credit also passports the pensioner to other benefits, such as housing benefit if they are rent payers and an annual credit towards their heating costs. This retirement income compares with the median weekly pay for full-time employees which was £611 at April 2021.[48]

The rise in home ownership and rising incomes over their lifetimes in the generation now in receipt of SP means that many are now better off than any previous generation in that age group. But for lower lifetime income earners the rates of SP mean they will be living in pension poverty for the rest of their lives. The Joseph Rowntree Foundation report on poverty for 2020–21 states 1.9 million pensioners are living in poverty.[49]

Median income for people living in retired households fell by an average of 1.1 per cent between financial year end 2018 and financial year end 2020, compared with 1.8 per cent growth per those living in non-retired households.[50]

The tax regime on pension funds is designed to give substantial incentives to save.

There is a tax-free allowance on earned income of £12,570 for people earning less than £125,140 per annum. Between £12,571 and £50,270 the tax rate is 20 per cent, between £50,271 and £150,000 the rate is 40 per cent and over £150,000, it is 45 per cent.[51] The tax rate only applies to the relevant band of income, not to the whole of the income. This is a progressive tax regime, the higher the income the higher the tax rate.

Pension contributions attract very favourable tax relief. Tax relief is available on 100 per cent of annual earnings up to a limit of £40,000 per annum and a lifetime limit of £1.073 million.[52] Tax relief is applied to pension contributions automatically, either if they are deducted by the employer before income tax or otherwise by the pension provider if the applicable tax rate is 20 per cent. The tax relief is paid on the whole of the contribution, not just that portion which would have been subjected to tax.

Additional relief can be claimed if completing a self-assessment tax return at 20 per cent of the amount of any income that has attracted the 40 per cent rate and 25 per cent at the 45 per cent rate.

For example, on £60,270 40 per cent tax will be deducted from £10,000. If £15,000 is paid into a private pension, tax relief at source of 20 per cent will be on the full £15,000. An extra 20 per cent tax relief on £10,000 (the full amount higher rate tax was paid on) can be claimed through a tax return. No additional relief will be paid on the remaining £5,000 which is deemed to have come from the lower tax band. If just £10,000 is paid in there will be a total of 40 per cent tax relief paid on the full amount, 20 per cent at source, 20 per cent through self-assessment.

To generate a retirement pension income which reaches the 40 per cent tax band, estimates from annuity providers range from a pension pot of between £780,000 and over £1 million. Pensions including the SP are taxable. Even those who have been in receipt of the tax relief at 40 per cent are unlikely to exceed the 20 per cent band once past pension age because of the total pension savings required to achieve it. Tax relief on pension savings is therefore regressive, with higher-income taxpayers likely to pay lower taxes on their retirement income than they have received in tax relief on the savings. Higher earners also get greater personal benefit of tax relief by making larger pension contributions and having all the tax relief at the higher marginal rate.

In its macroeconomic context, the pension savings themselves are deferred income. This reduces aggregate spending. High taxpayers have credit added to their pension funds at the highest rate of tax on the whole of the contribution which falls within this bracket. This turns every £100 paid from that bracket into £140. Amounts that fall within the lower rate receive £20 for every £100.

In the political context, the stated aim is to balance the budget through a combination of taxes and reductions in spending. In the case of pension savings, the government has repaid tax to savers at an increasingly advantageous rate in higher-income groups, thereby depriving their account of receipts now and receiving lower taxes on the deferred claim on the subsequent pension income later. While gifting these subsidies to the rich they have reduced the living conditions of the poor.

12.3   INCOME SUPPORT

The macroeconomic purpose of the Job Guarantee is not as a government job creation scheme but rather as an automatic stabiliser for the economy. It is an effective way of keeping the total rate of spending at a level that means all current goods and services produced can be bought at whatever the current prices are which would buy them all.

In the same way, the macroeconomic purpose of income support or social security is to act as an economic stabiliser, albeit an inefficient one. Current policy treats benefit payments as a form of charity to the poor, the poorly paid or unemployed and is focused on whether the amount they are paid is fair to workers who are 'paying for it' and the extent to which it affects the deficit. But through the MMT lens, the government is effectively employing claimants to maintain the rate of spending. They may or may not fulfil that purpose either in terms of income sufficiency for claimants or aggregate spending depending on the levels set.

Tax-free savings initiatives have also been aimed at children, although deferring expenditure from inadequate incomes is hardly possible and reduces aggregate spending. Child Trust Funds (CTF) were introduced in 2005 for children born between 1 September 2002 and 2 January 2011. They were to encourage long-term saving and give all children a financial asset by the time they reach 18. The government contributed a minimum of £250 for all children and a further £250 at age 7. Children whose parents were in receipt of income-based benefits each received £500 per payment. The scheme closed on 2 January 2011. Those who reached age 7 after the closing date of the CTF scheme did not receive the second payment, meaning that instead of being a universal payment the amounts received varied from £250 to £1000 per child. Very few accounts which were set up for the children in households in receipt of benefit have saved much beyond the initial government deposits, with the median amount held being around £650[53] because they have no surplus income.

The savings funds indicate the shift away from Beveridge's principle over the last 40 years, that to flourish, people's first need is the assurance of an adequate minimum income. The DWP emphasises 'improving financial resilience' through placing the responsibility on the individual to cope better, rather than on the government to ensure provision. Rather than ensuring that children do not live in poverty, the emphasis is on administering a 'child maintenance system' so that the non-resident parent pays where family breakdown has occurred rather than increasing benefit levels. The financial foundation for retirement is focused on creating private savings.[54]

Just as Beveridge assessed the pre-1942 web of income support available to be complex and unwieldy, so the Coalition government assessed that administering the benefits system had become too costly. Iain Duncan Smith, Secretary of State for Work and Pensions (2010–16), considered the level and range of benefits available to be a large part of the problem and the solution proposed was a new single benefit to replace six others. The stated aim was to enable people to move off benefits into work without a loss of income, which the government had concluded had created a dependency culture in which people were trapped. The objective of the changes was to 'make work pay'.

Though the rhetoric surrounding Universal Credit (UC) appeared to recognise the health and social benefits of work, it also promoted the idea that people in receipt of benefits had chosen a lifestyle. In a speech in 2014, Duncan Smith attacked the idea that poverty is about money, claiming that state money could not solve it.[55] The following year, addressing the free-market lobby group Reform he said that welfare expenditure 'cost every household in Britain an extra £3,000 a year'.[56] He argued that the changes being made would lead to £50 billion savings 'for the taxpayer'.

UC was introduced in 2013 and the in- and out-of-work benefits it was designed to replace were child tax credit, housing benefit, income support, jobseeker's allowance, employment and support allowance and working tax credit.[57] Instead of the traditional weekly or fortnightly payments to claimants, UC was to be paid monthly to mimic the salary payment of workers and to encourage the unemployed to maintain a working mentality.

Change to social security policy is based on the principle that it is better for people to be in paid employment than not.[58] The employment rate in August 2019 (pre-pandemic) was 75.9 per cent, the highest number since 1971. The unemployment rate was 3.9 per cent. The economic inactivity rate (those who cannot work for reasons of health or disability, who have family caring responsibilities or those who have been discouraged from actively seeking work) was 21 per cent.[59]

The Office for National Statistics bulletin[60] for Employment in the UK showed that of the estimated 32.72 million people in employment for December 2018 to February 2019, 6.3 per cent, or approximately 2,094,080 people, worked between 1 to 15 hours a week. UC covers working people with a tapered reduction in the benefit as they earn more. In July 2019, 2.3 million people were receiving UC, 33 per cent of whom were in work; 1 hour a week counts as work for these purposes. Approximately 20 per cent of claimants were exempt from demands to look for work because of significant disability or caring responsibilities.

Understanding the distribution of economic activity is relevant to policy decisions around social security reform. The distribution of employment and employment opportunity across the UK is not uniform. Data from the Organisation for Economic Co-operation and Development (OECD)[61] and The Centre for Cities reveals a range of economic inactivity figures showing Liverpool with the highest, at 12 per cent, Crawley at 2 per cent and Oxford and Exeter below 5 per cent. The report states that in 25 of the 32 cities (78 per cent) with an economic inactivity rate higher than the national average, the mining, manufacturing and logistics sectors accounted for more than 50 per cent of all jobs in 1951. In these areas, the share of people who are economically inactive because of long-term sickness is much higher than in the rest of the UK.

The new UC regime allowed the state to put much more stringent requirements on claimants. Sanctions are imposed which reduce or stop benefits. These might be for turning up late for appointments or not providing sufficient evidence of looking for work. Those who are working few hours must prove they have sought more hours or taken on additional employment.

In 2016, a new Act of Parliament, the Welfare Reform and Work Act, brought in even more stringent conditions. The DWP did not make the required impact assessment of the combined effect of the changes and The Equality and Human Rights Commission (EHRC) wrote to the Public Bill Committee expressing concern that neither the Impact Assessments on individual clauses nor the Human Rights Memorandum accompanying the bill 'examine equality impact in the depth required by section 149 of the Equality Act 2010 ... and are therefore unlikely to help Parliamentarians fully understand and debate the different provisions contained within the Bill'.[62]

A benefit cap was in place from 2013, which had been set at £26,000 per annum. This was designed to make sure that no household on benefits ever received more than the median salary for a single person. The average (mean) amount of Universal Credit paid to households on UC was £9,480 per annum.

in May 2021.[63] The cap affected relatively few families, but those were the families with the greatest number of children or the greatest need.

However, setting the cap made a political impact with media stories. Not only did the press pick up on the dependency culture, but also on the idea that there were very large families living on benefits who were not prepared to support their own children. Chancellor George Osborne, in a speech in April 2013[64] stated,

> For too long, we've had a system where people who did the right thing – who get up in the morning and work hard – felt penalised for it, while people who did the wrong thing got rewarded for it. When I took this job, I discovered there were some people who got £100,000 a year in Housing Benefit. No family on an ordinary income could ever dream of affording a rent like that.

In fact, the very rare instances of very high housing benefit came from the pressure on London councils to house the homeless on their waiting lists in private accommodation due to the shortage of affordable housing. There had been no large-scale replacement of council housing after the Right to Buy scheme.[65]

The DWP's impact assessment in 2016 said that capping benefits in this way had been shown to 'strengthen work incentives'. Its rationale also stated that it was helping to tackle the deficit by reducing expenditure and helping the government to 'return to sustainable public finances'. They evaluated that this was improving work incentives, promoting fairness between those on out-of-work benefits and taxpayers and delivering savings. Therefore, a further reduction would work better and stated '£20,000 in Great Britain and £23,000 in Greater London builds on this, delivering further positive change.'[66]

The same arguments were used in support of the Act's freeze on certain benefits for a four-year period. DWP's impact assessment states that the primary objectives are to

> Deliver savings to Government that contribute to a reduction in spending on welfare to tackle the deficit, increase work incentives and contribute to the suite of policies designed to rebalance the welfare state to support the vulnerable. The policy's aim was to gradually build the incentive for people to make the choice to move into work.

The assessment reported that there was no direct effect on business from the policy but that there could be

> An increase in labour supply as a result of claimants responding to incentives to move into employment. The 4-year freeze of benefit rates is expected to save £3.5bn in 2019/20. These savings will continue in future as increases will be from a lower base level and savings will increase in cash terms.[67]

Yet, despite this, the National Audit Office (NAO) report on UC[68] indicated that neither the DWP nor the NAO could confirm whether the programme would achieve its objective of increasing employment. Similarly, its report said that analysis of both the cap and conditionality have also called into question the effectiveness of these measures in moving people into work or of in-work progression.

Frank Field, chair of the Work and Pensions Select Committee (2015–19), said that Beveridge, 'will be rolling in his grave'[69] at the failure to produce evidence to back up the key economic assumption of universal credit.

In keeping with Iain Duncan Smith's idea that poverty is not about money, the Act also abolished most of the 2010 Child Poverty Act and renamed it the Life Chances Act. According to Duncan Smith, the only difference between poor and rich children was their start in life which he believed could be overcome by opportunities for social mobility. He expected wealthy individuals and large firms to put money into 'social enterprises' in deprived areas to offer these opportunities.

The Cambridge Centre for Housing and Planning Research (CCHPR) conducted in-depth research for the DWP with people affected by the cap which was published in 2014.[70] This was used as evidence in the impact assessment for reducing the cap in the 2016 Act and indicated that the changes to the cap may not be beneficial. 'Some people reported that they had sacrificed longer-term career aims or getting qualifications in favour of accepting low-skilled work to avoid the Cap.'

When the DWP had assessed the impact of the 2013 cap they stated, 'there is evidence that some households have responded to the benefit cap by moving house'. The CCHPR report for the DWP does not entirely support this position,

> Some households had moved to lower cost housing to avoid the Cap. Some still affected by the Cap wanted to move but found that a lack of suitable accommodation, especially social housing, was a barrier. Many of those still capped did not want to move and this was usually because their current housing option, they believed, was already the cheapest in their local area and they could not access social housing.

The OBR reported in 2018 on the savings from UC as claimants transferred from the legacy benefit system. It states that there is only a marginal saving which 'reflects the fact that UC is less generous on average'[71] but that this saving will increase over time. In contrast to UC's stated aims of saving money by simplifying the system and more people moving into work, the savings come from reducing the benefit itself. Concern about the system impoverishing claimants is widely represented in Parliament. A parliamentary inquiry by the House of Lords' Economic Affairs Committee stated, 'Cuts to Universal Credit have been partially restored but they, along with problems of design and implementation, have had lasting consequences by increasing poverty and hardship among many claimants.'[72]

For Friedman, philanthropy, funds provided by the rich directly for the provisioning of those in great personal hardship was the best way to deal with poverty. When fiscal policy is seen as money constrained and balancing the budget is the highest priority, the emphasis falls on reconsidering the government's total expenditure and which elements might be paid by the private sector rather than the public.

The severe reduction in disposable income for individuals and families on UC is evidence of this transfer of responsibility as food insecurity (the inability to afford the minimum calorific intake) has become widespread. Foodbanks were negligible until 2010–11[73] when the Trussell Trust, the UK's largest network of charitable foodbanks, distributed 61,000 food parcels. In 2016 after the caps to UC were imposed, that rose to 1.2 million and has continued to rise to 2.54 million in 2020–21.[74] The Trust noted that the need for foodbanks increased by an average of 30 per cent where UC had been rolled out compared to 12 per cent in areas where legacy benefits were still in place. Part of the increase in hardship was the six-week wait for payment for UC claimants.

The use of foodbanks to fill the gap in income sufficiency leaves problems for social policy analysts. It leaves gaps in data collection and there is poor ability to judge need, which is addressed ad hoc according to who is willing to run the foodbanks. The Trussell Trust is highly organised, but there is a range of local organisations around the country which have no formal records. Items for foodbanks also include essential sanitary products for babies and adults. Collections are made at schools, businesses and churches as well as supermarkets having donation points where shoppers can put a contribution to the foodbank as they do their weekly shopping.

This chapter has explored the moral and political drive behind social policies and asked how the arguments made to promote them stand up against modern money realities.

Paradoxically it was during the real financial and resource constraints of the 1940s that decisions were made based on the impact on inflation and resource distribution. Increasingly aggressively during the fiat currency period, the overriding concern for government has been to keep the deficit low and to frame all public spending in terms of its cost to the taxpayer and unaffordability.

People are portrayed as enjoying the luxury of a benefits lifestyle, in contrast to Alston's report on the extremities of homelessness and poverty that have been created. Government departmental and select committee reports have shown policies to be unable to achieve their stated ends and are only succeeding in driving people into poverty. Yet, in an echo of Friedman, senior Conservative Jacob Rees Mogg said on LBC radio, 'to have charitable support given by people voluntarily to support their fellow citizens I think is rather uplifting … Inevitably, the state can't do everything, so I think there is good within food banks.'[75]

Yet the assumption that there is reduced state intervention in this situation is inaccurate as the policies are interventions to shape a desired outcome. Governments cannot shrug off their fiscal responsibilities. Spending has increased the retirement savings of the better off and decreased the ability to live a life free of anxiety for the poorest. Both the Covid-19 pandemic and the 2008 banking crisis have shown how deep government pockets really are, but as yet this has not translated into a serious challenge to the tax-and-spend narrative.

If Beveridge was to ask if 'British provision for security, in adequacy of amount and in comprehensiveness, will stand comparison with that of any other country' in 2022 he would have to answer, 'it does not'.

NOTES

1.   Moggridge, 2010.
2.   Bhullar, 2018.
3.   Harvey, Chapter 6, this volume.
4.   Harold MacMillan, former Conservative Prime Minister (1957–63), was not expressing disapproval of the privatisation of state industries. But at a dinner of the Tory Reform Group in 1985 he compared what Margaret Thatcher was doing to a family encountering severe financial difficulties, selling assets including 'the Georgian silver'. Subsequently, in the House of Lords where he sat as the 1st Earl of Stockton, he clarified that it was not private ownership he was alluding to but the conversion of capital to use as income (Hansard, 1985).
5.   According to the Chartered Institute of Public Finance and Accountancy annual survey of libraries, December 2020, 773 libraries – almost a fifth – closed between 2010 and 2019 as a result of decreased funding of local authorities. See Flood, 2019.
6.   Moggridge, 2010.
7.   Alston, 2018.
8.   Beveridge, 1942.
9.   Bevan, 1952.
10.   Bevan, 1951.
11.   Bevan, 1952.
12.   Thatcher, 1979.
13.   Friedman, 1962, pp. 190–1.
14.   Day, 2017.
15.   Day, 2017.
16.   Alston, 2018.
17.   Leeson, 2018, pp. 327–72.
18.   Kelton, 2020.
19.   Thatcher, 2013, p. 349.
20.   Excess mortality England and Wales +55 per cent (Ansart et al., 2009).
21.   Lange, 2021, p. 149.

22.   Tudor Hart, 2010, p. 23.
23.   Index of Cabinet Conclusions, 1947.
24.   Bevan, 1951.
25.   Bevan, 1951.
26.   Mitchell et al., 2019.
27.   Horton, 2017, quoted in Fletcher, 2021.
28.   This changed with the introduction of charges in the Immigration Act 2014.
29.   Cameron, 2010.
30.   Mitchell et al., 2019, p. 499.
31.   Hood, 1991.
32.   Conservative Party, 1976.
33.   Bourdieu, 1986; Putnam, 1995.
34.   McCafferty, 2017.
35.   HM Treasury, 2010.
36.   Dunhill, 2018.
37.   Lerner, 1943.
38.   Beveridge, 1942.
39.   Department for Work and Pensions, 2021a.
40.   Office for National Statistics, 2018.
41.   Disney and Luo, 2016.
42.   Mitchell et al., 2019, pp. 499–501.
43.   Mitchell et al., 2019, pp. 499–501.
44.   Mitchell et al., 2019.
45.   Office for National Statistics, 2019a.
46.   House of Commons Library, 2021a.
47.   House of Commons Library, 2011.
48.   House of Commons Library, 2021b.
49.   Joseph Rowntree Foundation, 2021.
50.   Office for National Statistics, 2021.
51.   Income Tax Rates and Personal Allowances, 2022.
52.   Tax on Your Private Pension Contributions, 2022.
53.   Crawford and Emmerson, 2020.
54.   Department for Work and Pensions, 2021a.
55.   Duncan Smith, 2014.
56.   Duncan Smith, 2015.
57.   Universal Credit, 2022.
58.   See Mosler's 95 bones for 100 dogs, which explains that the government decides
      whether the jobs are available or not (Mosler, 2015).
59.   Office for National Statistics, 2019b.
60.   Office for National Statistics, 2019c.
61.   Barr et al., 2019.
62.   Welfare Reform and Work Bill Committee, 2015.
63.   Department for Work and Pensions, 2021b.
64.   HM Treasury, 2013.
65.   Solomon, 2013.
66.   Department for Work and Pensions, 2016.
67.   Department for Work and Pensions, 2015.
68.   National Audit Office, 2018.
69.   Guardian, 2018.
70.   Department for Work and Pensions, 2014.

71. Office for Budget Responsibility, 2017.
72. House of Lords, 2020.
73. House of Commons Library, 2021c.
74. Bramley et al., 2021.
75. LBC, 2017.

REFERENCES

Alston, P. (2018) Statement on Visit to the United Kingdom. https://www.ohchr.org/en/statements/2018/11/statement-visit-united-kingdom-professor-philip-alston-united-nations-special (accessed 29 September 2022).

Ansart, S. et al. (2009) Mortality burden of the 1918–1919 influenza pandemic in Europe. *Influenza and Other Respiratory Viruses*, Vol. 3, No. 3: 99–106. https://www.ncbi.nlm.nih.gov/pmc/articles/PMC4634693/ (accessed 9 September 2022).

Barr, J., Magrini, E. and Meghnagi, M. (2019) Trends in economic inactivity across the OECD: The importance of the local dimension and a spotlight on the United Kingdom. OECD Local Economic and Employment Development (LEED) Working Papers. https://read.oecd-ilibrary.org/industry-and-services/trends-in-economic-inactivity-across-the-oecd_cd51acab-en#page1 (accessed 9 September 2022).

Bevan, A. (1951) Resignation speech 23 April 1951, reproduced from Hansard HC Deb vol 487 cc34–43. https://www.nyebevan.org.uk/speeches/resignation-speech-23-april-1951/ (accessed 9 September 2022).

Bevan, A. (1952) *In Place of Fear*. Chapter 5 – A Free Health Service. https://www.sochealth.co.uk/national-health-service/the-sma-and-the-foundation-of-the-national-health-service-dr-leslie-hilliard-1980/aneurin-bevan-and-the-foundation-of-the-nhs/in-place-of-fear-a-free-health-service-1952/ (accessed 9 September 2022).

Beveridge, W. Social Insurance and Allied Services. Presented to Parliament by Command of His Majesty (November 1942) HMSO Cmd 6404, reprinted under Open Government License by Socialist Health Association. https://www.sochealth.co.uk/national-health-service/public-health-and-wellbeing/beveridge-report/ (accessed 8 September 2022).

Bhullar, I. (2018) William Beveridge and his Report. https://blogs.lse.ac.uk/lsehistory/2018/01/31/william-beveridge-and-his-report/ (accessed 9 September 2022).

Bourdieu, P. (1986) The forms of capital. In: John G. Richardson (ed.), *Handbook of Theory and Research for the Sociology of Education*. New York: Greenwood Press, pp. 241–58.

Bramley, G., Treanor, M., Sosenko, F. and Littlewood, M. (2021) *State of Hunger: Building the Evidence on Poverty, Destitution and Food Insecurity in the UK*. Trussell Trust Year Two Main Report. https://www.trusselltrust.org/wp-content/uploads/sites/2/2021/05/State-of-Hunger-2021-Report-Final.pdf (accessed 9 September 2022).

Cameron, D. (2010) Speech in Liverpool, 19 July 2010. https://www.gov.uk/government/speeches/big-society-speech (accessed 9 September 2022).

Conservative Party (1976) The Right Approach. Conservative Central Office, London.

Crawford, R. and Emmerson, C. (2020) Coming of age: Labour's Child Trust Funds. Institute for Fiscal Studies Publications. https://ifs.org.uk/articles/coming-age-labours-child-trust-funds (accessed 29 September 2022).

Day, C. (2017) The Beveridge Report and the foundations of the Welfare State. https://blog.nationalarchives.gov.uk/beveridge-report-foundations-welfare-state/ (accessed 9 September 2022).

Department for Work and Pensions (2014) In-depth interviews with people affected by the Benefit Cap. Research Report No. 895. https://assets.publishing.service.gov.uk/government/uploads/system/uploads/attachment_data/file/385901/rr895-benefit-cap-indepth-interviews.pdf (accessed 9 September 2022).

Department for Work and Pensions (2015) Welfare Reform and Work Bill: Impact Assessment of the Benefit rate freeze. https://www.parliament.uk/documents/impact-assessments/IA15-006C.pdf (accessed 9 September 2022).

Department for Work and Pensions (2016) Welfare Reform and Work Act: Impact Assessment for the Benefit cap. https://assets.publishing.service.gov.uk/government/uploads/system/uploads/attachment_data/file/548741/welfare-reform-and-work-act-impact-assessment-for-the-benefit-cap.pdf (accessed 9 September 2022).

Department for Work and Pensions (2021a) DWP annual report and accounts 2020 to 2021. https://assets.publishing.service.gov.uk/government/uploads/system/uploads/attachment_data/file/1005399/dwp-annual-report-and-accounts-2020-2021-web-ready.pdf (accessed 9 September 2022).

Department for Work and Pensions (2021b) Universal Credit statistics 29 April 2013 to 8 July 2021. https://www.gov.uk/government/statistics/universal-credit-statistics-29-april-2013-to-8-july-2021/universal-credit-statistics-29-april-2013-to-8-july-2021 (accessed 9 September 2022).

Disney, R. and Luo, G. (2016) The Right to Buy public housing in Britain: A welfare analysis. Institute of Fiscal Studies Working Paper W15/05, December. https://ifs.org.uk/publications/right-buy-public-housing-britain-welfare-analysis-0 (accessed 29 September 2022).

Duncan Smith, Iain (2014) A welfare state fit for the 21st century. Speech to the Centre for Social Justice, 23 January 2014. https://www.gov.uk/government/speeches/a-welfare-state-fit-for-the-21st-century (accessed 9 September 2022).

Duncan Smith, Iain (2015) Work, health and disability. Speech at an event hosted by Reform and Barclays, 24 August 2015. https://www.gov.uk/government/speeches/work-health-and-disability (accessed 9 September 2022).

Dunhill, L. (2018) Following the money: Rise of the OBR means less power for the NHS. *Health Service Journal*, 20 March.

Fletcher, A.N. (2021) What is evidence as evidence used? A case of dualism? *Social Theory and Health*, October.

Flood, A. (2019) 'Britain has closed almost 800 libraries since 2010, figures show', *Guardian*. https://www.theguardian.com/books/2019/dec/06/britain-has-closed-almost-800-libraries-since-2010-figures-show (accessed 20 February 2022).

Friedman, M. (1962) *Capitalism and Freedom*. Chicago, IL: University of Chicago Press.

Guardian (2018) Universal credit all-party report raises fears over workability of system, 8 February. https://www.theguardian.com/society/2018/feb/08/universal-credit-all-party-report-raises-fears-over-workability-of-system (accessed 9 September 2022).

Hansard HL. Deb vol 468 cc388–98 14 November 1985. https://api.parliament.uk/historic-hansard/lords/1985/nov/14/new-technologies (accessed 9 September 2022).

HM Treasury (2010) Chancellor announces policies to enhance fiscal credibility. Press Notice 1 October. https://www.gov.uk/government/news/chancellor-announces-policies-to-enhance-fiscal-credibility (accessed 9 September 2022).

HM Treasury (2013) Chancellor's Speech on changes to the tax and benefit system, 2 April 2013. https://www.gov.uk/government/speeches/chancellor-speech-on -changes-to-the-tax-and-benefit-system (accessed 9 September 2022).

Hood, C. (1991) A public management for all seasons? *Public Administration*, Vol. 69, No. 1: 3–19.

House of Commons Library (2011) Pension Credit – background. Standard Note CBP-01439, 14 December. https://researchbriefings.files.parliament.uk/documents/ SN01439/SN01439.pdf (accessed 9 September 2022).

House of Commons Library (2021a) State Pension uprating. Briefing Paper No. CBP-5649, 2 February. https://researchbriefings.files.parliament.uk/documents/ SN05649/SN05649.pdf (accessed 9 September 2022).

House of Commons Library (2021b) Average earnings by age and region. Research Briefing CBP-8456, 1 November. https://commonslibrary.parliament.uk/research -briefings/cbp-8456/ (accessed 9 September 2022).

House of Commons Library (2021c) Food banks in the UK. Research Briefing CBP-8585, 14 July. https://commonslibrary.parliament.uk/research-briefings/cbp -8585/ (accessed 9 September 2022).

House of Lords (2020) Universal Credit isn't working: proposals for reform. Economic Affairs Committee. HL Paper 105. https://publications.parliament.uk/pa/ld5801/ ldselect/ldeconaf/105/10502.htm (accessed 9 September 2022).

Income Tax Rates and Personal Allowances (2022) https://www.gov.uk/income-tax -rates (accessed 22 February 2022).

Index of Cabinet Conclusions 1 January–31 December 1947 (C.M. (47) 1st–96th Meetings). https://www.nationalarchives.gov.uk/ (accessed 9 September 2022).

Joseph Rowntree Foundation, Evidence and Impact Team (2021) *UK Poverty 2020–2021*. https://www.jrf.org.uk/report/uk-poverty-2020-21 (accessed 9 September 2022).

Kelton, S. (2020) *The Deficit Myth: Modern Monetary Theory and How to Build a Better Economy*. London: John Murray Press.

Lange, K.W. (2021) Rudolf Virchow, poverty and global health from 'politics as med- icine on a grand scale' to 'health in all policies'. *Global Health Journal*, Vol. 5, No. 3, September: 149–54.

LBC (2017) Jacob Rees-Mogg: Increased use of food banks is 'rather uplifting', 14 September. https://api.lbc.co.uk/radio/presenters/nick-ferrari/jacob-rees-mogg -increased-use-food-banks-uplifting/ (accessed 9 September 2022).

Leeson, R. (ed.) (2018) *Hayek: A Collaborative Biography*. London: Palgrave Macmillan.

Lerner, A.P. (1943) Functional finance and the federal debt. *Social Research*, Vol. 10, Note 1: 38–51.

McCafferty, I. (2017) Twenty years of Bank of England independence: The evolution of monetary policy. Speech at the 38th Robert Warner Lecture, The Worshipful Company of Founders, City of London, 5 October 2017. https://www.bankofengland .co.uk/-/media/boe/files/speech/2017/twenty-years-of-boe-independence-the -evolution-of-monetary-policy.pdf (accessed 9 September 2022).

Mitchell, W., Wray, L.R. and Watts, M. (2019) *Macroeconomics*. London: Red Globe Press, an imprint of Springer Nature.

Moggridge, D.E. (ed.) (2010) *Keynes on the Wireless: John Maynard Keynes*. London and New York: Palgrave Macmillan.

Mosler, W. (2015) The dogs and bones story. https://www.youtube.com/watch?v =dHIuK5xNi-Q&list=PLDUvqM-JGl097YQ9_vOOjfcBYUIOirfaV&index=52 (accessed 9 September 2022).

National Audit Office (2018) Rolling out Universal Credit. https://www.nao.org.uk/wp -content/uploads/2018/06/Rolling-out-Universal-Credit.pdf (accessed 9 September 2022).

Office for Budget Responsibility (2017) Universal Credit and the legacy benefits in 2017–18. https://obr.uk/box/universal-credit-and-the-legacy-benefits-in-2017-18/ (accessed 9 September 2022).

Office for National Statistics (2018) How do the post-world war baby boom generations compare? https://www.ons.gov.uk/peoplepopulationandcommunity/birthsdeathsand marriages/ageing/articles/howdothepostworldwarbabyboomgenerationscompare/ 2018-03-06 (accessed 9 September 2022).

Office for National Statistics (2019a) Pension wealth in Great Britain April 2016 to March 2018. https://www.ons.gov.uk/peoplepopulationandcommunity/personala ndhouseholdfinances/incomeandwealth/bulletins/pensionwealthingreatbritain/ april2016tomarch2018 (accessed 9 September 2022).

Office for National Statistics (2019b) Labour market overview, UK: October 2019. https://www.ons.gov.uk/employmentandlabourmarket/peopleinwork/employm entandemployeetypes/bulletins/uklabourmarket/october2019 (accessed 9 September 2022).

Office for National Statistics (2019c) Employment in the UK: April 2019. https:// www.ons.gov.uk/employmentandlabourmarket/peopleinwork/employmentandempl oyeetypes/bulletins/employmentintheuk/april2019 (accessed 9 September 2022).

Office for National Statistics (2021) Average household income, UK: Financial year 2020. https://www.ons.gov.uk/peoplepopulationandcommunity/personala ndhouseholdfinances/incomeandwealth/bulletins/householddisposableincomeandi nequality/financialyear2020 (accessed 9 September 2022).

Putnam, R.D. (1995) Bowling alone: America's declining social capital. *Journal of Democracy*, Vol. 6, No. 1: 64–78.

Solomon, V. (2013) Housing homeless families in London. London Councils Member Briefing.

Tax on Your Private Pension Contributions (2022) https://www.gov.uk/tax-on-your -private-pension/pension-tax-relief (accessed 22 February 2022).

Thatcher, M. (1979) Speech to Conservative Party Conference, 12 October 1979. https://www.margaretthatcher.org/document/104147 (accessed 9 September 2022).

Thatcher, M. (2013) *Margaret Thatcher: The Autobiography*. London: HarperCollins.

Tudor Hart, J. (2010) *The Political Economy of Health Care: Where the NHS Came from and Where It Could Lead*, 2nd edn, Bristol: Policy Press.

Universal Credit (2022) https://www.gov.uk/universal-credit (accessed 22 February 2022).

Welfare Reform and Work Bill Committee (2015) Written evidence submitted by the Equality and Human Rights Commission (EHRC) (WRW 85). https://publications .parliament.uk/pa/cm201516/cmpublic/welfarereform/memo/wrw85.htm (accessed 9 September 2022).

Postscript: thoughts on MMT's insights

L. Randall Wray

The economics of the mainstream is in disarray. As Frank Hahn[1] remarked four decades ago, "The most serious challenge that the existence of money poses to the theorist is this: the best developed model of the economy cannot find room for it." He was speaking of General Equilibrium theory, but his claim applies equally well to Dynamic Stochastic General Equilibrium theory, which is used by all the major central bankers of the world to model the economy. Let that sink in. Our central bankers use a model that has no money, no banks, and no financial system to understand the economy in order to formulate policy. Queen Elizabeth II asked why none of the mainstreamers foresaw the Global Financial Crisis coming. Their failure was baked into their model.

Remarkably, even insiders at the Fed recognize the dismal failure of orthodoxy. Rudd[2] begins a recent Fed research paper with this: "Nobody thinks clearly, no matter what they pretend ... that's why people hang on so tight to their beliefs and opinions; because compared to the haphazard way they're arrived at, even the goofiest opinion seems wonderfully clear, sane, and self-evident." He goes on to list ideas that "'everyone knows' to be true but that are actually arrant nonsense":

- Aggregate production functions ... provide a good way to characterize the economy's supply side;
- Over a sufficiently long span ... the economy will return to a state of full market clearing; and
- The theory of household choice provides a solid justification for downward-sloping market demand curves. (p. 1)

All arrant nonsense. All accepted as dogma.

To paraphrase what Keynes[3] said almost nine decades ago, mainstream theory's application is not only limited to a special case (i.e., an economy that does not use money), but is also dangerous when applied to the "facts of experience" to formulate policy. The evidence is plain to see all around us: in an era of multiple pandemics that threaten the continued existence of human life on planet earth, we are stymied by imaginary constraints concocted by economists.

Over the past quarter century, MMT got much of it right. Its proponents foresaw the fatal flaws of the euro.[4] They foresaw the oncoming Global Financial Crisis.[5] They warned that the policy response to that crisis would be insufficient, meaning that recovery would take many more years than necessary.[6] And when the COVID pandemic hit, they offered a policy response.[7]

In that last case, it is probable that at least some policymakers listened to MMT. Congressman John Yarmuth, Chair of the House Budget Committee, had embraced MMT and helped to usher through trillions of dollars of pandemic relief without worrying about "pay-fors". As he correctly argued:

> Historically, what we've always done is said, "What can we afford to do?" And that's not the right question. The right question is, "What do the American people need us to do?" And that question becomes the first question. Once you answered that, then you say, "How do you resource that need?"[8]

He went on to argue that as the US government issues its own currency, finance is never the problem. What matters is resource availability. As MMT predicted, those trillions of dollars of "deficit spending" did not cause interest rates to spike, did not cause the dollar to crash, did not cause attacks by bond vigilantes, and did not force the US government into default. All the finance was keystroked into existence, all the treasury's cheques cleared, all the bonds offered were gladly taken up, and the dollar remained strong. The deepest recession on record was reversed with the fastest recovery on record. MMT was in the news, again, but this time occasionally with a positive spin. The pandemic response was claimed to be the first real-world experiment that applied MMT.

However, the pandemic lingered on far longer than most thought it would – with continued supply chain disruptions, new viral outbreaks, organized political resistance to science, and price-gouging by mega-corps with pricing power. Inflation rose. MMT was blamed.[9] In truth, the policies adopted were not those MMT advocated – the spending was not well targeted, jobs were not created directly, capacity was not enhanced. As Yarmuth warned, all eyes need to be focused on resources, not on finance.

A chief architect of the dominant neoliberal world order, Larry Summers, announced with fury that he was offended that the "newspaper of record" (*New York Times*) would devote space to MMT: "I am sorry to see the @nytimes taking MMT seriously as an intellectual movement. It is the equivalent of publicizing fad diets, quack cancer cures or creationist theories."[10] Jason Furman – a favourite of administrations headed by Democrats – also weighed in: "I don't think MMT as an economic theory makes any sense. I also don't think it's played a role in shifting us on deficits."[11]

A favourite complaint of MMT's critics (both orthodox and heterodox) is to make the claims that (a) MMT has no coherent model, and (b) MMT is not published in any refereed journals. Both of these are thoroughly dishonest claims – as this volume makes clear. In these pages, you have seen discussion of models of price formation, exchange rate formation, and exchequer (treasury) spending. A recent macroeconomics textbook builds a complete Keynesian model that is thoroughly MMT-consistent – for the first time.[12] Hundreds of academic articles have been published laying out the MMT approach, as well as many dozens of books. Beginning with a handful of developers a quarter century ago, MMT now has thousands of followers.

This volume continues to expose the falsehoods. Many heterodox economists have tried to claim that MMT applies only to the US – the issuer of the international reserve currency. Several of the chapters here make it clear that is false; and, of course, it should always have been recognized as false because one of the main developers of the approach is Bill Mitchell, who hails from a tiny open economy (Australia). Increasingly, MMT has been adopted by economists from developing countries, including Ngongo Samba Sylla. Chapters in this volume assess the UK as well as the Economic and Monetary Union (EMU) from the perspective of MMT.[13] Relations of a sovereign currency nation with the external economy are also addressed by several chapters. MMT alternatives to "beggar thy neighbour" (and thyself!) mercantilist policy are explored.

Several chapters address resource constraints – both of developed and of developing nations – and how to relax them. Others go more deeply into the role that taxes play in MMT. There is an exhaustive review of British history – showing that the history of the exchequer *is* the history of money. And MMT's favourite policy recommendation – the Job Guarantee (JG) – is treated to both historical and theoretical explication.

Conventional macroeconomic theory – of both the orthodox and (unfortunately) of much of the heterodox variety – takes an excessively "high in the sky" view. Unemployment is caused by too little spending. Inflation is caused by too much. Keeping taxes aligned – more or less – with government spending ensures it will not be inflationary. The solution to inflation is to cut spending or raise taxes. MMT is dangerous because it lets the cat out of the bag: taxes do not finance government spending. This gives politicians a licence to run up the spending that will cause inflation. Best to keep the wool pulled over the eyes and insist on tax "pay-fors".

MMT's view is quite different. The composition of both taxes and spending matters. So there are two reasons that trying to match them is misguided: government doesn't need the revenue and there is absolutely no reason to believe that matching them means that government's impact approaches neutral. Spending on unemployed resources will put them to work with little inflationary consequence. Spending on a fixed price-floating quantity basis reduces further the inflationary danger. (That is precisely what the JG does – government offers a fixed wage and provides jobs to all who want to work at that wage.) Spending to increase productive capacity also reduces the danger of inflation, and can even present the danger of deflation. Clearly, no tax hikes are required – we might even need tax cuts (eventually) if productive capacity grows to exceed what can be supported by spending.

Likewise, it matters what kind of tax is imposed. A financial transactions tax, or a billionaire wealth tax, or a tax surcharge on millionaires is unlikely to take a significant amount of demand out of the economy – no matter how much revenue they raise – so are not likely to reduce inflation. On the other hand, a broad-based income or consumption tax will reduce demand significantly. Other methods can also be used, if desired: rationing, patriotic saving, or postponed consumption.[14]

All this is important if we are to introduce something like a Green New Deal plan – or any other large-scale government initiative. As Yarmuth insisted, we need to identify the resources needed and then release them from current use as necessary. We can use taxes for that purpose, although we might need to include other methods – such as banning oil drilling and fracking, or conscripting resources – to obtain the resources needed for the public purpose. We then spend to put those resources to use. If we have matched resources to purposes well, then there will be no significant inflationary pressures no matter what the budgetary outcome might turn out to be.

This is the sort of analysis that must be undertaken, but it scares both orthodox and heterodox economists used to relegating decision-making to the "invisible hand" of the market. Yes, planning will be required. Yes, it is difficult. Yes, mistakes will be made. But there is no alternative. A half century of neoliberalism has brought the world to the brink of collapse. Only concerted effort and cooperation by the world's governments provides any chance of survival.

Understanding MMT does not make this easy. But it helps us to recognize what the true constraints are: resources, initiative, politics, imagination.

NOTES

1.   Hahn, 1983, p. 1.
2.   Rudd, 2021.
3.   Keynes, 1964, p. 3.
4.   See Mitchell and Fazi, 2017; Papadimitriou and Wray, 2012.
5.   See Godley and Wray, 1999; Papadimitriou and Wray, 2007.
6.   See Wray, 2009; Tymoigne and Wray, 2009.
7.   See Nersisyan and Wray, 2020a, 2021.
8.   Wray, 2021.

9. Smialek, 2022.
10. Summers, 2022.
11. Furman, 2019. The New York Times article also quotes him as saying: "M.M.T. was already pretty marginal", noting that, in his view, most policymakers and prominent academics ignored it already.
12. Mitchell, Wray, and Watts, 2019.
13. See Wray and Liu, 2014 for an analysis of China's prospects from the perspective of MMT.
14. Nersisyan and Wray, 2020b.

REFERENCES

Furman, J. 2019. Tweet. https://twitter.com/jasonfurman/status/1083394281547722752 (accessed 5 September 2022).

Godley, W. and Wray, L.R. 1999. *Can Goldilocks Survive?* Policy Note 1999/4, Levy Economics Institute of Bard College. https://www.levyinstitute.org/publications/can-goldilocks-survive (accessed 5 September 2022).

Hahn, F. 1983. *Money and Inflation*, MIT Press, Cambridge, MA.

Keynes, J.M. 1964. *The General Theory of Employment Interest, and Money*, Harcourt, Brace, Javonovich, New York and London.

Mitchell, W. and Fazi, T. 2017. *Reclaiming the State: A Progressive Vision of Sovereignty for a Post-Neoliberal World*, Pluto Press, London.

Mitchell, W., Wray, L.R. and Watts, M. 2019. *Macroeconomics*, Macmillan/Red Globe Press, London.

Nersisyan, Y. and Wray, L.R. 2020a. *The Economic Response to the Coronavirus Pandemic*. One-pager No. 60, Levy Economics Institute of Bard College. https://www.levyinstitute.org/publications/the-economic-response-to-the-coronavirus-pandemic (accessed 5 September 2022).

Nersisyan, Y. and Wray, L.R. 2020b. *Can We Afford the Green New Deal?* Public Policy Brief No. 148, Levy Economics Institute of Bard College. https://www.levyinstitute.org/publications/can-we-afford-the-green-new-deal (accessed 5 September 2022).

Nersisyan, Y. and Wray, L.R. 2021. *Can Biden Build Back Better?* Public Policy Brief No. 155, Levy Economics Institute of Bard College. https://www.levyinstitute.org/publications/can-biden-build-back-better-yes-if-he-abandons-fiscal-pay-fors (accessed 5 September 2022).

Papadimitriou, D. and Wray, L.R. 2007. *The April AMT Shock: Tax Reform Advice for the New Majority*, Policy Note 2007/1, Levy Economics Institute of Bard College. https://www.levyinstitute.org/publications/the-april-amt-shock (accessed 5 September 2022).

Papadimitriou, D. and Wray, L.R. 2012. *Euroland's Original Sin*, Policy Note 2012/8, Levy Economics Institute of Bard College. https://www.levyinstitute.org/publications/eurolands-original-sin (accessed 5 September 2022).

Rudd, J.B. 2021. *Why Do We Think That Inflation Expectations Matter for Inflation? (And Should We?)*, Finance and Economics Discussion Series (FEDS) 2021-062, Washington, DC: Board of Governors of the Federal Reserve System.

Smialek, J. 2022. Is This What Winning Looks Like? *New York Times*, 6 February. https://www.nytimes.com/2022/02/06/business/economy/modern-monetary-theory-stephanie-kelton.html (accessed 5 September 2022).

Summers, L.H. 2022. Tweet. https://twitter.com/LHSummers/status/ 1490424193611141121 (accessed 5 September 2022).

Tymoigne, É. and Wray, L.R. 2009. *It Isn't Working: Time for More Radical Policies*, Public Policy Brief No. 105, Levy Economics Institute of Bard College. https://www.levyinstitute.org/publications/?docid=1206 (accessed 5 September 2022).

Wray, L.R. 2009. *The Return of Big Government: Policy Advice for President Obama*, Public Policy Brief No. 9, Levy Economics Institute of Bard College. https:// www.levyinstitute.org/publications/the-return-of-big-government-policy-advice-for -president-obama (accessed 5 September 2022).

Wray, L.R, 2021. *What Is MMT's State of Play in Washington?* E-Pamphlets, August, Levy Economics Institute. https://www.levyinstitute.org/pubs/e_pamphlet_2.pdf (accessed 5 September 2022).

Wray, L.R and Liu, X. 2014. *Options for China in a Dollar Standard World*. Working Paper No. 783, Levy Economics Institute. https://www.levyinstitute.org/ publications/options-for-china-in-a-dollar-standard-world-a-sovereign-currency -approach (accessed 5 September 2022).

Index

Tithe Act 193 208
tobacco plain packaging 117
total expenditure 100
trade 95
   deficit 75, 77–8, 98, 102, 103
   and developing countries 108–10
   in output and income generation
      100–101
traditional tax return 225
transaction taxes 211
Treasury bills 18, 22–6, 28, 29
Treasury Orders 43, 47
Treaty of Lisbon 170
Treaty of Rome 155–6
Treaty on the Functioning of the
   European Union (TFEU) 161, 165
Trichet, Jean Claude 164
Triffin, Robert 154
Trump, Donald 70, 77
Trussell Trust 282

UC *see* Universal Credit (UC)
UKIP 174
underlabouring function 188–91, 201
unemployment 31, 79, 81, 100, 120, 131,
      141, 159, 227, 228, 231–7, 239,
      242, 247
   and COVID-19 pandemic 254–9
unemployment insurance 255, 256
United Kingdom (UK)
   Exchequer's functioning 12–20
   financial system 2–4
   full employment 31–4
   government
      and banking system 20–22
      constraints on 28–30
      debt 22–4, 27, 29, 30
      macroeconomic context 26–8
      monetary circuit 24–6
      policy 28–34
      securities 21, 23, 24, 28–30
      spending 4–12, 21, 28–30, 32,
         141
   macroeconomic stability 32–4
   political taxes 208–9

United States (US)
   budget deficits 70, 71
   COVID-19
      job loss due to 255
      response to 80
      salary support in 254
   dollar 77–8, 82
   Modern Monetary Theory (MMT)
      73–4, 80–82
   resource constraints 79–82
   tax liabilities 89, 90
   trade deficits 82
Universal Basic Income 245
Universal Credit (UC) 32–3, 38, 278–82
US dollar 98, 135, 154

VAT 213, 223, 224
Velasquez, A. 213
Vlieghe, Gertjan 23
Vtyurina, S. 213

wages 92
Ways and Means Account 8, 10–11,
      16–17, 19, 23, 24, 30, 36, 57
Ways and Means bills 52–3
Weimann, J. 215
Welfare Reform and Work Act 279
Werner Report of 1970 156, 157, 169
William III 44
Wilson, Harold 112
workforce profile 237
working-age group 274
   income support 275
World Bank 109, 111–13, 118, 119
World Trade Organization (WTO)
      117–20
Wray, L.R. 78, 214
WTO *see* World Trade Organization
   (WTO)
Wyplosz, C. 106, 158

Z-D diagram approach 130–38
zero bound limit 166